George G. Higgins and the Quest for Worker Justice

George G. Higgins and the Quest for Worker Justice

The Evolution of Catholic Social Thought in America

John J. O'Brien

A Sheed & Ward Book

ROWMAN & LITTLEFIELD PUBLISHERS, INC.
Lanham • Boulder • New York • Toronto • Oxford

A SHEED & WARD BOOK

ROWMAN & LITTLEFIELD PUBLISHERS, INC.

Published in the United States of America
by Rowman & Littlefield Publishers, Inc.
A wholly owned subsidiary of The Rowman & Littlefield Publishing Group, Inc.
4501 Forbes Boulevard, Suite 200, Lanham, Maryland 20706
www.rowmanlittlefield.com

PO Box 317
Oxford
OX2 9RU, UK

British Library Cataloguing in Publication Information Available

Library of Congress Cataloging-in-Publication Data

O'Brien, John J., 1941-
George G. Higgins and the quest for worker justice : the evolution of Catholic social thought in America / John J. O'Brien.
p. cm.
"A Sheed & Ward book."
Includes bibliographical references and index.
ISBN 0-7425-3207-0 (alk. paper) — ISBN 0-7425-3208-9 (pbk. :alk. paper)
1. Higgins, George, 1916–2002. 2. Church and labor—United States. 3. Church and social problems—United States—Catholic Church. 4. Christian sociology—Catholic Church. 5. Civil religion—United States. 6. Christian sociology—United States. I. Title.
HD6338.2.U5O24 2004
261.8'5—dc22 2004014128

Printed in the United States of America

™ The paper used in this publication meets the minimum requirements of American National Standard for Information Sciences—Permanence of Paper for Printed Library Materials, ANSI/NISO Z39.48-1992.

In memory of those who lived on the side of the angels

Ramona Dolan, S.B.S.

George Gilmary Higgins

Kathleen Meyer

John M. and Kathleen O'Brien

Grace M. Vera

Joan Walsh

May they rest in peace.

Contents

~

Preface

This work began with two questions. First, how do the gospel and the marketplace relate to each other? Second, how does the Spirit act in the liturgy to convert the human heart and commit the church to worker justice? This inquiry led me to the person, the writings, and the work of Monsignor George G. Higgins. One of the most important public intellectuals in the United Sates in the 20th century, Higgins promoted the church's involvement with workers. He was steeped in the history of organized labor, American church history, and Catholic social teaching. Higgins reverenced the dignity of the worker, and he negotiated responsible stewardship by people in management, government, and church to promote a happy and just society. This work investigates the church's involvement with workers through the lens of the life, career, and writings of Monsignor Higgins.

My study has left me indebted to many people. First, I am grateful to Monsignor Higgins for his insight and advice. It seems fitting that God called him to eternal life on May 1, 2002, the day international workers celebrate their cherished place in society. Second, I am grateful to the Department of Archives at the Catholic University of America in Washington, DC. In particular, I thank Dr. Timothy Meagher, director of the archives, and, most especially, Dr. W. John Shepherd, assistant director. Dr. Shepherd has offered invaluable advice and insight into the Higgins' holdings.

I thank my sisters and brother and their families, Peggy Mulholland, Helen Kelly, and Luke Driscoll; the Passionist community; the faculty at Weston Jesuit School of Theology; Dr. James F. Keenan, S.J., the director of the doctoral program at Weston; and my colleagues in doctoral study for their support and guidance during my years of study and research. In particular, I am profoundly indebted to Dr. Margaret Eletta Guider, O.S.F., my dissertation director, for her insight and kindness, her breadth of learning, her commitment to scholarship, and her orthopathy. She made me investigate questions that I would have never thought of on my own. I am also grateful to Dr. Roger Haight, S.J., the first to suggest that I consider the work of Monsignor Higgins, Drs. Thomas Massaro, S.J., and Thomas Shannon for their part in shaping this project. My esteem also goes out to the superb library staff at Weston Jesuit and Episcopal Divinity School, especially Gene Fox.

I want to thank those who have stood by me in moments of darkness, especially the Servants of the Paraclete in Saint Louis, Tim McAuliffe and Millie Cargas, and the Sisters of the Holy Redeemer. I am grateful for colleagues and friends who have encouraged this work, especially Drs. Robert Carbonneau, Elizabeth E. Carr, Joseph A. Fahy, Janice Farnham, Paul Fitzpatrick, Edward Hall, Stephen A. Marini, William J. Meyer, Patrick Sullivan, Stephanie Terril, Theodore Vitali, and Paul J. Wadell. I want to acknowledge the support of fellow Passionists, especially Richard A. Burke, Michael Higgins, Robert Joerger, Joseph R. Jones, John F. Kobler, Terrence Kristofak, Gerald Laba, David G. Monaco, William J. Murphy, John T. Render, Robin Ryan, Michael J. Stengel, and Donald Ware. Finally, my thanks to dear friends: Doreen and Tim Bottone, Helen Byrne, Patrick Caughey, John E. Cockayne Jr., Mary and Ruben Espinosa, George and Jan Gentile, Barbara Gindhart, Laura Jefferson, Melissa McDiarmid, June McLoughlin, Larry and Nancy Manning, Gerri Meier, William Meyer Sr., Barbara Rilling, Cornelia Roy, Judith Smeltz, Jim and Linda Sullivan, Helen Stuart, Judy Talvacchia, Patrick Tarrant, Joseph Vujs, and Joseph Walsh.

Finally, Jeremy Langford and Katie Lane and the staff at Sheed & Ward deserve my gratitude for their attention to this project and for their help in publishing this work. Their courtesy and professional skill have been outstanding.

Monsignor Higgins always put it best when it came to people of character. All of the aforementioned are "on the side of the angels." "May their tribe increase!"

Introduction

On May 20, 2001, the University of Notre Dame awarded its Laetare Medal to Monsignor George Gilmary Higgins.[1] "The long career of George Higgins shows how an ardent embrace of Catholic doctrine intensifies the hunger and thirst for justice," said Holy Cross Father Edward A. Malloy, Notre Dame president.[2] Upon reception of the award at the 156th commencement, Higgins spoke about the church's relationship with working people, its concern for immigrants, and its solidarity with the poor.

> Exactly fifteen years after John Gilmary Shea received the first Laetare Medal, James Cardinal Gibbons . . . submitted to the Vatican his historic memorandum in defense of the Knights of Labor which the late historian, John Tracy Ellis, characterized as the single most important document in the entire history of the Church in the United States.
>
> Gibbons wrote in part in 1887, ". . . Since it is acknowledged by all that the great questions of the future are . . . the social questions, which concern the improvement of the condition of the great masses of people, it is evidently of supreme importance that the Church should always be found on the side of humanity, of justice to the multitudes who comprise the body of the human family." That remains as true today as it was at the end of the 19th century.
>
> One fears that today when many, but by no means all American Catholics are more prosperous than their immigrant forebears, we may fail to realize that poverty is still endemic in our society especially, but not exclusively, among minorities. We may also fail to realize that we are still a nation of immigrants—perhaps even more so than we were at the end of the 19th century.[3]

Higgins also spoke about the evangelization of the poor and the new immigrants.

> There are those among us who argue that evangelization of the poor and also of the new immigrants must be exclusively spiritual. That's a seductive half-truth. . . . To state simplistically that the Church's evangelization should be exclusively spiritual finds no support anywhere in the entire corpus of Catholic social teaching, least of all in the social teaching of Pope John Paul II. John Paul . . . comes down strongly in favor of a preferential option for the poor, not only in Third World countries but also in the industrialized countries of the West.[4]

The Laetare Medal was the last award accorded to Higgins in 2001. He was previously honored on three other occasions. First, on February 4, 2001, the United Auto Workers (UAW) recognized his work with the Public Review Board (PRB) at a luncheon at the Marriott Warden Park Hotel in Washington, DC.[5] Higgins served as a member of the board from its inception in 1957 and was its chair from 1966 until his retirement from the board in September 2000. Second, on September 3, 2000, Cardinal James A. Hickey presented Higgins with the Cardinal O'Boyle Medal at the annual Washington Archdiocesan Labor Day Mass. This medal, the Washington archdiocese's highest honor, is named after Cardinal Patrick O'Boyle, a stalwart advocate of social justice, civil rights, and labor. It was given to Higgins for his life of outstanding service to the church.[6] Third, President William Jefferson Clinton presented the Presidential Medal of Freedom to Higgins and fifteen outstanding citizens during ceremonies at the White House on August 9, 2000. Reverend Jesse Jackson, noted Harvard economist John Kenneth Galbraith, former senator George McGovern, Senator Daniel Patrick Moynihan, former Johnson and Johnson chief executive officer James Burke, and UAW union organizer Mildred McWilliams Jeffrey joined him in receiving the nation's highest civilian honor. "For more than 60 years now, he has organized, marched, prayed and bled for the social and economic justice for working Americans," President Clinton said in conferring the award on Higgins.[7] The award citation focused on Higgins' participation in Catholic–Jewish relations, civil rights, the promotion of religious tolerance, and organized labor.

What influenced Higgins to commit his priestly life to building bridges between Catholics and Jews, between African Americans and others, between Catholic social teaching and economic citizenship for the working poor? What caused him to become a spokesperson for human and civil rights? What piqued his interest in the unions and his commitment to a vital labor movement? What inspired him to become a Catholic journalist for fifty-six years?

This study investigates the social theology of Msgr. Higgins. Its principal sources for this theology are the annual *Labor Day Statements* (1946–2001); the *Yardstick* columns (1945–1994); and selected sermons, invocations, eulogies, and lectures. Chapter one discusses the concepts of civil religion and public theology in order to place Higgins's social theology within a larger religious and intellectual context. Civil religion undergirds the foundational myth of the United States as a redeemer nation. Its principles have enabled African Americans to search for freedom, the right to vote, and the right to work. Its ideals have attracted immigrants to these shores. Its inspiration has encouraged rural farmers, urban factory workers, and frontier people. Its hopes have strengthened women to seek the right to vote, the opportunity to own property, and the chance to become leaders. It has provided a basis for patriotism and a distinctive ethos throughout the nation's history. Civil religion has been a significant resource for public life and the common coinage that binds people together. In recent years, civil religion has come under attack. Critics ask: Is it in crisis? Is the covenant irrevocably broken? Even if its shards were reconfigured, are its tenets accessible to citizens who lack historical consciousness and prize individualism? Is it still capable of unifying the nation? Questions about civil religion are urgent because its critics claim that the public square is naked. They wonder: What are resources that will bring people together in debate, discussion, and decision making? What social glue will unite the many publics that make up the nation? Is there a public theology that can serve the commonwealth, provide moral substance, and rekindle hope for the future?

The churches and synagogues have historically engaged civil religion in fruitful dialogue. Public intellectuals such as Benjamin Franklin, Jonathan Edwards, Reinhold Niebuhr, H. Richard Niebuhr, Abraham Joshua Heschel, John A. Ryan, and John Courtney Murray have contributed to public discourse. They have provided a reasoned critique of the social order and have built bridges between the religious communities and society. They have recommended remedies for the nation's ills and have suggested pathways for achieving a more just, good, and happy society. This book argues that Monsignor George G. Higgins stands in the company of these public intellectuals. His social theology has built bridges between Catholic social teaching and the workplace.

Chapter two introduces Higgins to the reader. It begins by presenting a biographical sketch of his formative years (1916–1944). Higgins was a bridge that linked the social teaching of the late 19th century and the present. The second part of chapter two considers the church and organized labor in the late 19th century. It investigates the history of work in the years following the Civil War; the founding of the National Labor Union and its leader, William H. Sylvis; and the immensely popular Knights of Labor. It looks at the church's pastoral and institutional response to the social question. Cardinal Gibbons and Catholic activists encouraged workers to become involved in the labor movement. Gibbons' letter to the Holy See in support of the Knights forestalled papal condemnation. The working class remained connected to the church. *Rerum Novarum* strengthened the church's bond with workers and, with the 1919 Bishops' Statement, outlined the social agenda that developed in the early decades of the 20th century. The third part of chapter two investigates the work done by the Social Action Department (SAD) of the National Catholic Welfare Conference (NCWC).[8] SAD provided the church with a structure for pursuing the social apostolate. John A. Ryan, Raymond A. McGowan, and Linna E. Bresette laid the foundations for industrial democracy and economic citizenship. Higgins built on their foundation during his years in the social apostolate.

Chapter three investigates the development of Higgins' social theology in his early years in the social apostolate (1945–1962). The *Labor Day Statements* and the *Yardstick* columns consider the social agenda for labor–management cooperation and the reconstruction of the nation's economic life after the Second World War. Organized labor flourished during these years. Workers enjoyed unprecedented prosperity and power. Higgins worked to establish his credentials with organized labor and build bridges between the church and the unions. The 1950s were the era of the McCarthy hearings. Much of the Catholic press became militant supporters of Senator McCarthy and attacked Left-led labor unions. Higgins maintained a prudent balance and encouraged labor unions in their efforts to rid themselves of Communist influence, racketeering, and corruption. Chapter three concludes with the first session of the Second Vatican Council, in 1962. As a participant in the council, Higgins found it to be a turning point in his life.

Chapter four investigates the development of Higgins' social theology in his mature years in the social apostolate (1963–1980). The *Labor Day Statements* and the *Yardstick* columns consider the social teaching of Pope John XXIII, Pope Paul VI, and the Second Vatican Council. The council profoundly shaped Higgins. The *Yardstick* columns address such new issues as Catholic–Jewish relations, racism in the unions and in the society, Higgins' concern for the poor, and the renewal of organized labor. Bishop Joseph F. Donnelly and Higgins worked tirelessly in the 1970s to bring justice to the farmworker of California. Both supported Cesar Chavez and Dolores Huerta in their efforts to organize agricultural workers under the banner of the

United Farm Workers (UFW). Chavez said that the union could not have succeeded without Higgins.

Higgins became the leading Catholic liaison with organized labor. His was a powerful voice of conscience in the church, the unions, and society. The restructuring of the United States Catholic Conference (USCC) departments and the fact that Higgins had reached the mandatory retirement age of sixty-five enabled church authorities to retire him from his position at USCC. His retirement took effect on Labor Day 1980. A number of friends protested his retirement. Higgins, ever the priestly gentleman and loyal to the institutional church, never used the *Yardstick* columns to comment on his retirement. His retirement did not become a public issue. Higgins moved on. He continued to serve the social apostolate, and he maintained close ties with the labor movement at home and abroad. He was called on to teach, lecture, advise, and write. The *Yardstick* columns continued to promote economic citizenship and social justice.

Chapter five examines the development of Higgins' social theology in his later years in the social apostolate (1981–1994). The annual *Labor Day Statement* (*LDS*; 1981–2001) considers the significance of the labor movement in the 1990 *LDS* and Bishop John Ricard devoted the 1993 *LDS* to Higgins' public writing. Higgins also considered the issues of work, the economy, and the vitality of organized labor in the *Yardstick* columns (1980–1994). He supported the work of Solidarity, the Polish labor movement, from its beginnings. He applied the principles of social theology to the inner life of the church. In particular, the *Yardstick* columns support teachers and health care workers in their efforts to form unions in Catholic schools and hospitals. Church, academic, and labor leaders continued to seek his advice. He lent his name to institutions devoted to labor relations and research. He kept close ties with the rank and file and with local unions.

The conclusion estimates Higgins' contribution to the church's social apostolate. His thought and social ministry made the nation a better place. What an anonymous African American fieldworker said about the world could easily epitomize Higgins' social theology and apostolic labors: "But you know what I really think? I really think that one day the world will be great. The world gonna be great someday."[9]

CHAPTER ONE

The Movement from Civil Religion to Public Theology

Chapter one investigates the meaning and function of civil religion and public theology. It considers the dynamic movement that characterizes civil religion vis-à-vis public theology. This provides the context for the social theology of Monsignor Higgins. The first part of this chapter inquires into the origins of civil religion.[1] It asks a series of questions: What is civil religion? What is its function for the society? How has it shaped the foundational myth of the United States as a redeemer nation? What is its present vitality? What crisis does it now face? What significance does it have for the future? The second section examines civil religion vis-à-vis public theology. It, too, asks a series of questions: What is public theology?[2] What is its task? What does it offer society in its search for a moral vision? The final section presents Higgins' contribution to public theology—that is, the social theology that he developed over a fifty-year period. His thought is rooted in Catholic social teaching. The concept of economic citizenship is the foundation of his social theology and the principal metaphor that guides his social vision for a better, happier, more just society.

Civil Religion

Civil Religion in Historical Perspective

Many immigrants came to the United States for religious reasons. Some left situations of oppression and persecution. They sought religious freedom, the ability to worship God as they wished, and a life where they could live in communion with like-minded believers. These people were chary of any state religion that might dominate public life. Others came to establish the earthly Jerusalem. These people wanted to forge a harmony between religion and society, to foster the good life, to promote public well-being, and to taste the kingdom of God.

Prejudice and suspicion from the old country also migrated to these shores. Catholics experienced exclusion, oppression, and organized xenophobia. Nativists considered the Catholic Church a threat to civic solidarity and charged "that the Catholic Church was an institution incompatible with the American spirit of democracy."[3] Nonetheless, people in the United States esteemed religion and considered themselves religious. No one church became the established church. Each church and each religious group enjoyed equal status. Each person enjoyed a freedom of conscience to belong to any religion or to none.

Alexis de Tocqueville and *Democracy in America*

Religion deeply influenced the social and the political life of the early republic. The religious mores and the spirit of equality in the United States deeply impressed Alexis de Tocqueville. In 1831 he and Gustave de Beaumont came from France to visit the United States and Canada. In their travels, they hoped to accomplish three goals. First, they wanted to observe the penitentiary system. Second, they wanted to study the mores, the political institutions, and the style of democratic governance on the opposite side of the Atlantic. Third, they wanted to compare democracy in the United States with democracy in France.

Beaumont and Tocqueville used their aristocratic backgrounds to gain access to the intellectual circles in the United States. Their interviews and investigations "centered on the social structure and its relationship to social and political institutions. Economic matters played no part in the study except as they affected the way people conducted their lives."[4]

On January 23, 1835, Tocqueville published the first part of his observations. *Democracy in America* is considered "probably the greatest work ever written on one country by the citizen of another."[5] Tocqueville noted how well people of various backgrounds and classes mingled with each other in a spirit of equality.

> No novelty in the United States struck me more vividly during my stay there than the equality of conditions. . . . I soon realized that the influence of this fact extends far beyond political mores and laws, exercising dominion over civil society as much as over the government; it creates opinions, gives birth to feelings, suggests customs, and modifies whatever it does not create.

> So the more I studied American society, the more clearly I saw equality of conditions as the creative element from which each particular fact derived, and all my observations constantly returned to this nodal point.
>
> Later when I came to consider our own side of the Atlantic, I thought I could detect something analogous to what I had noticed in the New World. I saw an equality of conditions which, though it had not reached the extreme limits found in the United States, was daily drawing closer thereto; and that same democracy which prevailed over the societies of America seemed to me to be advancing rapidly toward power in Europe.
>
> It was at that moment that I conceived the idea of this book. A great democratic revolution is taking place in our midst; everybody sees it, but by no means everybody judges it in the same way.[6]

Democracy in America considered the social and political structures that ensured democracy's vitality. First, Tocqueville noted the importance of political parties, the press, and voluntary associations. His training as a lawyer and a magistrate helped him understand how political power was shared. An independent judiciary served as a check on legislative power and minimized tyranny.[7] Second, the laws and the institutions supported republican and democratic mores. He described these mores as "habits of the heart" and as the foundational ideas that shaped mental habits. These mores indicated the moral and intellectual state of the people.[8] Third, he considered religion to be the primary political institution: "The religious atmosphere of the country was the first thing that struck me on my arrival in the United States. The longer I stayed in the country, the more conscious I became of the important political consequences resulting from this novel situation."[9] Religion inspired patriotism and liberty. Patriotism fueled the fires of religious zeal. Religion was the institutional force that provided stability for the people. It strengthened whatever in democracy was fragile.

Tocqueville thought that Catholicism was the religion most congenial with the promotion of equality. However, he acknowledged that all the religious groups served to instruct the people about their duties to one another and their responsibility to live a moral life.

> America is still the place where the Christian religion has kept the greatest real power over men's souls. . . . [Religion] does direct mores, and by regulating domestic life it helps to regulate the state. . . . When the American returns from the turmoil of politics to the bosom of the family, he immediately finds a perfect picture of order and peace. There all his pleasures are simple and natural and his joys innocent and quiet, and as the regularity of life brings him happiness, he easily forms the habit of regulating his opinions as well as his tastes.[10]

Organized religion has been so influential that the British commentator G. K. Chesterton described the United States as a "nation with the soul of a church."[11] Every church promoted virtue, involvement in society, loyalty, and patriotism. The churches offered saving grace within their own denominations. They also contributed to the nation's birth, its development, and its progress in democracy: "The most dynamic movements in the early republic were expressly religious."[12] Church polity reflected the republican spirit and values.[13]

> Religion experienced vigorous growth during the Revolutionary period. It occupied a prominent place in public culture and a disproportionately large number of religiously active men served in the new nation's constituent assemblies. In a host of ways, both practical and intellectual, the church served as a school for politics.[14]

The Meaning and Function of Civil Religion

The founders of the nation were aware of the importance of religion in forming a responsible citizenry. They drew on the values, symbols, and heroic figures of Protestant Christianity. Furthermore, they borrowed vocabulary and concepts from the churches to create a national identity. The founders saw the United States as the redeemer nation. This nation was truly a new beginning, a *novus ordo seclorum*. The nation's true meaning and purpose was supported by a religious mythology. Borrowing a concept from the philosopher Jean Jacques Rousseau, Robert N. Bellah refers to this as *civil religion*.

> There actually exists alongside of and rather clearly differentiated from the churches an elaborate and well-institutionalized civil religion in America. . . . This religious dimension has its own seriousness and integrity and requires the same care in understanding that any other religion does. . . .
>
> This public religious dimension is expressed in a set of beliefs, symbols and rituals that I am calling the American civil religion. . . .
>
> Civil religion at its best is a genuine apprehension of universal and transcendent religious reality as seen in or . . . as revealed through the experience of the American people.[15]

Subsequent writers describe civil religion similarly. Robert Wuthnow says that civil religion "is a set of cultural symbols that draw connections between a nation and some conception of the sacred. These symbols usually consist of beliefs and practices that make explicit reference to a divine being."[16] Ronald C. Wimberley and William H. Swatos Jr. maintain that civil religion is a concept that refers to a "transcendent universal religion of the nation. . . . Civil religiosity is posited to be a common . . . set of beliefs in transcendent principles and reality against which the historical experience and actions of the nation should be evaluated."[17]

Civil religion is a phrase that originated with Rousseau. According to the analysis by Wuthnow, Rousseau presented the concept of civil religion as a way

> to understand the social principles underlying democratic societies. . . . In traditional societies a common religion had often provided such beliefs, but in modern nations a unifying set of beliefs needed to be found that would not exclude citizens who ascribed to minority religions or who were nonreligious. . . . Rousseau suggested that nations would (and should) develop a civil religion that would embrace all citizens, giving them reasons to practice civic virtue and to be patriotic.[18]

Rousseau outlined the simple dogmas of the civil religion in chapter 8, book 4, of *The Social Contract*. These common beliefs

> include belief in the existence of a divine being or order characterized by its power, wisdom, and goodness. They should also include some conception of the future, of justice, and of punishment, and they should emphasize the sanctity of the social bonds that link people together and the laws to which they are subject. . . . [It] should promote tolerance. The divine being . . . is thus a symbol that crystallizes the qualities people should admire in their nation and willingly commit themselves to upholding. Insofar as the divine being is both benevolent and just, and insofar as the life to come . . . is regarded positively, citizens will presumably be motivated to think well of their society.
>
> This concept of reality nevertheless legitimates the basic institutions of the nation by encouraging citizens to realize their dependence on a sovereign power, the ways in which their dependence on one another is conducive to achieving their higher values, and their need to be tolerant of one another.[19]

According to Bellah, the founders did not use the phrase *civil religion*, but they did use ideas similar to Rousseau's.[20] They thought that the country rested on the pillars of belief in God, religion, and morality. They also shared a consciousness that people in the United States would perceive and believe in God and in the religious symbols that were embedded in the culture.

Civil religion provides a national myth of origins. It envisions the United States as God's chosen people, as one nation under God and guided by God: "In God we trust." Civil religion sets forth the principles on which the nation was founded. It provides the nation with inspirational heroes and leaders, such as Benjamin Franklin, George Washington, and Abraham Lincoln.[21]

The presidency has symbolic and "religious significance even if the inhabitant of the office does not act in a particularly religious manner. Presidents have been inclined to invoke one of two different versions of civil religion."[22]

First, presidents have sometimes functioned in a high priestly or sacerdotal role. Here the emphasis is on the altruistic nature and the moral virtue of the divinely blessed nation.[23] The United States is at center stage in the concluding act of world history.[24] Second, other presidents have emphasized a prophetic role. Here the stress is on calling and challenging the nation to follow a righteous path.[25] Martin E. Marty notes that "the priestly will normally be celebrative, affirmative, culture-building. The prophetic will tend to be dialectical about civil religion, but with a predisposition toward the judgmental."[26]

George Washington functioned in a high priestly or sacerdotal role and in a prophetic way. The words of his first inaugural address on April 30, 1789, were of priestly utterance. He offered:

> My fervent supplication to that Almighty Being who rules over the universe, who provides in the councils of nations, and whose providential aids can supply every defect, that his benediction may consecrate to the liberties and happiness of the People of the United States a Government instituted by themselves for these essential purposes, and may enable every instrument employed by its administration to execute with success the functions allotted to his charge. . . .
>
> No people can be bound to acknowledge and adore the Invisible hand which conducts the affairs of man more than those of the United States. Every step by which we have advanced to the character of an independent nation seems to have been distinguished by some token of providential agency. . . .
>
> The propitious smiles of Heaven can never be expected on a nation that disregards the eternal rules of order and right which Heaven itself has ordained: and since the preservation of the sacred fire of liberty, and the destiny of the republican model of government are justly considered, perhaps, as *deeply*, perhaps as *finally*, staked on the experiment entrusted to the hands of the American People.[27]

The words and acts of the nation's founders fashioned the form and tone of priestly civil religion. Washington proclaimed November 26, 1789, as the first celebration of Thanksgiving Day. The words of Washington's Farewell Address on September 19, 1796, formed a prophetic utterance. They challenged the country to become a union at home and advocate independence abroad.[28] He called the citizenry to virtue and personal character, to harmony and peace, to religion and personal morality.[29] He recommended that the country remain faithful to its national character, "to observe good faith and justice towards all Nations."[30]

Washington and the early founders believed that the nation would be blessed with prosperity. According to Robert Bellah, "The God of civil religion is not only rather 'unitarian,' he is also on the austere side, much more related to order, law, and right than to salvation and love."[31] God was actively interested and involved in history; the Almighty had special concern for this nation. Bellah writes:

> What was implicit in the words of Washington . . . became explicit in Jefferson's second inaugural when he said: "I shall need, too, the favor of that Being in whose hands we are, who led our fathers, as Israel did of old, from their native land and planted them in a country flowing with all the necessaries and comforts of life." Europe is Egypt; America, the promised land. God has led his people to establish a new sort of social order that shall be a light unto all the nations.[32]

Civil religion provided the citizens with the beliefs, symbols, and rituals it would need to secure democracy. It shared much in common with Christianity. But it was neither sectarian nor Christian. Civil religion did not rival or compete with Christianity and the churches. Each had its own clear and distinctive role for the nation.

> Under the doctrine of religious liberty, an exceptionally wide sphere of personal piety and voluntary social action was left to the churches. But the churches were neither to control the state nor to be controlled by it. The national magistrate, whatever his private religious views, operates under the rubrics of the civil religion as long as he is in his official capacity.[33]

Civil religion interpreted the founding event of the American Revolution. This event was described in biblical language. The new nation was the final act of the Exodus from the old lands across the Atlantic. Its sacred texts were the Declaration of Independence and the Constitution.[34]

When George Washington died in his bed at Mount Vernon on December 14, 1799, the nation mourned the loss of its acknowledged Moses. James Madison and Henry Lee declared:

> Our Washington is no more! The hero, the patriot, and the sage of America, the man on whom, in times of danger, every eye was turned, and all hopes were placed, lives now only in his own great actions, and in the hearts of an affectionate and afflicted people.[35]

The nation mourned his death during the month of January 1800. Many towns conducted simulations of his real burial through public obsequies, observances, and ceremonies. These acts of communal solidarity helped the nation mourn together as if the body were present. Washington was enshrined in the imagination of the young nation.

> Symbols that linked Washington to the mythic themes at work in the republic included an eagle with a laurel wreath in its beak, various military trophies, and stripes from the U.S. flag. . . . [His death] was . . . transformed into a heroic event that regenerated and rejuvenated the body politic. . . . [He] continued to be imagined as an agent of Providence. . . . In death he was not only a unifying symbol that bound disparate sections of the nation together, he was also the personification of a model citizen. His virtuous, revered life was held up for all citizens to emulate.[36]

The Civil War was the second great event that involved national self-understanding. This was a time of testing. It raised the deepest questions about national meaning. Abraham Lincoln embodied the war's meaning. His prophetic task was to enable the nation and the churches to face "the original sin and curse of slavery."[37]

The new theme that now emerged in civil religion was death, sacrifice, and rebirth. Lincoln epitomized this death and resurrection theme. He was murdered on Good Friday, April 14, 1865. His life and death were the supreme sacrifice offered for the rebirth of the nation. What Christ's death symbolized for the Christian churches, Lincoln's death symbolized for civil religion.

William H. Herndon, Lincoln's law partner, wrote:

> For fifty years God rolled Abraham Lincoln through his fiery furnace. He did it to try Abraham and to purify him for his purposes. This made Mr. Lincoln humble, tender, forbearing, sympathetic to suffering, kind, sensitive, tolerant, broadening, deepening and widening his whole nature; making him the noblest and loveliest character since Jesus Christ. . . . I believe that Lincoln was God's chosen one.[38]

Lincoln was the martyred president. His death was like those of the soldiers who had died in the war. The living God had used Lincoln for divine purpose. He had been the one through whom the nation saw the light of God in its darkest hour. God was at work in American history. Lincoln was God's agent in facilitating national reconciliation. Sacrifice was indelibly inscribed in civil religion. Lincoln, the savior of the nation, and Washington, the father of the country—"the Peter and Paul of American patriotism"—were twinned in popular culture and in art.[39]

The new symbolism found expression in the establishment of national cemeteries for the war dead. The Arlington National Cemetery became civil religion's most hallowed monument. Memorial Day observations reinforced the theme of death, sacrifice, and rebirth. This day, especially in small-town America, was a community rededication to the martyred dead, to the spirit of sacrifice, and to the vision of democracy. Just as Thanksgiving, securely institutionalized as an annual national holiday via Lincoln, served to integrate the family into civil religion, so Memorial Day integrated the local community into the national cult. In addition, the Liberty Bell and the Statue of Liberty became symbols for a vital civil religion.

People saw no conflict between civil religion and Christian faith. Thus civil religion and the churches effected a strong sense of national solidarity. Civil religion remained a vital force in the 20th century. Woodrow Wilson used the tradition of civil religion to promote his vision of a nation transformed. Wilson thought that people would promote the common good. According to Gregory S. Butler, Wilson thought that the United States

> would play a central role as the vanguard of humanity. . . . America and mankind were moving to a world-immanent transfiguration of the human condition. "We think of the future," said Wilson, "not the past, as the more glorious time in comparison with which the present is nothing." American history, he remarked, "seems like a plain first chapter in the history of a new age."[40]

Wilson saw the nation as sent on a holy mission: to rid the world of tyranny and injustice and to redeem the world by giving it liberty and justice.[41]

When the nation faced the darkness of the Great Depression, Franklin Delano Roosevelt invoked the tenets of civil religion and its heroic figures to describe the symbolic role of the presidency. Shortly after his first election, he declared:

> The Presidency is not merely an administrative office. That is the least of it. It is preeminently a place of moral leadership.
>
> All our great Presidents were leaders of thought at times when certain historic ideas in the life of the nation had to be clarified. Washington personified the idea of Federal Union. Jefferson practically originated the party system as we now know it by opposing the democratic theory to the republicanism of Hamilton. This theory was reaffirmed by Jackson.
>
> Two great principles of our government were forever put beyond question by Lincoln. Cleveland, coming into office following an era of great political corruption, typified rugged honesty. Theodore Roosevelt and Wilson were both moral leaders, each in his own way and for his own time, who used the Presidency as a pulpit.

> That is what the office is—a superb opportunity for reapplying, applying to new conditions, the simple rules of human conduct to which we always go back.
>
> Without leadership alert and sensitive to change, we . . . lose our way.[42]

Roosevelt brought leadership and optimism to the presidency. He used the press conference and thirty fireside chats to challenge and encourage the nation. The measures he took during the first hundred days brought hope to the nation. The policies he endorsed strengthened ordinary citizens. The structures he set up put government on the side of workers for the first time in the history of the country. Roosevelt was the first president to consult public intellectuals for solutions to the nation's woes. In addition, senators Robert F. Wagner and Robert F. LaFollette Jr. became key figures in national recovery. The ideals of civil religion had been epitomized in the person of the president from George Washington to Franklin Delano Roosevelt. Roosevelt's actions and style now ensured that those ideals would be embodied in the institution of the presidency.

Church religion and civil religion were brought together and influenced the nation in the 1950s.

> President Eisenhower served for eight years as a prestigious symbol of generalized religiosity and America's self-satisfied patriotic moralist. The president even provided a classic justification for the new religious outlook. "Our government," he said in 1954, "makes no sense unless it is founded on a deeply felt religious faith—and I don't care what it is."[43]

This continued into the Kennedy administration. After his death the nation faced a time of trial. The civil rights movement, the plight of the poor, and the Vietnam War exposed the nation's moral decay and its wounds. Religious leaders such as Robert McAfee Brown, Abraham Joshua Heschel, and Philip and Daniel Berrigan challenged and questioned the vitality and the viability of civil religion. Martin Luther King Jr. and other religious leaders used the language of biblical and civic republicanism to challenge the nation to a new moral purpose.[44] Jesse Jackson also relied on this tradition in the presidential election in 1984.[45]

The presidency still provides leadership in the public faith of civil religion.

> As the national pastor, he provides spiritual inspiration to the people by affirming American core values and urging them to appropriate those values, and by comforting them in their afflictions. . . . To carry out these religio-political duties, the American people want a president who is religious and moral—but

> not too Christian and not too pious. Therefore, the national leader should be able to speak in public with feeling about God in general but not mention Jesus Christ in particular in order not to offend. . . . Most Americans want somebody in the presidential office who can verbalize religious sentiments, speak with a certain amount of moral authority, and thereby carry out the civil religion duties of the presidency. . . . When the presidents themselves possess a measure of religious understanding and personal faith, the expression of civil religion sentiments and dogmas seems more natural and can be very potent.[46]

Civil religion continues to function as a cultural, mythic, and ideological influence on national life. Some citizens, deeply aware of its importance, assume that everyone knows the narratives, understands the rhetoric, venerates the heroes, celebrates the rituals, observes the holidays, and visits the shrines of civil religion.

Civil religion has never functioned in isolation. It has always been in conversation and dialogue with organized religion. This partnership has provided a critique of civil society, and it has contributed to national vitality. But the crisis of the 1960s has left doubts and wounds. Some of the bands of civil religion seem to have unraveled.

The Crisis in Civil Religion

Scholars such as Robert N. Bellah, Richard John Neuhaus, Philip E. Hammond, and Andrew Delbanco have commented on the crisis the nation currently faces. Bellah thinks that the crisis of the 1960s has brought about a new trial for civil religion. The Vietnam War raised serious doubts about the meaning of the United States as a redeemer nation and as a chosen people. In 1975 Bellah stated that the covenant had broken:

> Today the American civil religion is an empty and broken shell. It was from the beginning an external covenant. That in itself is no fault, for external covenants are necessary. Until we are all as angels, external law and restraint are essential for any kind of social existence. But in a republic an external covenant alone is never enough. It is of the nature of a republic that its citizens must love it, not merely obey it. The external covenant must become an internal covenant and many times in our history that has happened. In a series of religious and ethical revivals, that external covenant has become filled with meaning and devotion. Even though that inner meaning and devotion has often been betrayed, genuine achievements have been left behind. It is better that slavery has been abolished. It is better that women have the vote. But the internal covenant can never be completely captured by institutions; its life is that of the spirit and it has its own rhythms.[47]

In a recent essay, Bellah considers what role the public institutions of the state, the market, education, and television played in the creation of a new common culture:

> The United States, surely, has an exceptionally powerful institutional order. The state in America, even though it is multileveled and, to a degree, decentralized, has an enormous impact on all our lives. . . . If the state intrudes in our lives in a thousand ways, the market is even more intrusive. There is very little that Americans need that we can produce for ourselves anymore. We are dependent on the market not only for goods but for many kinds of services. Our cultural understanding of the world is shaped every time we enter a supermarket or a mall. . . .
>
> Education . . . and television (and increasingly the Internet) linked to the market are enormously powerful purveyors of common culture, socializers not only of children but of all of us most of our lives.[48]

These public institutions mediate the common culture of radical autonomy and expressive individualism. Modern individualism has produced a way of life that can ignore the public good. People can find themselves without common bonds. The split between the public and the private is evident in the way that the market, education, and television function in contemporary society.

The contemporary market is a place for competitive and individualistic enterprise.[49] Alexis de Tocqueville anticipated this when he observed two tendencies in the United States during the Jacksonian era. The first was an acquisitive materialism and a restlessness that came with prosperity.[50] The second was individualism.[51]

> Individualism is a calm and considered feeling which disposes each citizen to isolate himself from the mass of his fellows and withdraw into the circle of family and friends; with this little society formed to his taste, he gladly leaves the greater society to look after itself.[52]

Education today trains people to become efficient managers. It equips them with skills that will help them function on the job. Bellah and his colleagues identify the manager as a distinctive character type in modern society and thus offer this description:

> The essence of the manager's task is to organize the human and non-human resources available to the organization that employs him so as to improve its position in the marketplace. His role is to persuade, inspire, manipulate, cajole, and intimidate those he manages so that his organization measures up to criteria of effectiveness shaped ultimately by the market but specifically by the expectations of those in control of his organization—finally, its owners.

> The manager also has another life, divided among spouse, children, friends, community, and religious and other nonoccupational involvements. Here . . . another kind of personality is actualized. . . . "Public" and "private" roles often contrast sharply, as symbolized by the daily commute from green suburban settings reminiscent of rural life to the industrial, technological ambience of the workplace.[53]

Television and the Internet reinforce isolation and individualism. Robert D. Putnam states that television has been the primary factor in the recent decline of citizen involvement in politics, in secondary associations, and in volunteerism.[54] This decline has weakened social trust and eroded social capital.[55]

When a nation's social capital diminishes, the nation loses common purpose. It becomes no more than an aggregate of unencumbered individuals. Some individuals may thrive in this setting, but the body politic does not. It flourishes only when the structures for civil conversation, the institutions for public debate, and the forums for reasoned discourse function credibly and well. When they do not, civil religion loses its vitality and viability. Furthermore, when religion is privatized, it loses its public voice and becomes unable to contribute to the commonweal. It no longer inspires; it ceases to be a resource for moral leadership. The public square is left empty. Other forces, such as the judiciary and the market, then move in and fill the vacuum. They replace religion's role. When religion is not a partner in the public debate, the cost to society is high. When possessive individualism is the regnant habit of the heart, the nation's social and spiritual capital diminishes.[56]

Religion does not have to remain a private matter. It can have a contemporary public role. Religious language is increasingly becoming the language of conscience in the public square.

> Nothing, however, stands in the way of religion's efforts to persuade, in those that are acceptable (or should be acceptable) to all. . . . Religion, then, is not merely tolerated in the public square but has the liberty to pursue its objective, provided only that it recognize that, in the interests of religious liberty for all, the ground rules are secular. . . . True religious liberty leads not to a secularist state devoid of spiritual values but to a secularist state of vibrantly contending spiritual values, reflecting convictions of conscience deeply held.[57]

Religion can challenge the conscience and the values of the nation. It can provide the consumer culture with a new collective vision of a better future. It can offer hope.

> The good society cannot exist without institutions built on the principle of service rather than profit. It must provide for its losers, not only for their sake, but . . . for the sake of the souls of the winners.

> This communitarian countertheme to American individualism has been . . . implicit in Lincoln's vision of a sacred republic. It was revived by . . . the Salvation Army and the Red Cross . . . as well as in the broader ameliorative program that came to be known as the Social Gospel. Even as Americans lived more and more by the logic of the marketplace, revulsion was building at the life of untempered greed. . . .
>
> What Christianity and democracy share is the idea that to live in a purely instrumental relation with other human beings, to exploit and then discard them, is to give in entirely to the predatory instinct and to leave unmet the need for fellowship and reciprocity.[58]

The Catholic imagination provides a unique vision. It upholds the dignity of the individual and the common good.[59] It serves as a vital resource for public life by providing foundational principles for political and economic citizenship.

> The prophetic role of religion requires a public religion, one that dares to stand with the secular. . . . Prophetic religion requires that religion be on the side of the oppressed, the dispossessed, the disinherited, and the discriminated. Prophetic religion refuses to be captive of any given culture, society, or socioeconomic class. It refuses to identify wealth and poverty in terms of moral superiority and inferiority. Prophetic religion seeks to advance justice and human rights for all members of society, even when in conflict with long established social patterns and traditions that run counter to these goals. . . . The prophetic role of religion in society means far more than mere involvement of religion in society. Furthermore, the church is called to be not a sectarian but a *public* witness to the Gospel.[60]

Public theology provides a vision for society. The next section considers its role.

Public Theology

In 1981 Martin E. Marty described public theology as

> an effort to interpret the life of a people in the light of a transcendent reference. The people in this case are not simply the church but the pluralism of peoples with whom the language of the church is engaged in a larger way. The *public church*, then, is a specifically Christian polity and witness.[61]

Religious faith functions in two spheres. First, each religious community derives its inner life from saving faith. But, second, its mission in the world and its public theology are due to an ordering faith that "helps constitute civil, social, and political life from a theological point of view."[62] Its task is to analyze the common bonds of people, to influence their lives together, and to transform public life.[63]

Numerous public thinkers have provided their visions for a better, happier, more just society. Benjamin Franklin, Jonathan Edwards, Reinhold Niebuhr, H. Richard Niebuhr, Abraham Joshua Heschel, John A. Ryan, and John Courtney Murray, among others, have written on the role that religion plays in the public realm.[64] Public theology promotes the practice of civic virtue among its members. It also makes connections between citizenship and discipleship.

> To act as a public church means to engage in public discourse, advancing reasoned argument based on the common good to justify positions on national morality. . . . In contrast to the private church, which like the family provides a comfortable haven from worldly cares, the public church must appeal in its political argument to that search for larger meanings that goes on even at the heart of the therapeutic personality. For only breadth of vision can finally transform private virtue, associated exclusively with self-interest, into public virtue directed toward the common good. . . . The public church remains today the primary means whereby private morality can be refocused upon the public sphere.[65]

In its social teaching, the Catholic Church has developed a public theology. Its cornerstones have been a respect for personal dignity and an appreciation of the common good. Catholic social teaching provides a leaven for a new social capital. It continues to build bridges between the church and society.

Catholic social teaching has traditionally used the language of natural law to engage in public discourse, which has enabled it to reach the widest possible public, to dialogue with a wide variety of thinkers and policy makers, and to avoid sectarian thinking. Catholic public theology is

> a self-consciously religious effort to form and mold American culture and politics so that they conform more fully with God's plan of salvation. . . . It regards American society and indeed all societies as subject to an enduring order of justice which calls all nations to self-criticism and reform. [Public theology] seeks to create a new unity among the American people through civility and discourse; but it proceeds from the belief that the ultimate measure of public dialogue is . . . its ability to restore to the U.S. as a nation a spiritually-rich vision of society. It seeks to formulate a common religiously-based frame of reference . . . which brings to the most important debates on American public policy the spiritual values which can alone add unity and depth to cultural and political discussion.[66]

This vision has been communicated to the public through theologians and social activists, public statements and pastoral letters, newspapers and journals, schools and universities. Catholic social teaching has been publicized and developed by staff members at the Social Action Department (SAD).

The Social Theology of George G. Higgins

Monsignor George G. Higgins related the principles of Catholic social teaching to workplace issues such as the meaning of work, the rights and responsibilities of workers, the role of organized labor in American democracy, labor–management cooperation, and justice for the poor. His social theology rests on the idea of economic citizenship.

Archbishop Rembert Weakland used Higgins' idea of economic citizenship to discuss the plight of the poor. In his address to an urban ministry conference in Milwaukee in October 1996, Weakland acknowledged that the economy was working well for many. He noted, however, that it was not benefiting welfare recipients and the working poor. The poor believed that they had no voice in the decisions that affected their work, families, and security. In short, Weakland indicated that the working poor and those on welfare did not enjoy economic citizenship. He quoted from a recent lecture that Higgins had given in Washington:

> As Msgr. George Higgins has so often said, many people simply do not feel that they enjoy "economic citizenship," i.e., the right to make decisions that affect their economic security. Msgr. Higgins wrote: "Economic citizenship requires a voice in the decisions that shape your life and your livelihood—a voice in your job, your community and your country. Economic citizenship requires a sense of recognition and respect—for the work you do, the contribution you make and your inherent dignity as a child of God."[67]

Democracy flourishes when people enjoy full citizenship. The vitality of a democracy depends not only on voting rights but also on the ability of the masses to earn a living. In fact, those who are not able to earn a living are not inclined to vote or participate in the democratic process. They often feel alienated from the political process.

Judith N. Shklar indicates that citizenship can be democratic only in principle:

> The dignity of work and of personal achievement, and the contempt for aristocratic idleness, have since Colonial times been an important part of American civic self-identification. The opportunity to work and to be paid an earned

> reward for one's labor was a social right because it was a primary source of public respect. . . . Paid labor separated the free man from the slave. The value of political rights was enhanced for the same reason. The ballot has always been a certificate of full membership in society, and its value depends primarily on its capacity to confer a minimum of social dignity.[68]

Social dignity has been tied to having a job. Work is a mark of self-respect and recognition, of civic dignity and social status. Work enables families to feel secure because the members of the family are earning a living.

> The struggle for citizenship . . . has, therefore, been overwhelmingly a demand for inclusion in the polity, an effort to break down excluding barriers to recognition, rather than an aspiration to civic participation as a deeply involving activity.[69]

Some people have envisioned work as a criterion of citizenship. They consider people who earn a job to be good citizens. Those who do not or cannot work are considered a disgrace, a failure, a burden to society. When work disappears from a neighborhood, a town, or a city—or when people cannot work because of a temporary or permanent disability—the unemployed can be stigmatized or demonized. They come to be treated as less than citizens.

The struggle for economic citizenship has a long history. Chapter two traces that history. It begins by introducing George G. Higgins. Much in Higgins' formative years—in his family and in the seminary—prepared him for his lifelong work in the social apostolate. The chapter then investigates the social and historical heritage of the late 19th and early 20th centuries. This study explores the meaning of work in the United States in the 19th century, the birth and the development of organized labor, the pastoral involvement of the Catholic Church in the social question, and the development of an institutional structure to serve the social apostolate.

CHAPTER TWO

The Historical Development of American Catholic Social Teaching

Chapter two begins with a brief sketch of George G. Higgins' formative years to allow the reader to situate Higgins within a larger history of 19th- and 20th-century America. This chapter then investigates the changes that took place in the activity of work and the workplaces, the birth of national labor organizations, the Knights of Labor, church–labor relationships, and Catholic social teaching. In general, this section chronicles the story of Irish and German immigrant males who worked in the mines and the factories. It tells the tale of pro-labor Catholic priests who supported their people through the turmoil of riots and strikes. The issuance of Pope Leo XIII's *Rerum Novarum* inspired the vision of priests such as Peter C. Yorke, Peter E. Dietz, and John J. Burke; the work of Catholic laywomen in the labor movement; and the social action of Catholic religious women. As the church grew in self-confidence and overcame the animus of 19th-century nativism, it created institutional structures for its work in the social apostolate.

George G. Higgins: The Formative Years (1916–1944)

George Gilmary Higgins, the oldest son of C. V. (Charles Vincent) Higgins and Anna Rethinger Higgins, was born on January 21, 1916. His parents had met in Springfield, Illinois, where they married in 1912. They moved north to Chicago and then to LaGrange, Illinois, in 1923. They were blessed with four other children: Anna, born in 1914; Bridget Elizabeth, known as Betty, born in 1918; Eugene, born in 1920; and Mary Catherine, who died in 1926 at the age of three. C. V. and his brothers, during their Springfield years, worked as machinists, firefighters, and engineers on the railroad. All were strong union men. Although his schooling ended in the eighth grade, C. V. had broad intellectual interests. He exposed his children to a variety of people, intellectual pursuits, politics, and church life. He worked with Jews in the post office and cultivated a warm regard for them. He brought young George into the Jewish settlement in the Near West Side of Chicago and exposed him to another culture and way of life. George accompanied C. V. to lectures given by G. K. Chesterton, Hilaire Belloc, and John A. Ryan. They also went to political events for Al Smith in 1928 and to the Democratic convention in Chicago Stadium in 1932, where Franklin Delano Roosevelt was chosen as presidential candidate.

C. V. Higgins was an avid letter writer. He read widely in literature and poetry and in the works of Chesterton, Belloc, Jacques Maritain, and Christopher Dawson. He constantly kept a copy of *The Divine Comedy* with him and read it many times. C. V. worked the night shift at the post office in LaGrange. Each noon young George would join him for lunch and a thorough reading of the latest issues of *America* and *Commonweal*. Higgins remembered his father's passion for the visual arts. He subscribed to *Liturgical Arts*, a journal that promoted liturgical art and architecture. At the time, Dom Virgil Michel—the Benedictine monk from Saint John's Abbey in Collegeville, Minnesota—was a prominent figure in relating the liturgy to daily life and in bridging liturgy and social justice. Michel, with many of the early liturgical pioneers in the 1920s and 1930s, considered the liturgy to be the basis for social action. Higgins said:

> Michel believed that the Catholic social action movement symbolized by Ryan had concerned itself too much with reform of social and economic institutions and not enough with moral and spiritual reform. . . . He believed activists of his time paid too little attention to the liturgy, which, he constantly insisted, is the indispensable basis of Christian social action. It has served as a constant reminder throughout my own social ministry.[1]

Father John Henry Nawn played an important part in Higgins' life. A one-time Shakespearean actor from Massachusetts, Nawn was pastor of Saint Francis Xavier parish in LaGrange. He was well read and shared his library with C. V. and his son. After the eighth grade, George entered Quigley Preparatory Seminary in the Near North Side of Chicago. Higgins enjoyed his years at Quigley. His seminarian classmates found him to be knowledgeable about world and national events. They liked his genuine, open, and friendly manner.[2]

After Quigley, Higgins entered Saint Mary's Seminary in Mundelein, Illinois. There he met Monsignor Reynold Hillenbrand. Born in 1904, Hillenbrand was ordained to the priesthood in 1930 and appointed rector of Saint Mary's in 1936. These were significant years for developments in Catholic social action and the passage of labor legislation under President Roosevelt. Invigorating the social apostolate were *Quadragesimo Anno*, the encyclical issued by Pope Pius XI on May 15, 1931; the enactment of the so-called Wagner Act in 1935; the establishment of the National Labor Relations Board; and other pro-labor union initiatives. Hillenbrand inaugurated a kind of ecclesial New Deal at Saint Mary's. He supplemented the seminary curriculum with documents such as *Rerum Novarum* and *Quadragesimo Anno* as well as the U.S. bishops' 1919 "Program of Social Reconstruction" and other statements issued by the bishops. He connected the liturgical reform with the social apostolate, interracial and social justice, and the lay apostolate. He inculcated a sense of personal responsibility in his seminarians for effecting change and social transformation. Social action was not marginal to the vocation of the priest. It was at the heart of priestly ministry.

During his seminary days, Higgins told his friend Jack—the late Monsignor John J. Egan—that "you have to learn to fight injustice wherever you find it."[3] Higgins developed a sense of personal responsibility and an overwhelming interest in the social teaching of the church, economics, laws governing everything from wages to working conditions, labor organization, race relations, poverty, and parliamentary law.[4]

Archbishop Samuel Stritch, Cardinal Mundelein's successor, ordained Higgins and his class to the priesthood in 1940. At Hillenbrand's suggestion, Stritch sent Higgins and eleven other priests to study at the Catholic University of America in Washington, DC.[5] Higgins concentrated on economics, political science, and sociology. During these years of graduate study Higgins met Monsignor John A. Ryan, Father Raymond A. McGowan, Father Francis J. Haas (later Bishop), and Father John Hayes (a fellow Chicago priest at SAD). Each brought a distinctive outlook regarding the social apostolate. Ryan supported legislation and unionization as pathways to justice. McGowan stressed the importance of organization and of cooperation among groups representing labor, management, and government. He constantly kept in touch with representatives from organized labor and with the employers' associations in the United States and in Latin America. He advocated a reform of the entire capitalist system. Haas endorsed the labor movement and believed that workers, as social beings, had an obligation to join unions. Hayes concentrated on educating and forming the clergy for the social apostolate.

Higgins completed the master of arts degree in May 1942. His dissertation investigated and elucidated the underconsumption theory of John A. Ryan. Monsignor Ryan took this economic theory from John A. Hobson, an English economist at the turn of the 20th century, and promoted it in *The Living Wage* in 1906. He thought that underconsumption and oversavings were the basis for economic depressions and unemployment. Consequently, he studied and wrote extensively on underconsumption. Higgins' dissertation was expository. He presented Ryan's thought without proffering a personal critique. Ryan's thought on unemployment, economic recovery, and government spending as the "the necessary means to an economy of abundance for all the people"[6] influenced the direction of Higgins' thought.

In his doctoral dissertation, "Voluntarism in Organized Labor in the United States, 1930–1940," Higgins traced the shift in trade unionism from labor voluntarism to a greater reliance on the state and its regulatory activity. He contrasted the problem of the two labor federations: the American Federation of Labor (AFL) and the newly established Congress of Industrial Organization (CIO). The AFL, strongly committed to labor voluntarism from the time of its founder, Samuel Gompers, grudgingly came to accept government involvement and regulatory interference in the process of collective bargaining. The CIO, in contrast, was more congenial to government's regulatory role in labor–management negotiation. The so-called pro-union Wagner Act provided the CIO with the opportunity to unionize the nation's mass-production workers. When the National Labor Relations Board was created in July 1935, the government became partners with labor and management in the process of collective bargaining. Unions increasingly turned to political action to preserve their interests and hard-earned gains. Higgins, as demonstrated by the *Yardstick* columns, continually returned to the role of government in labor–management cooperation. He promoted collective bargaining as the best way to achieve the common good and a just social order.

After the Catholic University of America awarded him the doctoral degree in 1944, Higgins expected to return to an assignment in Chicago, but this never occurred. When tuberculosis caused Father John Hayes to resign his post, SAD invited Higgins to replace him.[7] One of his first tasks was to accompany John A. Ryan on his flight home to St. Paul, Minnesota, where he died a few months later. Father Raymond A. McGowan succeeded Ryan as director of SAD in 1945. Humble and self-effacing, McGowan mentored Higgins as his assistant. The social apostolate called forth Higgins and his warm and gregarious people-skills in various ways.[8] His personal interest in organized labor led him to devote many hours to building relationships and to earning his credentials in the 1940s and the 1950s. He established friendships with union leaders and rank-and-file members. SAD engaged his well-honed intellectual gifts. Higgins spent hours studying, thinking, and writing. He began writing the series Social Action Notes for Priests, a project that Hayes had begun in 1940. This service continued for twenty-eight years and ended with the January–February 1968 issue. He maintained a considerable correspondence and began to collaborate with McGowan in writing the *Yardstick* columns. Higgins wrote nine *Yardstick* columns in 1945. He then assumed full responsibility for the weekly column in 1946. Thus began Higgins' career of fifty-six years in Catholic journalism.

Higgins spent hours in serious study to write the *Yardstick* columns. Since so many of them were devoted to labor–management relations, Higgins cultivated a profound historical consciousness by reading widely in the history of organized labor; labor–management cooperation; labor legislation; and other topics in Catholic studies, economics, and sociology. Doing so helped him to understand the development of workplace justice through collective bargaining and the importance of organized labor in a democratic society.

Changes in the Activity of Work in 19th-Century America

The United States underwent profound change in the 19th century. Immigrants came from northern Europe (especially Ireland and Germany) between 1840–1860 and from eastern and southern Europe between 1880–1910. They sought work, a living wage for themselves and their families, and economic citizenship. They brought their culture, religion, and family heritage across the Atlantic and adapted to a new world. Developments in the nature of work itself and in the growth of the labor movement, with political and religious change in Europe, influenced Catholic social teaching.[9] Dramatic changes occurred in the use of machinery, the workplace, transportation, working conditions, geography, and the employer–employee relationship. Steel machines replaced iron. Electric-powered machines rendered water-driven wheels, domestic looms, and hand tools obsolete. The workplace changed. Before the Civil War most people worked on the farm, in the home, and in local shops.

> Nine out of ten people lived on the land in 1790 and just about eight out of ten were still there in 1860. . . . On the eve of the Civil War, most Americans lived in the countryside, wedded to a distinctive way of life contemporaries called the "household factory" and some present-day historians refer to as the "household economy" or "household production." . . . Spinning and weaving were essential household activities for yeomen and planter households alike. . . . Farm chores, however, were primary.[10]

Skilled local entrepreneurs had some degree of economic citizenship. These artisans trained their own apprentices, hired semiskilled journeyworkers, and established mutual aid societies. This marked the beginnings of local trade unions.[11]

Significant changes in transportation occurred. Wagons traversed better roads; boats used the new canals to bring products to local and regional markets. Skilled workers enjoyed a modest living in good times. Unskilled workers left farms and homesteads to find work in cities and at sea. They took high-risk jobs for meager pay in good times and for terrible wages in bad times.[12] Many resented the skilled workers and barely survived the depression years of 1819 and 1837.[13] Immigrants, the unemployed, and African American slaves were among the poor. Industrial slavery and African American slavery gnawed at the nation's conscience. Former slaves experienced economic apartheid long after the Civil War.

The urban factory system dominated the lives of workers and their families. Workers spent long hours at work, toiled for six or seven days per week, and received meager wages. Work was hazardous, safety was ignored, sanitation was poor, health was precarious, and housing was inadequate. Families survived because women and children worked. Owners threatened their workers' security. They locked out, fired, or replaced workers capriciously. Managers demanded that workers be on time and efficient. Workers were denied leisure, education, family life, and religious practice.

The country expanded further into the West. Inventions such as the telegraph and the railroad revolutionized communications and transportation. More products became available as America developed into a land of comfort. Advertising capitalized on the wants of a growing consumer culture.[14] Magazines pandered to sexual desire. Catalogues offered products giving vitality, pleasure, and a richer life. Ingenious empire builders such as Jay Gould, John D. Rockefeller, Andrew Carnegie, and J. P. Morgan reaped rich rewards. The rich grew enormously richer. The rest lived insecurely. Skilled workers faced job-related problems such as fatigue and injury. They feared that they would lose their jobs to unskilled immigrants. Unskilled workers lived on the margins of poverty. Male workers sought solace and companionship in saloons. Intemperance threatened the fabric of 19th-century America. Poverty, hard times, and despair preyed on most workers and their families. The relationship between owners and workers changed when national labor unions emerged and developed (see table 2.1). Some of these unions were short-lived. Nevertheless, both the male and female workers' impetus to unionize indicated a desire for economic citizenship.

Table 2.1. National Labor Unions

Union (date begun)	*Founder*	*Members*
National Labor Movement (1866)	William H. Sylvis	Men
Knights of St. Crispin (1867)	Group of shoemakers	Shoemakers
Ladies of St. Crispin (1869)	Carrie Wilson	
The Knights of Labor (1869)	Uriah S. Stephen	All workers
American Federation of Labor (1886)	Samuel Gompers	Men: crafts
Union for Industrial Progress (1886)	Mary Kimball Chew	Women: crafts
Women's Trade Union League (1903)	Mary Kenney O'Sullivan William English Walling	Working-class women
Industrial Workers of the World (1905)	Eugene B. Debs	Socialists
Congress of Industrial Organizations (1938)	John L. Lewis	Men: mass production

The National Labor Movement and William H. Sylvis

National labor unions were born after the Civil War, and they flourished during the Gilded Age.[15] Unions gave workers a voice. Owners attempted to silence that voice. They locked workers out, refused to negotiate with unions, and hired nonunion replacements ("scabs") during times of labor unrest. Sometimes owners signed contracts with unions and agreed to the closed shop, then funneled their work to shops employing nonunion workers. Owners frequently spread false rumors about union workers, planted evidence that discredited employees, and created a climate of fear and panic in neighborhoods. Workers endured court hearings, incarceration, violence, and death. The laws, the courts, and the police sided with ownership.

Skilled craft workers responded by unionizing. The Knights of Labor and the socialist Industrial Workers of the World (IWW), the latter founded in 1905, sought systemic change. Both groups worked to educate the public to change the foundations of laissez-faire capitalism. They organized to force owners to recognize their right to form associations, guarantee the closed shop, and negotiate with fairness. The AFL concentrated on practical goals for the rank and file—namely, the eight-hour workday, higher wages, safety in the workplace, and better working conditions for women and children.

The time was ripe for political agitation. The country faced depressions in 1873, 1877–1878, 1884, and 1893–1894. Smaller recessions were commonplace. Unions sought public support and sympathy in the general press and in workers' newspapers. Many newspapers, including those under union auspices, created public support and sympathy for workers. Workers protested in the stockyards; marched in the streets; and engaged in work stoppages, boycotts, and strikes. Strikes easily turned into violent clashes, with workers on one side and police, militia, and private detectives on the other. Owners thwarted strikes by obtaining injunctions. Between 1890 and 1920 state and federal courts issued 2,095 injunctions. Owners established the National Association of Manufacturers (NAM) in 1895 to maintain their power over labor and to promote the open shop.[16]

William H. Sylvis, the son of a wagon maker, led the effort to create the first national trade union.[17] Born in western Pennsylvania in 1828, Sylvis spent his youth working in a local iron foundry. He completed his apprenticeship in the 1840s and quickly became a journeyman molder. He joined the local Journeymen Stove and Hollow-Ware Molders Union in Philadelphia and became an active labor organizer.

> He threw his boundless energy into the tasks of bringing all the city's molders into the organization and of communicating with unions of the trade in other cities for the purpose of establishing a national union. Thirty-two delegates from nine different unions gathered in Philadelphia on July 5, 1859, and drafted plans for the National Union of Iron Molders. At the formal founding convention early in 1860, Sylvis was made treasurer, and he wrote the preamble to the union's constitution.[18]

The molders organized to protect their jobs and

> "to elevate the moral, social and intellectual condition of every Moulder in the country." Delegates to the 1860 convention denounced piece work, the employment of "bucks," and unrestricted employment of apprentices.[19]

Sylvis lost the national treasurer's job. The new organization collapsed with the Civil War. In 1863 the revived Iron Molders' International Union became the National Labor Union (NLU), and Sylvis was elected its president. By 1865 his indefatigable organizing made this the strongest and most close-knit labor organization in the United States. Union members paid taxes, built up a strike fund, issued union cards, and guaranteed a closed shop when a scab album was published in the labor press. Sylvis supported collective bargaining and discouraged strikes except as last resort. He worked for more-general labor reforms, such as the eight-hour workday, the formation of cooperatives, and currency reform. Literally worn out from intense union organizing, Sylvis died a premature death in 1869. The NLU collapsed in 1872. Despite its fragile and short life, the NLU "was a workers' organization—the first, enduring nationwide institution created by the American working class."[20] The NLU encouraged all workers to join unions; it promoted currency ("greenback") reform; and it raised important issues that would concern the labor movement for years to come.

First, the NLU raised the issue of workday hours. It worked to reduce the ten- or twelve-hour day. Eight-hour leagues and advocates lobbied to persuade Congress to make the eight-hour day a legal day's work. They argued that increased leisure would bring increased spending.[21] Big business countered by reducing hours and wages. Second, the NLU supported the development of cooperatives. Big business opposed them. One by one the cooperatives died, partly due to the inefficiency of union officials. Third, the NLU highlighted the need for currency reform, the social and political rights of women, the earnings and organization of wage-earning women, and political action on behalf of organized labor.[22] Fourth, the NLU faced the vexing issue of racial discrimination. Isaac Myers, a black ship-caulker who founded a dry-dock company for black artisans driven from jobs by returning Confederate soldiers, summed up the racial situation at the National Labor Congress on September 4, 1869. In his speech, Myers

> praised the memory of Sylvis and hailed the NLU for "taking the colored laborer by the hand and telling him that his interest is common with yours." He went on to stress the common interests of workers of both races in organization, good wages, and shorter hours, but he emphasized the point that white workers who barred blacks from employment erected an impassable barrier in the path toward unity. "If American citizenship means anything at all," Myers explained, "it means the freedom of labor, as broad and universal as the freedom of the ballot."[23]

However, more than any issue, the state of the economy determined the life and death of unions. The panic of 1873 and the depression of the 1870s brought hard times and contributed to the decline of the NLU.

The Knights of Labor

The Knights of Labor became the second national labor organization.[24] On December 9, 1869, nine veterans of the Garment Cutters' Association met in Philadelphia. On December 28, 1969, seven of those men met again and launched the Noble and Holy Order of the Knights of Labor. Soon six more members joined them. Uriah Stephens provided inspirational leadership. The Knights were at first a secret society. New members were ritually initiated. This kept them free from employer interference.

The Knights remained small in number. Their members were politically conservative skilled white craftsmen. A second local assembly was formed in 1872, and a district assembly was created in 1873 to coordinate the efforts of all locals. The Knights expanded beyond Philadelphia when the New York City gold beaters formed Local Assembly 28 in early 1874.

The Knights changed when they expanded into the mines and the mills. In 1875 local assemblies were created in Pittsburgh and in northeastern Pennsylvania. In 1876 Local Assembly 222 elected Terence V. Powderly, a twenty-seven-year-old machinist, as its master workman.[25] Two years later he was elected mayor of Scranton on the Greenback Labor Party ticket. He served from 1878 to 1884.

The Knights survived the brutal railroad strikes of 1877 and called their first convention in Reading, Pennsylvania, on January 1, 1878. The grand assembly produced a preamble and a constitution. More copies of its ritual book, the *Alephon Kruptos*, became available in 1878. Still, the Knights remained a small group with big ideas. When Uriah Stephens resigned so that he could run for U.S. Congress in 1879, the grand assembly chose Powderly as the new grand master workman. This was the turning point for the Knights.

Powderly, an Irish Catholic, never liked the order's secrecy. Under his leadership the Knights became increasingly public.

> The future of American labor in the mid-1880s appeared to lie with the Knights of Labor. For the first time a labor organization seemed strong enough to challenge industry on its own grounds. . . . The Noble and Holy Order was in reality an indigenous response to American conditions and, much as had been the National Labor Union, a combination of trade union and general reform philosophy. Its leaders looked forward to a "corporate commonwealth." However hazy their goals may have been, they stressed organization, education, and political agitation as the best means to build a new society. The Knights insisted that the existing economic system could only be changed peaceably, and this often led them to oppose strikes.[26]

The 1880s were a volatile and revolutionary period. A general depression led to unemployment and reduced workers. More and more workers unionized. The Knights organized, planned, and thought out their goals. Membership grew to 42,517 in 1882 when Joseph Buchanan organized Western railroad men and miners. The first test of the Knights' solidarity came in the 1883 when telegraphers lost their strike with Jay Gould and Western Union. The Knights grew to over 74,000 members in 1884 and to more than 111,000 in 1885.

> One reason for its growth, despite meager results, is that the Order sought to bring fringe groups to its center and into accord with the rhetoric of its constitution. In theory, only bankers, lawyers, gamblers, speculators and liquor tradesmen were banned from KOL membership. By the early 1880s, the KOL was already a diverse assortment of Marxists and Lasallean socialists in New

York City, anarchists in Chicago and Denver, Germans in Cincinnati, French Canadians in New England mill towns, and scores of reformers, temperance advocates, socially conscious ministers, ritualists, small employers, and trade unionists. . . . In addition, the Order took in women and African Americans. The first women Knights were organized into an all-female local in 1881 when Mary Stirling and Harry Skeffington organized Philadelphia shoe operatives in Local Assembly 1684. . . . The first confirmed black assembly was of coal miners in Ottumwa, Iowa.[27]

The next test for the Knights came in 1885 when shopmen on the Wabash Railroad spontaneously struck against Jay Gould's Southwest System. Engineers joined in the strike. Union Pacific railroad workers who were Knights contributed monetary and organizational support. Local assemblies of the Knights organized thousands of new members. The railroads fired the shopmen on the Wabash, closed their shops, and then reopened with militant, armed strikebreakers. In reply, all the Knights of Labor on the Wabash struck. Gould met with the executive board of the Knights and agreed to the board's demands.[28] The victory was decisive for the Knights. The order grew to 729,677 members in a single year. Robert E. Weir estimates that over one million called themselves Knights.[29]

Why did the Knights of Labor attract so many workers? First, they supported the eight-hour workday. Second, they ran for elected office and won. In the November 1886 elections, candidates from the Knights, independent labor parties, and socialist groups won local and state offices. Third, they cultivated unity and solidarity through a vibrant musical, literary, and material culture. Labor music played a significant role in minimizing individualism and developing a communal identity. Group singing cultivated the values, principles, and beliefs of the rank-and-file members. Music encouraged the practice of virtues that overcome intemperance, corruption, greed, hypocrisy, and tyranny.[30]

> Music reinforced the call to remake American society and place producerist Christians in charge. . . . Songs echoed motifs of Jesus the carpenter, the sanctity of toil, and Christ the condemner of Mammon worship. Just as Christ cleansed the temple to prepare for his own Passion, so too would the Knights cleanse American society to prepare it for labor's dawn. . . . Knights celebrated True Christianity and the eight-hour day.[31]

This musical tradition among the Knights gave birth to the songs of the IWW and the CIO.[32] Poetry, newspapers, short stories, novels, and serialized fiction entertained and promoted labor identity and solidarity. The Knights produced badges, banners, pins, and pictures of Uriah Stephens, Terence

Powderly, and other leaders. The unity of the Knights was most evident in this material culture.

Despite the success of the Knights, Powderly found himself overwhelmed by the order's growth. Success masked the order's divided ideological factions. The Haymarket Square riot of 1886 frightened many people. Some identified the Knights with the Molly Maguires and with anarchists. Despite the fact that many Knights were Catholics, many priests were suspicious. The practice of secrecy and oath taking reminded them of the Masons. Powderly constantly worked to gain the Catholic Church's support for the Knights.

These factors, especially the decision to make the Knights a secret society again, contributed to a decline in membership in the 1890s. More important, the power of big business and the depression of the 1890s contributed to the decline of the Knights, the rise of Samuel Gompers, and the AFL.

The Knights of Labor and the Catholic Church

Catholicism in the last decades of the 19th century was a minority church struggling to find its place. On the institutional level, the hierarchy wanted to demonstrate that Catholics supported republican ideals, maintained peace and order, practiced virtue, and were good citizens. On the practical level, pastors promoted personal holiness and the avoidance of personal sin, greed, and dishonesty. Preachers at parish missions inveighed against intemperance and indolence. Charity for the poor and needy was promoted rather than justice, systemic change, or social reform.[33]

The Catholic Church faced a dilemma in its relationship with the Knights of Labor. The order's initiation ritual and oath had a quasireligious character. The Knights appeared to be similar to fraternal organizations such as the Odd Fellows, the Knights of Pythias, and the Freemasons. The church in the United States and Europe feared and suspected Freemasons the most. Many of the clergy preached against them and discouraged followers from joining them. Masonic lodges reached America by 1730, little more than a decade after the founding in 1717 of the London Grand Lodge from which all modern Masonry stems. Freemasonry derived many of its symbols and the idea of a secret initiatory lodge from the occult tradition, combining them with ideals from chivalry and the free-thinking spirit of the Enlightenment. The lodges were a spiritual home for progressive-minded middle-class business and professional men. They often were hotbeds of anticlericalism and advanced thinking about democracy and the "rights of man." Freemasons, it seemed, stood for all that the church opposed: human reason, liberalism, and democracy; secrecy and oaths; occult and ancient wisdom; and an eclectic religiosity.[34] The church faced a critical choice. Should it oppose

Catholic membership in the Knights, or should it support a fraternity that would probably have been condemned in Europe? In Quebec, Cardinal Elzear-Alexandre Taschereau succeeded in having the Knights condemned. James Augustine Healey—the bishop of Portland, Maine, and the first African American bishop in the United States—threatened to excommunicate members of the Knights. He treated them as Freemasons.

Many priests refused to support the Knights. They suspected that all labor unions were filled with anarchists and socialists. One exception was Father Cornelius O'Leary, pastor of a railroad parish in DeSoto, Missouri. He supported workers in his parish. When the Knights went on strike in March 1886, O'Leary stood by them. Later he testified on behalf of the Knights before the Curtin Committee. In November Archbishop Peter Richard Kenrick reassigned him to a parish in Webster.[35]

Some priests were openly hostile to the Knights. Powderly's correspondence indicates that he suffered abuse from priests who misinterpreted the order's insignia pin. Other priests used the pulpit to rail against Powderly and the order. Powderly disdained what he called "Churchianity" and its displacement of genuine Christianity. Nevertheless, Powderly constantly tried to gain favor with the church because so many Knights were Irish Catholic.[36]

Commitment to labor and reform was reinforced by Irish nationalism. The Irish in the United States were committed to the cause of the Land League in Ireland. Charles Stuart Parnell sought to transfer the ownership of Irish lands from the aristocratic families to the tenant farmers. The New York newspaper *Irish World* and Powderly linked Irish land reform with social issues in the United States. When the Land League collapsed in the 1880s, Henry George combined the promotion of land ownership with social reform.[37]

> For George, the root cause of social disorder and distress was the ability of a few landowners to profit from rising land values. To correct this injustice and thus achieve a more equal distribution of wealth, George proposed a single tax. This single tax on the 'unearned increment' of the land—that rise in land values caused by market demand, rather than by any improvement the owners made—would bring in sufficient money to ensure social progress. Utopian though it was, George's program attracted an enthusiastic response, and his book *Progress and Poverty* was widely read.[38]

Terence V. Powderly and the Knights of Labor, the socialists, Samuel Gompers and the AFL, and Father Edward McGlynn supported George's ideas. They actively campaigned for him when he sought election as mayor of New York in 1886.[39] McGlynn was a gifted speaker and an intellectual.[40] His thought was rooted in Jeffersonian ideals and in Thomistic theology.

> George and McGlynn represented the Jeffersonian, equal rights, and anti-monopolist tradition in the United Labor Party. Just as they battled against capitalist monopolies, they also battled against the socialist desire to make the state a national monopoly. . . . McGlynn stressed that his social reform was gradualist, i.e., to educate the people with an organic social vision that prompted their moral imaginations to see beyond self-interest to self-donation for the common good.[41]

His principles for social reform reflected his theology.

> McGlynn perceived in George's Single Tax program that economic plan which affirmed the image of God in humankind and constructed a policy built upon a stewardship of use, productivity, exchange and human cultivation.[42]

McGlynn served as the beloved pastor of Saint Stephen, a parish known throughout New York City for its charity and its commitment to the poor, the orphaned, and the needy. He worked indefatigably for the temporal and spiritual needs of Irish American workers. McGlynn came into conflict with Archbishop Michael Augustine Corrigan over his support for the public school system in New York and for his political activism on behalf of Henry George.[43] When McGlynn refused to go to Rome to represent his views, Corrigan succeeded in having him excommunicated. The excommunication was lifted in 1892. McGlynn became reunited with the church and made pastor of the parish of St. Mary in Newburgh, New York, in 1894. He continued to speak at civic and labor meetings and remained active in the single-tax movement. "He made his last great speech at the funeral of Henry George on October 31, 1897, where he uttered those famous words, 'There was a man sent from God, and his name was Henry George.'"[44]

The debate in the church concerning the Knights of Labor, Henry George's social reform, and the celebrated McGlynn affair highlighted the serious plight of the Catholic working classes in the late 19th century. Would the church support or condemn Catholic membership in the Knights of Labor? The answer would play a role in determining whether the working poor would be loyal or lost to the church.

Cardinal James Gibbons "had begun his career among working people. He understood that blue-collar families were the Church's core membership, and he feared that . . . a condemnation would be a public relations disaster."[45] When he visited Rome in 1887 to receive the Cardinal's red hat, he presented a lengthy statement that defended the rights of workers to organize and he urged that the Knights of Labor not be condemned.

Gibbons began by stating that the Catholic social teaching of Pope Leo XIII had served as a guide for the U.S. bishops at their October 1886 meeting.

> In weighing this question I have been very careful to follow as my constant guide the spirit of the Encyclicals, in which our Holy Father, Leo XIII, has so admirably set forth the dangers of our time and their remedies, as well as the principles by which we are to recognize associations condemned by the Holy See. Such was also the guide for the Third Plenary Council of Baltimore.[46]

He then indicated that only two of U.S. archbishops had voted to condemn the Knights. Then Gibbons stated the reasons that determined the vote of the majority of the committee. He addressed the internal structure and practices of the Knights. He indicated that the order was not hostile to the faith.

He then addressed social evils, the public injustices, and "the heartless avarice which, through greed of gain, pitilessly grinds not only the men, but particularly the women and children in various employments [which] makes it clear that it is . . . the right of the laboring classes to protect themselves."[47] He concluded that association was the most efficacious, natural, and just means to remedy the avarice, oppression, and corruption of individuals and corporations.

The report spoke about the consequences that would occur "from a lack of sympathy for the working class, from a suspicion of their aims, from a hasty condemnation of their methods."[48] First, the church would not be considered a friend of the people. It would lose their hearts. Second, the church would be seen as un-American and alien to the spirit of the nation. Third, the church would risk losing the Catholic working class. Finally, Gibbons indicated that it was foolish to condemn the Knights, an organization that would eventually die out. He requested that Rome exercise prudence and not condemn the Knights.[49]

Gibbons' memorandum marked a turning point for labor and social reform. Higgins said that Father John Tracy Ellis considered it

> the most important document in the history of the Catholic Church in the United States. . . . Had Rome condemned the Knights of Labor in the United States, the church in our country would have lost the allegiance of many, perhaps the majority, of Catholic immigrant workers. The relationship of church and organized labor would have soured, resulting in a permanent rift.[50]

Once the Vatican lifted the ban on the Knights, the church was perceived as being officially on the side of labor. The church in the United States would now be able to create its own social gospel tradition.

Pope Leo XIII and *Rerum Novarum*

The second half of the 19th century was a time of revolutionary social, economic, and religious change in Europe. Serious issues such as the consolidation of nation-states, the emergence of individualism and liberalism, and the attractive nature of socialism underlay struggles between the rich and the poor.[51] The Catholic Church lost its political power, and the papal states shrunk, finally reduced to the Vatican alone. The church was losing its connections with the working-class poor in urban areas. Catholic clergy and laity puzzled over ways to minister to the working poor and their families. Catholic intellectuals and pastoral agents sought a *via media* between the Charybdis of industrial capitalism and the Scylla of socialist anarchy.

Social Catholicism responded to the plight of the urban poor in three ways: paternalism, corporatism, and Christian democracy. Each of these, according to Mary Elsbernd, differed in its goal and method:

> The paternalists sought the universal application of charity through the moral transformation of industrial employees into patrons. The corporatists sought a total restructuring of economic society through the enforced collaboration of employers and workers in the corporative system. The Christian democrats sought to give the initiative and responsibility for the reformation of the economic system back to the workers through a system of trade union and legislative participation.[52]

The Renewal of Thomism: Paternalism

Paternalism was aptly named. It maintained the hegemony of the aristocracy. Its role was to take care of workers through charity. Workers were recipients, not agents of their destiny. Paternalism "had enjoyed a certain favor since the midpoint of the century. Spurred on by the theory of LePlay it strove 'to make the ruling classes generous but firm guides of a docile proletariat.'"[53]

Albert de Mun, a French aristocrat with a social conscience, responded to the plight of the poor by founding charitable societies and the *oeuvre de cercles catholiques*. These associations were intended to bridge the gaps separating the French aristocracy, the factory owners, and the workers. Artisans and industrial workers were included. These circles were examples of organized social effort, places

> where workers could gather to relax, to get counseling and material help. They would be equipped with reading rooms and gymnasiums and would provide games of all kinds, even concerts. He was acutely aware of the Church's failure in regard to the poor.[54]

De Mun was instrumental in passing social legislation on behalf of working women and children and including reduced workday hours; Sunday rest; and insurance for workers who suffered from disease, accidents, and old age. "Like-thinking French employers formed a union, *Patrons du nord*, which worked diligently to create associations and services for their employees."[55]

In Italy, Catholic social action functioned along paternalistic lines with the *Opera dei ongressi*. Similarly Belgian social Catholicism promoted an economic liberalism and political monarchism.

> The trend became known as the School of Angers since the disciples of [Charles] Perin and [Frederic] LePlay met there under the patronage of Bishop [Charles-Emile] Freppel. The school stood for freedom of association when it was understood as the association of free individuals for the mutual defense of individual rights; free and spontaneous charity was their goal and motivation; above all they rejected state and ecclesiastical intervention into labor problems.[56]

Paternalism did not attract the industrial workers, because it envisioned no change in the economic system and because it provided no place for their participation in decision making. It denied them economic citizenship.

Corporatism

The corporatists realized that poverty did not result from a breakdown of morals or from a lack of benevolence by the affluent. They did not believe that the working class had an aptitude for self-determination. They also distrusted the liberal economic system. Therefore, they promoted an enforced collaboration of employers and workers.

The principal sowers of corporatist social Catholicism were Wilhelm Emmanuel von Ketteler, the Bishop of Mainz, and Count Rene de la Tour du Pin.

Ketteler was a gifted pastor. He realized that the church had to bring fresh thinking to the issues of church/state and labor/capital. In the 1850s Friedrich Pilgram, a writer for the influential Catholic periodical *Historisch-politische Blatter,* further influenced Ketteler. Pilgram was trying to find ways to reassociate capital and labor without subjugating labor to capital. Ketteler realized that the church could not remain satisfied with the social and political institutions of a bygone era. These institutions needed to improve and change to respect the rights and the dignity of the working class.

Ketteler was also a gifted thinker. He espoused the natural law thinking of the neo-Thomists. He consulted the opinion of the socialist leader Ferdinand Laselle. Ketteler presented his proposals for aiding the industrial working class in 1864 in his book *The Labor Problem and Christianity*. There he suggested that the church champion human dignity and encourage charitable institutions for the sick, the poor, and the aged. Second, it should support the primary institution of Christian marriage and home life and provide education in economic skills and in the realm of culture and values. Finally, it should organize systemic change through productive cooperatives financed by the voluntary cooperation of Christians. Labor would then no longer be treated as just another commodity.

In an address at the celebration of the Kolping Journeymen's Association in Mainz, Germany, November 19, 1865, and more publicly in 1869, Ketteler admitted the need for government intervention, religious and moral support, and opportunities for self-help and association. In a sermon preached to thousands of workers in 1869, Ketteler embraced the labor movement and endorsed the right of the workers to organize and be organized. He called for government social policies that favored workers. He recommended that a number of priests be trained in economics and become familiar with the factory system. He endorsed church support for Catholic lay leaders in the labor movement.[57]

Count Rene de la Tour du Pin was an associate of Albert de Mun. The Austrian Karl von Vogelsand introduced him to Ketteler's thought. La Tour du Pin suggested the corporatist system as a Christian restructuring of society through a transformed and adapted guild system. He envisioned that workers of a particular profession would join in local units with employers at the head. Workers would share profits by having shares in the corporation. Local, regional, and national units would make binding decisions regarding the conditions of labor, wages, employment, and dismissal.

In addition to the corporative theory, la Tour du Pin and his *Conseil des etudes* held that private property could be limited and that the state had a right to intervene in economic affairs. The corporatists considered their position to be an alternative to liberalism and socialism. Between 1884 and 1891 corporatists from France, Belgium, Germany, Austria, and Italy met under the presidency of Swiss cardinal Gaspard Mermillod "to work out a version of the corporatist theory adapted to the needs of the modern world."[58] Pope Leo XIII regularly received reports concerning the results of their meetings. They eventually moved beyond the mixed corporation and decided to support separate associations for workers and management. In addition, they affirmed insurance programs for employees as well as international legislation for workers' rights and wages.

The Fribourg Union, founded in 1884, promoted corporatist thinking. It was immensely loyal to the papacy and represented an attempt to establish modern structures based on the medieval guild system. It called on the state to intervene to safeguard justice and the common good. But it also endorsed the initiative of individuals and the actions of mediating organized bodies. Thinkers in the Fribourg Union gave birth to the principle of subsidiarity.

> The legacy of the Fribourg Union remains a mixed one. Its concrete proposals proved inadequate in the face of the vast changes taking place in industrial society. . . . [It] successfully preserved vital elements of the traditional Christian vision of a good society: the social purpose of property, the positive but limited role of the state, the centrality of justice, the primacy of duties over rights, the principle of subsidiarity, and most importantly, the crucial role of the common good as the unifying force of the political community.[59]

Christian Democracy

Christian democracy was the last trend to emerge. It accepted the techniques and principles of political republicanism. It also thought that the legislative process was the best means toward achieving a just socioeconomic structure. This trend sought to involve workers in taking responsibility and initiative to change the economic system. The Christian democratic movement identified with and encouraged workers' unions. It did not seek to replace existing economic structures with Christian alternative institutions, nor did it accept extant structures.

> Franz Hitze, . . . a co-founder with Ludwig Windhorst of the *Volksverein*, gave the following description of his aim in life and political career—an aim which probably summarized that of many others.
>
> "Now began a new philosophy and a new program for my life with the aim of devoting all my attempts to the lifting up of these masses [of workers] by means of a comprehensive *social reform*, systematic institutions for their education and self-training, to make them economically, morally and mentally capable of *co-operating in state and society* as mature and responsible persons. . . ."
>
> Hitze and the *Volksverein* gave leadership to the Christian trade union movement beyond the German borders.[60]

The *Volksverein* educated Catholics in Germany and in the United States. It had eight hundred thousand members by the beginning of the First World War. Its courses and publications trained Catholic activists in social and economic ethics, in local level organizations and unions, in legislative participation, in local organizations, and in unions for the people and by the people.

During the pontificate of Leo XIII, clergy and laity involved themselves concretely in social action on behalf of the working poor. Leaders such as Cardinal Henry Edward Manning in England courageously espoused the cause of the poor.[61] Manning said, "My politics are social politics . . . my radicalism [goes] down to the roots of the sufferings of the people."[62] Manning took up the cause of the workers: "Whatever rights capital possesses, labour possesses."[63] His decisive intervention and advocacy on behalf of the dock strikers in London in 1889 endeared him to workers. They formed a great cortege at his funeral and carried his picture with that of Karl Marx.[64]

Devoted Catholic laity served the poor directly through local units of the Saint Vincent de Paul Society, founded by Fredric Ozanam, yet another luminary of 19th-century social Catholicism.[65] Study circles trained workers in social ethics and economics. Associations grouped farmworkers and factory workers together. Politicians were advocates for legislative change, for better wages and working conditions, for fewer working hours and Sunday's rest, and for the rights of women and children.

All the while, two significant shifts were gradually developing. The first shift was perceptual. It dealt with how members of the working class were perceived. Earlier in the century workers were envisioned as recipients of the charity rendered them by the aristocracy. By century's end workers started to gain a voice as agents and participants in shaping their own well-being.

The second shift was relational. It dealt with the relationship of church and state. Earlier Catholic teaching posited that the church, because it possessed the truth, should enjoy a preferential role in Catholic countries. As secularization and industrialization developed, the church lost its privileged position. The state became autonomous. Sometimes it was antagonistic or indifferent toward the church. By century's end the church struggled to relate its moral vision to the aspirations of a secularized modern world. Pope Leo XIII's espousal of natural law philosophy provided a vocabulary elastic enough to offer universal moral principles. These principles were then applied on the local level to benefit the workers and the common good.

Pope Leo XIII—while still Vincent Joachim Pecci, archbishop of Perugia and papal nuncio in Brussels—had observed the impact of industrial capitalism on the working-class poor. In an effort to find a solution, he studied Ketteler's writings. After becoming pope, several events influenced him and propelled him to publish *Rerum Novarum*. These included the position of the United States bishops regarding the Knights of Labor; the influence of Henry George in England, Ireland, and the United States; the transatlantic connection between Cardinal Manning in England and Father Edward McGlynn in the United States; and Manning's intervention on behalf of the workers in the London dock strike of 1889. Pope Leo XIII also met with workers whom Leon Harmel brought on pilgrimage to Rome. He kept informed about discussions concerning the degree of state intervention in economic matters and the thinking of various members of the Fribourg Union.[66]

Pope Leo XIII drew from several sources as he oversaw the drafting process of *Rerum Novarum*. The Jesuit Thomist Matteo Liberatore prepared the first schema.[67] Cardinal Tommaso Zigliara, also a Thomist, followed with a second schema. This was then redacted by Liberatone and Cardinal Camillo Mazella before being translated into Latin by Alessandro Volpini.[68] Gabriele Boccali did further editing. Although the pope did not write a single line, the encyclical reflected his thinking and bore his mark throughout.

> Leo approached the encyclical from a position in reaction to the extremes of socialism and liberalism and based on the authority of Scholastic tradition. . . . The significance of *Rerum Novarum* lay in its existence and in its mediating position between liberalism and socialism. . . . The primary value of *Rerum Novarum* was less what was said about the conditions of labor than the fact that a pope, Leo, addressed the issue in such a way that the movement known as social Catholicism was given tacit papal approval. As such, *Rerum Novarum* not only militated against general Catholic indifference toward socio-economic problems, but also put the Church on the side of industrial labor in attempting amelioration of the situation. . . . The very existence of such a papal document gave the stamp of approval to Catholic involvement in the resolution of socio-economic problems associated with industry and placed the Church's point of entry into the arena as one of reaction to both economic liberalsim and socialism.[69]

Rerum Novarum begins with an impassioned description of the signs of the times, especially regarding class conflict and the gap between the fortunes of the few and the poverty of the many. The first part of the encyclical upholds the natural right of individuals to acquire private property. It presents the family as the primary foundation of society.[70] The encyclical then proceeds to offer its solution to working-class poverty. The answer is found in the mutual recognition of the duties of capital and labor. The encyclical argues that the church contributes to civil society in its role as the guardian of the natural law and the interpreter of true religion. Its model of society is "inspired by an image of medieval unity within which classes live in mutually interdependent order and harmony."[71] Capital and labor need each other

> to maintain the equilibrium of the body politic. Each requires the other; capital cannot do without labor nor labor without capital. Mutual agreement results in pleasantness and good order; perpetual conflict necessarily produces confusion and outrage.[72]

The encyclical then enumerates the duties of workers and employers. Workers are obligated to do the work that they have agreed to in justice; to respect the property and the person of the employer; and to eschew violence as the means to redress conflict. Employers need to respect that "their [workers] are not their slaves; that they must respect in every man his dignity as a man and as a Christian."[73] Employers are also responsible to ensure that workers have time for religion, that workers are not subject to corrupting influences and occasions, and that they attend to their home and family without squandering their wages. The actions of the rich and the poor are to be guided by justice and motivated by love. Justice demands that employers pay a just wage.[74] "Endorsement of the just wage and protective labor legislation, moreover, implies at least nascent recognition of the fact that some of the deepest problems of the Industrial Revolution were structural and institutional as well as religious and moral in nature."[75]

The social role of the church and state is the next topic addressed. The church has the obligation to preach the Gospel, promote virtuous living, and to attend to the material and external conditions that enable a virtuous life. It is an advocate for and a servant of the poor.[76] The state's primary role is to promote the common good as well as "the interests of the poor."[77] It is to exercise distributive justice to each and every class.

> Justice, therefore, demands that the interests of the poorer population be carefully watched over by the administration, so that they who contribute so largely to the advantage of the community may themselves share in the benefits they create—that being housed, clothed, and enabled to support life, they may find their existence less hard and more endurable.[78]

State intervention is necessary when the good of a particular class, especially the poor, or the common good is threatened with harm and no other solution is possible.[79]

Issues such as the right to strike, the length of the workday, child labor, and a just wage are considered with the state's responsibility to protect the rights of workers and the common good. Leo XIII endorses workers' associations, those with religious foundations as well as those with secular unions.[80] He did not think that unions were socialist or radical. Instead, in light of the history of the medieval guilds, he thought that workers would naturally desire to associate with one another and would cooperate with employers to promote their own good and the good of society.

> The grand hope expressed in *Rerum Novarum* is that, by the cooperative and mutually reinforcing work of the state, unions and intermediate associations, and the church, the working class can be elevated out of poverty, the tensions between the classes can be resolved, and society can be returned to a state of order, harmony, and justice inspired by Christian love and safeguarded by fidelity to the church, offered a social vision.[81]

The vision that *Rerum Novarum* proposes is indebted to the thought of Ketteler, the Liege School and its promotion of state intervention, and the social program of Cardinal Gaspard Mermillod and the Fribourg Union. The social program of the Fribourg Union influenced the direction of subsequent Catholic social thought in the following ways:

1. Some form of nuanced endorsement of the right to own private property
2. Rejection of the idea or necessity of class struggle
3. A critical appraisal of capitalism as a system opposed to the medieval organic model of society, but with no formal condemnation of it
4. An emphasis on workers' rights
5. Strong support for unionization and workers' associations
6. A "just wage" sufficient for a laborer's family[82]

Rerum Novarum became the foundation for the church's involvement in the social question. It became the church's public theology, enabling it to engage in dialogue and partnership with state and society. Its principles became the guide for the church's practical and pastoral ministry at the dawn of the 20th century.

> By his support of the cause of labor as in *Rerum Novarum* and of scientific advance as in *Aeterni Patris* on Christian philosophy and *Providentissimus Deus* on biblical studies and through the opening of the Vatican archives to historians, Leo and the Catholic Church officially recognized the modern world, its problems and needed solutions, but claimed the legitimacy of interpretations and solutions other than the socialist approach.[83]

Rerum Novarum became the basis for Catholic social action in the United States. Its cause was taken up by a variety of priests and lay activists.

Catholic Activists

The Response to *Rerum Novarum*

The initial reaction to *Rerum Novarum* in the United States was favorable. Labor unions had a basis for their cause. Church leaders were enthusiastic. Bishop Spalding of Peoria, Illinois, indicated that the encyclical showed that the mission of the church was the salvation of souls and the salvation of society. Bishop McQuaid of Rochester, New York, directed that the encyclical be read from the church pulpits on successive Sundays. Catholic newspapers publicized its message. African American and white lay Catholics became more deeply aware of their leadership role in fostering social justice and action. They also espoused the Saint Vincent de Paul Society and the cause of temperance. However, "within a few years it was put on the shelf to gather dust. There were several reasons why the encyclical failed to ignite a Catholic crusade for social justice."[84]

First, the church was dealing with too many internal issues to make social justice a priority in the 1890s. The hierarchy was divided into factions. The more conservative German American bishops distrusted the ecclesial politics and the Americanizing tendencies of some of the liberal Irish American bishops. In addition, the church was still struggling to find its place in society. Groups such as the American Protective Association (APA) exhibited strong anti-Catholic sentiment. A rich devotional Catholicism fostered personal piety. Catholic priests preached individual conversion during parish missions.[85] Catholic spirituality reinforced a dichotomy between the sordidly evil workplace and the wholesome domestic hearth. It defined traditional gender roles in society.[86] In short, religion's social consequences were confined to charity and philanthropy, not justice and systemic change. A public theology of social justice would develop only later.[87]

Second, many of the Catholics who came to the United States between 1890 and 1920 were from eastern and southern Europe. They were poor and needed to find employment, housing, education, and health care for their families. The church had little time or energy for theory. It was practical by necessity. The moral life was orientated to the individual. The social dimension developed later.

Third, the church had not yet developed the intellectual tools and structures that would enable it to adapt and apply the abstract principles of *Rerum Novarum* to the American scene.

> Its leaders were not a minority of articulate prophets challenging accepted beliefs, but numerous clergy and laypersons who seldom understood or proclaimed their activities as a distinctly religious response to industrialization. Many Catholics, therefore, had a long experience in coping with social problems before they began to reflect on them.[88]

Finally, the church lacked a national organization for the promotion of its social doctrine.[89] Some bishops clung tenaciously to their role as authoritative teachers of the faith and as guides for the moral life in their dioceses. They were chary of anything that might weaken their position. Save for infrequently called national plenary councils, there was no corporate structure for promoting Catholic social teaching. Social justice ministry depended on the personal charisma and individual initiative of the Catholic clergy, the members of religious communities, and the lay organizations.

Activist Clergy: Thomas J. Hagerty and Thomas McGrady

The bishops and priests that studied *Rerum Novarum* found ample material to combat socialism. Ignoring Pope Leo XIII's criticism of capitalism and the call for social reform, many clergy distrusted labor unions and waged their own crusade against socialism. This intensified when the International Workers of the World was founded and when the Socialist Party entered the political arena. German Catholics in particular feared socialism, distrusted the motives and the politics of Irish American Catholics, and tended to work independently of any other ethnic group. They channeled their efforts at social reform through their own organization, the Central-Verein. The Central-Verein, or Catholic Union of America, was founded in Baltimore in 1855 to support German American Catholics in cases of poverty. At the turn of the 20th century the Central-Verein found new purpose as a proponent of social reform. Reorganized in 1905—with a central bureau in Saint Louis, under the directorship of Frederick Kenkel—the Central-Verein educated American Catholics about the church's social teaching, especially as it related to the competing evils of socialism and capitalism. It sponsored classes and provided pamphlets on the social questions of the day. In 1909 the central bureau of the Central-Verein began publishing its own journal, *Central Blatt and Social Justice*. An affiliated organization for women, the National Catholic Women's Union, was formed in 1916. The male and female organizations eventually assimilated into the mainstream of U.S. Catholicism, but the *Social Justice Review* continued to exist and promote social reform.[90]

Several Irish American Catholics became leaders in the militant socialist industrial unions and the state federations of the Socialist Party in Wisconsin, Iowa, Colorado, and Minnesota. A few priests espoused socialism. Father Thomas J. Hagerty became ordained in Chicago and then moved to Texas and eventually to Our Lady of Sorrows parish in Las Vegas, New Mexico. He was attracted to socialist ideas through his ministry to Mexican American railroad workers. He soon began to travel for the American Labor Union and became a leader of the socialist left wing. "His radicalism, like that of Bill Haywood, leader of the Western Federation of Miners and later of the Industrial Workers of the World, was formed in the violent atmosphere of the Rocky Mountain mining camps."[91] He saw the conflict between Marxism and Christianity. He favored a form of worker ownership. Hagerty used his brilliant intellectual and rhetorical gifts to advance labor and socialist issues. He edited the *Voice of Labor*. In 1905 he helped draft the IWW platform.

Father Thomas McGrady—a native of Lexington, Kentucky, and ordained in 1887—did pastoral work in Galveston, Texas, until 1891. He then became a pastor in the Lexington, Cynthiana, and Bellevue areas of Kentucky. Because the great famine had driven his parents from Ireland and because of the influence of the working class in the mill and factory town of Bellevue, McGrady began a program of self-study to examine the theoretical basis for capitalism. His thought was influenced by utopian anarchists; Christian socialists; single taxers; Populists; followers of Ferdinand Lasalle and their Social Democratic Party; and the writings of Robert Gronlund (*Cooperative Commonwealth*), Robert Blatchford (*Merrie England*), Henry George (*Progress and Poverty*), Edward Bellamy (*Looking Backward*), and Karl Marx (*Capital*). He also recognized his indebtedness to the Catholic predecessors and the social democracy of Ketteler, Decurtins, Moufang, Hitze, Kopling, and Weiss.[92]

McGrady thought that socialism and Catholicism were complementary. Nevertheless, he believed that *Rerum Novarum* and its acceptance of profit-driven capitalism did not provide practical answers to the problems of industrialization. McGrady's books and pamphlets criticized Catholic views toward socialism and Catholic leaders' acceptance of the free-market system and the disparity that it caused.

In 1900 he became a lecturer and propagandist for various Socialist Party locals in 1900. At six-foot-three and 280 pounds, McGrady was an imposing presence. He was also a powerful speaker who traveled around the country promoting socialism and supporting local Socialist Party leaders. McGrady came into conflict with fellow socialists David Goldstein and Martha Moore Avery.[93] His bishop, Camillus P. Maes of Covington, and his fellow priests condemned his views concerning the social duty of the priest. In fact, Maes' lack of support, bad faith, and harassment wore McGrady down.[94]

In 1902 he resigned from pastoral ministry to devote himself full time to Socialist Party work. He remained a Catholic and a priest in good standing. He moved to San Francisco and worked as a lawyer. During the ten years of his socialist career, McGrady dedicated himself to showing that socialism was acceptable within the limits of Catholic teaching. He died in 1907 at the age of forty-four and was buried in the Catholic cemetery in Lexington.

McGrady was much more than an activist. He wrote seriously about issues such as private property, the significance of the profit motive in economics, the inadequacy of guild unionism, the need to expand unions to include the unskilled industrial worker, and the role of pacifism as an antidote to violence.[95]

> American Catholic historians Abel, Hennessey, and Dolan locate McGrady outside of the parameters of American Catholic social thought. Their critical assessments . . . are predicated upon the official Catholic judgment that socialism was antithetical to Catholicism. . . . [They] depict him as a socialist

> active priest who separated himself from the Church and converted to socialism as if socialism were an alternate religion competing with Catholicism in the spiritual marketplace.[96]

However, McGrady's social democratic Catholicism was formulated within a neoscholastic metaphysics. He rooted his social thought in his Christology and an apocalyptic understanding of history, religion, and science.

> McGrady's social vision offered an incarnational, apocalyptic, yet empirically verifiable Catholic and democratic social perspective that was a Catholic alternative not only to the moral and eschatological Protestant social gospel, but also to progressive and corporative social Catholicism. His social democratic Catholicism represents the American Catholic pastoral inclination toward a sacramental theology in which the Church mediated redemptive grace to individuals who . . . became the constituency of a constitutional democratic state. It was the constitutional democratic state, constituted by a redeemed citizenry, which established a cooperative political economy that reflected the providential intention for loyalty to the God, the common good, justice, and personal liberty. . . . McGrady attributed to the state a mediating role . . . in the Christocentric and apocalyptic plan of God for the defeat of social evil.[97]

Throughout his career McGrady sought the political–economic system through which God would prepare the world for the millennium and the coming reign of Christ. He found that system in democratic socialism. His writings and his activism were an apologetic promoting democratic socialism as the way to economic citizenship.[98]

Peter C. Yorke

Peter Christopher Yorke was "unquestionably one of the more charismatic labor priests at the turn of the century."[99] He was born in Galway, Ireland, in 1864. He received a classical philosophical and theological education. During the years Yorke studied classics at St. Jarlath's in Tuam, Bishop John McHale impressed him and engendered a profound sense of Irish nationalism. This remained an inflammatory issue throughout his life.

He began his studies for the priesthood at St. Patrick's in Maynooth. His family encouraged him to seek a mission in the San Francisco area. Therefore, he completed his seminary education at St. Mary's Seminary in Baltimore in 1886. Cardinal Gibbons ordained him for priestly ministry in the archdiocese of San Francisco a year later.

His early priestly career augured a promising future. Archbishop Riordan noted his intellectual ability and sent him to study with scripture scholar

Henry Hyvernat in Washington. Yorke was in the first class in 1889 at the new Catholic University of America. Yorke excelled so well in Semitic languages that Hyvernat wanted him to become a faculty member. But Yorke was unhappy at the university. After completing the licentiate in theology in 1891, he returned to San Francisco and became appointed to St. Mary's Cathedral. Three years later he became chancellor of the archdiocese, secretary to Archbishop Patrick Riordan, and editor of the archdiocesan newspaper *The Monitor*.

Yorke soon became a leading figure in church life as a pastor, an educator, a liturgist, a journalist, and a social activist. He published textbooks that adapted the Baltimore catechism for different grade levels. Yorke was instrumental in the formation of the National Catholic Educational Association in 1904. As pastor of Saint Peter's from 1913 until his death in 1925, he introduced significant liturgical reform and encouraged active participation by the laity.

As a journalist, Yorke founded *The Leader*, a local Irish newspaper, in 1902. It promoted a free Irish state and supported trade unionism. He edited this paper until prominent clergy and laity pressured the apostolic delegate and archbishop Riordan to replace him. Yorke severed ties with the newspaper in 1909.

He vanquished the anti-Catholic nativists, the APA, through a spirited defense of Catholicism in the pages of *The Monitor*. The height of his polemical career was between 1894 and 1898. *The Monitor* became the voice of religious and ethnic liberty in San Francisco. Yorke played an important role in the municipal election of 1898 in which the reform democratic ticket of James Phelan defeated the APA ticket.

After the election of 1898 and after his subsequent conflict with Archbishop Riordan, Yorke resigned from *The Monitor* and the chancellorship. He took a year's sabbatical and traveled in Europe during 1899. Pope Leo XIII granted him an audience and praised him for his defense of the faith against the APA. Yorke also visited Ireland and helped Irish patriot Padraig Pearse turn the tide in favor of an Irish republic.

Unlike Edward McGlynn and Thomas McGrady, who were sympathetic to the modern age, Yorke recognized the irreconcilable difference between the church and the unwarranted optimism of the social, economic, and political reformers of the Progressive Era. He upheld Pope Pius X's assessment that the agenda of Pope Leo XIII had not realized a synthesis between theology and science, and he maintained that the church had the responsibility to restore all things in Christ. Yorke was

> the premier neo-scholastic controversialist in the greater San Francisco area during the progressive era. His vocation . . . brought him face to face with the

> social disease wrought by the excessive optimism of the age. . . . That disease was manifest most destructively in the economic injustice of the San Francisco Labor crisis between 1901 and 1911. Economic injustice prompted him to formulate a theological expose of the sin of American progressivism. Yorke's social criticism served as the intellectual ferment in which he developed a conversionist theological remedy for the disease.[100]

Yorke promoted economic citizenship by becoming a social activist and by developing a theology of social conversion. He emerged as a social activist between 1900 and 1910, and he became the spiritual leader and principal advocate for the right of workers to form and join unions and obtain equitable wages. The struggle, as he envisioned it, was between the rich and the poor.

> Siding with the poor . . . Yorke worked tirelessly to rally the cause of labor in its struggles with the employers of San Francisco. Yorke . . . used the principal concepts of *Rerum Novarum*, anti-socialism, social justice, right of organization, and State and Church relations to labor, to promote labor and work toward a more equitable society for all people.[101]

Yorke first applied the principles of *Rerum Novarum* to the great teamsters strike on the San Francisco waterfront in the summer of 1901. His oratory and his editorials supported the workers' cause and the attempt of unions to achieve fair wages and hours, including one day's rest in seven. The central question in the strike was

> Shall men for whom Christ died to teach them that they were free, men, with free men's rights, be crushed beneath the foot of the least bright of all angels that fell from heaven, Mammon, the spirit of Greed?[102]

Yorke held that all workers had an obligation to join an honest union to protect their rights. The Employers' Association finally agreed to recognize the Brotherhood of Teamsters as part of the strike settlement.

The power of labor and unionism grew greatly after the 1901 strike. Employers were not able to crush labor's presence and spirit.

> While its only immediate gain was the avoidance of defeat, the labor movement soon emerged victorious. The Employers' Association dissolved within a year, while the closed shop swept through most of the businesses which had so bitterly opposed it. The actions of Phelan's police had won public sympathy for the embattled unions; during the next twenty years, organized labor would be the pivotal factor in San Francisco's politics.[103]

Yorke was also involved in the street-car strikes of 1906 and 1907. These strikes focused on work hours and fair wages. Yorke maintained the same attitude toward labor that he had shown in 1901. The conflicts were perceived as struggles between the rich and the poor.[104]

Yorke's social theology was a neo-Thomist offensive against the progressives' identification of the state as the agent of moral regeneration. He invited Catholics and other citizens to turn away from the personal isolation caused by individualism and the social regression caused by competitive commercialism. He believed that the regenerative turn to Christ was the best hope for liberty. He held that

> the hunger for justice and charity would be satisfied only through the works of a people regenerated through the sacramental graces of the Church. . . . Yorke acted as a neo-scholastic bridge between the organic social theology of Orestes Brownson and the sacramental neo-thomistic social theology of Virgil Michel. . . . The point of greatest coincidence between supernature and nature (the point of conversion) resided in the Catholic sacramental transformation of Jeffersonian individualism from its atomistic and contractual understanding of citizen and society to a social organicism in which each individual was a vital member of a national communion.[105]

Yorke's theology attempted to interpret Jeffersonian constitutional democracy as the remedy for social injustice and the reconstitution of individuals and society in Christ.

Peter E. Dietz

In 1901 forty laymen met in Boston to organize the American Federation of Catholic Societies. Its purpose was to foster

> Catholic interests and works of religion, piety, education, and charity; the study of conditions in Catholic social life; the dissemination of the truth and the encouragement of Catholic literature and of the circulation of the Catholic Press.[106]

After 1903 bishop James A. McFaul of Trenton and archbishop Sebastian G. Messmer of Milwaukee gave it enthusiastic support. The federation grew rapidly. It harmoniously incorporated middle-class men and women of Irish, German, Italian, Polish, and Bohemian heritage. It promoted social reform based on *Rerum Novarum*. It had 1.5 million members by 1906, and it reached its peak of three million members in 1912. The federation hoped to create a Christian nation based on Catholic social principles and the moral renewal of society. After 1919 it promoted social reform and the labor issue based on *Rerum Novarum*. The person most responsible for this shift was Peter E. Dietz.[107]

Dietz, the son of immigrant German parents, was born in New York City in 1878. He "acquired an interest in the plight of labor at an early age when he accompanied his father to meetings of the fledgling labor movement. These formative experiences gave direction to his adult commitments as a priest."[108] Dietz entered the seminary at sixteen. He began to envision a vocation that combined priesthood with an active commitment to economic reform. During his time of study in Germany (1900–1902) he became convinced that the democratic tradition of the United States made economic reform possible if based on Catholic social teaching. He completed seminary studies at the Catholic University of America in 1903. A year later Cardinal Gibbons ordained him for the diocese of Cleveland.

Dietz joined the local and national activities of the Central-Verein. Frederick P. Kenkel, the progressive leader of the Central-Verein, envisioned social reform through a restructuring of society; a reordering of attitudes and values lived out in an organic, integrated community; and labor legislation on behalf of workers' health, life, and limb. It promoted the eight-hour workday; the abolition of unnecessary Sunday work; a living wage; just compensation for injury; proper moral and sanitary conditions in the home, shop, mine, and factory; and legislation that would safeguard the physical and moral well-being of the young. The Central-Verein worked to educate Catholics through social libraries, social study circles, and the German English magazine *Central Blatt and Social Justice*.[109]

Dietz was not an academician. He was a practical agitator, pragmatic organizer, and insightful journalist. He devoted these talents to persuading Catholics in the United States to conform themselves to the social teaching of Leo XIII. Specifically, Dietz concentrated on the role of labor unions in solving social problems. Dietz published his plan for social reform in the English edition of *Central Blatt and Social Justice*. He exhibited social zeal, profound knowledge of industrial conditions in the country, and an appreciation of the momentous task facing his fellow Catholics. Dietz constantly sought to create programs that would include practical directions for implementing theory.

Dietz established direct Catholic influence among labor union leaders. In 1910 he founded the Militia of Christ for Social Service.[110] Membership in the militia was open to Catholics active in the AFL and in other trade unions. Its membership was concentrated in Chicago, Milwaukee, and St. Louis. Dietz envisioned that the militia would confirm the church's defense through a plan of social reform. He also hoped that Catholics in the unions would counter anti-Catholic attitudes of Protestant and socialist unionists. Dietz sought an official alliance with the AFL, but labor leaders never supported an official link.

In 1910 he attended the AFL convention as a representative of the American Federation of Catholic Societies (AFCS). When the AFCS established a Social Service Commission in 1912, Dietz became its secretary. The Militia of Christ's labor program exerted vast influence on the church's life through the Social Service Commission. He edited *Social Service*, the militia's official organ, which appeared in the AFCS bulletin under "Newsletter."

Dietz sought a national Catholic voice for social reform through an integration of the militia and the Social Service Commission of the AFCS. This never occurred, partly because of Dietz's inability to compromise and his rebarbative personality. He met with frustration when he did not receive episcopal support for a plan to implement social and economic reform. Still, Dietz remained steadfast in his commitment to practical reform. In 1915 he began the American Academy of Christian Democracy in Hot Springs, North Carolina. The setting was ideal for his purposes, though the amenities were spartan. The school was to train the laity in Catholic social teaching and in the democratic principles undergirding the political and economic system of the country. Dietz appreciated the need to equip his students professionally, and he imbued the graduates with a profound understanding of the spiritual implications of social service.

In 1922 Dietz received financial backing from the AFL and transformed the women's academy into the American School of Labor with the purpose of educating Catholics in the Church's social teaching. Dietz's plan remained unfulfilled because of conflict with Archbishop Henry Moeller of Cincinnati. Moeller, under pressure from powerful business interests in Cincinnati, asked Dietz to leave his diocese.

Dietz returned to Milwaukee in 1922 and to a quieter parish life. He moved to Whitefish Bay, a suburb of Milwaukee, and became founding pastor of Saint Monica parish. The parish established its own credit union in 1928, the first in Wisconsin. Other parishes used his procedure in setting up their credit unions.

Peter Dietz was admired for his zeal and for his dedication to organized labor and the practical implementation of Catholic social teaching. He was respected for his asceticism and holiness. Dietz was a man ahead of the times. Having great ability as an organizer, he demonstrated that businesses in a profit-driven economy only change when there are organized efforts on behalf of economic justice. In many ways, he anticipated the practical plan of the 1919 Bishops' Statement and the creation of the Social Action Department of the National Catholic Welfare Conference. His lay schools anticipated the Catholic labor schools by twenty years. The Association of Catholic Trade Unionists could trace its objectives back to his Militia for Christ.

Though his aspirations always outstripped his resources, he clearly laid the groundwork for those who enlisted the church in the work of economic and social reform. The inscription on Dietz's gravestone, "Champion of Labor—Founder of St. Monica's congregation," captures precisely his life's work.[111]

Labor Priests and Strikes

Labor priests such as Hagerty, McGrady, Yorke, and Dietz shaped the church's involvement in labor reform and trade unionism. Hagerty and McGrady took a socialist pathway in their service to the working poor. Yorke applied the principles of *Rerum Novarum* to support waterfront and street-car union workers during the virulent strikes in San Francisco. Dietz created organizations to instruct Catholics in social principles and to equip laity for professional social service.

Just as important, other priests supported the cause of labor during the anthracite strike in 1902, the Lawrence textile strike in 1912, and the steel strike in 1919. These priests identified with their people because they were often sons of working-class families and some had worked in the mines and mills. These priests also showed compassion and acted as advocates for justice.

The Anthracite Strike (1902)

The anthracite strike in eastern Pennsylvania in 1902 was one of the most dramatic strikes in the nation's industrial history. John Mitchell came to the area in the fall of 1899 to form a local of the United Mine Workers of America (UMW). Mitchell met miners in halls and in open fields; he visited their homes.

> Just as the American colonies secured their independence in the Revolutionary War, but did not secure its confirmation until the War of 1812, so the anthracite mine workers of Pennsylvania gained their liberty in 1900, but did not firmly establish it until 1902.[112]

Mine workers met in Shamokin, Pennsylvania, March 13–24, 1902, and passed resolutions embodying their demands. These included an increase in wages; a decrease in the hours of work, from ten hours to eight; the payment for coal by weight; and recognition of the union, a written contract, and a satisfactory method for settling disputes.[113] Arbitration failed and the strike began in May.

Because of his friendship with J. F. Power, a priest in Spring Valley, Illinois, Mitchell sought the friendship and support of local clergy in Pennsylvania. Many priests of the Scranton diocese stood behind the strikers. Father James V. Hussie in Hazelton urged the miners to adhere to the resolution adopted at the convention. Mitchell set up his headquarters in Wilkes-Barre, where he received the counsel and active support of Fathers John J. Curran and John J. O'Donnell. Both attempted unsuccessfully to persuade management to meet with Mitchell. Curran also met with J. Pierpont Morgan in New York and Theodore Roosevelt in Washington in an attempt to settle the strike.

When Roosevelt set up a commission to end the strike, all three priests testified about the desperate poverty of the miners.[114] They continued to support organized labor and remained friends with John Mitchell. When Mitchell died on September 9, 1919, and his solemn requiem Mass was offered on the morning of September 12,

> Father Curran, his friend of twenty years, was the celebrant of the Mass. Rev. T. J. Comerford, who baptized him, was Deacon, and Father John J. McCabe, the pastor of St. Ursula's parish in Mount Vernon, to which the Mitchell family belonged, was Subdeacon. Father John J. O'Donnell was the Master of Ceremonies. Bishop Hoban gave the final benediction.[115]

The Textile Strike (1912)

Work in the textile mills of Lowell, Lawrence, and Fall River, Massachusetts, was hard, and the pay was low. Many died under the cruel and grueling conditions of life. Mill owners imported bosses from Manchester, Birmingham, and the mining districts of England. They drove the immigrant Irish workers mercilessly. The workers, first almost entirely Irish and later French Canadian Catholics, were treated as if they were part of the machinery. Work began at six in the morning and ended at seven at night. High brick walls surrounded the mills and gates. At five minutes past six these gates were closed. If workers were even a few minutes late, they were docked a day's pay. If workers were tardy more than twice, they were fired.[116]

Thousands of workers in the cotton, woolen, and worsted mills went on strike for nine weeks in Lawrence, Massachusetts, in 1912. The conflict started when the managers of the mills reduced the earnings of the workers. This action was taken because the state legislature had passed a law that, in 1911, reduced the hours of work for women and children under eighteen. In 1912 the mill managers applied the law to all workers. However, they did not state how the shortened week would affect wages; instead, they cut the wages of the largely immigrant workforce.

The IWW formed locals comprising workers with Franco-Belgian and Italian roots. The nine weeks were filled with violence and intrigue. The strikers demanded higher wages, double pay for overtime, the abolition of the premium system, and an assurance that there would be no recrimination against the strikers.[117]

The most prominent priest in Lawrence was Father James T. O'Reilly, O.S.A. He was pastor of Saint Mary's church from 1886 to 1925. Mill owners such as William N. Wood consulted Father O'Reilly whenever there were troubles at the mills. Encouraging the strikers were O'Reilly; Fathers James A. McDonald, O.S.A.; Timothy J. Regan, O.S.A.; Mariano Milanese, O.S.A., the pastor of the Italian Holy Rosary church; and Vasile Nahas, pastor of the Syrian Saint Joseph's church.[118]

On January 20, seven strikers were blamed when sticks of dynamite were discovered in the strike district. The strikers claimed that agents of management had planted the dynamite, a claim that was later proved true. A few days later a false report circulated that an agreement had been reached and that the strike had been called off. The strike committee ordered a parade to take place on Monday morning, January 29. There was rioting throughout the day. In the evening a striker, Anna LoPizzo, was shot and killed. Two IWW leaders, Joseph J. Ettor and Arturo Giovannitti, were accused of the shooting and jailed. Father Milanese visited and supported them.[119]

On February 7, a reception was given in honor of Cardinal O'Connell's elevation to the cardinalate. Governor Eugene E. Foss asked the cardinal to help in solving the strike. On February 8, the cardinal directed Monsignor Michael J. Splaine to enter into the Lawrence controversy. O'Connell enlisted the help of O'Reilly and Milanese. Splaine and others helped in negotiating with the mill owners on a just settlement.[120]

The strike finally ended in mid-March. The priests had played a significant role on behalf of labor throughout the strike. They supported their people, set up relief funds, preached encouraging words, and promoted the just demands of their people.

The bitterness and violence of the strike were slowly salved by the return to the prosperity of the 1920s. Cardinal O'Connell carefully refrained from speaking out on the issue for two years. Finally, he issued a pastoral letter for Advent, "Relations between Employers and the Employed." The letter was published on November 23, 1921.[121] O'Connell used the principles of *Rerum Novarum* to indicate that the worker "must support his family; and the living wage which he has a right to demand . . . is the one which will maintain his family in frugal and reasonable comfort. The man who accepts less through necessity or fear of harder conditions is the victim of force and injustice."[122] The worker could protect this right by combining

> with others to enforce it and form a union with his fellow workers to exert the adequate moral power to maintain it to better his conditions within the limits

> of justice. To deny him this right is tyranny and an injustice. He has no other way to safeguard his interests. The rich and the powerful have many ways which they do not hesitate to employ to protest their investments; the workingman has only the support of peaceful combinations.
>
> Moreover, workmen's associations may peacefully agitate and seek to mould public opinion in their favor to bring about a redress of real grievances. A campaign of this kind must, however, be legitimately conducted, free from violations of justice and of charity and of the public peace. Finally, the worker . . . has the right to refuse to work, that is to strike, and to induce by peaceful and lawful methods others to strike with him when this extreme measure becomes necessary to mitigate unendurable conditions, or to wrest from an unreasonable employer just compensation for his labor, after all other measures have failed.[123]

The pastoral letter was significant when viewed in light of the events that had occurred since the preceding January: the strike, Governor Foss' address, the mediation of the clergy in the strike by express order of the cardinal, and the success of the clergy in bringing about peace. The pastoral letter was issued at the same time as the court was considering the case of Ettor and Giovannitti. They were acquitted on November 27. The following day, Thanksgiving, witnessed the close of the series of celebrations for God and country.[124]

The Lawrence textile strike of 1912 was a victory for labor because of the support of labor priests. On November 29 the *Lawrence Tribune* published a personal letter that the cardinal had sent to Father O'Reilly. He wrote:

> I need not assure you that I have followed with interest the recent demonstrations by which the citizens of Lawrence so effectively displayed their loyalty to God and country and incidentally destroyed the false impression given by a few socialistic and atheistic disturbers at the time of the recent labor troubles.
>
> The magnificent parade on Columbus Day was a display of reverence for the flag of our country, which brought words of commendation and approval on all sides; and I feel sure that the religious sentiments that will be manifested in the Thanksgiving celebration will eliminate the last vestiges of any suspicion that the motto "No God, No Master" finds any sympathy in the hearts of the citizens of Lawrence.[125]

The Steel Strike (1919)

Melvyn Dubofsky aptly described 1919 as an *annus mirabilis*.[126] The nation mourned the death of Theodore Roosevelt on January 6. A flu epidemic that had begun in the fall of 1918 continued into the winter of 1919. Cities were hit hard: five hundred thousand people died. In addition, African American migration into northern cities sparked two major race riots in Washington, DC, and Chicago. In all, there were over twenty-five incidents of racial violence during the summer. Many of those who were victimized or lynched were veterans of the First World War. Scandal also tainted baseball when the Black Sox scandal in Chicago became public.[127]

Getting the soldiers home, finding them jobs, and paying bills strained the economy as the year began. The first overseas contingents arrived home in April. Spring and summer featured parades in New York and other cities. By August most soldiers had returned to the United States. The last units did not leave Germany until 1925.

The returning doughboys tried to find work. They faced price inflation. President Wilson ordered all price controls and profit restraints lifted. Prices shot up. The reconstruction project was a battleground of conflicting interests. Management wanted to roll back the gains that the unions had achieved during the war. Owners resisted union efforts for recognition and higher wages. The National Association of Manufacturers (NAM) presented the open shop as "the American way."[128] They believed that unions subverted the nation's cherished values. Employers also used injunctions against organized labor to undermine the purpose of the Sherman Antitrust Act.[129]

The labor movement remained confident that it had secured a place in the economy because of its gains during the two decades of the Progressive Era. It was eager to push its agenda further in 1919. Samuel Gompers was optimistic that the federal government would remain positive toward labor. He had hailed the Clayton Antitrust Act of 1914 as "labor's *Magna Carta*."[130] Organized labor supported the Democratic Party in the 1912 elections and the 1916 reelection of Woodrow Wilson.

However, the events of 1919 demonstrated that no real systemic change was imminent. Big business still had powerful allies in the federal government and in the courts. William B. Wilson, a former UMW official who was the secretary of labor, faced conflict with attorney general A. Mitchell Palmer.[131] Palmer, the head of the Justice Department, triggered a Red scare during the year. His animus was aimed at Eugene V. Debs, the socialists, and the IWW anarchists in the labor movement.

The *annus mirabilis* began for labor in February 1919 when shipyard workers started a general strike in Seattle. Over sixty thousand workers stayed away from their jobs. Mayor Ole Hansen, a former progressive, thought that the strikers were IWW anarchists. He called out federal troops to supplement the city's police force. The strike ended nine days later when the AFL refused to support the strike.

However, rank-and-file workers pushed for higher wages, shorter hours, and union recognition. Over four million workers participated in strikes in 1919, a number never before reached and not to be exceeded until 1946. Strikers sought shorter hours, wage increases to match inflation, and union recognition. In sum, 20 percent of the industrial workforce was involved in twenty-six hundred work stoppages.

In September 1919 three-quarters of Boston's fifteen hundred police went on strike in a dispute over wages and their union's efforts to affiliate with the AFL. Governor Calvin Coolidge sent in the state militia and emerged as the hero of the affair. Coolidge held that "there is no right to strike against the public safety by anybody, anywhere, any time."[132]

Textile workers in Lawrence struck again under the radical leadership of A. J. Muste. Railroad workers, though they did not strike, endorsed government ownership of the railroads. Working-class militancy soared and union membership grew.

In the fall of 1919 over three hundred thousand soft-coal miners walked out of the pits and defied the federal government and court injunctions. UMW president John L. Lewis called off the strike after a direct plea from President Wilson. Rank-and-file members proved recalcitrant. They later voted that the UMW seek the nationalization of the coal mines.[133]

Finally, on September 22, 1919, over three hundred thousand steelworkers stopped working as part of an AFL drive to organize the steel industry. This strike spread to fifty cities in ten states. The strike shocked the nation. It resisted arbitration. The steel companies unleashed a national propaganda barrage that portrayed the steelworkers as content with their jobs and accused the unions of serving Bolshevik masters. Workers simply lacked the power to defeat the antiunion and open-shop industry. Management also pitted craft union workers against semiskilled or unskilled workers. It used ethnic, gender, and racial diversity to divide workers against themselves.

As had been the case in the 1902 and 1912 strikes, a number of priests supported their people during the strike. Father E. A. Kirby, pastor of Saint Rose's church in Girard, Pennsylvania, said:

> The steel strike is a continuation of the struggle of the masses of the common people against autocracy. The World War decided the people's right to political democracy but the people have yet to win economic victory. . . .
>
> If the AFL is not allowed to plead the workingman's rights in the way it has outlined, there is only one alternative and that is Bolshevism. . . .
>
> The Catholic Church always sympathizes with the down-trodden and in this case the offensive steel corporations are not the down-trodden.[134]

A number of prominent priests supported the strike and encouraged the strikers. Father John V. R. Maguire, C.S.V., of St. Viator's College, Bourbonnais, Illinois, went on speaking tours in Pittsburgh, South Chicago, and Gary, Indiana. Mother Jones and Father George Barry O'Toole, professor of philosophy at St. Vincent's Seminary, Latrobe, Pennsylvania, also took to the platform. Father John A. Ryan addressed a public meeting in Johnstown, Pennsylvania, during the conflict.

Pastors also acted on behalf of the strikers. Father Adelbert Kazincy, the pastor of Saint Michael's Church in Braddock, Pennsylvania, was a mainstay for the strikers. His school was a center for food distribution. His preaching attracted and sustained Catholics as well as Protestants. When the U.S. Senate ordered the Committee on Education and Labor to investigate the strike, Kazincy testified in Pittsburgh on October 11, 1919. He indicated that the laborers were so overworked that they had to work on Sundays and could not go to night school to become citizens. He also spoke about their deplorable housing and work conditions. Father Stephen A. Ward, pastor of Saint John's Church in Johnstown, Pennsylvania, quietly supported his people and encouraged them to remain united.[135]

During the 1919 strikes, workers knew that they could count on the church and some of its priests to support solidly workers and their unions. When the strike ended in 1920, the country prepared to return to "normalcy" as a mature industrial society. Changing the country were the pivotal years of 1900 to 1920 and the First World War. The United States moved into the 1920s as a country that was urban and industrialized.

> For the first time, . . . reported the 1920 census, urban population outstripped rural population. The blue-collar labor force in . . . manufacturing, mining, and logging had reached a peak it would not again touch or exceed except for a brief period during World War II. . . . Fewer Americans than ever were self-employed, and fewer people worked on the nation's farms. . . . The typical worker was a semiskilled machine operator who labored for wages in the mass-produced industries—autos, electrical goods, and petrochemicals—which would characterize the economy of the 1920s.[136]

Lay and Religious Women

Catholic laywomen and religious women contributed significantly to the labor movement and in direct service to the poor. Many were immigrants and poor. Their faith and courage led them to break new ground for women workers. Single Irish and German women worked as domestic servants in the cities. The latter also worked on rural farms. Single Italian and Polish women worked in factories. After marriage the latter took in borders; did piecework at home; and cleaned offices, schools, churches, and hotels. French Canadian women found work in mills. Mexican American women,

> often the most economically disadvantaged, were forced into whatever unskilled labor they could find, including farm work, domestic service, and work in garment or food-processing plants. . . .
> [Women] experienced firsthand the deplorable conditions, instability, and inadequate pay of the working class in late nineteenth-century America. It is thus no surprise that many Catholic women supported and even led the labor movements of their day.[137]

Mary Harris (Mother) Jones

The most prominent woman in organized labor was Mary Harris Jones. Jones was born in Cork, Ireland, on May 1, 1830, and was baptized a Catholic. "A social and theological analysis of Jones's autobiography and selected correspondence uncovers the chronological definition of her concept of labor. . . . Familial and religious influences consecrated her to the pursuit of social justice."[138]

The Harris family came to the United States when Mary was a child. Her father's work in railroad construction took the family to Canada. Mary attended high school and teacher preparatory school in Toronto. Once she left home, she severed all ties with her family. She was trained in elementary education by Mother Theresa Maxis, the African American founder of the Sisters Servants of the Immaculate Heart of Mary. Her family and friends confirmed her gift for teaching. Mary taught briefly in Monroe, Michigan, and in Memphis, Tennessee.

In 1861 she married George Jones, an iron molder and labor organizer. His zeal for unionism taught her the psychology of the worker on a grassroots level. Mary lost her husband and four children in a yellow fever epidemic that broke out in Memphis in 1867.[139] She interpreted her escape from the plague as a message from God. God was calling her to serve the laborer. "The world is suffering today from an industrial yellow fever, not less fatal, but, I am certain, as preventable."[140]

She returned to Chicago and worked as a dressmaker. She lost all her belongings in the Great Chicago Fire of 1871. She found refuge in the Knights of Labor and became a lifelong friend of Terence Powderly. For the next quarter of a century the only anchor in her nomadic life was Chicago.

From 1880 on, Mother Jones found new purpose in the labor movement. She instantly attracted workers by her person and rhetoric. She became "Mother," and the workers became "her boys," a kind of extended family. "Her fiery rhetoric, laced with religious allusions, mesmerized and inspired the miners. Her ability to empathize with the workers' suffering and to verbalize eloquently their pain convinced many that Jones had holy gifts."[141]

Her career as a labor organizer had three distinct periods. First, Mother Jones was an organizer and a crusader from 1890 to 1903 in West Virginia and in Pennsylvania for the United Mine Workers Association (UMWA). She then became an independent organizer from 1903 to 1910. For a short time she participated in the formation of the socialist IWW; however, they were too revolutionary for her. She returned to the UMWA when John P. White became president in 1910. She continued to organize and crusade for the UMWA until her death in 1930. On one hand, faith motivated and sustained her social action. On the other hand, faith provided a basis for her critique of the church's lack of commitment to social justice. Jones

> was not indiscriminately antagonistic toward the Catholic Church. She denounced the Church's social paternalism because it inculcated social passivism. Jones believed that the marriage between ecclesiastical paternalism and unregulated or welfare capitalism reduced the laborer to an economic instrument. That reductivist tendency led to the conclusion that the welfare of the worker must be sacrificed in order to insure the advancement of the race and prosperity of the nation. . . . She called for laborers to attain a bit of heaven here before they died. . . . Jones's criticism of social and ecclesiastical paternalism stemmed from her sense of egalitarian principles expressed in biblical narratives. . . .
>
> According to Jones the Catholic clergy had forgotten the evangelical preference for the poor, choosing instead to process down the aisles to sanctuaries built with the profits of despotic commercial sovereigns. . . . Jones contrasted the Christ of the poor with the Christ of the social and ecclesiastical paternalist. The former Christ was the Lord of life. The latter Christ was the parasite.[142]

Mother Jones returned to the church in the final years of her life. Father William Sweeney, one of her religious associates, gave her the last rites on September 14, 1930. Mother Jones died on November 30, 1930. A high requiem Mass was celebrated in Washington, and she was buried near the bodies of the five miners who were killed in a massacre of October 12, 1899.[143]

Leonora Barry, Mary Kenney O'Sullivan, and Agnes Nestor

Leonora Barry, Mary Kenney O'Sullivan, and Agnes Nestor were also prominent labor leaders. Leonora Barry was born in Ireland in 1849 and came to the United States in 1852. She married William Barry in 1871 and gave birth to two children. She was widowed in 1881. She joined the Knights of Labor with the hope of raising women's wages and bettering women's deplorable, unhealthy, and dangerous working conditions. Rising to leadership in the Knights, Barry was elected head and general investigator for the Department of Women's Work in 1886. Despite opposition from male workers and some priests, and despite apathy from many women, Barry wanted to organize women workers. In 1890 she married again and withdrew from active labor work. However, she continued to be active in Catholic charitable organizations and in support of temperance and women's suffrage.[144]

Mary Kenney O'Sullivan was born in Hannibal, Missouri, in 1864. At fourteen she left convent school in the fourth grade and entered the workforce, first as an apprentice dressmaker and later as a printer. After her father died a few years later, Mary supported herself and her invalid mother as a printer. When the company went out of business, she moved to Chicago and worked for a large printing-press company.[145] A deeply religious Catholic, her faith shaped her social-reform endeavors and taught her a sense of outrage because of the terrible working conditions that women endured. Organizing female workers, she discovered, was the only way for them to obtain better hours and working conditions. Her work in the printing and binding trade brought her into the Ladies' Federal Labor Union no. 1703. She helped organize the Chicago Bindery Workers' Union and formed unions of women cloak makers, box makers, laundry workers, and shirt makers. These women worked in sweatshops. In 1891 she became the first woman general organizer for the AFL. She soon left the post, frustrated by the lack of support from male union members and leaders.

Kenney returned to Boston. In 1894 she married John O'Sullivan, who died tragically eight years later. During those years, she reared four children and continued to work in the labor movement. With William English Walling, an economist and wealthy young socialist, she founded the Women's Trade Union League (WTUL) in 1903. She served as secretary, treasurer, and vice president from 1903 to 1911. She began the Boston WTUL in 1908.

While closely linked to the AFL, the WTUL differed from it in two ways. The WTUL organized unskilled female workers. It had a republican conception of unionization. Kenney worked for better working conditions, salary, and working hours. She encouraged individual responsibility and group solidarity. The WTUL supported strikes and legislative advocacy. Kenny was at the forefront of the 1912 textile strike in Lawrence, Massachusetts. Inspired by the 1919 Bishop's Statement, Kenny was an advocate for the Child Labor Amendment; an eight-hour workday for women; and a legal minimum, living wage. Until it disbanded in 1950, the WTUL was *the* voice that spoke out for women seeking entrance into AFL unions.[146]

Agnes Nestor was born in 1880 in Grand Rapids, Michigan. Thomas Nestor, her father, was a member of the Knights of Labor. When the family moved to Chicago in 1897, Agnes went to work in a glove factory at age fourteen. She worked a ten-hour day, six days a week. In 1898 she led coworkers out on strike. They demanded an end to machine rent, raises for lower-paid workers, and a union shop. The strike ended after ten days with a labor victory. Nestor decided to dedicate her life to the organization of women workers.

Nestor was a devout Catholic. She got involved with the Central-Verein and became one of the early vice presidents of the Conference on Industrial Problems. She chaired the Committee on Women in Industry of the National Council of Catholic Women (NCCW) and taught at the Institute on Industry sponsored by the NCCW and the National Catholic Welfare Council (NCWC).[147]

Nestor joined the Chicago WTUL in 1904 and eventually became its president. She was elected to the national executive board in 1906 and held a national office in the WTUL until her death in 1948. She worked indefatigably to organize female workers in support of better working conditions, a reduced working day, and a living wage. The trade union, as Nestor envisioned it, was a school that trained women in the civic virtues that would ensure industrial democracy and their participation in the common good.[148]

Nestor was a pioneer in workers' education. She stood by the most disadvantaged workers, and she directed the WTUL to support new, fledgling unions; unemployed women; immigrant female workers; and those who went out on strikes. She often collaborated with John A. Ryan and SAD.[149] Mary Kenney O'Sullivan and Agnes Nestor "envisioned the labor union as a democratic structure that fostered civic virtues and which had a special concern for the most disadvantaged in society."[150]

Roman Catholic Sisters

Roman Catholic religious women were committed to the most disadvantaged in society. In addition to teaching and nursing, 19th-century sisters ran day care centers, infant and maternity homes, homes for the aged, mental institutions, settlement houses, residences for working women, and houses for unwed mothers. They challenged feminine stereotypes by opening industrial schools, which provided young women with apprenticeship in the trades and enabled them to be self-supporting.[151] Sisters in social service were creative, imaginative, and risk taking. Their public service broke stereotypical models of women's roles in late-19th- and early-20th-century Catholicism. Their dedication to the poor, their commitment to social justice, and the witness of their lives won over their skeptical Protestant neighbors.[152]

The 1919 Bishops' Statement

From 1891 to 1919 the Catholic Church struggled to find its place and voice in the United States. When the United States entered World War I in 1917, every part of the church hastened to do its share to assist the government. The archbishops sent a letter from their annual meeting in April 1917 to President Wilson. They pledged the loyalty of the Catholic people in the national effort for liberty.

> We affirm in this hour of stress and trial our most sacred and sincere loyalty and patriotism . . . We bow in obedience to the summons to bear our part in it, with fidelity, with courage, and with the spirit of sacrifice, which as loyal citizens we are bound to manifest for the defense . . . and the welfare of the whole nation. . . . We pledge our devotion and our strength in the maintenance of our country's glorious leadership in those possessions and principles which have been America's proudest boast. . . . We stand ready . . . to co-operate in every way possible . . . to the end that the great and holy cause of liberty may triumph, and that our beloved country may emerge from this hour of test stronger and nobler than ever. Our people, as ever, will rise up as one man to serve the nation.[153]

The NCWC also began in 1919. Its purpose was to "unify, coordinate, encourage, promote and carry on all Catholic activities in the United States, to organize and conduct social work; . . . to aid in education; to care for immigrants, and generally to enter into and promote by education, publication and direction the objects of its being."[154] The NCWC provided a forum in which the bishops could act together in counterbalancing the political influence of the Protestant Federal Council of Churches. Its administrative vision came from its first secretary-general, Paulist Father John J. Burke.

> The key to understanding Burke was his vision of the Church as the Mystical Body of Christ of whom each Christian was a member. For the organic unity of the body to become visible, it needed structure, organization. While the international organization of the Church was apparent in its hierarchical structure and the adherence of all Catholics to the pope, there was no such organization at the national level, nothing to unify the Catholic body as a dynamic force in the life of the country. To meet this need, Burke established the War Council and encouraged the formation of its peacetime counterpart, the

> NCWC. . . . Burke never lost sight of the essential reality that the Spirit must enliven the members of the structure with the life of Christ.[155]

On Lincoln's birthday, February 12, 1919, the administrative committee of the NCWC issued a statement entitled the "Program of Social Reconstruction."[156] Father John A. Ryan had prepared the document after studying a number of plans in Britain and the United States.[157] The program presented the practical measures that were necessary, desirable, and obtainable for social reconstruction. It stated the principles that would guide the state, business, and labor into the postwar period. Paradoxically, the program espoused Progressive Era ideas at the era's tail end.

The bishops' program advanced many of the ideas for social reform that Ryan had been advocating for years.

> These included legislation for a minimum wage and child labor; social insurance against unemployment, sickness, accidents, and old age; public housing projects; legal enforcement of the right of labor to organize; control of monopolies, and curtailment of excess profits. The Bishops' Program also recommended the retention of the War Labor Board for settling industrial disputes, and the maintaining and increasing of the war time level of wages. Perhaps the most significant proposals, and those which caused the greatest amount of comment, were the ones which advocated that the workers should be given a "proper share in industrial management"; that they "become owners, or at least in part, of the instruments of production," and that they be given a larger share of the product of industry.[158]

Two particular aspects of the bishops' program, the role of women in the workplace and the significance of the farm, were traditional and forward looking. First, while acknowledging the contribution that women had played in industry during the First World War, Ryan continued to envision a domestic role for women. He warned women that some occupations might harm their health and morals. At the same time, he was adamant that women and men should be paid equally for their work.

Second, the program recommended that those who returned from the war be given the opportunity to establish themselves as farmers. Implementing this policy would increase the number of farm owners and independent farmers. It would lower the cost of living by increasing the quantity of agricultural products. This suggestion revealed a deeply ingrained cultural preference for the land over the city.

> Deists such as Thomas Jefferson and Benjamin Franklin connected this emerging vision to the democratic nature of the new nation: rural

> America—civilized by small-scale farming—fostered a virtuous utopia free of the artificiality characteristic of city, and particularly aristocratic life. . . . Jeffersonian agrarianism seemed incongruent with the realities facing the nation, yet it was clear that a number of groups used Jefferson's rhetoric to address those very problems. . . . Catholic agrarians . . . sought to use this vision to "ruralize" the Church while the Church, in turn, Catholicized the countryside. It is clear that Catholic agrarianism's rural nostalgia was characterized by a bitter anti-urbanism. Startling in its own right, . . . Catholicism was overwhelmingly urban in the United States. In the mind of Catholic agrarians, though, the city stood as the incarnation of everything wrong with American life.[159]

The National Catholic Rural Life Conference, with the green revolution of Peter Maurin and *The Catholic Worker*, promoted a return to the land. So, too, did Virgil Michel and the Benedictine monks of Saint John's Abbey in Collegeville, Minnesota; the members of the grail movement in Ohio; and influential thinkers such as Herbert Agar and Allen Tate.

Ryan judged that the three chief defects in the economic system were the inefficiency in productions and the distribution of goods; insufficient incomes for most wage earners; and unnecessarily large incomes for a small minority of privileged capitalists. He recommended such new measures as cooperatives and copartnership, increased income for labor, and the abolition or control of monopolies to restore competition. Most of all, he wanted a reform in the spirit of labor and capital.

The public response to the bishops' program depended on the social location of a given observer. Michael Williams, press secretary of the NCWC, promoted the program through a massive publicity campaign. Others welcomed the proposals and considered them revolutionary, a Catholic miracle. Yet, the program was no miracle. It was the result of three decades of commitment to the reconstruction of society.

Others responded negatively. Many priests did not understand, appreciate, or sympathize with the aspirations of economic democracy. Other concerns—such as pastoral care, the Irish question, and the fear of socialism—consumed their interest. NAM and big business thought that the program favored labor and socialism. Many middle- and upper-class Catholics did not like Ryan's brand of liberalism. They criticized the program, and they opposed Ryan and the work of SAD. Ryan's vision of cooperation between labor and management failed to attract those in management as well as Catholics whose concerns lay elsewhere.

> The thrust of church teaching and pastoral activity identified the church with religion and religious education, located moral responsibility largely around

sexuality and family life, and thus made social and political matters at best interesting material for ethical reflection, at worst simply irrelevant to what it meant to be a Catholic Christian. Then and later the marginalized and discontented would look to the church for aid in changing social practices and institutions, but those who had benefited, or had hope to benefit, from those practices and institutions, were not inclined to enter into a dialogue still located at the margins of church life.[160]

On September 26, 1919, the bishops issued a pastoral letter. Its tone was conservative. "It warned of increasing bureaucracy and reliance on government and gave special attention to . . . materialism and permissiveness, posing dangers to the family."[161] Section 10 of the letter addressed industrial relations. The bishops returned to Leo XIII and *Rerum Novarum*.

> That the spirit of revolutionary change which has long been disturbing the nations of the world, should have passed beyond the sphere of politics and made its influence felt in the cognate sphere of practical economics, is not surprising. The elements of the conflict now raging are unmistakable, in the vast expansion of industrial pursuits and the marvelous discoveries of science; in the changed relations between masters and workers; in the enormous fortunes of some few individuals, and the utter poverty of the masses; in the increased self-reliance and closer mutual combination of the working classes; as also, finally, in the prevailing moral degeneracy. The momentous gravity of the state of things now obtaining fills every mind with painful apprehension; . . . and actually there is no question that has taken a deeper hold on the public mind.[162]

The pastoral letter then went on to enunciate the moral and religious aspects of the social question. It stated that industrial strife, the conflict between labor and capital, the attitudes of the wealthy few vis-à-vis the working-class poor, and the moral principles were the same as they had been in 1891.

The bishops were keenly aware that the "unnecessary strikes . . . within the last few months"[163] were unjust. While they may have seemed to involve only the rights of labor and capital, they affected the rights and needs of the public and deprived the people of what they needed for reasonable living.

The pastoral letter asserted the community's right to order and tranquility. It encouraged cooperation between labor and management because of their interdependence within the economic system. It stated that the role of religion was to bring the rich and the breadwinner together, to remind capital and labor of their mutual duties and the obligation of justice.[164] The bishops reiterated the value and worth of the worker and the dignity of human labor. They recommended that there should be

> directive principles in industry. . . . By treating the laborer . . . as a man, the employer will make him a better working man; by respecting his own moral dignity as a man, the laborer will compel the respect of his employer and of the community.[165]

The bishops reaffirmed that industrial problems could be settled if labor and capital would "meet each other in a friendly spirit. . . . The evidence of such a disposition would break down the barriers of mistrust and set up in their stead the bond of good will."[166]

The pastoral letter spoke of the reciprocal rights of labor and management. Workers had the right to organize in associations and unions that promoted their welfare. They had a right to a living wage, with its content and universality clearly spelled out.[167] They also had the right to secure benefits for sickness, disability, and retirement. Capital had a right to expect labor unions to honor contracts and agreements, to receive a fair day's work for a fair day's pay, and to profits that "stimulate thrift, saving, initiative, enterprise, and all those . . . energies which promote social welfare."[168]

The pastoral letter also returned to one of the favorite themes of *Rerum Novarum*, labor–management solidarity through "associations and organizations which draw the two classes more closely together."[169] The bishops supported the development of associations as a way to combat the socialist influence in the unions, the Red scare, and the kind of violence that the nation had witnessed in 1919.

> While the labor union or trade union has been, and still is, necessary in the struggle of the workers for fair wages and fair condition of employment, we have to recognize that its history, methods and objects have made it essentially a militant organization. The time seems now to have arrived when it should be, not supplanted, but supplemented by associations or conferences, composed jointly of employers and employees, which will place emphasis upon the common interests rather than the divergent aims of the two parties upon cooperation rather than conflict.[170]

These associations would benefit the worker, the management, and the consumer. Worker participation in industrial management would increase personal dignity and responsibility, would foster interest and pride in work, and would bring about efficiency and contentment. Employer participation would promote cooperation and harmony with employees. The consumer would benefit because this arrangement would bring about improvements in production. "In a word, industry would be carried on as a cooperative enterprise for the common good, and not as a contest between two parties for a restricted product."[171]

The pastoral letter recommended the industry council plan—that is, that workers would share in ownership. The bishops saw this as something that would give stability to industrial society. They also expressed confidence that the nation would never choose revolution or violent radicalism as a way to solve industrial and social problems. Instead, education, organization, and legislation would be sufficient to right social wrongs.[172]

The bishops' "Program of Social Reconstruction" and their pastoral letter of 1919 gave the church a public voice in the social question. This voice would continue through SAD.

The Social Action Department

When the NCWC created SAD, it established for the church an organized and consistent public voice. According to Higgins, SAD served as a clearinghouse for

> the distribution of the best Catholic study in the social action field and, thus, is primarily educational in its purpose. [Its] continuing task [is] to observe, appraise, and to seek to influence along Christian lines the great changes of our day. Its goal is a society permeated with the ideals of justice and charity, directed toward the aim of restoring all things in Christ. The Department seeks to influence the thinking of individuals and their conduct. But even more, its goal is to seek a form of social organization which, by itself, conduces to virtue and Christian living. We cannot escape the fact that we are profoundly affected by our environment. Free will does not operate in a vacuum. We feel that it is our task to seek an environment of attitudes, customs, institutions and laws which help people to be better as individuals and as members of society. We seek to strengthen the home, industrial society, our political institutions and indeed the society of nations so that the ideals of Christ may prevail.[173]

SAD had offices in Washington, DC, and Chicago from 1920 to 1928. John A. Ryan directed SAD's work in industrial relations at the Washington, DC, office. Dr. John A. Lapp directed SAD's work in civic education and social welfare at the Chicago office. Father Edwin V. O'Hara directed a third division, the Rural Life Bureau.[174] The two offices merged after the Chicago location closed in May 1927. Ryan directed SAD from 1920 to 1945. He selected as his assistant Father Raymond A. McGowan, a gifted intellectual, writer, and organizer.

Ryan had a passion for social justice, dating back to his seminary studies in St. Paul, Minnesota, and his study of *Rerum Novarum*. The social gospel theologians, especially Richard T. Ely, influenced his thinking on the primacy of morality over economics. After ordination, Ryan attended the

Catholic University of America in Washington, DC, where he studied under the noted Belgian moral theologian Father Thomas Bouquillon.[175] From 1889 to 1902 Bouquillon developed a distinctive kind of moral thinking. He integrated neo-Thomistic theology, the historical method, and the empiricism of the social sciences. This revolutionized moral theology in the United States. Bouquillon's moral thinking and methodology influenced Father William J. Kerby, the first proponent of professional social work and an organizer of Catholic Charities,[176] and John A. Ryan, the most influential figure in American Catholic social thought in the first half of the 20th century. Ryan developed a practical vision of social reconstruction based on natural law theology, the social principles of *Rerum Novarum*, and the empiricism of economics. Ryan and McGowan worked well together at SAD. "Ryan interpreted and defended American reform in terms of Catholic thought. McGowan reversed the process, rigorously measuring reform proposals against 'the yardstick' of papal teachings and seeking to develop an independent Catholic program based on the occupational group idea."[177] SAD promoted the laity's role as agents of social change who were called to apply the principles of Catholic social teaching to their local workplaces.

Ryan received help and advice from an executive committee. Its first members were Monsignor Splaine, Father Kerby, Father Frederick Siedenburg, S.J., Father William A. Bolger, C.S.C., Father Edwin V. O'Hara, Dr. Charles P. Neill, James E. Hagerty, Frederick Kenkel, and George J. Gillespie. SAD's Washington, DC, office was ably staffed by Elizabeth Sweeney, Rose McHugh, and Linna E. Bresette.[178]

Ryan and McGowan began producing a variety of educational literature. McGowan wrote a weekly news sheet that was sent to all Catholic newspapers, major labor journals, and international Catholic organizations. It covered current economic happenings, and it related Catholic social principles to social and industrial problems. McGowan consistently supported labor's right to organize and to collective bargaining for better wages and working conditions. SAD was one of the first organizations to speak against the so-called open-shop campaign:

> The open shop drive . . . threatens not only the welfare of the wage earners, but the whole structure of industrial peace and order. . . . It is not merely against the closed shop, but against unionism itself and particularly against collective bargaining. . . . The open shop drive masks under such names as The American Plan and hides behind the pretense of American freedom. Yet its real purpose is to destroy all effective labor unions.[179]

SAD produced a monthly magazine, *Catholic Action*, and a series of twenty-three pamphlets on the labor question. In Chicago Dr. Lapp published five books in the Social Action Series. In 1933 McGowan began a weekly newspaper column, *The Yardstick*. NCWC News Service distributed it to local Catholic newspapers.

Joint social statements were issued under Catholic, Jewish, and Protestant auspices—respectively, from SAD, Central Conference of American Rabbis, and the Federal Council of Churches.[180] These statements supported the reduction of working hours from twelve to eight hours per day. SAD developed materials on Catholic social teaching for lay study groups and collaborated with the National Councils of Catholic Men and Women. Bibliographies and outlines on industrial subjects were sent out to Catholic colleges, seminaries, and Newman clubs. Ryan, Lapp, and Bresette traveled around the country giving lectures. Ryan, McGowan, and Bresette worked directly and indirectly for social legislation through public forums, senate hearings, and writings on such subjects as the minimum wage, public works, and old-age security. Linna Bresette helped set up the Parish Credit Union National Committee.

McGowan and Bresette collaborated closely in the creation and development of the Catholic Conference on Industrial Problems (CCIP). This national organization, begun in 1922, devoted itself to the study of industrial problems. It conducted national and local conferences for owners, managers, workers, religious and civic leaders. These conferences provided a forum for learning, discussion, and practical solutions in economic life.

After March 1933, SAD related its program to evaluating and promoting New Deal legislation. Ryan supported two of President Roosevelt's positions.

> In the ethical field, President Roosevelt had accepted the rights of all persons to a minimum decent degree of welfare; in the economic field, he had accepted the theory that a lack of purchasing power had caused the depression. In view of this approach to the social problem, it was not surprising that the Social Action Department hailed both the objectives and the methods of the New Deal as a step towards the Catholic program of social justice. But support for the New Deal was always qualified by criticism of its inadequacies . . . The Department vigorously defended such major New Deal laws as the Agricultural Adjustment Acts, the National Industrial Recovery Act, the act establishing the Tennessee Valley Authority, the Social Security Act, the National Labor Relations Act, and the Fair Labor Standards Act. Indeed, Father Ryan considered the last three laws as having done "more to promote social justice than all the other Federal legislation enacted since the adoption of the Constitution."[181]

SAD encouraged Catholic participation in unions and collective bargaining. It applied the principle of subsidiarity to the local union. It trained labor priests to work in the social apostolate.[182] Labor priests opened schools that equipped workers with skills that they would need in labor organization, public speaking, running meetings, and holding fair union elections. SAD made Catholic social teaching a constitutive part of Catholic life and spirituality. It provided Catholic workers with a practical theology for the workplace.

CHAPTER THREE

~

Higgins' Early Years in the Social Apostolate: 1945–1962

Chapter three considers Higgins' early years in the social apostolate, his work at SAD, and the foundations of his social theology. First, it investigates the annual *Labor Day Statements (LDSs)* from 1946 to 1962, which summarized the main social concerns of SAD in the post–Second World War era and which outlined the salient social principles promoted by NCWC. Second, the chapter analyzes the *Yardstick* columns that Higgins wrote for Catholic newspapers from 1945 to 1962. These columns developed and expanded the social principles found in the *LDSs*. Third, the chapter summarizes the main points of Higgins' emergent social theology.

The Labor Day Statements (1946–1962)

The Labor Day Statements

Labor and management had worked with the Roosevelt administration to meet the production needs of the military during the Second World War. Women entered the workforce. The war brought the economy out of the Great Depression. It unified the country and reaffirmed the nation's purpose. Dan Wakefield caught the spirit of this era in his novel *Under the Apple Tree: A Novel of the Home Front*. The story is set in Birney, Illinois, and ten-year-old Artie Garber muses about the war; the heroism of his brother, Roy, who has gone to war; and the mythical meaning of the nation.

> In the crisp clear days of October, America was beautiful, just like in the song. Artie had never been "from sea to shining sea," nor had he seen "the purple mountain's majesty" but he knew they were out there, believed in them, and

> saw every day with his own eyes the beauty of the gentle hills, the creeks and cornfields, the solid old white frame houses and the ancient oaks of Town. He believed, in fact, that God had "shed his grace" on this land, that this grace was tangible, visible, in the arch of rainbows over wet fields, the slant of shed sunlight on the sides of old barns. His pride in his country was sustained by the signs of nature and the symbols of men, not only the bright stars and stripes that flew from public buildings and hung from private porches but the comforting, everyday emblems of home: Bob's Eats, Joe's Premium, Mail Pouch Tobacco. This was what Roy and all the other boys were fighting to save, preserve, and protect, along with the people who were lucky enough to live in and of it, and all this was sacred, worthy of any sacrifice, including life itself, for without it, life would be hollow and dumb.
>
> Sometimes home seemed so beautiful and right it was hard to believe the War was really going on out there in the fringes of the world, the bleak foreign battlefield and alien oceans.[1]

When the war ended, the country discovered that the idyllic picture of America the beautiful was hollow. God's grace was not self-evident for the working poor and for the African American. Many questions loomed large. Would returning military personnel find jobs? Would workers on the home front lose jobs? Would women workers stay on the job or return to the home? Would racism thwart African Americans and deny them economic citizenship? Would the labor unions continue to be a powerful force? Would labor–management negotiations pander self-interest or promote the common good? SAD decided that the time was opportune to explain Catholic social principles through an annual *LDS*. McGowan wrote the first *LDS* in 1946. Each *LDS* celebrated the achievements of organized labor, encouraged workers in their efforts, suggested practical action, and promoted a variety of spiritual practices.

The McGowan Years (1946–1954): The Meaning of Labor Day

Workers in Europe set aside May 1 to celebrate working people and their achievements. Since May Day was associated with communism, workers in the United States set aside the first Monday in September as Labor Day. Congress established this holiday in 1894 to express the nation's "fundamentally Christian attitude towards employer-labor relations."[2] Its principal proponents, Peter J. McGuire and his colleagues, "wanted a labor holiday that would signalize the dignity of work, emphasize just rewards for labor's dignity and activity and proclaim full partnership of labor in economic life."[3] Labor Day became a time to thank God for blessings received, an occasion when workers could "join their bishops and priests in offering the Sacrifice of the Mass for the advancement of the cause of social justice and social charity."[4] Labor Day reaffirmed the nation's trust in the Providence of God.

> When you are fearful for yourselves, when you worry about the lot of your dear ones, when you feel anxious as to what might happen in the world: let not your heart be troubled. . . . every thing is in the hands of God. . . . Sometimes you will have to struggle to defend your right to live and to work. But this will not upset your peace of mind, because . . . you always place your trust in your Father Who is in heaven.[5]

Each *LDS* promoted Labor Day as a spiritual and moral event.

> Neither collective bargaining nor arbitration nor all the directives of the most progressive legislation will be able to provide a lasting labor peace unless there is also a constant effort to infuse the breath of spiritual and moral life into the very framework of industrial relations.[6]

The Postwar Agenda

Each *LDS* connected the spiritual and moral aspects of labor justice with the practical. The 1946 *LDS* spelled out the postwar agenda. First, it encouraged labor to organize the unorganized so that clerical and supervisory workers, as well as those in the service occupations, would benefit. Second, it stated the responsibility of organized labor and its accountability to workers and employers and to general economic welfare. Third, it addressed the ethical responsibility that unions had to eliminate racial and religious discrimination, to live up to the ethical principles on which unionism was founded, to eradicate racketeering, and to eliminate socialist influences among the rank and file through the democratic process. The statement told unions to honor their responsibilities to employers and to live up to collective-bargaining contracts. In short, workers should give a fair day's work for a fair day's wage and should respect others' property.[7]

Cooperation and the Industry Council Plan

The nation's economic vitality required the cooperation of organized labor, management, consumers, and the government. The 1946 *LDS* pointed out each group's role. First, organized labor must move beyond the confines of collective bargaining over wages, hours, and working conditions. It must develop labor–management cooperation through an organized system of industry councils.[8] Second, social justice required that organized labor and organized management

> come together in an occupational group system—an organized system of cooperation for the solution of all of the major problems of economic life. In each industry the occupational group should include all interested parties: labor as well as capital, employees as well as employers.[9]

While management and labor would still meet separately and maintain their own organizational identities, the occupational groups would seek to modify competition by maintaining standards of fairness regarding wages, hours, prices, and business practices; avoid private industrial dictatorship by enabling labor to share in all industrial policies and decisions; and exclude political or bureaucratic industrial dictatorship by keeping the immediate control in the hands of the agents of production. They would be prevented from injuring the consumer or the common good by governmental action "directing, watching, stimulating or restraining, as circumstances suggest or necessity demands."[10] The occupational group system would aim to bring into industry sufficient self-government

> to reduce to a minimum the conflicting interests of the various industrial classes, to place industrial direction in the hands of those most competent to exercise it, and to permit only that amount of centralized political control which is necessary to safeguard the common good.[11]

Third, consumers must have some form of representation in governing the occupational groups. Fourth, the only alternative to organized cooperation would be legislation. Relying on legislation was seen as an irresponsible and inadequate solution because it expected the government to do what it was incapable of doing—namely to reconstruct economic life according to Christian principles.

> Legislative reforms . . . cannot and will not get to the heart of the difficulty. Legislation can assist in the solution of the labor problem, but to rely exclusively on legislative devices and techniques is to shirk our common responsibility for the basic reconstruction of economic life along more Christian and more democratic lines. Thus far the American people have been unwilling or unable to substitute organized cooperation for the rule of competitive individualism and private monopoly.[12]

The Role of Government

Nevertheless, McGowan clarified the positive resources that government could offer. It could encourage cooperation, and it could craft laws that would remove the causes of industrial conflict. Legislation could extend coverage and enhance the benefits of minimum wage, social security laws, and effective price controls. Furthermore the government could provide for adequate housing; support labor and management in administrating economic programs; and call for a national meeting of representatives from organized labor, management, agriculture, and the professions to discuss the establishment of the industry council system. In this last item, the statement envisioned labor, management, and the government working in a congenial and democratic way to establish industry councils. This system promoted the common good by giving labor, management, agriculture, the professions, and the government a voice in economic planning, in reducing labor–management conflict, in creating labor–management harmony, and in solving practical problems. This partnership would promote full and steady employment, continuous and efficient production, an improved standard of living, and greater equity for all. The industry council system would be a sign of democracy's strength.[13]

The Role of Organized Labor

The first nine *LDSs* explored the sacred character of Labor Day to celebrate the dignity of the individual and the kinship people share.

> Labor Day is a Social Justice Day because of two facts of human nature. One is the great worth of the individual. . . . [The other is that] we . . . depend on one another. We are extraordinarily important individuals; but we are interdependent by our very nature. That interdependence is ennobled by kinship: we are children of Our Father, and we have an adopted son-ship through Christ our Brother. We are born to be brothers. . . . Labor Day is really a holy day dedicated to individual dignity and human brotherhood for human welfare. May God Who made us as we are and Christ Who showed us our dignity and brotherhood help us to dedicate Labor Day to man's dignity and man's brotherhood—a dignity and a brotherhood that come from our kinship with God, confirmed and heightened by Christ, our Lord.[14]

This kinship and call to a shared life is evident in organized labor. Unions exist for much more than pragmatic reasons. First, unions promote a vision. "The labor movement fixes as its goal nothing less than the complete richness of life, without limitation of any kind, the attainment of the complete human ideal, in all of its economic, ethical and spiritual implications."[15] Second, unions extend this vision by organizing the unorganized. This is "an absolutely necessary prerequisite to the establishment of industrial peace and economic justice."[16] Third, they preserve this vision "when they correct the internal faults and defects of their unions and when they eliminate Communist Party influence in their locals."[17] Fourth, they demonstrate their role when workers responsibly and actively participate "in union meetings and affairs, by studying Catholic Social Teaching, and by working for a Christian reconstruction of the social order."[18] Ultimately, from Higgins' perspective, the vitality and the hope of the labor movement are in the hands of the rank and file and in organizational structures that reverence the dignity of the individual and the value of brotherhood. These values are spiritual. They are learned at the foot of the cross.

> There are few things more important in our times than the dedication of the economic world itself to the practical realization of all that the dignity and brotherhood of man require. This does not mean antipathy to government's place as a protective, regulative and cooperative agency. It means simply that the center of responsibility is in economic life itself among the people who give their lives to it. The men of our time and country who are advancing the spirit of Christ in their work and ownership are among our greatest benefactors and are heralds of a better future.[19]

The words of Pope Pius XII were a source of encouragement and hope for the working people of the United States and of the world.

> In your workshops and factories, under the sun in the field, in the darkness of the mines, amid the heat of the furnace, wherever the word of Him Who commands may call, may there descend upon you the abundance of His favors which may afford you help, safety and solace and make meritorious of eternal happiness all the hard work in which here below you spend and sacrifice your life.[20]

The Higgins Years (1955–1962): Labor–Management Cooperation

When Higgins became SAD director in 1955, he became responsible for the annual *LDS*. The *LDSs* from 1955 to 1962 continued the theme of labor–management cooperation. Their tone was optimistic because organized labor had come of age. The AFL-CIO merger in 1955 was a sign of maturity. Furthermore, there was confidence that common sense and a common vision would prevail through voluntary discussion and collective thinking, joint action, and further developments in collective bargaining. Ultimately, the issues of the day—namely, economic renewal, automation, unemployment, poverty, corruption, and apathy among rank and file—were rooted in moral and spiritual matters.

Envisioning the Future

The 1955 *LDS* expressed "guarded optimism" because of the gains that labor and management had accomplished in collective bargaining over the past decade. The future of collective bargaining augured well for two reasons. First, the merger of the two labor federations would make it easier to organize people in the service, trades, and manufacturing fields; to eliminate jurisdictional disputes between competing unions; and to unify the union movement's opposition to communism. Second, the automobile industry powerfully negotiated the guaranteed annual wage, which gave workers a measure of a secure income and stable employment. Labor and management had settled their own issues without government intervention. The 1956 *LDS* remained

> "fairly optimistic" because, according to many experts, the nation was about to enter an entirely new era characterized by an unprecedented degree of industrial peace and labor-management cooperation. . . . Be that as it may, the recent merger of the American Federation of Labor and the Congress of Industrial Organizations is one of several indications that we have reached an important turning point in the history of industrial relations.[21]

Organized labor could now concentrate on "its essential role in the economic life of the nation, which is to cooperate with management, as an equal partner, in applying the principles of social justice."[22] Labor and management began to look at the impact of automation on unemployment and their joint responsibility for the whole economy.

The Responsibilities of Organized Labor

At this time, organized labor began to address its internal issues. First, the AFL-CIO's Ethical Practices Committee and the rank and file would need to work together to eliminate "the cancer of racketeering."[23] Second, workers would need to recommit to giving a fair day's work for a fair day's wage and to cultivating a respect for the rights of employers and consumers. Third, social progress, justice, and charity would require the rank and file to participate actively and regularly in union meetings, serve on committees, and take the initiative in eliminating abuse and racketeering on the local level.[24]

> The problem of apathy or indifference—the willingness . . . to surrender their conscience to their union—is basically a religious problem. The only effective remedy is a genuine and moral revival, . . . a profound renewal of the Christian spirit based on the persevering practice of prayer and penance and a thorough training in the essentials of Catholic social teaching. . . . In other words, the only adequate solution to the crisis currently confronting us . . . is a profound renewal of moral and spiritual values which . . . will never come to pass unless employees and workers throw themselves on the mercy of God in a spirit of humble prayer.[25]

A commitment to internal policing and correction, a greater involvement by rank-and-file union members, and a greater trust between labor and management would reduce cynicism and suspicion of each other's motives. Good-faith collective bargaining and labor–management cooperation would minimize the use of economic and political pressure and would maximize the use of collective bargaining to achieve industrial peace.[26] Industry-wide conferences or councils would allow labor and management to relate their wage–price decisions to the public interest and to the effective promotion of overall economic welfare.[27] Labor–management cooperation could be the bridge to public interest and the common good; it could counteract the influence of communism and the Cold War; and it could foster economic growth and progress for everyone.[28]

The *LDSs* presented the agenda that occupied the staff at SAD. The columns highlighted the issues that the *Yardstick* columns would develop during these years. In short, the *LDSs* pointed out how organized labor could be a vital participant in democracy through the active participation of the rank and file; through collective bargaining and moral integrity; through labor–management cooperation and economic planning; and through the elimination of apathy, racketeering, and communism. In addition, the *LDSs* indicated that the economic issues had a moral and spiritual dimension. They suggested a variety of spiritual disciplines that could fortify economic citizenship.

The *Yardstick* Columns (1945–1862)

A General Overview

Higgins authored the *Yardstick* column for fifty-six years. The Department of Archives and Manuscript Collections at the Catholic University of America in Washington, DC, holds the entire collection of Higgins' writings. It has catalogued and titled approximately twenty-two hundred *Yardstick* columns between 1945 and 1994.[29] His first column was written for the week of January 8, 1945, and his last column was written for the week of July 25, 1994. Columns written between 1995 and 2001 are still being processed by the Department of Archives and Manuscripts. Illness forced him to retire from writing. His final column was appropriately written on Labor Day 2001, appearing in Catholic papers on September 25, 2001.

Higgins decided the topic of each *Yardstick* column. The length of each column varied between 600 and 950 words, with a typical column averaging 750 words. Remarkably, in an era before fax machines and e-mail, Higgins rarely missed a column. When he was unable to write the column, a guest writer substituted—usually someone involved in the social apostolate. The archival holdings have copies of 103 columns written by thirty-four guest columnists between 1949 and 1977.[30] NCWC News Service distributed the *Yardstick* column, as well as other news items, to Catholic newspapers a week before its publication. The local Catholic paper decided whether it would use the column or not. It also was free to choose the title: *The Yardstick* (or just *Yardstick*), *Tests of a Catholic Social Order*, or a title based on the contents of the article. Higgins indicated that at least twenty-odd newspapers carried the column regularly.[31]

What did Higgins want to accomplish through the *Yardstick* columns? The column attempted to educate its readers about the social order, but in reality, the column did much more. Higgins offered his readers information about current and timely topics. He presented a perspective drawn from Catholic social teaching. This provided readers with principles that they could reflect on and then apply practically in the marketplace. He encouraged his readers to actively participate in society according to their gifts and vocations.

The column connected the church's social teaching with issues of public significance. Higgins wanted the column to be as objective as possible, to serve as a yardstick for his readers, a way to measure social justice and social charity. Higgins genuinely respected others' opinions and ideas. Therefore, the column sought to build bridges between a range of scholarship in ethics, theology, sociology, economics, labor–management relations, and the relationship between labor history and the church's magisterium. Higgins' perspective was rooted in the church's natural law tradition. His intellectual integrity demanded nothing less than a search for the truth. Borrowing a phrase from Al Smith, the columns "look at the record," are "for the sake of the record," and "put the record straight." Higgins' fairness and objectivity are evident in the way that Higgins described himself and his readers. He referred to himself as "the writer," "the present writer," and the "writer of this column"; he referred to his readers as "the reader."

The column taught a way of thinking about personal well-being and the common good.[32] Those who read the *Yardstick* column regularly cultivated an

> intellectual solidarity—a willingness to take other persons seriously enough to engage them in conversation and debate about what they think makes life worth living, including what they think will make for the good of the polis. . . . It does not seek to eliminate pluralism through coercion. . . . [It seeks] positive engagement with the other through both listening and speaking. It is rooted in a hope that understanding might replace incomprehension and . . . seeks an exchange that is a *mutual* listening and speaking. . . . When such conversation about the good life begins and develops a *community* of freedom begins to exist. And this is itself a major part of the common good.[33]

The *Yardstick* columns provided its readers with grist for serious thinking, reflection, and action.[34] Readers occasionally wrote to him about a particular column, and Higgins often responded personally. Sometimes he devoted a follow-up column to recognize his readers' opinion, to clarify his position, to apologize, or to offer a new perspective.

The column sought to connect theory and practice. The column was action-based thought, the product of his engagement with labor leaders, the rank and file, and the working poor. These provided him with the narratives and the insights that were as foundational for his thought as the principles of Catholic social theory. In short, the *Yardstick* column promoted economic citizenship and manifested Higgins' lifelong commitment to a strong labor movement. Ultimately, economic citizenship depended on a vital labor movement.

> The labor problem is not a matter of ancient history. It is an ongoing problem that calls for an active involvement on the part of those who believe in social justice. While organized labor is undoubtedly far from perfect—I even have intimation at times that my own church is far from perfect—no other movement in sight would enable American workers to protect their legitimate economic interests. No other movement would enable American workers to play an effective and responsible role in helping to promote the general economic welfare both at home and abroad.
>
> At the height of the Great Depression, in one of his many books on industrial ethics, Msgr. John A Ryan wrote two sentences that sum up his views on labor. This is my credo, as well as his.
>
> "Effective labor unions are still by far the most powerful force in society, for the protection of the laborer's rights and the improvement of his or her condition. No amount of employer benevolence, no diffusion of a sympathetic attitude on the part of the public, no increase of beneficial legislation, can adequately supply for the lack of organization among the workers themselves."
>
> I have spent my life saying this, in one way or another. I believe it remains true, and I hope the religion-labor dialogue will help us see the relevance of Ryan's words to the problems of today.[35]

The *Yardstick* Columns (1945–1962): Setting the Agenda

Higgins wrote nine *Yardstick* columns in 1945. These initial columns presaged his major concerns in the postwar years and beyond. His first column, "We Can No Longer Tolerate Discrimination," addressed racial prejudice in the workforce.

> The fact remains that racial prejudice is seriously hindering essential war production. . . . It must remain a serious blot on our Patriotism that thousands of qualified Negro workers have been denied the opportunity (a better word would be the *privilege*) of contributing to the war effort. And why? Purely because of the blind and the unreasoning racial prejudice of certain groups, which, often as not, are the boldest in the parade of Patriotism.[36]

The column then pointed out the role that Fair Employment Practice Committee (FEPC) had played in "rooting out this cancer of racial and religious discrimination in job opportunities in war industries."[37] Higgins endorsed the bills that would go to Congress to make the FEPC a permanent agency. "We cannot tolerate a continuation of racial discrimination which will delay final victory."[38] He aligned his position with testimony given by Archbishop Lucey, Bishop Haas, Monsignor Ryan, and Father John LaFarge, S.J.

The next three columns focused on organized labor. "Unionism for White-Collar Workers" addressed the plight of unorganized white-collar workers during the Second World War. "It's common knowledge that 'white-collar' workers have probably suffered more than any other economic group."[39] Higgins indicated that the solution

> to the peculiar problems of this group is organization into *bona fide* trade unions of their own choosing. If trade unionism is sound both economically and ethically, there is no good reason why any large segment of American industry should refuse to profit from it. If it should refuse to organize, . . . it may reasonably expect to remain at the bottom of the economic ladder.[40]

The column then used bold-face type to offer what Higgins considered an even more compelling reason for organizing.

> Catholic social teaching . . . calls for a system in which all economic groups will be organized according to their particular function in economic society. The so-called "Vocational Groups" system or "Industries and Professions" system of Pius XI's *Quadragesimo Anno* cannot even begin to function effectively until the majority of workers (and employers, and farmers, and professional people) are so organized.
>
> We are not contending that every last worker has a moral obligation to join a trade union. But we are saying that those who dissuade any group of workers from organizing are postponing the fulfillment of Papal directives for the Christian reorganization of economic and social life. "White-collar" workers would do well to examine the credentials of some of their friends.[41]

In "Labor Leads the Chase" Higgins addressed the comments of Stuart Chase, the author of *Democracy under Pressure*. Higgins set out to refute Chase's claim that industry, agriculture, and labor were pressure groups selfishly endangering the public welfare.

> All of us, to be sure, may be grateful to the author for putting the finger on the selfishness of pressure groups wherever and whenever he uncovers it, let the chips fall where they may. But some of us, including certain responsible spokesmen for the American labor movement, have a feeling that he tries to do too much. It's one thing to call a spade a spade and to castigate the labor movement for its weaknesses—for war-time strikes, for "featherbed" rules, for restrictions on output. . . . But it's quite another thing to leave the impression . . . that these

> abuses . . . are the rule rather than the exception. . . . Labor has its faults . . . but organized labor has done more to secure benefits for the American workers than have all other groups combined.[42]

The column then indicated that labor, especially through the CIO's industry council plan, would lead the way in the postwar economic reconstruction of society. Higgins reinforced labor's right to organize into free unions of its own choosing, to bargain collectively, and to have an effective voice in the decisions of management that affect their personal and family welfare.[43]

Three columns in August and September considered postwar reconversion and the urgent issues of full employment for the returning veteran vis-à-vis the existing worker; superseniority, that is, a job preference for veterans regardless of their employment seniority; and how to achieve economic vitality through the cooperation of industry, labor, and agriculture. First, an untitled column looked at how the nation would deal with full employment for the returning veteran vis-à-vis employment for the existing worker on the home front. Higgins cited the testimony of Phil Murray, who supported the full employment bill, unemployment compensation for war workers, a sixty-five-cent minimum-wage law, the Wagner-Murray-Dingell social security bill, a permanent FEPC with statutory powers, and a series of similar measures.[44] Second, he stated that superseniority would treat the civilian worker unjustly and would "separate the veteran from the rest of the population and create artificial schisms."[45] Third, in "Preface to the Agenda," Higgins commented on the upcoming labor–management conference. He suggested that both groups needed to look beyond strikes and lockouts to the deeper economic problems of the nation. "The central problem today is full employment, arrived at not by haphazard guess-work, not by chance, nor by government decree, but by the democratic cooperation of the functional groups in American economic life."[46] The column concluded with the advice that Bishop Haas offered to American industry in his Labor Day sermon for September 1945 at the Cathedral of the Holy Name in Chicago:

> Let us not minimize this point. There is no need to talk about cooperation, joint action and working together in industry for a common purpose—to say nothing of building a permanent economic society that will enable business men as well as wage earners to live Christian lives—unless employers regard the right of workers to organize democratically, and to deal collectively through their own representatives, as "finished business." Unfortunately a considerable group of American employers do not regard this right as "finished business."[47]

Haas spoke bluntly because NAM, the U.S. Chamber of Commerce, and leaders in business and industry had never really accepted the National Labor Relations Act, the right of workers to organize, and the process of collective bargaining. Management's begrudging compliance with the act signaled its opposition to labor–management cooperation in planning the economy and the goal of full employment.

The columns for December 17 and 31, 1945, investigated the government's role in legislation and in guaranteeing the right to organize. "Less Rhetoric, More Common Sense" considered government intervention and legislation on behalf of health insurance. Higgins used the principle of subsidiarity to indicate that compulsory health insurance was not socialistic and unethical per se. He quoted the norms that Popes Leo XIII and Pius XI had given:

> If, therefore, any injury has been done to or threatens either the common good or the interests of individual groups which injury cannot in any other way be repaired or prevented, it is necessary for public authority to intervene (Leo XIII).
>
> Just freedom of action must, of course, be left both to individual citizens and to families, yet only on condition that the common good be preserved and wrong to any individual be abolished (Pius XI).
>
> Just as it is gravely wrong to take from individuals what they can accomplish by their own initiative and industry and give it to the community, so also it is an unjust and at the same time a grave evil and disturbance of right order to assign to a greater and higher association what lesser and subordinate organizations can do (Pius XI).[48]

The column concluded by Higgins' stating his conviction that a reasonable middle position between freedom and regulation would best serve the common good.[49] "Natural Rights Are Not for Hire" pointed out the natural right of workers and foremen to organize to protect and advance their own economic welfare. "Their right to organize and to bargain collectively is a natural right, the expression of which the State is obliged to protect."[50] The promotion and the protection of this right formed cornerstones of Catholic social teaching. "The social encyclicals look forward to a new economic order in which labor will be given a partnership in profits and ownership and, within reasonable limits, in management as well."[51]

The 1945 columns outlined the agenda that the *Yardstick* columns would repeatedly turn to for the rest of the decade and through the 1950s. These included issues such as full employment for veterans and workers on the home front, the responsibility of labor to organize the unorganized into unions of their own choice, the promotion of collective bargaining to achieve economic justice, and the elimination of racial and religious discrimination in unions. Beyond these issues lay the more complicated and difficult tasks of establishing the cooperation of industry, labor, and agriculture to plan the economy, develop some version of the industry council plan, and clarify how government and legislation enter into labor–management relations.

Postwar Reconstruction

On November 5, 1945, representatives from the AFL, CIO, Mine Workers, and Railroad Brotherhoods met in Washington with people from NAM and the U.S. Chamber of Commerce to lay the foundation for labor–management cooperation on the home front. The hope was that what the United Nations conference in San Francisco had done for world peace, the National Labor–Management Conference (NLMC) would do for industrial peace. The NLMC did not, however, achieve industrial peace. Instead it revealed the anxieties and disagreements that existed between the labor and management. Even before the conference had adjourned, General Motors (GM) began a strike on November 21.[52] The *Yardstick* quickly identified the central issue in the strike—namely, GM's outmoded and reactionary economic philosophy. This philosophy denied the social nature of property and insisted that costs, wages/prices, profits, schedules, and investments were the responsibility of management alone.[53] GM's philosophy denied that workers had the right to share in ownership, management, and company profits. The column concluded by quoting *Quadragesimo Anno* (no. 88):

> Just as the unity of human society cannot be founded on an opposition of classes, so also the right ordering of economic life cannot be left to a free competition of forces. For from this source, as from a poisoned spring, have originated and spread all the errors of individualistic economic teaching. . . . Free competition, while justified and certainly useful provided it is kept within certain limits, clearly cannot direct economic life.[54]

Organized labor had grown in power between the mid-1930s and the mid-1940s. Its postwar goals were clear:[55] equal and full employment, the expansion of collective bargaining to include pensions, health insurance,[56] higher wages (without raising prices), and a greater voice in cooperation with management in planning overall economic policies.[57] Could organized labor achieve these goals? Could it maintain the loyalty that it had achieved among working people during the war? David Brody noted the changes that J. B. S. Hardman, the labor intellectual, witnessed in the labor movement.

> After World War II, union membership stood at fifteen million, a five-fold increase since 1933. Among production workers in manufacturing, over two-thirds

> came under collective bargaining. In transportation, coal and metal mining, steel, automobiles, meat packing, rubber and other basic industries, union coverage was complete or nearly so (80–100 per cent organized). . . . The first years of peace confirmed the durability of labor's gains. After V-J Day, a great strike wave swept the country, causing 4,630 work stoppages in a single year, bringing out 4.9 million workers, and costing the nation 119.8 million man-days of lost production. Only the labor upheaval of 1919 was comparable, but with this difference: after World War I, government and industry had crushed the unions. Witness both to 1919 and 1946, Hardman noted the change. "One was determined and ruthless, the other circumspect and mindful of a kind of protocol of civilized behavior." Strikebreaking had fallen out of favor. Nor would labor's strength be confined to its traditional sphere. . . . "American labor unions have become a social power in the nation and are conscious of their new import."[58]

The postwar years were a time that tested the ability of organized labor to effect change. The turning point came in 1946–1948,

> when a still powerful trade movement found its efforts to bargain over the shape of the postwar political economy decisively blocked by a powerful remobilization of business and conservative forces. Labor's ambitions were thereafter sharply curbed, and its economic program was reduced to a sort of militant interest group politics in which a Keynesian emphasis on sustained growth and productivity gain-sharing replaced labor's earlier commitment to economic planning and social solidarity.[59]

Dreams of labor–management cooperation and planning were dealt a severe blow when Congress passed the Taft-Hartley Act.[60] Despite its faults, and acknowledging the need to eliminate abuses, Higgins advocated a strong labor movement in the pursuit of justice and postwar reconstruction.

> The author of a column of this type is occasionally accused of having a pro-labor bias in the reprehensible sense of the term and, superficially at least, the criticism seems to have some merit. But only superficially, I think, for it would appear that the balance of power is still so decidedly weighted in favor of management and ownership in American economic society that . . . an attitude of doctrinaire impartiality would be nothing but a rather transparent subterfuge for an anti-labor bias.
>
> The social encyclicals are admittedly impartial in the sense that they stand for even-handed justice, but they are not by any means neutral or impartial . . . in their presentation and appraisal of the facts of modern economic life. They recognize and flatly affirm . . . that labor does not yet enjoy equality of status and power with organized capital. The encyclicals unashamedly take the side of organized labor in its quest . . . for an expanding participation in ownership, profits, and management.[61]

The *Yardstick* columns consistently promoted the legitimacy and the necessity of trade unions

> for the protection of the rights of labor, but, even more important, as a necessary step towards the establishment of a Christian social order. . . . Catholics ought to be straining every effort to expand the membership of American unions. This is not to say . . . that Catholics are obliged to defend the closed shop; but it's perfectly obvious that those who are opposed to the closed shop do so because they are opposed to the further extension of the side of the angels.[62]

Democracy and Organized Labor

The *Yardstick* column "Organized Cooperation in Economic Life" addressed the crisis that the nation faced in 1946. Could the democratic system of grassroots cooperation and participation work? Could business and organized labor foster an egalitarian society, a mutual accountability, and a common good? Higgins suggested that farmers, labor, management, and consumers could use the means at hand for teamwork and cooperation. "The major decisions in American life ought to be made from the ground up through the mechanism of organized cooperation between the functional groups at the industry level, the regional level, and finally at the national level."[63] He supported a strong labor movement, cooperation in place of competition, and a more egalitarian society that would manifest the oneness of the human race and the unity of Christ's mystical body.[64] Big business needed to be more accountable to the public, and organized labor needed to find ways to make unions and labor leaders effective servants of the public interest.[65] Democracy flourished when organizations of mutual help and service worked together to overcome selfish individualism.[66] The democratic system needed a vital labor movement. Labor was essential "for the working people of this country [and] the very cause of democracy."[67] Democracy's issues were ultimately moral and spiritual issues.

> Democracy is based on a sense of the priceless dignity and worth of the individual man, coupled with a sense of the dependence of all men on one another—a sense of working together to make it succeed. It is a government of, by, and for the people—not as isolated or atomized individuals, but as brothers living and working together with a minimum of external compulsion, for the common temporal good of all. . . . Democracy cannot long survive without the help of God or . . . unless the rank-and-file get down on their knees with some regularity and humbly and fervently say their prayers.[68]

Higgins believed that economic citizenship was possible if labor, management, and government cooperated freely in planning the future.

> America will not be able to meet this challenge unless . . . it is prepared "to raise up the religious and spiritual potential of its democracy to the height of the cross." And it cannot do this unless the Catholics of the United States provide the leadership which can rightly be expected of them. . . . Our Lord said, "And I, if I be lifted up . . . will draw all things to myself"—all things, political life included. . . . It is our inestimable privilege as members of His Mystical body to cooperate with Him in this holy work of universal restoration and redemption.[69]

The Purpose of Unions

The labor movement, from its very beginnings, was pragmatic. Unions protected the interests of workers and promoted the value of workers and their work. They gave workers a voice to protect their rights and their dignity; to earn a living wage; to provide housing, health care, and other benefits for their families; and to have a modicum of security so that they could enjoy life.[70] The local union was the place where the rank and file could exercise responsibility and fulfill their social and communal humanity. The union fostered solidarity and gave working people a firm footing to engage in collective bargaining.[71] The *Yardstick* column for August 11, 1947, commented on the purpose of unions.

> What is the purpose of labor unions? There are several answers to the question.
>
> 1. The purpose . . . is purely defensive—to bargain collectively with employers or their representatives over wages, hours and working conditions, and to defend the special interests of the workers. . . .
> 2. The purpose . . . is in large measure, if not predominantly, political—to prepare the ground for the establishment of a labor government through which and through which alone . . . the interests of labor can be adequately provided for.
> 3. The purpose . . . is partly defensive, but principally cooperative—to cooperate in an organized fashion with management and with the government for the particular common good of each industry, and for the general economic welfare of the whole community.[72]

Catholic social teaching saw collective bargaining as the foundation for, and the stepping stone toward, the establishment of the occupational group system, which would enable organized labor and organized management to work together in solving the major problems of economic life.[73] A concrete example of mutual cooperation occurred in 1953. When the AFL Hatters Union began negotiations with the Hat Corporation of America in Norwalk, Connecticut, the company informed the union that competitive conditions would require moving a large part of its straw-hat production to Tennessee as well as building a new factory for finishing low-price felt west of the Mississippi. This meant that many longtime employees would not only lose their jobs but would also find it difficult to find another occupation. The union called a strike. It lasted from July 9, 1953, until the end of May 1954. Both sides negotiated in good faith, and eventually the Hat Corporation decided to remain in Norwalk.[74] The time had come for labor and management to work together, to avoid self-centered isolation and economic individualism, and to contribute to the common good.[75]

Particular Unions

Higgins devoted a number of *Yardstick* columns to the unions of longshoremen, teachers, transport workers, and farmworkers.[76] He considered the needs of migrant workers and women, and he wrote on the right to association for police, postal, and federal employees.[77] All of these groups sought a greater measure of economic citizenship and workplace justice.

Jesuit Father John M. Corridan, the associate director of the Xavier Institute of Industrial Relations in New York, served as a guest columnist in 1949. He alerted *Yardstick* readers to the problems longshoremen faced. Longshoremen were responsible for breaking out or stowing away cargo on the docks of New York. They averaged 2.5 days of work per week. The system of hiring did not guarantee them work. The shape-up devalued them as persons and deprived them full employment.[78] In addition, the work was dangerous. Every year one out of every five hundred longshoremen was killed or completely disabled for life; one in forty received a permanent physical impairment; and one in four would lose thirty-four days because of temporary injury. The core issue was the unjust method of hiring. Corridan indicated that the only solution lay in a drastic reform of labor practices. Reform required government investigation and remedial legislation.

Higgins, too, encouraged a change in the system of hiring. He used this issue to encourage personal moral reform among the laity. "The average person engaged in economic life cannot perfect himself in the spiritual life, as an individual, unless he devotes himself unselfishly to the reconstruction of the social order. It should also be pointed out, too, that social reconstruction is primarily the responsibility of the laity."[79] In fulfilling this responsibility, the laity need the support of the clergy.

> The role of the priest is paramount. It is his duty and his privilege to form the laity spiritually and supernaturally for their difficult apostolate in the social order. In the final analysis, however, the distinction between the role of the clergy and that of the laity fades into insignificance in view of their common responsibility to restore all things in Christ. . . . Let all strive according to the

> talent, powers, and position of each to contribute something to the Christian reconstruction of human society.[80]

Priests in the social apostolate were called to inspire, energize, and stimulate the laity by their example. The clergy and the labor schools had the same goal. They aimed at "the systematic training of deeply motivated and spiritually inspired lay leaders in the ranks of labor and management."[81]

The *Yardstick* column also addressed teachers' unions. "Should Teachers Strike?" asked:

> Do teachers have the right to join a union? Do teachers have the right to strike? These are two separate and distinct questions which ought to be answered separately and on their own merits. And they ought to be answered calmly in the light of ethical principles.[82]

Higgins maintained that teachers had as valid and as sacred a right to join a union as did carpenters or bricklayers. "It can even be argued . . . that teachers *ought* to join a union" to advance their economic welfare.[83] At the same time, teachers should belong to professional educational associations. If the two organizations did not remain distinct, the professional association became a company union. "And company unionism, even for teachers, is downright hypocrisy."[84] Higgins thought that teachers ought to voluntarily surrender their right to strike.

> It then becomes the duty of their public employers to provide an adequate alternative or substitute for the weapon of the strike. Methods will have to be developed by which teachers and other public employees can effectively appeal their economic grievances without the necessity of resorting to the strike. That such methods . . . are not in existence today is amply demonstrated by the startling fact that some 350,000 teachers have deserted their chosen profession in discouragement and despair to go into other types of better-paid employment. A similar condition prevails, for the same reasons and with even more disastrous results, in the nursing profession.
>
> What's the answer? The answer is unionization plus a change of heart on the part of public administrators. The problem isn't going to be solved by piously telling teachers . . . that teachers who think of ideals before pay checks do not join such organizations [unions]. The members of the American Federation of Teachers—AF of L—are just as idealistic as their sentimental critics and much more realistic. . . .
>
> If the public has some rights, it also has some duties. And if teachers have some duties to the public, they also have some rights. It is suggested again that they have to unionize if they want to protect these rights and if they want to advance their economic welfare.[85]

Higgins' support of the right to organize and the value of unions did not blind him to labor's faults or its high-handed behavior. "Speaking of Labor Unions" took on the Transport Workers Union, CIO. Higgins bluntly denounced the public irresponsibility of its leaders, who threatened to strike against New York City's transportation system if city officials opposed a referendum to privatize the municipally owned power plants. He suggested that the union leaders be disciplined.[86]

The plight and the poverty of migratory farmworkers, Mexican and Mexican American, and their radical need for unionization attracted Higgins' attention. Fifteen *Yardstick* columns served as a prelude to the significant commitment Higgins would make to the unorganized and unprotected working poor in the next phase of his priestly career at SAD.[87] The June 2, 1960, conference "America's Woman-Power Future," in honor of the fortieth anniversary of the Women's Bureau of the U.S. Department of Labor, occasioned the column entitled "America's Working Women." The column reported on undersecretary of labor James T. O'Connell's opening address. Higgins wrote, "O'Connell . . . sounded a very timely warning against the danger of overemphasizing the economic role of women in the labor market at the expense of their spiritual and educational role in the family and the home."[88] Furthermore O'Connell indicated that the correct balance between these two roles would be difficult to define because "the woman is the keystone of home and family."[89] Higgins acknowledged that O'Connell's presentation was consonant with Catholic social teaching. However, Higgins added:

> the fact is . . . that the church has . . . emphasized . . . that, while family life is the normal vocation of women, it is not . . . the only calling which is open to them. Moreover, the church is doing everything within her power to encourage all women . . . to play an active role in the civic and social order.[90]

Higgins then went on to quote the words that Pope Pius XII addressed to women:

> Be present everywhere for the Faith, for Christ, in every way and to the utmost possible limit, wherever vital interests are at stake, wherever laws bearing on the worship of God, marriage, the family, the school, the social order are proposed and discussed.[91]

In short, the column supported the reconstruction of the social order and the active participation of women in the reform. Ever the thoughtful gentleman, Higgins concluded with congratulations and prayerful best wishes to Mrs. Alice Leopold, director of the Women's Bureau, and to her associates. He acknowledged the contribution that these women made to improve the economic and social status of female workers. "God bless them, one and all."[92]

Finally, the *Yardstick* columns addressed the responsibility of the government to recognize the right of police, postal, and other federal employees to organize.[93]

> Approximately 50 years ago the Congress . . . enacted a law [the Lloyd-LaFollette Act] permitting Government employees to join unions of their own choosing. Since that time a number of unions have been formed in the government service. But while many agencies deal with these unions unofficially, they have never been formally recognized by the Executive Department.
>
> The Government has a duty to recognize the right of its own employees to organize, not only in theory but in practice. The right to organize is a natural right of every human being. It does not depend upon the nature of the work in which a person is engaged. . . . The various agencies of the Federal Government have a responsibility to set an example for private industry in the field of labor relations. . . . Up to the present time they have failed to carry out this responsibility.[94]

In short, these *Yardstick* columns addressed the rights and responsibilities of organized labor. They demonstrated a vision of social reform and reconstruction in which the rank and file, the poor, the female workers, and the other workers might overcome economic injustice through organization. They provided a theology from below that gave workers an active role in shaping their lives and in using their voice to achieve economic citizenship.

Structures of Cooperation

How would labor–management cooperation be achieved? This topic received constant treatment in the *Yardstick* columns. The topic had intrigued Higgins from the days of his doctoral dissertation. Not only was he familiar with the CIO's industry council plan, but he was also a keen interpreter of the papal encyclicals.[95] The *Yardstick* columns repeatedly returned to the industry council plan as the ideal program for economic planning and as a middle way between free competition and collectivism, between economic individualism and state intervention/control.[96]

> This means that all of the people engaged in a given industry or profession (workers and employers alike) are intended by nature to cooperate with one another for the good of their own industry or profession and for the good of the whole economy. Nature itself intends them to organize for this purpose—to "form guilds or associations" and through these self-governing associations to regulate economic life according to the requirements of social justice. Each industry forms a separate "order" (or "guild" or "occupational group" or "industry

> council") and the various industries, thus organized, are to work for the common good. Together they form the Social Order whose function it is in cooperation with government, to "give form and shape to all economic life."
>
> These "orders" are not the creatures of government. They are natural organizations and . . . they are to be self-governing—subject to the over-all supervision of the State, which has the final responsibility for coordinating the activities of all subordinate groups in the interest of the common good.
>
> It is very important to emphasize . . . that this organized system of cooperation among the various self-governing "orders" is not a distinctly Catholic program, but rather one which is based upon the natural law—upon the nature of man and the nature of society—and therefore ought to recommend itself to all right-thinking Americans, whatever their religion.[97]

What was the basis for the industry council plan? The principle of subsidiary, one of the major contributions of *Quadragesimo Anno* to Catholic social teaching, was the foundation for the industry council plan.[98]

> One of the cardinal principles of Catholic social teaching is the so-called "principle of subsidiarity" . . . [which states that] "just as it is gravely wrong to take from individuals what they can accomplish by their own initiative and industry and give it to the community, so also it is an injustice and at the same time a grave evil and disturbance of right order to assign to a greater and higher association what lesser and subordinate organizations can do."[99]

Organized labor, government, and economic groups in the community were to apply the principle of subsidiary to solve their problems through a structured cooperation. Government was to assist and advise, not dominate and control. The efficient operation of the industry council plan would eliminate the necessity for direct government intervention and would promote the common good of the country. Industry-wide collective bargaining was a step in the right direction toward economic cooperation.

A second sign of cooperation was the importance of the CIO in encouraging rank-and-file participation, in overcoming apathy, and in extirpating communist influences in the various locals. On the eve of the merger that would create the AFL-CIO, Higgins reflected on the importance and the place of the CIO in shaping economic citizenship. "In our opinion, the establishment of the CIO in the middle '30s was one of the most important landmarks in the history of the United States. It was truly a great step forward in the development of human progress."[100] The CIO had contributed to the promotion of social justice; to the strengthening of democracy; and to the material standard of living by improving the wages, hours, and working conditions of workers in the mass-production industries. In addition, the CIO had contributed spiritually to the causes of interracial justice, human freedom, human brotherhood, and self-government in industry. Workers were then "able to stand on their own feet as mature citizens of a developing economic democracy which . . . is an indispensable bulwark or support of political democracy."[101] Finally, a third sign of cooperation was the merger of the two organizations and the creation of the AFL-CIO in December 1955. Higgins attended the separate AFL and CIO conventions in New York City, December 1–3, and then attended the joint AFL-CIO unity convention, December 5–10. He considered the merger to be "the most important development in the history of organized labor in the United States."[102] He gave the invocation at the final CIO convention. He also delivered the invocation at the opening session of the AFL-CIO convention in Atlantic City on December 5, 1957. He prayed that the delegates would be given strength of character and would be guided in their tasks in organized labor.

> Ours is indeed a noble calling and a very sacred trust. We are the elected representatives of millions of men and women who look to us not only for efficient service but for inspiration, too, and for an example of perfect integrity and completely unselfish devotion to the cause of justice and human brotherhood.
>
> There can be no double standard of morality, no conflict of interests in our lives. We are no longer private citizens; we are public servants pledged to serve our members and our fellow-citizens above and beyond the call of ordinary duty.[103]

The International Union Movement

Higgins' work at SAD brought him into contact with the international labor movement. Throughout this period Higgins was establishing bonds with labor organizations in Australia, Canada, Germany, Italy, France, and England.[104] He was able to compare how other union movements operated and how they were similar to or different from organized labor in the United States. He noted in particular the conflicts between Christian and socialist unions in Europe. He was aware of the benefits enjoyed by organized labor in the United States due to their neutrality and their freedom from religious coercion. He strongly supported the work of the International Labor Organization (ILO).[105] Higgins recommended that the United States retain its membership in the ILO despite the influence of communist members and the presence of representatives from the Soviet Union.[106] In short, contact with international labor taught Higgins the value and strength of U.S. labor, especially in collective bargaining, and it strengthened his resolve to work with other economic and political systems on behalf of an international common good.

The Virtue of Social Justice

Pope Pius XI first used the term *social justice* in the encyclical *Divini Redemptoris* (no. 51). Quoting Pius, Higgins wrote, "The virtue of social justice is easy to talk about but difficult to define, and even more difficult to put into practice. . . . [Social justice] is that virtue which demands 'from each individual all that is necessary for the common good.'"[107] Furthermore, the term "designated the objective norm of all social and economic activities, relations, and institutions. The concept of the common good is intimately part of the notion of social justice."[108] People need to pray for this virtue; then they need to incorporate it into their spirituality and integrate it into their action.[109] Workers can put this virtue into practice through their involvement in their local unions, their support for labor–management cooperation, and their collaborative service with others in the mystical body of Christ. This virtue is essential for those who are committed to the long haul and to the gradual development of a just social order. It is concretely exercised through cooperation with others for systemic change in society and the flourishing of social charity.[110] An active and intelligent participation in the liturgy of the church sustains those who strive for and thirst for social justice.

> It is the Mass that matters most even in the political order and especially in a democracy. Democracy is based on a sense of the priceless dignity and worth of the individual man coupled with a sense of the dependence of all men on one another—a sense of working together to make it succeed.[111]

A sense of community and fellowship, experienced and cultivated in the Eucharist, bears fruit in the supernatural order and in the political order.

> The spiritual force for the development of this fellowship comes from Christ, from the Mystical Body. The great embodiment of this force in the world today is the liturgy and especially the Mass, which is Christ and people acting together.
>
> The Mass shows forth the supreme worth of the individual. The individual is present at Mass as a divinized creature, and the Mass in turn enhances that divinization, that supreme worth. But the individual is also present at Mass as a member of the group—acting, giving, receiving, worshiping together with his fellow Catholics.
>
> This corporateness, this sense of a fellowship of all in relation to all, must be carried into the political order where a man's individual contribution is more important than he thinks it is. Who can estimate the importance of a single vote, even in the primaries, at a time when . . . "the quality of elected representatives is a matter of life and death in a democracy."[112]

Obstacles to Organized Labor

Higgins was deeply aware of human limitations and selfishness. He encouraged the rank and file to become involved in their local unions and to overcome their tendency of indifference and apathy. Unionists that simply paid their dues and received material benefits missed the moral and spiritual meaning of work and union membership. Union membership demanded more. It called for a perspective large enough to include concern and action on behalf of the common good. Economic citizenship required active participation in the affairs of the union and the society. When organized business or organized labor sought only its own economic or political goals, it risked losing a sense of community and solidarity. It also risked the intrusion of the government into its affairs and the loss of self-governance and autonomy. Unions and union leaders had public responsibilities: to extirpate communist influence in their ranks and to eliminate racism, xenophobia, racketeering, and the abuse of power.[113] Higgins recognized the complexity of these issues, but he also realized that solutions were available.

Allies and Adversaries

The *Yardstick* columns revealed Higgins as a man of gratitude. He was grateful for the work of theologians, labor historians, pastors, and activists who toiled for workplace justice and the creation of a new social order. The *Yardstick* columns mentioned people, organizations, and movements that were allies in promoting social justice as well as those that opposed it.

Higgins found support for his work from colleagues in the social apostolate. The *Yardstick* columns introduced readers to those involved in the social apostolate, including Cardinal Edward F. Mooney, Archbishop Robert E. Lucey, Bishops Francis J. Haas, and Joseph F. Donnelly. All involved themselves in serving the cause of working people, organized labor, and individual workers. Higgins paid tribute to Fathers John LaFarge and Raymond A. McGowan as well as Linna E. Bresette and John Cort. Each was professionally dedicated to the cause of worker justice and transformative change. Many *Yardstick* columns featured Catholic activists, labor priests, and directors of labor schools—such as John Boland, Phil Carey, John M. Corridan, Carl Hensler, William Hogan, Luigi E. Ligutti, Bill Smith, Mrs. Robert A. Mahoney, and Sister Thomas Aquinas. Higgins constantly studied the writings of Jacques Maritain, Yves Simon, Cardinal Emmanuel Suhard, M-D Chenu, Yves de Montcheuil, and others involved with the *nouvelle theologie* in France. He incorporated their thought into the *Yardstick* columns. Higgins was spending the time to earn his credentials and to establish his credibility in the house of labor. He befriended local and national labor leaders, the rank and file, and people involved in the Department of Labor. Higgins' great mentor and example had been Monsignor Reynold Hillenbrand, from whom Higgins learned to appreciate the transformative value of the liturgical movement and the lay retreat movement. Both helped Catholics, those lettered and unlettered, to relate the Gospel and their spiritual life to public witness and social justice.

Higgins faced a number of formidable opponents during these years. Their opposition was usually not directed at him personally. It was directed at the liberal Catholic stance that he espoused. The *Yardstick* columns engaged his opponents' thought. Higgins continually battled with Paul Blanshard, a nationally known Protestant writer. Blanshard manifested strong anti-Catholic animus. His books constantly portrayed the Catholic Church as a foreign intrusion into the United States and as an institution incompatible with a democratic process and way of life.

Higgins responded to the thought of John T. Flynn and Westbrook Pegler. Both were nationally known columnists that opposed socialist tendencies in organized labor and the influence of communists in the CIO. In fact, Pegler's anticommunist attacks were so irrational and vitriolic that a number of papers dropped his column and accused him of plagiarism and falsehood. *The Wanderer*, *Twin Circle*, and the *National Catholic Register* opposed labor's participation in economic planning, railed against communist influence in the unions, and espoused the interests of big business. They opposed Higgins' pro-labor position and thought his social theology too liberal. The *Yardstick* columns never maligned these adversaries personally, nor did they besmirch their reputation. Higgins attacked ideas, not personalities. He was gracious to his opponents and consistently set the record straight by proposing and applying the principles of Catholic social teaching.

NAM, Higgins' principal opponent, emerged in the late 1940s and in the 1950s as the major advocate for big business and its interests.[114] Committed to an economic individualism, it provided pro-business information, lobbied against collective bargaining, and courted antiunion politicians. Higgins accurately estimated the role that NAM, the U.S. Chamber of Commerce, and big business played in obtaining the passage of the Taft-Harley Act in 1947.[115] This legislation dealt a severe blow to organized labor. Despite later efforts to repeal Taft-Hartley, Higgins and many colleagues in the social apostolate and in the labor movement came to accept it as the inevitable law of the land.

Conclusion

Higgins bridged a pre– and post–Second Vatican Council church and theology. The liberal Catholicism of the church in Chicago shaped his theological formation. It enabled him to link the spiritual and the temporal. Higgins was much more than a liberal New Deal Democrat dressed in ecclesiastical garb. The *Yardstick* columns revealed his social theology. What did his social theology look like? What was its underlying theological anthropology? What were its foundations and its implications for economic citizenship and marketplace justice? What commitments did his theology make of him?

The *Yardstick* columns put the human person at the center of Higgins' theological anthropology. Each person possesses personal dignity and worth. Each person is inherently social and naturally inclined to build community and to create bonds of sisterhood and brotherhood. The inclination to organize and form associations for one's own good and for the common good is inscribed onto the tablets of the human heart. Higgins was a realist in his anthropology. He understood that humans could yield to selfishness, individualism, and personal sin. He recognized that there was a tendency to "let George do it." He knew that apathy and avarice could stalk the human heart. People could be tempted to see prestige over the common good. A wounded humanity was disposed to privilege, racial arrogance, racketeering, selfish individualism, and consumerism. These vices break down the bonds of community and solidarity.

Higgins' social theology, rooted primarily in the natural law tradition of the papal encyclicals, recognized that grace and redemption are offered in community. Unions are necessary for personal and communal well-being. Individual and social goals are realized by organizing the unorganized. People, by reason of their social nature, are obliged to form associations and unions to achieve social, economic, and political goals. The labor movement is more than New Deal pragmatism. Unions have moral and spiritual dimensions. They put workers on firm footing with business through collective bargaining. Collective bargaining becomes a first step toward full cooperation between labor and management, a partnership designed for responsible economic planning and the common good. Unions give the working poor a chance for economic citizenship and a voice that each could not have individually. Union leaders are public servants. They have a noble calling and a sacred trust.

Higgins' social theology committed him to disciplined study and an intellectual life. He modeled civility by respecting others' opinions, even when these opinions were opposite his. He was resolute in his commitment to promote a strong labor movement for people in industry, in the professions, in agriculture, and in service occupations. He expected that the church would honor the principle of subsidiarity by supporting organized labor. He paid personal attention to the suffering and plight of the working poor. He saw them as children of God living in the shadow of the cross. Ultimately, the goal of his social theology is the reconstruction of the social order, the restoration of all things in Christ, and the flowering of social justice and social charity in an American context.

Higgins' idea of church was the mystical body of Christ, clergy and laity working together for the reform of society. Christians possess the spiritual disciplines of personal prayer and liturgy. Breaking the bread of the Eucharist has economic and political consequences for Christians that live out their vocation with a devotion to Christ. Christ draws all people to himself and involves all people in the mystery of the cross. Higgins summed this up well in his column "Lay Spirituality," which appeared on October 29, 1951. He expanded on an idea that Yves de Montcheuil developed in his book *For Men of Action*:

> There is no enlightened sanctification without attention not only to the state of individual relationships with our neighbor, but also to the state of social relationships and the institutions which express them.

The column concluded with a section titled "Scandal to the Gentiles":

> This means . . . that "the all-out struggle against injustice should be inculcated in all Christians. It should appear so established a duty that it becomes inconceivable that there could exist a deep Christian life which might fail to take an interest in it. . . ." Our Christianity would then 'be different,' Father de Montcheuil concludes, and we would no longer be faced with the paradox and/or scandal, so common in modern times, of "Christians of incontestable virtue who [pass] through the midst of the gravest social injustices almost without seeing them, trying, it is true, to comfort the afflictions which they [meet], but without wondering about their deep causes." The virtue of these people is "incontestable" surely; but, as Father de Montcheuil reminds us, it is "regrettably misguided."
>
> Misguided? Maybe that means that we priests—the shepherds of the flock—are the ones who ought to study Father de Montcheuil's little treatise. After we ourselves are persuaded of the "necessary union" of the spiritual and the temporal, we will be better prepared to persuade the laity. Until that time we will have no reason to be surprised when we read that Catholics, too, discriminate against the Negro without any qualms of conscience and in other ways give scandal to the Gentiles.[116]

CHAPTER FOUR

~

Higgins' Mature Years in the Social Apostolate: 1963–1980

Chapter four considers the development of Higgins' social theology during his mature years in the social apostolate, 1963–1980. Higgins went to Rome as a *peritus* at all three sessions of the Second Vatican Council and served on the commission that investigated the role of the laity in the church. The council ended in 1965, the same year as Higgins' silver anniversary of ordination to the priesthood. After serving the council he served as temporary secretary for the group that initiated and developed Catholic–Jewish dialogue. He returned to Rome in 1971 and participated in the Synod of Bishops. These experiences of the worldwide church broadened his horizons. During these years the *Yardstick* columns reflected his involvement in movements that would irrevocably affect church and society. He traveled frequently between Washington, DC, and California to represent the U.S. Bishops Committee on Farm Labor and to help agricultural workers in their quest for social justice. His presence in the fields, union halls, negotiating sessions with growers and union officials, and the liturgy bore a strong and hopeful witness. The *Labor Day Statements* and the *Yardstick* columns promoted a new social vision for the issues that faced the nation and the church in the tumultuous 1960s and 1970s.

This chapter first looks at his *Labor Day Statements*. These annual statements interpreted questions and issues that the *Yardstick* columns would take up more extensively. How could racism be eliminated in the workplace? What was the relationship of racism and poverty? What should the church do to ameliorate the plight of the working poor in the midst of plenty? What would organized labor have to do to remain credible in society and enable workers in making the transition from manual to automated work? How could labor, industry, government, and church collaborate to guarantee agricultural workers the right to organize into a union of their own choice? How would the church practice what it preached by allowing Catholic teachers and health care workers to unionize?

This chapter then considers the *Yardstick* columns from 1963 to 1980. These columns addressed not only issues that would transform church and society in the United States but also concerns explored by the Second Vatican Council and the postconciliar period. What role might the church play in healing the wounds of the modern world? What role did the laity play in renewing church and society? What kind of relationship might develop between Catholics and Jews? What methods would the church use to ameliorate the life of the poor and promote human rights and religious freedom?

Finally, this chapter sums up the principal developments in Higgins' social theology during this period.

The *Labor Day Statements* (1963–1980)

Racism

In the 1930s and 1940s SAD concerned itself with the plight of minority workers. Edgar Schmiedeler and Francis J. Gilligan wrote essays describing the plight of African American farmworkers and factory workers during the years of the Great Depression.[1] Forty women and men attended a SAD-sponsored seminar in Washington, DC, July 2–5, 1946, which considered economic life, civil rights, housing, and social and health services in the African American community.[2] SAD published a report of the meeting and its goals.[3] SAD was also concerned with Latinos in the United States and with issues that affected organized labor in North and South America.[4] Furthermore, the *LDSs* manifested Higgins' concern for the systemic racism that affected minority and poor workers in factories, fields, and farms.[5] The problems of racism, poverty, and unemployment were cut from the same cloth. How the nation—in particular, how the unions—would deal with racism constituted the great test for democracy.[6] Although the Civil Rights Act (1964) was a first step in remedying this social injustice, it was only a first step in the right direction. Unfortunately, it was not enough.

> No greater mistake could be made than to think that this problem, the sheer magnitude and tragedy of which we have yet fully to grasp as a nation, was taken care of once and for all by the enactment of the Civil Rights Act of 1964. The passage of this statute was truly history-making in its implications, but, in the long run, the Act could prove to have been a curse, rather than a

> blessing, if the hopes and expectations which it has aroused among our Negro fellow citizens are frustrated, not so much by the uncompromising opposition of those who opposed its enactment in the first place as by the careless apathy and indifference of those who favored its adoption.[7]

What would be required to eliminate racism? First, citizens needed to recognize and acknowledge the presence of racism in the nation and in the workplace. Second, citizens needed to mobilize. The issue was so serious that no one could remain a passive spectator on the sidelines. Third, people needed to be open to the kind of conversion that regarded people of minorities positively.

> That this will require special attention to the dismal plight of our Negro fellow-citizens and the members of other minority-groups is self-evident. . . . It must be emphasized that a purely impersonal interest . . . is far from being adequate. Much more is demanded of all of us. We are called upon to perform the corporal and spiritual works of mercy on a person-to-person basis and to do so with profound respect for the dignity and the sensibilities of those whom we are privileged to serve in the name of the Lord. We will . . . fail to meet this challenge effectively if we think of the poor and the underprivileged only as some many digits in a cold statistical abstract and fail to see them in all their dignity as the favorite children of God.[8]

Fourth, owners, managers, and unions needed to honor aspirations for racial equality, shared responsibility, and participatory democracy concretely and practically.[9] Industry would have to eliminate discrimination in hiring practices and institute more fair promotion policies. Unions would need programs and policies that would encourage minority workers and promote racial justice in jobs and work roles.

> Indeed [labor, industry, management] are all in the same boat—all of us, clergymen included—and unless we make up our minds to bring about complete racial equality now—and not ten years from now—we may be heading for a national catastrophe.[10]

Poverty and Unemployment

Racism degrades people, erodes their self-esteem and self-confidence, and renders them powerless. Having no job and being poor entail a further kind of powerlessness. The poor and the unemployed have no voice. Higgins' writings contributed to the national war on poverty.[11] He began to address poverty by turning to the examples of Moses and Jesus in the 1965 *LDS*.

> Moses told his followers on the threshold of their entry into the Promised Land that "there will be no lack of poor men in the land that is to be thy home. I

> must needs warn thee, then to be openhanded towards thy brother, thy fellow-countryman, when he is poor and in want. . . . It may be that one of thy brethren . . . will fall on evil days. Do not steel they heart and shut thy purse against him; be generous to his poverty."
>
> Christ came into the world not to destroy the law of the Old Covenant, . . . but to perfect and fulfill it. "By this," he said, "shall all men know that you are my disciples, that you have love one for another," adding very solemnly, in another context, that on the last day our love of God will be measured strictly by the degree to which we have ministered—or failed to minister—to the material as well as the spiritual needs of our neighbor.[12]

The statement then compared the situation of the ancient Jews with that of people in the United States. Moses commanded an openhanded generosity because Jews and their neighbors were surrounded by abject poverty. Jews might be tempted

> to steel their hearts and close their purses against their less fortunate neighbors. Poverty . . . was the perennial and almost irremediable lot of all but the favored few. Our own situation in the United States at the present time is vastly different. We are the wealthiest and most prosperous people in the history of mankind. Never before have so many people enjoyed such a high standard of living. . . . The law of Moses and the subsequent teaching of Christ on the virtue of charity . . . are . . . more important today than ever before. This is true . . . because . . . there is less excuse today for the continuation of widespread poverty, and infinitely less excuse on our part for steeling our hearts and shutting our purses against its unfortunate victims.[13]

Who are the poor in the United States? Higgins identified them as "able-bodied Americans [who] are unemployed through no fault of their own, and millions more [who] are the victims of the most degrading kind of poverty—all the more degrading because it so often gets unnoticed in a land of bounteous plenty."[14] The poor are white-collar and blue-collar, skilled and semi-skilled people; African American workers in factories and on farms; small family farmers and their families; and Latino migrant men, women, and children who work in the factories and in the fields. "American agricultural workers, . . . for 100 years or more, have been among the most disadvantaged and most exploited workers in the American economy."[15] Finally, the poor are working-class ethnic white people in our cities. These frequently are the second- and third-generation descendants of various ethnic groups. Some are families who are not earning middle-class salaries. Many are elderly people living in abject poverty or are youths disillusioned by poverty and unemployment.

> For many years, we have tended to set aside or ignore ethnic differences in this country as though they were no longer consequential. We have allowed ourselves to believe that our society is divided principally on black-white lines, with a nod toward the Indian and the Spanish-speaking population. The large white majority of working people—whether poor or middle class—is thought of as being a homogeneous mass lacking in its own internal divisions and its own peculiar problems. . . . The continued neglect of the white ethnic working class is bound to bring disastrous results in its wake.
>
> Many mixed ethnic communities are commonplace in the larger cities. . . . Some Irish, French, Polish, Slavic, Italian, Syrian, German, Jewish, and other ethnic enclaves are still plainly visible in the social pattern. More often, we tend to think of these people as being able to solve their own problems, which in large measure they do. There are, however, tensions within and between the ethnic groups and the black and brown communities which are potentially very dangerous. Ethnic communities and neighborhoods must be considered as a social asset, for they provide security and stability. . . . When . . . they are faced with rapid social change, . . . they can produce confrontations that are socially destructive.
>
> It is difficult to rationalize neglect of these citizens, given their number and their strategic location in our urban areas. . . . A large number are blue-collar workers. They are the backbone of the labor force in most of our industrial cities, mining towns, and manufacturing centers. They still reside in older, mixed-ethnic neighborhoods, or have relocated in predominantly blue-collar suburbs. The needs, frustration, and problems of these largely working class people are urgent and varied. We reject the widespread accusation that these people are the primary exponents of racism in our society, although we do not deny that racism exists in their ranks.
>
> The urban crisis, at its core, is a human and a moral crisis. . . . The Church in this country has traditionally been an urban church. Its institutions represent a crucial force that might well be decisive in restoring our cities and determining the future life-style of urban Americans.[16]

What was causing poverty in the United States? The *LDSs* indicated a number of reasons for poverty. First, negative attitudes breed poverty and thwart change. Some people refuse to admit that there are poor or unemployed people in the land.[17] The poor and the jobless remain invisible. Others do not perceive the link between poverty and its racist roots. They stereotype the poor as incompetent and indolent. Still others lack moral courage.[18] They simply turn the other way and ignore working-class people. Second, many workers lack resources to effect systemic change. They may be unorganized or afraid of reprisal if they organize. Agricultural workers in particular lacked legal rights because the 1935 National Labor Relations Act gave collective bargaining rights only to workers in industry.[19] Third, groups with power have resources to maintain the status quo. Growers representing vineyards in California, Arizona, Texas, and Florida court powerful allies in Congress.[20] Fourth, groups with social capital—such as organized labor, organized business, and religious institutions—refuse to collaborate, and they expect that the government will solve poverty and unemployment through legislation and other kinds of controls.

Who is affected by unemployment? Higgins and John Carr, coordinator for urban issues at the United States Catholic Conference, devoted the 1977 *LDS* to full employment. In general,

> last year, over twenty million individual Americans were unemployed. Almost one-third . . . were touched by joblessness within their own families. . . . Our current battle with massive unemployment is more severe in its extent and duration than in any period since the great depression. . . . High employment is a continuing failure in our nation. It requires a long term and comprehensive response. . . . Massive unemployment represents the most serious threat to human dignity and the most serious violation of social justice in our economic life.[21]

In particular,

> as the last hired and first fired, minorities have been especially victimized by the six recessions since World War II. . . . One out of five teenagers was jobless. . . . Women are more likely to be jobless than men. . . . Female unemployment cannot be treated lightly because millions of women work to provide essential support for themselves and their families. . . . Moreover, many working class families would be unable to make ends meet without the assistance of working wives. . . . Blue-collar workers are much more prone to joblessness than white-collar workers. . . . The costs of unemployment are enormous. . . . Economic costs are serious. They contribute to larger governmental deficits at all levels, lost productivity and greater inflation. However, these costs pale before the human and social toll of joblessness.
>
> The human costs of unemployment cannot be measured in similar quantitative terms, but any sensitive observer can appreciate the devastating impact of joblessness. The loss of income leads to serious problems in meeting basic housing, food and health needs. Less obvious are the personal and psychological consequences of the loss of a job. Long-term unemployment destroys hope and confidence. It diminishes self-respect and ambition. In our culture, persons without employment lose a critical measure of their place in society and a source of individual fulfillment. They perceive that society has no productive role for them or that there is no contribution they can make. . . . Alienation and loss of confidence intensify and lead to increased anxiety and anti-social behavior.[22]

Joblessness contributes to poor health, the unraveling of the social fabric, family dysfunction, and a scapegoat mentality that pits domestic workers against undocumented workers, women, minorities, and young people. Joblessness also raises moral questions about peoples' worth and social status, about national purpose and identity. Higgins and Carr concluded that unemployment is a form of oppression and injustice.[23]

> An effective national commitment to full employment is needed to protect the basic human right to useful employment for all Americans. It ought to guarantee . . . that no one seeking work would be denied an opportunity to earn a livelihood. Full employment is the foundation of just economic policy; it should not be sacrificed for other political and economic goats.[24]

Solutions

Racism, poverty, inequality, and unemployment were the crises that confronted the nation. Their solution required that organized labor, management, government, and religious communities commit themselves in their own circles of influence and in collaboration with one another for the common good of a prosperous life.

The *LDSs* envisioned that organized labor would be faithful to its tradition of caring for the poor, that it would use its power and influence to eliminate racism, poverty, inequality, and joblessness. Critics of organized labor did not evidence the optimism of the *LDSs*. Many criticized organized labor because of its past history of discrimination. African American workers frequently faced unjust hiring practices, were used as strikebreakers, and were denied opportunities for promotion. African Americans, especially in northern industrial plants, would be militant in demanding change in the late 1960s and 1970s. Other critics perceived labor as big labor and its leaders as just another pressure group. Some depicted union leaders as self-interested, as lacking any concern for the general welfare of the nation. Many observed that the rank and file seemed to be greedy and uninvolved in their local unions. Labor's credibility was called into question. In fact, every worker had an indispensable role to play in the production of goods and services not only for the general welfare and for the common prosperity but also for the elimination of racism and inequality, which would require moral conversion.[25] While labor exerted immense power for change, for the common good, and for creating a better life, its critics wondered if it had the will to do so.

The *LDSs*, rooted in the tradition of subsidiarity, envisioned labor's continued commitment to active participation in union locals and to the process of collective bargaining. Unions were able to negotiate good wages for their members. But for many, life was not good. Unions would need to move beyond collective bargaining. Their future required new horizons. Unions would need to use their resources to research the impact of automation on jobs and work satisfaction, on worker boredom, and on rethinking the nature of work.[26] Although some work remained manual and menial, other jobs were moving from individual enterprise to collaborative work efforts. Unions had the financial and human resources to help the poor, to retrain the semiskilled, to offer apprenticeships to minorities, to support Cesar Chavez and the efforts of the United Farm Workers in their struggle to organize farmworkers, and to stand firmly with those on strike. Labor needed to recommit its efforts and energy to organize the unorganized.

Higgins reenvisioned management's role in solving these national crises. First, management would need to honor its commitments to collective bargaining and to maintaining its honesty and integrity in all negotiations.

> Given the scope, the depth and persistence of the current economic crisis, labor and management should now explore the possibility of expanding the scope of collective bargaining to include an even wider range of issues—plant closings and plant locations, investment policies, the democratization of corporate governance, job enrichment and various forms of work participation aimed at increasing productivity.[27]

Second, management needed to extend its hand to the poor by creating jobs; by attending to the workplace environment; and by cooperating with working peoples' aspirations for equality, responsible partnership, and a role in decision making.[28] Third, it could use its financial and human resources to investigate the changing meaning of work, to study the impact of technology on workers, and to promote common goals.[29] Management did not need to be labor's adversary. It could collaborate to attain the goal of full employment. Its policies and programs could strengthen the courage and the pertinacity of working people in pursuing mutual goals.

> One of the great mistakes made by American industry 50 years ago . . . was that it completely underestimated the intelligence, the determination, the skill, and the drive of the workers it was dealing with. This proved to be a costly mistake and one which the more intelligent leaders of American industry, by hindsight, have come to regret.[30]

Management would need to put aside its ideological and partisan considerations and set policies rooted in social justice, in creating jobs, and in aiming at full employment.

> Fundamentally, our nation must provide jobs for those who can and should work and a decent income for those who cannot. An effective national commitment to full employment is needed to protect the basic human right to useful employment for all Americans. . . . Full employment is the foundation of just economic policy; it should not be sacrificed for other political and economic goals.[31]

Social Vision

What is the proper role of religious communities in solving the social issues of racism, poverty, inequality, and unemployment? What resources can the church contribute? First, the church needs to attend to the biblical images that nourish faith and shape attitudes. The *LDSs* were anchored in three biblical images. The first image presents Moses and his words to the Israelites who have arrived at the threshold of the promised land. "Be openhanded towards thy brother, thy fellow-countryman, when he is poor and in want."[32] The second is similar in theme. Ezekiel 16 states that "this was the iniquity of Sodom . . . pride, fullness of pride, and abundance, and the idleness of her and her daughters: and they did not put forth their hand to the needy and the poor."[33] The third image is Jesus and the criterion of the corporal and spiritual works of mercy. "When you did it to one of the least of my brethren here, you did it to me."[34] In short, these images foster a preferential respect for the poor. The poor are not outsiders; they are brothers and sisters. The church is called to be aware of the poor; to promote and protect their rights, especially their right to organize; and to help people determine their own direction.

> The poor themselves . . . are helping us regain our sense of justice and compassion. They have acquired a new awareness of their own fundamental human rights, a new consciousness of their own dignity which has shaken them "out of any fatalistic resignation and [has spurred] them on to liberate themselves and to be responsible for their own destiny." In the process, they are challenging the nation to take off its moral blinders . . . and to look more honesty and more realistically than ever before at the darker side of American life—at poverty, racial discrimination, the ravages of war, the awful wastefulness of a suicidal arms race, the destruction of our natural environment, and other deep-seated problems in our society.[35]

Second, the church needs to continue to reflect theologically on the meaning of work. The 1972 *LDS* stated:

> Making work more human and more humane and making it possible to live not as machines but as men and women of dignity and worth will not be easily accomplished, but it goes to the heart of what we mean by social justice. . . . The

> Christian theology of work starts from the premise that people work . . . to earn a living, . . . to develop their own personal growth, . . . to addresses the needs of their fellowmen, . . . [and] to be partners in the work of bringing God's creation to perfection.[36]

Christians also act to humanize their workplaces, to ensure social justice, to bring about racial integration, to encourage hope, and to achieve common community goals.

Third, the clergy and other church ministers need to appreciate their leadership role in promoting the social dimension of the gospel. They need to know more about the history of the labor movement and its struggles to assist people in achieving a better life. They also need a lifelong commitment to serve the working poor, the least of their brothers and sisters. This commitment will flourish when fortified by prayer for the poor and by friendship with the poor.[37] What Geno Baroni wrote about the leadership of priests in initiating cooperation between minority and ethnic groups applies to all social ministry.

> The role of the parish priest also includes:
>
> a. Teaching ethnic groups how to respect the best of their own cultural heritage.
> b. Teaching these groups the real value of a free and open society in which all groups are equally respected.
> c. Isolating common community problems affecting all urban residents and uniting the various ethnic and minority groups in solving them.
> d. Preventing polarization and closed-mindedness among these groups.
> e. Developing an international awareness among Americans because of the ties of some ethnic groups with their relatives in other parts of the world.[38]

Finally, the church will only be credible when it practices what it preaches, when it honors the right of church employees to organize into unions of their own free choice for the sake of the common good.[39] In short, the cooperation of church and organized labor is still needed to ensure justice for all.

> There is no other movement in sight which could enable American workers to protect their legitimate economic interests and at the same time play an effective and responsible role, under a system of industrial democracy, in helping to promote the general economic welfare.
>
> The labor problem is not a matter of ancient history. It is a continuing problem which calls for active involvement on the part of dedicated and well instructed men and women who, while supporting the right to organize, will at the same time encourage organized labor to expand its horizons and help it to

play a more effective role, not only on behalf of its own members, but in support of the common good.[40]

The *Yardstick* Columns (1963–1980)

The Renewal of the Church

Higgins nourished his hopes for the renewal of church and society by years of serious study, writing, prayer, and action. His vision was broadened ever wider by the kind of renewal he witnessed unfolding in the church between 1962 and 1971. Higgins focused his *Yardstick* columns on four significant moments. First, he was deeply influenced by the papal teaching and the charismatic, prophetic qualities of Popes John XXIII and Paul VI. Second, Higgins went to the Second Vatican Council as a *peritus*. His keen mind, his penchant for supplying the press with information, and his convivial personality allowed him contact with a variety of people. The council became a milestone in his life and social theology. Third, Higgins' longstanding relationship with Jewish people in the labor movement and his work as the interim secretary for the commission that crafted *Nostra Aetate* were preludes to his postconciliar involvement in Catholic–Jewish relations. Finally, he participated in the 1971 Synod of Bishops. The synod document *Justitia in Mundo* expressed principles that he had learned in the labor movement. Higgins returned to the document to support his own position on worker justice in Catholic institutions.

Papal Social Teaching

The *Yardstick* devoted seventeen columns to the social encyclicals of Pope John XXIII.[41] Higgins did not attempt to give a systematic treatment of Pope John's social teaching. Instead, the columns responded to topics that appeared in a number of books and periodicals and that related to the social mission of the church and to the labor movement in the United States. In each instance, he treated each topic in its relationship to the social teaching of the papal encyclicals, especially *Mater et Magistra*.

First, the January 7, 1963, column considered the social mission of the church. The column assured readers that the Second Vatican Council would address the urgent social and economic problems of the day. In addition, it mentioned that the council members committed themselves to peace and social justice. However, Higgins indicated that the council would not present a final solution for these problems and would not break new theological ground. Instead, the church would act as a social critic and advocate.

> The doctrine outlined . . . clearly shows how the Church is needed by the world today to denounce injustices and shameful inequalities and to restore the

> true order of goods and things so that, according to the principles of the Gospel, the life of man may become more human.[42]

Since the council was pastoral, it was more concerned about

> how to motivate Catholics to want to acquire and then spread that social and community sense which . . . is "innate in true Christianity." It can also be expected to give new impetus to the lay apostolate.[43]

Higgins then returned to one of his favorite themes: the social action and mission of the laity.

> Pronouncements by the Fathers of the Council on specific social and economic problems will come in due time. They will not have their desired effect, however, unless the faithful acquire a deeper understanding and a greater love for the Church and are persuaded that it is of the very essence of the Church's mission to restore all things in Christ, including the social and economic institutions of mankind.[44]

Second, Higgins addressed those who used *Mater et Magistra* to oppose the system of trade unionism regnant in the United States. The April 14, 1963, column stated that the union shop was moral and that the neutral secular unions in the United States were acceptable to Catholic social teaching. Higgins reinforced his support with comments from a commentary on the encyclical by the esteemed Jesuit Oswald von Nell-Breuning:

> The term "Christian union" is not mentioned at all in *Mater et Magistra*; rather it speaks—as Pius XI did—of professional organizations and trade unions which are guided by Christian principles. . . . But beside trade unions "guided by Christian principles" there are other unions "which take their inspiration from natural law principles and show respect for freedom of conscience. . . ." Membership in trade unions which emphasize the natural moral law and in which the consciences of Catholics are not hurt is plainly left free—without special restrictions as, for instance, the requirement of simultaneous membership in a Catholic organization.[45]

Higgins' position continued to meet passionate opposition from those who favored unions based on Christian principles. He attempted to settle the matter conclusively in the column of February 17, 1964. First, for the record, he stated the facts.

> *Mater et Magistra* takes note of the fact that Catholics throughout the world are actively engaged in two different types of unions: (1) those that carry on their

activities in . . . explicit accord with the principles of Christian teaching and (2) those that follow the natural law and respect the liberty of individuals in religious and moral questions. . . . The first of these two categories is comprised of the Christian unions of Belgium, Holland, France, Switzerland, Latin America, and some parts of Asia and Africa. The second category includes the unions of the United States, Canada, England, and various other countries. . . . In summary, this dispute turns around the question as to whether or not Pope John meant to favor or to give preferential status to the so-called Christian unions.[46]

Second, he presented the opinion of an unnamed priest-scholar in Rome with whom he had consulted on this matter. In part, the scholar's letter of February 1, 1964, says,

I think I can say that the position stated by John XXIII in *Mater et Magistra* is a "de facto" position. He states that nowadays Catholics are present in the working world in two ways: *with Christian inspired syndicates* or *individually* working inside syndicates which are not linked to any faith or confession. He is only blessing and encouraging both, but he doesn't give any judgment on which way to prefer since, according to his ideas, the solution of such problems lies with the individual.[47]

Higgins knew individuals representing both styles of unionism that lived the social dimension of the gospel in their work and in their union activity. He spoke of them endearingly as the salt of the earth.

Third, the April 4, 1964, column opposed the adoption of wage–price guidelines that the Council of Economic Advisors had recommended to President Johnson. Instead, Higgins supported collective bargaining "conducted responsibly by labor and management alike and with due regard for the public interest." Here he stood in solidarity with remarks that George Meany, the president of the AFL-CIO, made at the United Auto Workers convention.

If collective bargaining is to be responsible bargaining, it must be free. And it cannot be free . . . if it is required to operate within the limits of predetermined wage-price guidelines, regardless of how or by whom these guidelines are established. . . . Experience has demonstrated the need for as much freedom and as much flexibility or elbow room as possible in collective bargaining. Experience has also demonstrated, however, that unlimited freedom in collective bargaining does not necessarily guarantee that labor and management will act responsibly and with due regard for the public interest. However, it is becoming increasingly clear that in an economy as complicated and as highly interrelated as our own, some way must be found to make collective bargaining

> serve the national economic interest more effectively. It is difficult to say how this should be done. . . . In summary, it seems to me that organized labor would be making a serious mistake if it were to plump for unlimited freedom in collective bargaining. In the long run this would be a futile gesture, for some degree of national economic planning is almost a necessity at the present time. Collective bargaining has its place, but of itself it cannot solve all of our economic problems.[48]

Collective bargaining is a step in the right direction because, through union negotiators, it enables workers to participate in the decisions that affect the economy and the public interest. It also gives a voice that will represent the rights, demands, and aspirations of workers. Collective bargaining ensures that deliberations are not confined to those who merely represent the interests of management. It is the primary, though not perfect, way to mutuality, labor–management cooperation, and social justice.

Last, two columns addressed the spirituality and language needed for the future development of the social mission of the church. The column of August 17, 1964, stated that the spirit of poverty, presented in Pope Paul VI's *Ecclesiam Suam*, could contribute to a spirituality of social justice and to the solution of social and economic problems.

> The spirit of poverty "makes us more sensitive to, and more capable of understanding the human aspects of economic questions, by applying to wealth and to the progress it can effect the just and often severe standard of judgment that they require, by giving to indigence our most solicitous and generous attention, and finally by expressing the wish that economic goals be not the source of conflicts, of selfishness and of pride among men, but that they be used in justice and equity for the common good and accordingly distributed with greater foresight."[49]

The column of August 19, 1968, indicated that *Mater et Magistra* and *Pacem in Terris* manifest a shift in the language and theological method used in papal social teaching. The classical period of Catholic social teaching, from Pope Leo XIII to Pope Pius XII, expressed itself in abstract, speculative thought. It was concerned with universal principles that could be applied anywhere and everywhere without reference to the vagaries of history.

> Catholic social doctrine, in the years that lie ahead, must be developed through a process of debate and dialogue and that this . . . must be conducted in a structured way. "Natural law . . . can no longer be regarded as universally binding when it is a case of specific, concrete issues. Catholic social doctrine must find a new way to prove its validity. . . . Most pronouncements have degenerated to the level of personal opinions, and such opinions of themselves

cannot have binding force. They acquire this force only if we know what group stands behind them. We must broaden the pluralistic base involved in the formulation of such opinions."[50]

Higgins understood this shift in terms of dialogue and debate. However, the shift—in its nature and in its implications—was a new, radical turning point. Catholic social teaching would broaden its base during the postconciliar period. Its method would be more pragmatic, historical, and empirical. Its language would attempt to integrate insights offered by the themes and principles found in the writings of the Scriptures and the early Christian writers; by the natural law theology of the human person-in-society and the common good tradition; by empirical data from the social sciences; and by testimony from people in the local churches. Its conclusions would be humble and open to ongoing dialogue, discussion, and revision.

The Second Vatican Council

Higgins attended all three sessions of the Second Vatican Council as a *peritus* for the Commission on the Apostolate of the Laity. Cardinal Cento chaired the commission. Although no laypeople were on the commission, lay organizations were represented by clerics. "Conspicuously absent were the theologians who in the previous decade had done the most to advance the theology of the laity: Congar, Philips, Rahner, Schillebeeckx, von Balthasar, Chenu."[51] The commission was a last-minute addition to the Preparatory Commission, whose task was to study

> the apostolate of the laity, religious and social Catholic action. The official *Quaestiones* set out three general areas of work: (a) the apostolate of the laity: its scope and purposes, its subordination to the hierarchy, and how it may be adapted to meet contemporary needs; (b) Catholic Action: the notion, scope and subjection to the hierarchy, adapting its constitution to present needs, the relation between it and other associations; (c) associations: how they can better accomplish their charitable and social activity. The clearest point in these brief topics was the subordination of the lay apostolate to the hierarchy; "today's needs" were left quite unspecified. No mention was made of the theological foundations of the question.[52]

Subcommittees worked on producing an initial document. The first *Schema* was completed in April 1962. Its last section dealt with the right and the duty of the church to participate in the Christian restoration of the natural order.

> In the course of elaborating this text, the principal subject of dispute was the participation of the laity in mixed or neutral associations for social justice. The

> final text came down on the side of the defenders of this practice, at least in certain places and circumstances.[53]

The commission continued to study the theology of the laity and the role of the laity in apostolic action.

> Although the Commission . . . could not be regarded as one of the stars of Vatican II, . . . neither could it be regarded as unimportant. The passage of time shows it to have had great qualities, the primary one being the sense it had of its own autonomy and proper authority as a organ of the Council. It was not inclined blindly to follow the directives of the General Secretariat, which told it to shorten its text (November 22, 1962) and to change the plan of the schema and introduce a section on "associations of the faithful" (December 1962). At the preliminary meeting in mid-January 1963 a plea from Msgr. Pavan, who stressed the special character of social action in the apostolate, was enough to obtain the rejection of these official recommendations.[54]

The commission met with representative laypersons on February 26 and 27, 1963, and at the end of April 1963. This laid the groundwork for Paul VI's decision to invite lay auditors to the council, a decision announced on September 14, 1963. Eventually five subcommittees were entrusted with the five chapters of *Schema XVII*. Monsignor Higgins was appointed to work on the fifth chapter—that is, "V. The order to be followed, as well as coordination and even cooperation with non-Catholics" (nos. 17–24).[55] The *Schema* that was sent to the council fathers on April 27, 1964, was the third one that the commission had developed.

> This third printed text staked out a line that the final text would follow, although profound changes would be made in it in response to the criticisms of the fathers that had already arrived in writing during the summer of 1964 or would be expressed orally during the public debate, October 7–13, 1964.[56]

The final "Decree on the Apostolate of Lay People," *Apostolicam Actuositatem*, was promulgated on November 18, 1965.

The *Yardstick* columns commented on four aspects of the Second Vatican Council: the apostolate of the laity; the church in the modern world; religious liberty; and Catholic–Jewish relations.

The goal of Schema 17, on the apostolate of the laity, and Schema 13, on the church in the modern world, is simply the well-being, the advancement, and the salvation of the world today. In his column for January 20, 1964, Higgins expressed his hope that the council would identify the problems that confronted the creative thought and imaginative action of Catholics and other people of goodwill.

> The most that we have any right to hope for is that the Schema will identify and dramatize the urgency of the principal problems confronting the modern world and will challenge Catholics and all other men of good will to work toward a speedy solution of these problems in the light of sound social problems.[57]

Higgins respected the complex nature of these issues. He expected the council to do good analysis of the issues. Solving the problems was an ongoing process and task.

> In the final analysis, however, these problems can only be solved by informed and zealous laymen—laymen who are at once technically competent and adequately instructed in the principles of social ethics and theology and who have a deep and abiding love for the world and are persuaded that their very Christian calling leaves them no choice but to be deeply concerned about the problems with which the world is presently confronted.[58]

Love for the world would inspire Christian laity to collaborate with other people of faith and goodwill. In particular, Higgins saw concrete evidence of service to human betterment in the council's affirmation of the union movement. *Gaudium et Spes* became a classical *locus theologicus* in Higgins' future writings.

> In business enterprises it is persons who associate together, that is, men who are free and autonomous, created in the image of God. Therefore, while taking into account the role of every person concerned—owners, employers, management, and employees—and without weakening the necessary executive unity, the active participation of everybody in administration is to be encouraged. . . .
>
> Among the fundamental rights of the individual must be numbered the right of workers to form themselves into associations which truly represent them and are able to cooperate in organizing economic life properly, and the right to play their part in the activities of such associations without risk of reprisal. Thanks to such organized participation, along with progressive economic and social education, there will be a growing awareness among all people of their role and their responsibility, and, according to the capacity and aptitudes of each one, they will feel that they have an active part to play in the whole task of economic and social development and in the achievement of the common good as a whole.
>
> In the event of economic-social disputes all should strive to arrive at peaceful settlements. The first step is to engage in sincere discussion between all sides; but the strike remains even in the circumstances of today a necessary (although an ultimate) means for the defense of workers' rights and the satisfaction of their lawful aspirations. As soon as possible, however, avenues should be explored to resume negotiations and effect reconciliation.[59]

Higgins cited this text in his column of January 24, 1966, to defend the rights of U.S. migrant workers who were on strike against grape growers and vineyard owners in Kern and Tulane counties in northern and southern California. The strikers sought better wages and a union contract. The growers refused to recognize the workers' right to organize because farmworkers are not covered by federal or state labor legislation. Eleven representatives from Catholic, Protestant, and Jewish communities sided with the strikers, commended their nonviolence, and recommended the following steps:

> 1. That the strikers continue their demands.
> 2. That the growers be urged to enter into negotiations with strike representatives.
> 3. That churches and synagogues . . . become involved in the strike through personal participation and through the donation of food and supplies.
> 4. That the Governor of California be urged to support state legislation to "ensure the right of collective bargaining" for farm workers in that state.
> 5. That President Johnson and the Congress be urged to enact federal legislation extending the National Labor Relations Act to include agricultural workers.[60]

Higgins supported the committee's recommendations. He also used this occasion to acknowledge the moral obligation of religious leaders to publicize their solidarity with the farmworkers. He envisioned the clergy and laity working for social and economic justice in distinctive yet complementary ways. At times, religious leaders would act boldly, speak prophetically, and offer practical and particular recommendations. But ordinarily they would contribute by stating general principles, by doing further study, and by participating in ongoing dialogue with the modern world.[61] Higgins sensed that a new era of dialogue was just beginning within the church, between the church and other religious bodies, and between the church and the modern world.

> History will undoubtedly say that the council's decision to adopt [*Gaudium et Spes*] was truly providential. . . . What a tragedy . . . if the Church had failed to take advantage of this long-awaited opportunity to engage in fraternal conversation with mankind. . . . [The Church's] desire . . . has been to be heard and understood by everyone; it has not merely concentrated on intellectual understanding but has also sought to express itself in simple, up-to-date, conversational style, derived from actual experience and a cordial approach, which make it more vital, attractive, and persuasive. It has spoken to modern man as he is. "The Council," as [Pope Paul VI] remarked, . . . "considers the world in all its realities with loving attention, capable of discovering everywhere traces of God and therefore of goodness, beauty and truth." This is not only its philosophy, but also its theology—a theology of profound Christian optimism.[62]

Gaudium et Spes marked a turning point in the relationship between the church and the world. The church stepped down from its role as a moral critic of individuals and institutions and began a pilgrimage of dialogue with the world.[63] Partnership between church and world now rested on two planks—namely, the church's commitment to social reform and religious freedom. The church's role in this partnership called for a life of profound interiority and a renewed experience of communion with God. Prayer would energize the church with charity, and charity would transform ecclesial renewal beyond a mere "tinkering with institutional or structural reforms. . . . The crisis . . . [was] too profound to be resolved by superficial reforms."[64]

Religious freedom anchored the new relationship between the church and the world because, at its center, the doctrine expressed respect for individual conscience and honored the dignity of the human person. Religious freedom was the pathway into the deeper issue, the effective presence of the church in the modern world. Higgins was personally interested in the progress and the promotion of this schema for a number of reasons. First, he personally esteemed Jesuit Father John Courtney Murray, the schema's principal architect. Both men resided at Casa Villanova, and Higgins was attentive to Murray and his precarious health. Second, Higgins recognized that the concept of religious freedom was the singular contribution that the United States church would make at the Second Vatican Council. He was pleased that the schema was not voted on until the last session. This allowed the council enough time for the widest possible consensus, and it ensured its mature development.[65] Third, Higgins revered the history of church and labor in the United States. This relationship had enabled the church to be present in society. Catholic working people were a Gospel presence in the house of labor. Higgins, because of his historical appreciation and pastoral instincts, knew that organized labor was an essential linchpin for the future of economic democracy. Its potential for effective change was enormous. The church–labor relationship was couched in a language of respect for human dignity, personal conscience, and concern for of the poor.

> Cardinal Gibbons . . . spoke about the practice of religious freedom as he knew it (in 1887) and . . . as we have known it ever since. . . . "For myself," he said, "as a citizen of the United States, without closing my eyes to our defects as a nation, I proclaim, with a deep sense of pride and gratitude . . . that I belong to a country where the civil government holds over us the aegis of its protection without interfering in the legitimate exercise of our sublime mission as ministers of the Gospel of Jesus Christ." For the great progress which the Church in the United States has made "under God and the fostering care of the Holy See, we are indebted in no small degree," he added, "to the civil liberty we enjoy in our enlightened republic. . . ."

> The principle of religious freedom, which derives from the essential dignity of the human person, can be and has been made to work successfully in practice, to the benefit not only of religion but [also] of civil society as well.[66]

When the council espoused religious freedom, a new era of the church's relationship with the world began. The church renounced all claims to special privilege and a preferential place in society.[67] The church and society became modern partners, mutual pilgrims humbly seeking to craft public policies through a dialogue characterized by civility and understanding. This was the way the church would apply the gospel of life to the wounds of the world.[68]

Catholic–Jewish Relations

The Second Vatican Council inaugurated a new relationship between the church and the religions of the world. *Nostra Aetate*, the declaration on the relationship of the church to non-Christian religions, was promulgated on October 28, 1965. The document recognized the workings of the Spirit in the great religions of the world. In particular, the council radically reshaped the church's relationship with Judaism.

> Since Christians and Jews have such a common spiritual heritage, this sacred Council wishes to encourage and further mutual understanding and appreciation. This can be obtained . . . by way of biblical and theological inquiry and through friendly discussions.
>
> Even though the Jewish authorities and those who followed their lead pressed for the death of Christ, neither all Jews indiscriminately at that time, nor Jews today, can be charged with the crimes committed during his passion. . . . Jews should not be spoken of as rejected or accursed as if this followed from holy Scripture. Consequently, all must take care, lest in catechizing or in preaching the Word of God, they teach anything which is not in accord with the truth of the Gospel message or the spirit of Christ . . . Indeed, the Church reproves every form of persecution against whomsoever it may be directed. Remembering, then her common heritage with Jews, . . . she deplores all hatreds, persecutions, displays of anitsemitism leveled at any time or from any source against the Jews. . . .
>
> There is no basis . . . for any discrimination between individual and individual or between people and people arising either from human dignity or from the rights which flow from it. The Church reproves, as foreign to the mind of Christ any discrimination against people or any harassment of them on the basis of their race, color, condition in life or religion.[69]

Higgins' family background, his relationship with organized labor, and his sense of history contributed to his passionate participation in Catholic–Jewish dialogue. His father had taught him respect for Jews and Jewish culture. He had close ties with Jewish labor leaders and rank-and-file union members. His historical sense enabled him to understand the heinous nature of nativist animus against 19th-century Catholic immigrants, anti-Catholicism, and anti-Semitism.[70] The July 31, 1978, *Yardstick* reiterated the history and the consequences of racial and religious bigotry.

> Al Smith's loss was not due to political factors, but religious prejudice. In 1928 the Ku Klux Klan, which attacked blacks, Jews, and Catholics with equal fervor, had six million members throughout the country. The anti-Semitic tract "Protocols of the Elders of Zion" was being distributed on a massive scale. And the infamous immigration quotas, designed to keep Southern and Eastern European Jews and Catholics out of the United States, were being enacted by Congress in a mood of near hysteria. (These quotas, it must be recalled, were still in effect in the late 1930s and 1940s, and were cynically applied to prevent both Jews and Catholics from escaping Hitler's master plan for "cleansing" Europe of its "undesirable" elements).[71]

The same column also pointed out the history of cooperation between Catholics and Jews in the National Conference of Christians and Jews, in the factories, and in political parties. Cooperation enabled both groups to achieve common social and political goals and to develop a unique theology from below. The following quote, though lengthy, captures the warmth of Catholic–Jewish friendship.

> A small group of prominent Americans banded together to form an organization to eliminate [any] intergroup prejudices which disfigure and distort religious, business, social and political relations. . . . This was the National Conference of Christians and Jews [NCCJ].
>
> The NCCJ was founded as a lay organization. Of its six original members, only two, one rabbi and one Methodist minster, could be identified as clergy. There were no bishops or priests, although the jurists, industrialists and scholars were deeply religious people. . . . There is something uniquely American about the success story of Jewish-Christian relations over the last 50 years. . . . The NCCJ merely formalized and made visible . . . an interfaith phenomenon already deeply embedded in the American socio-political cultural pattern. . . .
>
> While the various religious organizations were officially "ghettoized" each in its own little enclave of triumphalism in those narrow days before Vatican Council II, Americans were busily discovering each other in the factories and political parties.
>
> Catholics and Jews were perhaps especially involved in this "pre-dialogue" activity. Both were immigrant groups and highly urbanized as communities. The beginnings of the labor movement in this country are largely the fruit of

> Catholic-Jewish coalition that came together out of common hurts and desperate needs. . . . Catholics and Jews joined . . . together into coalitions to achieve the social and political goals that neither community could have won on its own.
>
> Here, the church had learned its theology from the grass roots up. In America, the coalitions and compromises, recognition of mutual agendas and shared priorities came first. Only later did the official dialogue begin. But when it began, in the late 1940s and 1960s, it had here . . . a solid base upon which to build. The network of personal and programmatic relationships . . . gives the Jewish-Christian dialogue in this country a style and a depth among the people nowhere else, perhaps, achievable.
>
> This fact, of realistic and self-aware intergroup activity on all levels of the religious communities involved, is perhaps America's greatest contribution to the interfaith movement in the world today. And the NCCJ stands as a fitting symbol of that contribution.[72]

The *Yardstick* columns outlined the constitutive elements for fruitful Catholic–Jewish dialogue.[73] First, biblical and theological studies provided a foundation for mutual knowledge, understanding, and conversation. Second, a spirit of humility and repentance helped the church purge the slightest trace of anti-Semitism from its heart.[74] Judaism was now mentor, and the church was listener and learner. Higgins rhapsodized that *Nostra Aetate* was

> writing finis, not to a book, but only to the preface of the first of a long series of volumes which will not be completed until the end of time. . . . What a proud boast it will be for the church in the United States if our own bishops, priests, and faithful step out in front and set an example for the rest of the world in this regard. The Church Universal has a right to expect this of us, for, in the Providence of God, approximately half of all the Jews in the world live in America. Working hand and hand with them as brothers, we have a glorious opportunity to transform the council's declaration . . . from a lifeless piece of paper into a living document which, in God's good time, can literally change the face of the earth.[75]

Third, *Yardstick* columns indicated the role and responsibility of the institutional church for initiating conversation,[76] for educating Catholics regarding the spiritual bonds and the common heritage uniting the two communities,[77] for communicating the profound significance of the land for Jews,[78] and for highlighting the commitment of both communities to promote social justice.[79]

Higgins tirelessly dedicated himself to participating in national and international initiatives on behalf of Catholic–Jewish relations. He served as the pro tempore secretary for the Subcommittee on Catholic–Jewish Relations of the U.S. Bishops Committee on Ecumenism and Interreligious Affairs in 1967 and chaired the advisory board of the Secretariat on Catholic–Jewish Relations in 1968. He attended two international gatherings of the International Catholic–Jewish Liaison Committee in 1976 and 1977.[80] In May 1978 the Synagogue Council sponsored an outdoor meeting at the foot of the Lincoln Memorial to celebrate the thirtieth anniversary of the State of Israel. Higgins was one of the invited speakers. "All of [the speakers] stressed . . . the life or death necessity of guaranteeing the security and integrity of the State of Israel against any and all aggressors."[81]

The 1971 Synod of Bishops

The five-week Synod of Bishops was held in Rome in October and November 1971. Higgins attended as a priest auditor and participated actively in the English-speaking group. The synod's two main topics—the ministerial priesthood and justice in the world—immensely interested him. He enjoyed the free, though frank and careful, discussions. He read eight to ten French-, Italian-, and English-newspaper accounts of the synod every day.

The synod considered the crisis in the ministerial priesthood. It investigated optional celibacy, the need for a greater diversity of priestly ministries, and the relationship between bishops and priests. It addressed the involvement of priests in secular occupations and party politics, and it explored the establishment of national or regional episcopal conferences.[82] Higgins thought that the synod had acted wisely in taking a middle-of-the-road position on the priest's role in social and political matters. The synod

> stressed the right and the duty of the Church, and of the ordained priest, to preach and give witness to justice at every level of society, to denounce violations of justice, to help promote the full development of persons and of nations—and to do all that this involves without fear or favor. But, it also noted that the institutional church "is not alone responsible for justice in the world" and has neither the competence nor the responsibility to offer concrete solutions to particular social problems.[83]

He was pleased that the synod reaffirmed the role of the laity as the primary agents for effecting structural changes in society. Their apostolic action was authentically rooted in their baptism and was no longer regarded as a participation in the hierarchy's mission. Laity acted as mature citizens and autonomous members of society. Higgins agreed with the direction that the synod had ultimately taken.

> My own feeling is that what the Synod said about the social mission of the Church and the specific role of the ordained priest in the field of social reform

> is reasonably adequate as a statement of general principles but is not and was never intended to be the final word on the matter. The Synod—to its credit, in this writer's opinion—deliberately refrained from getting bogged down in particulars. . . .
>
> The Church's involvement in action for justice will remain ineffective if it is not given flesh in the life of our local churches at all their levels. . . . The Synod . . . was opting for the principle of pluralism and for a large degree of local autonomy.
>
> It remains, then, for the local churches to take up where the Synod left off and to assume their own responsibility in the area of social reform and try to figure out . . . what needs to be done—and by whom and under what rubric—if the Church is effectively to carry out its indispensable role in the promotion of social justice. . . .
>
> Those who think that the document is too conservative shouldn't throw up their hands in despair. . . . They should roll up their sleeves and try to fashion local programs of social action which may be more to their liking.[84]

The local church was entrusted with the mission of promoting justice, proclaiming the Gospel, remedying injustice, and educating and forming the laity. Political action and programs that helped the poor and the weak became the means to social justice. The synod's affirmation of the laity, especially its role in transforming the temporal order, reinforced Higgins' conviction that the theology of the laity had to become part of the bloodstream of the church.[85] "The Synod, next to the Vatican Council itself, [was] the most interesting meeting I have ever been privileged to attend."[86]

Higgins did not agree with the negative press reports regarding the synod.

> When I had finished reading [the newspaper reports] half way across the Atlantic, I knew I had to ask the Sabina stewardess to bring me another martini to lift my normally optimistic spirits. . . . I can take almost any amount of pessimism in stride. But pessimism is one thing, and cynicism is something else again. . . . This writer has had all the cynicism he can take from his friends in the Fourth Estate.[87]

He returned home in an optimistic spirit. He immediately began to apply the social teaching of the synod to the internal life of the church. *Justice in the World* enunciated what would become one of the most frequently quoted principles of modern Catholic social teaching:

> While the Church is bound to give witness to justice, she recognizes that everyone who ventures to speak to people about justice must first be just in their eyes. Hence we must undertake an examination of the mode of acting and of the possessions and lifestyle found within the Church herself. . . . Those

> who serve the Church by their labor, including priests and Religious, should receive a sufficient livelihood and enjoy that social security which is customary in their region. Lay people should be given fair wages and a system for promotion. . . . The Church recognizes everyone's right to be heard in the spirit of dialogue which preserves a legitimate diversity within the Church.[88]

Higgins would return to this principle when he considered the church's responsibility to those employed in Catholic schools and hospitals in the 1980s and 1990s.

The Laity and the Church's Mission

Higgins wrote thirty *Yardstick* columns on the role of the laity in the social ministry of the church.[89] His work with the laity in organized labor and his position at SAD reinforced his conviction that the church's social mission belonged primarily, though not exclusively, to the laity. The *Yardstick* columns promoted the laity as agents of social change and advocates of workplace democracy. The laity incarnated the Gospel in the world. They were the hands that leavened the yeast of the Gospel in society and its structures. The church was now beginning to reenvision the vocational, charismatic, and functional roles of the clergy and the laity. The June 16, 1969, *Yardstick* column addressed the transition that was beginning to take place.

> The real stumbling block to putting the church at the service of the secular Christian . . . is the universal persistence, both inside and outside the church, of a 19th-century caricature of the church at a time when Christians ought to be rehearsing their roles for the 21st-century. The 19th-century caricature . . . [is based on] the idea that the church is to be regarded as something apart from the Christian.[90]

The mission of the church in the 19th-century model rested on a hierarchical and juridical ecclesiology from above. Those of the clergy were the professionals; those of the laity were the amateurs. The clergy formed the public face of the church. When activist clergy members were put in the front lines, the church looked good. Higgins named this the Selma syndrome.[91] The phrase serves as a metaphor, opening the way to some of his bedrock convictions. First, the clergy should not usurp the role of the laity in social action. Both should function according to their vocations and in ways that model the prophetic Christ. Second, the church should train and form the laity to take its rightful place as ecclesial representatives in social, racial, and workplace forums. Third, the cause of social justice demanded long-term commitment of the clergy and the laity to the cause of those that were marginalized and excluded from social, political, and economic citizenship. Higgins wanted long-distance runners. He was critical of those who lacked staying power, who committed only to short-term notoriety. He also criticized the kind of systemic paternalism that undercut the laity's role or belied the real order. "In the professional and occupational world the secular Christian is the 'native,' the priest a tourist or visitor."[92] He envisioned an alternative, 21st-century ecclesiology from below in which the clergy and the laity worked to prepare the way of justice and helped to inaugurate the reign of God.

> To prepare the way for Him who is to come—to be open to the Spirit and open to the future—entails a high degree of apostolic flexibility, a willingness to take prudent risks, and to change with the changing needs of the world and the Church. It also presumes a sense of dependence on the providence of God and a commitment to the virtue of evangelical poverty—poverty in the sense of being prepared to admit that the way we have done things in the past may . . . be outmoded and that new methods and new structures may have to be adopted if the Church is to effectively carry out its mission.[93]

The church stood at a turning point. Higgins believed that insights from the social sciences and from social theory could expand the church's intellectual capital.[94] A revaluation of the laity's social responsibility would require a program of lay formation and training for them to be witnesses of Christ in the social order. An affective and intellectual appreciation of social theology and ethics would help the laity to apply principles to practice in diverse cultural settings.[95]

For years the Catholic laity had been leavening the secular order through its participation in unions, employer associations, professional associations, and political parties. Catholics also helped improve the quality of life through their involvement in interreligious and secular organizations.[96] Higgins encouraged the laity to involve themselves ecumenically.[97] "The church isn't just something to which people go. The church is something that goes with them wherever they go."[98]

Higgins was concerned that an entire generation of lay leadership could be lost because the church was too preoccupied with internal affairs and its internal ministries and because it too little valued the laity's social ministry in effecting its mission in the secular world.[99]

> The Church . . . acts upon the world through her laity. . . . Without a dynamic laity conscious of its ministry to the world, the Church in effect does not speak or act. . . . It would be one of the great ironies of history if the era of Vatican II which opened [the] windows of the Church to the world were to close with the Church turned upon herself. Ecclesiastical chauvinism has no more to recommend it than civic or national super-patriotism.[100]

The church in the United States did engage the national issues of race, war, poverty, and work. It began to provide a contemporary catechesis for the church's social ministry and began to apply its teaching to the issues of race, housing, the welfare of people, and the plight of the poor and the underprivileged. Twelve *Yardstick* columns considered the theological and liturgical foundations for social action.[101] First, the incarnation became the theological basis for social action. The eternal Word became flesh in history. "Christ became one of us. If we can manage to think of Christ only as God, then we can close our eyes to the fact that we have to love every man if we are to love Christ."[102] Second, the teaching of the Gospel needed to be applied to every age. In particular, these columns related the incarnation to racism, poverty, and work. Higgins noted the existence of two separate and unequal societies: one being white, the other being black. He stated bluntly that all have had some part in white racism.

> No group of White Americans can reasonably expect to get off the hook so easily with regard to the matter of white racism. . . . All members of the white community—and especially those of us who have benefited most from the system—are responsible, in varying degrees, for the tragic plight of black Americans and must share the blame for the nation's failure to press for a national resolution of the racial crisis which was outlined so starkly in the Kerner report.
>
> This is not to say that our leaders in church and State are immune to criticism on the matter of race relations. . . . Constructive criticism implies a willingness on the part of those who are mounting the criticism to confess that we are all pretty much in the same boat. . . . The fact of the matter is . . . that all of us are responsible in more ways than we realize and certainly in more ways than we are willing to admit. . . . Unlike the Publican in the . . . parable, the Pharisee thought that he could get off the hook by rubbing his own guilt against others "the way we wipe dirty fingers on a rag." It didn't work in his case, and there is no reason to think that it will work in ours.[103]

Higgins also addressed the issue of poverty. The June 24, 1968, *Yardstick* column, written on the eve of the Poor Peoples' March in Washington, revisited the 1965 *LDS*. Higgins offered the example of the generosity of Moses and the presence of Jesus in the least, the last, and the left out. Both figures called the church to welcome the poor and to develop a solidarity with the poor.[104] Similarly, the January 1, 1973, *Yardstick* column revisited the 1972 *LDS* concerning job dissatisfaction, worker alienation, workplace boredom, the meaninglessness of dead-end occupations, and the low self-esteem of workers.[105]

The foundation for social action rested on the liturgical life of the church.

> Active, intelligent and truly informed participation in the sacred liturgy is the primary means of developing a social consciousness among Catholics. Too many Catholics . . . think of religion as worship of God that begins and ends in the privacy of the soul, and, while going to Mass regularly, are content to leave their neighbor out in the cold like the man in the Gospel who was left half-dead on the road to Jericho and was passed by without compunction by men who were thought to be—and presumably thought of themselves as being—holy men. . . .
>
> The liturgical practice of too many Catholics . . . is excessively individualistic and . . . falls short of the ideal recently set forth by the Church. . . . A congregation steeped in the liturgical life of the Church will be more socially conscious and will be better prepared to make sound moral judgments in economic and political life than one that is not. . . .
>
> In the words of St. Augustine, what the liturgy can and should teach us is that "it is not only your tongue that praises God; the works of your hands must be in tune with your voice. After a time, your tongue becomes silent; sing by your life, and your praise will never cease. . . . When you play the kettle-drum or the zither, your hands sing as well as your voice. When you sing 'Alleluia,' you must also feed the hungry, clothe the naked, and house the stranger. Then it is not your voice only that resounds; your hands keep time and tune with it."[106]

The Renewal of the Nation

Racism

The United States was remaking itself in the 1960s and the 1970s. The nation confronted its racism, its poverty, the war in Vietnam, and the plight of migrant agricultural workers. Higgins' lifelong commitment to racial equality was not based on any single event, person, or writing. It was simply a matter of doing justice. His study of U.S. labor history made him keenly aware that racism had profoundly affected working people of color. African American workers had often been hired as strikebreakers. They were also derided, attacked, and lynched. Even when they were members of a union, they often experienced racial prejudice from their rank-and-file colleagues in union locals. They were assigned jobs designated as "Negro jobs." There was little chance for promotion or ascension to leadership positions. A. Philip Randolph, the inspirational leader, and Milton P. Webster, the practical leader of the Brotherhood of Sleeping Car Porters, struggled tirelessly and tenaciously to unionize African American porters and maids. The brotherhood was recognized in 1935 when the AFL granted them a charter and acknowledged them as bargaining agents for porters and maids employed by the Pullman Palace Car Company. White union officials belatedly and begrudgingly accorded Randolph (and fellow African American Williard S.

Townsend) a leadership role on the federation's executive council. Asian workers had likewise endured discrimination, incarceration, deportation, and xenophobic anti-immigration legislation. Latino agricultural workers, the poorest of the poor, competed with imported Mexican workers for the same low-paying jobs, lived in inadequate and unsanitary housing, were denied benefits, and lived without legal protection. Minority women, relegated to gender-defined jobs, suffered low wages and inferior benefits because of the color of their skin. Higgins knew firsthand that people of color were denied economic citizenship.

SAD addressed racism in two ways. First, Father John F. Cronin, the Sulpician moral theologian at St. Mary's Seminary in Baltimore, worked for the passage of civil rights legislation. Second, Higgins devoted thirty-eight columns of the *Yardstick* to racism and to civil rights.[107] The *Yardstick* column for March 3, 1970, defined white racism.

> The best definition of racism is an operational one. This means that it must be based upon the way people actually behave, rather than upon logical consistency or purely scientific ideas. *Therefore, racism may be viewed as any attitude, action, or institutional structure which subordinates a person or group because of his or their color.* Even though "race" and "color" refer to two different kinds of human characteristics, in America it is the visibility of skin color—and of other physical traits associated with particular colors or groups—that makes individuals as "targets" for subordination by members of the white majority. . . . Specifically, white racism subordinates members of all these other groups primarily because they are not white in color.[108]

Higgins resonated with the impatience of black intellectuals and leaders.[109] The *Yardstick* column for June 24, 1963, stated, "Discrimination against Negro workers on the part of labor unions is clearly immoral and, given labor's traditional claim to leadership in the field of social justice, is also hypocritical." Combating racism was organized labor's most urgent issue.

> We are now at a turning point, however, in the history of the United States and also in the history of the American labor movement. This is the year of decision for all of us in the field of race relations and civil rights. . . . [The labor movement] must expect to be judged almost exclusively on its performance in the field of civil rights and must expect to be told, even by its friends, that its record on the issue of civil rights has been somewhat disappointing. . . . Negro leaders are also asking . . . when the labor movement is going to lower the boom on those unions which are still practicing racial discrimination. When an employer tries to discourage the organization of his workers or refuses to engage in collective bargaining, the labor movement will go to almost any length to bring him to time and, if necessary, will drive him to the wall. Negro lead-

> ers are disappointed that it tends to react much less vigorously when one of its own affiliates is guilty of practicing racial discrimination. . . . Many labor leaders have yet to grasp the depth and the passion of the present racial crisis. . . . This is the most serious problem with which the labor movement is presently confronted. . . . Labor would be well-advised to take a self-critical and ruthlessly honest look at this problem, which is largely of its own making. It can ill afford to get the reputation of being even partially out of sympathy with the Negro's legitimate and very belated demand for complete equality.[110]

Higgins acknowledged the gap that existed between the higher-echelon members of unions and the rank and file, between organized labor and African American intellectuals and leaders, and between the cities and the suburbs.[111] The urban–racial crisis threatened to destroy the nation.

He suggested resources and strategies for combating racism. First, he promoted ministries of the Word, such as preaching, education, and testimony. Catholic, Protestant, and Jewish communities were voices of conscience. Their participation in public discourse and in advocacy was based on the rich theological foundation of the human person.

> The American bishops have long since come out in favor of comprehensive civil rights legislation as a logical, not to say a necessary application, in our times, of basic Catholic teaching on the equality and dignity of all of God's children, regardless of their racial origin or the color of their skin.[112]

Church and synagogue exercised a distinctive voice of suasion in the public forum. During the week of July 21, 1963, representatives from the National Council of Churches, the Synagogue Council of America, and SAD testified before three congressional commissions in support of President John F. Kennedy's civil rights legislation. This was the first time in U.S. history that the three religious communities had "presented a united front in support of a particular legislative program."[113] Second, Higgins publicized concrete actions done on behalf of racial justice. The *Yardstick* of April 1, 1963, reported on the "battle, led by Monsignor [Jack] Egan, to force adequate relocation and housing provisions into the urban renewal plan for the Hyde Park-Kenwood neighborhood adjacent to the University of Chicago." Egan—with the support of unions, social reform organizations, and local religious communities—acted to protect poor African Americans in revitalizing the Hyde Park–Kenwood neighborhoods. He encouraged the collaborative efforts of religious and civic groups to achieve racial justice. The *Yardstick* of June 24, 1963, supported the picketing done by the National Association for the Advancement of Colored People (NAACP) in Philadelphia, which had thrown up a mass picket line around a federally financed construction project from which black workers were systematically excluded. The result was immediate. A few qualified African American craftspersons were hired. In addition, the federal government had begun to investigate "discrimination against qualified Negro workers on projects which are being paid for by Uncle Sam. . . . [The government] is no longer going to tolerate the exclusion of Negro applicants from Federally sponsored apprenticeship programs."[114] He endorsed public witness and stood with those who marched in Selma and Memphis. "Several thousand clergymen and nuns went to Alabama last month 'like the lame to Lourdes . . . sensing somehow that God was stirring the waters in Selma.'"[115] Higgins and John McCarthy joined other marchers in Memphis on April 8, 1968, the day before the funeral of Dr. Martin Luther King Jr. King had helped to forge a new coalition of civil rights activists and the labor movement in Memphis.

> [The sanitation workers] were his people—desperately poor Negroes fighting against almost impossible odds for elementary economic justice. They needed him and . . . he heeded their anguished plea for help even though he must have known that . . . he was putting his own life in jeopardy. His courage and sense of dedication will be forever held in highest honor. . . .
>
> Organized labor . . . also rallied to the cause. . . . Labor's belated but effective support of what started out as a largely Negro-oriented cause seems, anyway, to be an example of the kind of labor-Civil Rights coalition that is needed to get at the root causes of the racial crisis in the United States. . . .
>
> The unions . . . are, and will remain the largest institution in the country committed to domestic social reform. . . . The Seventies could see a vast growth in collective bargaining among groups which previously have resisted unionization . . . So perhaps there will be a new labor movement. . . .
>
> The revitalized unions could have a deep community of interest with the poor generally and with Negroes, since the work of destroying the ghettoes and building a decent America would provide full employment for a generation at least. The old-fashioned economic drives and reawakened conscience of the middle class might converge. The reinvigorated labor movement which could result would be a crucial element of a new political majority in America. . . .
>
> The garbage strike in Memphis will have been a major turning point in American social history, and Dr. King, God rest his noble soul, will not have died in vain.[116]

Higgins did more than write about racial equality. He lived it! Bishop John McCarthy said:

> Out of everybody I knew at the [Catholic] Conference George was the most pastoral. When maids were burying the 18-year-old boys who'd been shot by the police, George Higgins and I were at the funeral, or George by himself.

> And when a maid's daughter was getting married at the Antioch Baptist Church, George would be there. I'm not saying that no one else ever went to anything, but George had that real good feel for the role of the priest, especially in moments of sorrow and celebration in peoples' lives.[117]

Poverty and Unemployment

The nation began to confront the plight of the poor and the blight of poverty. In 1958 John Kenneth Galbraith, the prominent Harvard University economist, addressed an economics of abundance vis-à-vis inequality and the reality of islands of poverty.

> Poverty—grim, degrading and ineluctable—is not remarkable in India. For relatively few, the fate is otherwise. But in the United States the survival of poverty is remarkable. We ignore it because we share with all societies at all times the capacity for not seeing what we do not wish to see. Anciently this has enabled the nobleman to enjoy his dinner while remaining oblivious to the beggars around his door. In our own day, it enables us to travel in comfort through the South Bronx and into the lush precincts of midtown Manhattan. But while our failure to notice can be explained, it cannot be excused. "Poverty . . . is no disgrace but it is damned annoying." In the contemporary United States, it is not annoying but it is a disgrace.[118]

In 1962 Michael Harrington captivated the political and the popular imagination with the publication of *The Other America: Poverty in the United States*. The book, wrote Irving Howe, was "a *cri de coeur*, an appeal to the conscience of the country: how can you allow such a scandal to fester in this country?"[119] For the first time since James Agee's classic work *Let Us Now Praise Famous Men*, a writer had stirred scholars, politicians, and citizens with new insight.[120] Harrington did not dispassionately analyze the concept of poverty; he wrote about poor people living urbanwide and countryside. He provided new vocabulary. He said that the poor were invisible.[121] Harrington concluded that forty to sixty million people, out of a population of 180 million, were living in poverty in 1959. The poor were not a small and declining number; they would not disappear in the future. Roughly one out of three people lived below the standards that were regarded as the decent minimum for food, housing, clothing, and health. Harrington wrote without sentimentality about poor people living in "a culture of poverty."[122] Different kinds of poverty stalked the alcoholic poor, the hillbillies in city slums, the aging and the elderly poor, the poor living with mental illness, the workers who were shut out of their jobs by automation and technology. According to Maurice Isserman in *The Other American: The Life of Michael Harrington*, Harrington asked his readers to

> make use of their "vision"—in two senses. First, he asked them to "see through the wall of affluence" and recognize the true dimensions of poverty . . . and its cost in human dignity. Second, he declared that there must also be vision "in the sense of purpose, of aspiration." Michael summoned his readers to a "war on poverty" not just for the sake of the poor but for their own sakes. Ending poverty was not a question of charity. . . . Michael argued that Americans should be angry and ashamed to live in a society that . . . was instead divided into two nations.[123]

In his final chapter of *The Other America* Harrington writes:

> The decisive moment occurs after all the sociology and the description is in. . . . After one reads the facts, either there are anger and shame, or there are not. And, as usual, the fate of the poor hangs upon the decision of the better-off. If this anger and shame are not forthcoming, someone can write a book about the other America a generation from now and it will be the same, or worse. Perhaps the most important analytic point to have emerged in this description of the other America is the fact that poverty in America forms a culture, a way of life and feeling, that it makes a whole. It is crucial to generalize this idea, for it profoundly affects how one moves to destroy poverty.[124]

In 1960 John F. Kennedy was personally affected by the poverty he witnessed in West Virginia. During the campaign he declared that the war against poverty and degradation was not yet over. However, as president his commitment to the pursuit of liberal reform did not match his rhetoric. Harrington criticized Kennedy for his cautious approach toward the nation's problems. Kennedy's few legislative achievements had little impact on the poor. In the early months of his presidency, unemployment was at its highest level since the outset of the Second World War. After Kennedy's assassination, Johnson quickly declared an unconditional war on poverty as a way to secure legitimacy in the eyes of the country. However, the war in Vietnam eventually eclipsed his concern for the poor.[125]

Higgins' concern for the poor was cut from the same cloth as Harrington's.[126] Higgins' *Yardstick* columns identified the poor, addressed the causes of poverty, and offered solutions. First, he identified the poor as women (disproportionately African American), children, and the elderly.[127] They live in rural and urban settings, and they lack essential material goods.[128] Many work at full-time jobs that do not provide sufficient income. Others work occasionally or seasonally. These people are lonely wanderers, families living in cars and shelters, and migrant farmworkers and their families.[129] Still others are consistently unemployed. They often lack the training and education necessary for a job. Poverty robs them all of social status, economic strength, and political power. The culture of poverty deprives them of economic citizenship. They usually do not participate in the political processes that affect their lives. The culture of affluence marginalizes, excludes, rejects, and discriminates against them.[130]

Higgins addressed the causes of poverty. He stated that the underlying economic cause of poverty was unemployment.[131] Social conditions and unjust systems perpetuated poverty. Poverty, an intractable and virulent malaise, would only be eliminated through a moral and religious conversion.[132] People with power and privilege would only be moved to action when they actually saw the faces of people who were poor. This called for a new heart and a taste for the deeds of justice in the marketplace and in the neighborhood. Higgins offered practical ways to express personal concern and involvement. He promoted

> tithing in investment, i.e., the investment, by individuals or non-profit institutions, of about 10% of their available capital in non-segregated housing developments. Patterns of racial segregation in both housing and schools are in large part determined by investors in real estate. Investors of good will must be encouraged to make their dollars work for justice as well as for monetary return.[133]

He recommended economic and legislative reform. He steadfastly maintained that organized labor was the principal, and perhaps even the sole, institution capable of protecting the rights of workers in promoting a just minimal wage, in lifting workers out of poverty through collective bargaining, and in promoting the common good. In one of his last *Yardstick* columns during this period, he presciently identified the social composition for the 1980s.

> The fight against poverty in the '80s will, in many ways, be played out on a new battlefield. The great material consumption spree of the '60s and '70s, spurred by a seemingly endless tide of petroleum and an abundance of cheap raw materials has ended, and we have entered an economic era marked by limited resources, slower economic growth and the increasing internationalization of our economy.
>
> In short, the squeeze is on and it will have profound effects on the struggle to achieve economic justice. . . .
>
> The steady expansion of the economic pie in preceding decades made it easier to improve the lot of the poor. But as we enter the '80s, the pie isn't growing as rapidly. As a result, a partial dismantling of the social-welfare system put in place during the last 30 years of prosperity has already begun.
>
> Distribution, not growth, has become the key issue in fighting poverty. With a shrinking economic pie, who gets which slice will be crucial to anti-poverty efforts of the '80s.

> Making sure the poor get a fair slice . . . will be virtually impossible as long as the interests of the poor are assumed to be in conflict with the interests of the majority of Americans. And this is not going to happen without a new politics based on coalition building.
>
> Today the most significant economic border . . . isn't between the poor and the rest of us, but between the super-rich and the rest of us. This economic reality requires a new politics which can link the efforts of anti-poverty groups with those of organizations which represent "middle America"—consumer groups, labor unions and other public-interest organizations.[134]

He recognized the bonds of solidarity that the church was creating by initiating grassroots programs and by sponsoring the large-scale *Campaign of Human Development.* "If the Catholic community works together, it can fashion a vision for the 1980s as bold and creative as that which first created the *Campaign for Human Development.*"[135] Higgins challenged his readers to a spirituality of personal involvement in a passionate and lengthy *Yardstick* column:

> Our first obligation, as we examine our collective conscience, . . . is to force ourselves to realize that there is indeed no lack of poor people at the present time in almost every community. . . . Our recognition of this fact has been very slow in coming. As one experienced writer put it, "The poor have drifted out of the national consciousness. . . . This has happened not because Americans are cruel but because they are looking the other way."
>
> Thanks be to God, . . . this regrettable situation is beginning to change for the better. . . . The American people, thanks in part to the Poor Peoples' March, are gradually facing up to the fact that literally millions of their fellow-citizens have fallen on evil days through no fault of their own and are living in the most degrading kind of poverty.
>
> The poor . . . are finally beginning to drift back into our national consciousness, and in recent years we have belatedly begun to step up our efforts, through legislation and other appropriate means, to help them remedy their sad plight and to take their rightful place in American economic and social life.
>
> Whatever we may be able to do about the problem of poverty impersonally . . . by supporting needed reforms in our economic system, by adjusting our social and economic legislation to the needs of the times, and by contributing, according to our means, to organized appeals for the relief of the needy and the underprivileged is all to the good and should in no way be discounted or underestimated. On the other hand, it must be emphasized that a purely impersonal interest in the plight of the poor and the disadvantaged is far from being adequate. Much more is demanded of all of us. We are called upon to perform the corporal and spiritual works of mercy on a person-to-person basis and to do

so with profound respect for the dignity and the sensibilities of those whom we are privileged to serve in the name of the Lord. . . .

[The poor are not] so many unfortunates to be relieved. . . . [The poor are] persons to be courted. . . . This is our common responsibility and not merely an elective . . . for the few. None of us . . . is free to look the other way or to stand on the sidelines as a passive spectator. We are all called upon to become personally involved in helping the poor to help themselves.[136]

Vietnam and Domestic Issues

Higgins devoted several *Yardstick* columns to domestic issues, such as the war in Vietnam, birth control, abortion, and the changing role of women in society and in the church.

> For each issue on which he staked out a position, he drew on a background that combined a clear understanding of the Church's social doctrine and a sure knowledge of economic forces, fusing them into a broad vision of an ideal society in which labor, management, and the state would join forces to serve the common good of the people. . . . His guides were the great social encyclicals, the landmark 1919 bishop's program, . . . and the teaching of mentors such as Msgr. Ryan and Father McGowan.[137]

The teaching of the Second Vatican Council, especially on the role of the church in its mission to the modern world, guided his thinking.

The Vietnam War, America's longest war, went on for decades. U.S. involvement began in 1945 when U.S. Merchant Marine ships ferried French soldiers into the county in an effort to restore France's crumbling Indochinese empire. U.S. involvement and interest continued because Presidents Eisenhower, Kennedy, and Johnson, as well as secretary of state John Foster Dulles, believed that the United States had to take a stand and show itself opposed to communism. The United States could not afford to lose Vietnam to the enemy. In 1954 the United States expanded its role, hoping to prevent the victorious Vietminh from extending communist control throughout the country. America's slowly escalating presence in Vietnam in the early 1960s drew little public criticism, partly because the threat of communism seemed so great. Few Americans doubted that their country would prevail as long as its resolve remained strong. The toughest decision on the war fell to Lyndon Johnson soon after he took over the presidency in 1963. Johnson tried to manage the war on the side while he managed his war on poverty. In 1965 tens of thousands of American troops were rushed into the country and began an all-out bombing campaign against the North. Johnson hoped that the U.S. military would right the situation before too much had gone awry. Johnson's miscalculations cost him the presidency.

Small groups of pacifists and increasingly larger groups of university students began to oppose the war and to publicize facts that the government had trued to hide. By 1968 and 1969 the antiwar movement had become massive and militant. Protestors wanted the United States out of Vietnam. Reports of U.S. atrocities, the inability of the United States to win the support of South Vietnamese peasants, mounting deaths and casualties, and a weak South Vietnamese government fueled the antiwar protests. By 1970 opposition to the war was great. The U.S. military, for the first time in the nation's history, was unable to win this war. Never before had a war caused the nation so much disenchantment and fury. The effects were felt long after the war ended, and bitterness about the war continued into the 1990s. Higgins initially had supported the war. He honestly believed that the people of Vietnam wanted help from the United States. He admired President Johnson and considered him to be a man with compassion for the poor and an interest in the welfare of humanity around the globe.[138] Higgins continued his own questioning and scrutiny as the war dragged on, and people of conscience began to express moral reservations. His trip to the Far East in 1969 awakened him to the deep resentment others felt toward U.S. presence in the region. By 1972 Higgins had come to recognize the evil of the war, and he voiced his opposition, too.

> So far as this writer is concerned, there is enough information . . . to warrant the conclusion that the war in Vietnam is an evil of almost incalculable proportions. Please God, it will have come to a merciful end before we enter upon a second Respect Life Week in the fall of 1973. . . . I am not suggesting for a moment that we should soft-pedal our opposition to abortion. If anything, I think we should redouble our efforts to sensitize our people to this terrible evil. On the other hand, I am equally convinced that we will simply have to be consistent in the statement of our moral principles if we hope to retain a shred of credibility. Abortion is admittedly a clear violation of the moral law. But so is the bombing of innocent people in Vietnam. Why not say so, at long last, in quite specific terms![139]

He considered birth control, abortion, and the changing role of women to be important family- and work-oriented issues.[140] An occasional *Yardstick* column related birth control to social and union issues. He objected to an endorsement of Planned Parenthood by a union official and to a recommendation that the Planned Parenthood program would be incorporated into the social service program of organized labor. He stated that workers did not want their unions meddling in their personal, family, or religious affairs; and because the matter was personal and its scope was beyond the competence of the state, he did not want the federal government to intervene in family planning. "He saw the consolidation of birth control into the antipoverty programs as an insult to the poor and especially to Blacks."[141] Similarly, Higgins did not want the unions to include abortion as part of the medical benefits package when they engaged in collective bargaining. This could divide and destroy a local union.

Higgins consistently supported the vitality of the family and the just demands of women in the workplace.[142] He opposed policies and practices that discriminated against women and encouraged fairness in wages, hiring, promotion, training opportunities, and seniority. In the late 1960s and early 1970s his convictions and compassion brought him to the question of rights, especially for poor and underprivileged working women.[143] He supported the role of women in the workplace and encouraged them to participate in union locals and to assume leadership roles in organized labor.

The Renewal of Organized Labor

Labor leaders and their unions respected Higgins' knowledge, integrity, and fairness. These qualities enabled him to be a presence in the workplace. Higgins presented his principal concern during this period in the *Yardstick* columns. He promoted economic citizenship through collective bargaining, labor–management cooperation, and vigorous efforts to organize the unorganized. He worked tirelessly with the United Farm Workers to organize agricultural workers in California, and he supported the just demands of workers in the clothing and manufacturing industries.

Higgins steadfastly maintained that unions were essential and necessary for the well-being of the country and for progressive economic change.

> In our opinion unions are absolutely indispensable in our kind of industrial society. . . . Employers . . . have an obligation to welcome, or at least not to interfere with, their establishment. Until this principle is . . . universally taken for granted as a self-evident truth, labor and management will of necessity spend too much time and energy sparring with one another—time and energy which they ought to devote to carrying out the demands which social justice makes on both of them. Social justice . . . demands . . . that the two groups forget their petty differences and jointly try to figure out how they can best serve the welfare not only of their own members or stockholders, but of all their fellow citizens and especially the poorest of the poor.[144]

He proposed remedies that would renew the labor movement and move it beyond its travail. He recommended that labor unions find ways to organize, attract the young, and work to overcome their negative image.[145] He bluntly told the rank and file to support the agreements that their leaders worked out with management.[146] He called labor and management to responsible partnership and collaboration in planing the economy, securing full employment, and providing educational programs to train the un- and underemployed.[147] He lamented the energy that unions wasted on strikes and suggested that this energy be creatively redirected into discussion and cooperation.[148] Most of all, he promoted collective bargaining as the cornerstone of economic democracy and hoped that labor and management would commit themselves to make it work better.[149] When the U.S. Postal Service celebrated the issuance of a special stamp to commemorate the contribution of collective bargaining in the history of labor–management relations, it invited Higgins; President Gerald Ford; and some two hundred business people, labor leaders, government officials, and media representatives to a dinner. Higgins opened the gathering with an invocation that waxed eloquently on the merits of collective bargaining.

> O Lord, we come here to celebrate symbolically the progress we have made over the years . . . in democratizing industrial relations in this country through the institution of collective bargaining. With all its limitations, however, collective bargaining remains the most valid and the most successful approach for strengthening the essential components of our particular kind of economic system while . . . enhancing the dignity and the freedom of the industrial worker. . . . What is needed most of all is clearheaded recognition of the community of interest of many vital points between private needs and public policy. . . .
>
> [Collective bargaining] must continually adapt itself to new problems and to new needs and above all must work to achieve full employment and nondiscriminatory employment for all workers of every race, color, and creed. . . . Collective bargaining aims at achieving a realistic measure of democracy in American industry. . . . Democracy is very serious business. It does not come cheap. It demands a certain price . . . of those who claim it as their birthright. It demands that they pull together for the common good. . . .
>
> Give us the intelligence and the fortitude to work effectively for social and economic justice at home and abroad. Help us to be faithful to our religious convictions in the field of interracial justice. Grant that we may at last have the courage . . . to make this country a land of freedom, justice, and equality for all its citizens, regardless of their racial origin or the color of their skin.[150]

The *Yardstick* columns addressed issues such as the decline of union membership and the animosity that the press and popular opinion held toward unions.[151] Featherbedding, strikes, and labor's conservative position on Vietnam were all given as reasons for labor's travail. Organized labor was portrayed as a self-interest group. Big labor had joined the ranks of big business and big government.[152] Legislation still tended to favor big business, and in some circles there was opposition to the closed shop and to collective bargaining.[153] Higgins unmasked the superficiality of public opinion and countered with his own nuanced analysis of labor's problems. Labor's difficulties, he opined, were principally due to the impact of automation and technology on working people.[154] Rapid industrial change had surprised organized labor. The rise of global corporations had undermined its power. The consequences for working people in the United States were dire. Workers experienced decline in real wages, worsening income distribution, and a rising rate of unemployment. Furthermore, Higgins objected when television portrayed organized labor negatively or rendered it invisible. Programs did not mention its place in society, and it ignored the ways unions had improved the quality of life of working people and their working conditions. When television occasionally included working people, it tended to feature people in the service trades and neglect those who produced consumer goods. Some programs depicted union members as violent, clumsy, uneducated, and deficient in personality and leadership skills. In short, workers were portrayed as robots. They smoked and drank too much. Higgins told television that the time had come for it to mend its ways.[155]

He analyzed the ways that intellectuals and journalists depicted union leaders and rank-and-file members. Critics portrayed union leaders as conservative, self-serving, complacent, and lacking in missionary zeal for the cause of labor. They argued that unions were no longer capable of attracting new members. They contrasted the militancy and excitement of the 1930s and 1940s with the ultraconservatism and the insouciance of the 1970s. Labor leaders, they said, had sold out the rank and file. They lived too comfortably and too luxuriously. They began to write labor's obituary. Higgins did not agree. He maintained that unions were still necessary to promote human dignity, secure fair treatment for all workers, and avoid a return to 19th-century servitude.

> I have always felt it would be impossible to maintain a democratic society without free, strong unions. It seems to me that an attack against the unions should concern not just union people, but everyone dedicated to an open society. . . .
>
> The labor movement, as far as I am concerned, is the nation's most effective force for progressive social change.[156]

He told unions to widen their horizons, educate their own about the purpose of unions, instill idealism, and imbue a spirit of sacrifice.[157] He recommended that they rekindle an enthusiasm for social reform and that they refine their vision. Ultimately, labor renewal depended on the rank and file in union locals. Labor's problems could not be blamed on a so-called decadent and conservative leadership. In reality, Higgins thought that labor leaders were more progressive in attitude and thought than the rank and file and that their influence over the rank and file was exaggerated. In fact, the latter pressured leaders and stymied their attempts to eliminate featherbedding and to refrain from strikes. Rank-and-file apathy and opposition to their leaders thwarted unions in their efforts to organize the poor, fight for consumer protection, and develop a meaningful life for working people. He feared that the entire collective-bargaining process was threatened by the trend toward nonratification among the rank and file.[158]

Higgins lauded the labor and civil rights movements. He considered them the two most liberal and progressive forces in the United States.[159] The *Yardstick* columns chronicled important steps that organized labor undertook to guarantee real democracy for its own members. The United Auto Workers (UAW) inaugurated a seven-member, independent public review board (PRB) in 1957. The PRB watched over the ethical practices of the UAW and gave the rank and file an avenue of appeal. The American Federation of Teachers also set up a PRB. These steps set new standards of social justice, enabled independent action, and kept the courts and federal administration agencies from interfering with union affairs.[160]

The *Yardstick* columns reported on a variety of dinner meetings that Higgins attended. Promoting economic and racial justice, these events became occasions to remember. He attended a dinner in Detroit to commemorate the fortieth anniversary of the UAW–Flint strike against GM. The strike marked the beginning of the open shop in the United States. Some boycotted the dinner, calling it tuxedo unionism. Higgins' presence enabled him to honor a significant moment in labor history and to connect that history with the same hope for workers in the textile industry in the South. The Leadership Conference on Civil Rights honored Andy Biemiller and Higgins at a testimonial dinner in Washington on January 22, 1979. The Hubert H. Humphrey Civil Rights Award was presented to both men for their work in civil rights.[161] Higgins used the occasion to remind the audience of the church's commitment to civil rights and to labor–management relations, and he spoke about his own life and ministry in the social apostolate. Early in his prepared remarks, he quoted two of his favorite sentences from one of Monsignor Ryan's books written at the height of the Great Depression.

> "Effective labor unions are still by far the most powerful force in society for the protection of the laborer's rights and the improvement of his condition. No amount of employer benevolence, no diffusion of a sympathetic attitude on the part of the public, no piece of beneficial legislation, can adequately supply for the lack of organization of workers themselves." . . .
>
> We remain committed . . . to do whatever we can to help organize the unorganized, especially those whose right to organize is being openly violated by anti-union forces in our society. Despite the progress of recent decades, the

right of workers to organize is still a live issue. . . . In practice . . . workers still struggle against difficult odds to achieve the protection and benefits of collective bargaining long since enjoyed by their fellow workers in most of the basic industries in the United States.

We have no choice, in the light of our own tradition, but to continue to stand up and be counted in defense of labor's right to organize. There is one school of thought which says that, in doing so, we are beating a dead horse or, alternatively, that the labor movement is passe. We disagree with both arguments.

The labor problem is not a matter of ancient history. It is an ongoing problem which calls for active involvement on the part of those who believe in social justice. While the labor movement is undoubtedly far from perfect, there is no other movement in sight that would enable American workers to protect their legitimate economic interest and at the same time play an effective and responsible role in helping to promote the general economic welfare. . . .

R. H. Tawney, the great British economic historian and social ethicist, says that "if a man has important work and enough leisure and income to do it, he is in possession of as much happiness as is good for any of the children of Adam." I can only say with gratitude to God and to all of my superiors, colleagues, friends and associates that . . . I have been extremely fortunate. I have had important work to do during my entire priesthood, and sufficient leisure (if not always enough money) to do it. I have had as much happiness as is good for any of the children of Adam.[162]

United Farm Workers (UFW)

Higgins' words accurately described his life and ministry. His priestly work in the social apostolate was important work. His ministry and his writing enabled him to be a presence in the halls of labor, an advocate for the poor, and a prophetic voice for the church's mission in the world. "Religious activists, therefore, need to see themselves as 'long-distance runners'—content with modest gains, building for the long run without expecting many thanks for their efforts."[163] He showed himself to be an indefatigable "long-distance runner . . . content with modest gains" in his work on behalf of the nation's agricultural workers. Their quest for economic citizenship and workplace justice captivated the moral conscience of the nation in the 1960s and 1970s. Higgins contributed decisively to the success of the farmworkers and their cause. He devoted over one hundred *Yardstick* columns to *la causa*.[164] He presented his readers with a comprehensive analysis of the issues that affected the nation's agricultural workers and invited their participation in the struggle for social justice.

Higgins became involved with the UFW and its struggle for economic citizenship as a member of the Bishops Committee on Farm Labor. He reports his activity in the *Yardstick* columns and uses them to form the religious conscience of his readers. The story of the nation's agricultural workers begins with the governments of the United States and Mexico and their role in supplying guest workers for the fields of California, Texas, Arizona, and New Mexico. It continues with the genesis, growth, struggle, and eventual success of the UFW. The *Yardstick* columns revealed Higgins' thought and action on behalf of the poorest of the nation's working poor.

The Bracero Program

The so-called bracero program was officially known as the Farm Labor Transportation Program.[165] It began as an emergency measure during the Second World War.[166] As U.S. workers left the fields for the factories and the armed services, the demand for food and fiber production increased. Southwestern U.S. farmers, accustomed to using cheap Mexican labor, asked the federal government to relax its restrictions on immigration from Mexico. On June 15, 1942, the U.S. government formally requested Mexico's assent to the temporary emigration of its nationals under contract. The Mexican government was lukewarm to the idea because of a long history of U.S. exploitation of, and discrimination against, Mexican workers (*los braceros*). When the United States pledged itself to faithful performance of contracts entered into by each worker, the Mexican government moved beyond its original reluctance. On August 4, 1942, the two governments agreed to allow Mexican contract workers temporary employment. The agreement intended to have braceros supplement, not displace, the domestic labor force. The accord stipulated that guest workers were to be guaranteed transportation, a minimum wage of thirty cents an hour, unemployment compensation, housing, and medical treatment. The Farm Security Administration (FSA) of the Department of Agriculture administered the program and served as the official employer. It contracted with the individual worker and farmer, which avoided direct worker–grower contracts. The FSA provided some housing units with sanitation as well as health and medical associations. However, its efforts were insufficient.[167] Owners failed to live up to the contracts. Disputes arose regarding wages and unemployment. Workers complained about unsatisfactory, mosquito-infested housing; inadequate sanitary facilities; poor quality of food; and a lack of recreational and educational opportunities. Some workers, dissatisfied with arduous stoop labor and woeful working conditions, ran off before their contracts expired. In 1943 the Mexican government indefinitely suspended recruitment, which caused the United States to renegotiate its agreement with Mexico so that braceros would receive the same wages, housing, sanitary conditions, and medical care as U.S. agricultural workers. The bracero program continued after the Second World War under a proviso of the Immigration Act of 1917. It was codified as Public Law 78 on July 2, 1951. The program reached its peak between 1955 and 1959 when almost a half-million braceros worked on fifty thousand farms in thirty-eight states. The need for guest workers dwindled in the 1960s, and the program was thus terminated on May 30, 1963, although legislation extended it until 1964. In all, nearly five million braceros had worked in the United States between 1942 and 1964.

Higgins had always opposed the bracero program because he believed that it exploited the guest workers. It did not improve their economic or working conditions, and it made human beings Mexico's chief export.[168] Furthermore, it denied domestic workers the opportunity to obtain work, higher wages, and better benefits. It undermined their efforts to organize into unions of their own choosing. In short, the bracero program robbed Peter to pay Paul. It was a form of "indentured servitude that is contrary to American principles."[169] He continually opposed the powerful agribusiness lobby whenever it tried to revive the bracero program.[170]

At the time, the bracero program seemed to solve the need for sufficient seasonal workers. However, it really served the interest of the powerful farmers and growers. It masked deeper issues: racial and social injustice; and the plight, poverty, and penury of the nation's agricultural workers. Farmworkers were the poorest of the working poor because their wages were so low. The gap between farmworkers' wages and industrial workers' wages kept widening. Higgins supported the passage of legislation to amend the Fair Labor Standards Act and to raise the minimum wage for agricultural workers. When asked if this would increase food prices, Higgins said, "We do not choose to keep down our bills, especially our food bills, at the cost of overworking and underpaying human beings. We chose to pay the prices necessary to support an adequate wage."[171]

So long as the bracero program continued, a system of power, discrimination, and oppression continued. Owners arbitrarily hired and fired farmworkers. Too many were under- and unemployed. They had no voice in negotiating higher wages, better working conditions, and other legitimate benefits. Denied human dignity and fundamental rights, agricultural workers were portrayed as lazy, shiftless, ignorant, and unskilled. They were like farm implements. Higgins understood the serious nature of their situation. For years he had kept a file on all issues affecting them. He recognized that the time was ripe for organizing the nation's agricultural workers.

The Genesis and Growth of the UFW: Cesar Chavez and Dolores Huerta

Cesar Chavez and Dolores Huerta read the signs of the times. The birth of the UFW is the story of Chavez, Huerta, and their associates. The UFW began with their dream of organizing farmworkers. Their dream became a cause (*la causa*) and a crusade, then a moral and religious movement (*el movimiento*), and finally a union.

Cesar Estrada Chavez, son of Librado and Juana Chavez, was born on March 31, 1927, near Yuma, Arizona, on a farm that his grandfather homesteaded in the 1880s. The family lost the land in 1938 and moved near Oxnard, California. They later settled in a barrio called *sal si puede* (get out if you can) in San Jose. Chavez left school after the eighth grade in 1942 to work in the fields. He served in the U.S. Navy for two years (1944–1946) where he experienced discrimination and strict regimentation. He then returned to farm work in California. He married Helen Fabela, the daughter of Delano farmworkers, in 1948. They eventually had eight children.

Two men deeply influenced Chavez during these years. The first, Father Donald McDonnell, ministered in the barrio. McDonnell introduced him to Catholic social teaching. Chavez often said that his real education began with Father McDonnell. The second man, Fred Ross, was an activist with the Community Service Organization (CSO). He recruited Chavez into the CSO in 1952 and mentored him thereafter. From 1952 to 1962 Chavez organized twenty-two CSO chapters. The CSO became the most militant and effective Latino civil rights group in its day. Chavez helped people become citizens and registered voters. The CSO exposed police brutality and pressed for paved streets and other barrio improvements. Chavez spoke about his dream in a 1983 speech.

> All my life, I have been driven by one dream, one goal, one vision. To overthrow a farm labor system in this nation which treats farm workers as if they were not important human beings. Farm workers are not agricultural implements. They are not beasts of burden to be used and discarded. This dream was born in my youth. It was nourished in my early days of organizing. It has flourished. It has been attacked. . . . My motivation comes from my personal life—from watching what my mother and father went through when I was growing up, from what we experienced as migrant farm workers in California.
>
> That dream, that vision, grew from my own experience with racism, with hope, with the desire to be treated fairly and to see my people treated as human beings and not as chattel. It grew from anger and rage . . . when people of my color were denied the right to see a movie or eat at a restaurant in many parts of California. It grew from the frustration and humiliation I felt as a boy couldn't understand how the growers could abuse and exploit farm workers when there were so many of us and so few of them.
>
> Late in the '50s, I experienced a different kind of exploitation. In San Jose, in Los Angeles and in other urban communities, we—the Mexican American people—were dominated by a majority that was Anglo. I began to realize . . . that the only answer, the only hope, was in organizing. More of us had to become citizens. We had to register to vote. And people like me had to develop the skills that

> it would take to organize, to educate, to help empower the Chicano people. I spent many years—before we founded the union—learning how to work with people.[172]

Chavez resigned from CSO on his thirty-fifth birthday, March 31, 1962. Cesar and Helen moved their family to Delano to be near Helen's family and near Richard, Cesar's brother and colleague in *la causa*. Chavez began to organize in the spirit of Saint Francis of Assisi and the nonviolent philosophy of Gandhi. He rallied an impressive roster of colleagues: Chris Hartmire and Jim Drake, two ministers from the California Migrant Ministry; Fathers Mark Daly and LeRoy Chatfield; Manuel Chavez, his cousin; Gilbert Padilla and Dolores Huerta, both formerly CSO activists.

Dolores C. Huerta brought impressive organizational skills and energy to the National Farm Workers Association (NFWA), which she founded with Chavez in 1962. Huerta was born on April 10, 1930, in a mining town in northern New Mexico. Her father, Juan Fernandez, was a miner, field-worker, and union activist. He also served in the State Assembly. Her parents divorced when she was three. Her mother, Alicia Chavez, raised Dolores, her two brothers, and her two sisters in the central San Joaquin valley farmworker community of Stockton, California. She owned a restaurant and a seventy-room hotel. Farmworker families were often put up for free. Dolores' mother taught her the importance of sacrifice and service. Huerta left a teaching position to organize workers. She founded the CSO Stockton chapter in 1955, then founded and organized the Agricultural Workers Association in 1960. She lobbied fearlessly in Sacramento to get legislation passed that allowed voters the right to vote in Spanish and to take the driver's license exam in their native language. She lobbied in Washington in 1962 in an effort to end the bracero program. She negotiated contracts for the farmworkers, set up hiring halls and the farmworker ranch committees, administered contracts, and conducted over one hundred grievance procedures on the workers' behalf. These contracts established the first health and benefit plan for farmworkers. Huerta spoke out against pesticides; lobbied in Sacramento and Washington, DC; organized field strikes; directed UFW boycotts; and led campaigns for political candidates such as Robert F. Kennedy. As a legislative advocate, she became one of the most visible UFW leaders. In 1974 she helped secure unemployment benefits for farmworkers, and she directed the boycott of grapes, lettuce, and Gallo wines in the eastern United States. For more than thirty years she was Cesar Chavez's most loyal and trusted advisor.

The UFW in the 1960s and 1970s

The task of organizing farmworkers began slowly and humbly in 1962. The story of the UFW is the narrative of the farmworkers' struggle with the growers and with the major agribusiness companies between 1965 and 1980. The story includes strikes, picketing, and boycotts. The story chronicles the vicissitudes of the UFW: its success in winning contracts with the major growers and its setbacks at the hands of the Teamsters and pro-owner politicians. The story culminates in the passage of the California Agricultural Labor Relations Act in 1975 and the continuing fight for social justice from the late 1970s through the 1990s.

The NFWA held its first convention in Fresno on September 30, 1962. For the next three years Chavez met with and organized farmworkers. In 1965 the NFWA was drawn into two strikes. The first strike took place in McFarland. Farmhands at a rose farm asked the NFWA to help them gain a wage increase. The workers struck. They gained the increase but did not win union recognition. The second strike took place in the Coachella valley. The Agricultural Workers Organizing Committee (AWOC) led a walkout of Mexican and Filipino grape pickers. When Coachella growers attempted to pay local workers less than what they paid the braceros, the Filipinos refused to work. AWOC, led by Larry Itliong, struck nine farms in Delano on September 8 and asked NFWA to join the strike. NFWA members met at Our Lady of Guadalupe Church on September 16 and voted unanimously to strike. Thus began the historic five-year Delano grape strike. Chavez called on the public to boycott grapes. Volunteers were sent out to major cities, where they established boycott centers and promoted the grape boycott. Chavez dramatized the strike and the boycott by leaving Delano on March 17, 1966, to begin a three-hundred-mile pilgrimage (*perigrinacion*) to draw national attention to the suffering of farmworkers. The theme of the march was *perigrinacion, penitencia, y revolucion*. The marchers arrived at the steps of the state capital in Sacramento on Easter Sunday, April 10. During the march and after a four-month boycott, Schenley Vineyards negotiated an agreement with the NFWA. This was the first genuine union contract between a grower and a farmworkers' union in U.S. history. The NFWA boycotted the DiGiorgio Fruit Corporation during the spring and summer 1966. It forced the giant grape-grower to agree to an election among its workers. DiGiorgio countered by bringing in the Teamsters Union. The NFWA and AWOC then merged and formed the UFW. The union affiliated with the AFL-CIO. DiGiorgio workers voted for the UFW.

The UFW then struck the Giumarra Vineyards Corporation, California's largest table-grape grower. In response to a UFW boycott, other grape growers allowed Giumarra to use their labels. The UFW countered by boycotting all California table grapes. Strikes and boycotts continued from 1967 to 1970. Millions rallied to *la causa*. Victory came in the spring and summer of 1970 when most California table-grape growers sign UFW contracts.

Soon after achieving its goal with the grape growers, the UFW faced another crisis. Salinas valley growers signed contracts with the Teamsters Union in the summer 1970 to keep the UFW out of California's lettuce and vegetable fields. Ten thousand central-coast farmworkers responded by walking out on strike. Chavez called for a nationwide boycott on lettuce. Chavez was jailed in Salinas (December 10–24) for refusing to obey a court order to stop the boycott against Bud Antle lettuce. Coretta Scott King and Ethel Kennedy visited him and offered their support.

In 1971 the union moved its headquarters to La Paz. The UFW established table- and wine-grape contracts and reached agreements covering vegetable workers. Its membership grew to eighty thousand. In 1972 the AFL-CIO chartered the UFM. Despite these successes, the struggle continued. When the union's three-year table-grape contracts came up for renewal, owners signed contracts with the Teamsters without an election and without any representation procedure. This sparked a bitter three-month strike by grape workers in the Coachella and San Joaquin valleys. Thousands of strikers were arrested for violating antipicketing injunctions; hundreds were beaten; dozens were shot; and two were murdered. In response to the violence, Chavez called off the strike and began a second grape boycott. Between 1971 and 1973 seventeen million people boycotted grapes, lettuce, and Gallo wine. The boycott eventually persuaded growers to agree to a state law that would guarantee farmworkers the right to organize and bargain collectively. The landmark California Agricultural Labor Relations Act (ALRA) became law in June 1975 and the Agricultural Labor Relations Board (ALRB) was set up. Farmworkers, for the first time in U.S. history, were entitled to receive the same rights that had been accorded workers in the mining, steel, and auto industries for many years.

Hundreds of elections were held between September 1975 and January 1976. The UFW won the majority of the elections in which it participated. The ALRB, which enforced the law, shut down briefly when it ran out of money and after pro-owner lawmakers refused to approve an emergency appropriation. In the mid- to late 1970s the UFW continued winning elections and signing contracts with growers. In 1977 the Teamsters Union signed a jurisdictional agreement with the UFW and agreed to leave the fields. A year later the UFW called off its boycotts of grapes, lettuce, and Gallo wines. The UFW, in a bid to win decent wages and benefits, struck major lettuce and vegetable growers up and down the state in 1979. In September the UFW finally obtained significant pay raises and other contract improvements from SunHarvest, the nation's largest lettuce producer. Other growers soon settled. By the early 1980s, with election victories and contract negotiations, UFW contracts protected forty-five thousand farmworkers.

Union victories were short-lived. The growers' contribution of a million dollars to George Deukmejian's campaign helped elect him as governor. Between 1983 and 1990 Deukmejian thwarted the enforcement of the state's historic farm-labor law. Thousands of farmworkers lost their UFW contracts. Many were fired and blacklisted. Fresno-area dairy worker Rene Lopez, age nineteen, was shot to death by grower agents after voting in a 1983 union election. Chavez declared a third grape boycott in 1984. In 1986 Chavez inaugurated the "Wrath of Grapes" campaign and continued to press the grape boycott in the late 1980s and early 1990s. In the spring and summer 1992 Chavez and UFW first vice president Arturo Rodriquez led vineyard walkouts in the Coachella and San Joaquin Valleys, which enabled grape workers to achieve their first industry-wide pay increase in eight years.

The following year Cesar Chavez died peacefully in his sleep at the modest home of a retired San Luis, Arizona, farmworker while defending the UFW against a multimillion-dollar lawsuit brought against the union by a large vegetable grower. On April 29, 1993, forty thousand mourners marched behind Chavez's plain pine casket during funeral services in Delano. It was the largest funeral of a labor leader in the history of organized labor. After his death, a mourner told Helen Chavez that Cesar was finally with God. Helen replied that Cesar was always with God. Cesar Chavez's faith, courage, and perseverance had brought social justice to thousands of agricultural workers. On August 8, 1994, President Bill Clinton posthumously presented the Medal of Freedom to Cesar Chavez. Clinton compared Chavez to Moses leading Israel out of Egypt. Helen Chavez received the medal during the White House ceremony.

The Success of the UFW

Why did Chavez, Huerta, and their associates in the UFW succeed in organizing farmworkers when others had failed? Why were they able to combine the purposes of trade unionism with the ultimate ambition of altering the fundamental structure of U.S. society? Part of the answer lies in the context. The 1960s bore movements dedicated to radical social change. Many followers, especially the young, learned about the poor and became involved in their struggle to obtain civil and workers' rights. *La causa* awakened the nation's conscience and captivated its moral imagination. The other part of the answer lies with the charismatic personality, moral character, and courage of Cesar Chavez. The UFW might arguably be the best example of a union's personifying the identity, personality, values, and passion of its leader. In many ways the UFW was a corporate extension of Cesar Chavez himself. Chavez spoke about his passionate commitment to organize fellow farmworkers.

> Deep in my heart, I knew I could never be happy unless I tried organizing the farm workers. I didn't know if I would succeed. But I had to try. All Hispanics . . . are connected to the farm workers' experience. We had all lived through the fields—or our parents had. We shared that common humiliation.
>
> How could we prepare as a people . . . while the farm workers, men and women of our color, were condemned to a life without pride? How could we progress as a people while the farm workers . . . were denied self-respect? How could our people believe that their children could become lawyers and doctors and judges and business people while this shame, this injustice was permitted to continue?
>
> Those who attack our union often say, "It's not really a union. It's something else. A social movement. A civil rights movement. It's something dangerous." They're half right. The United Farm Workers is first and foremost a union. A union like any other. A union that either produces for its members on the bread and butter issues or doesn't survive. But the UFW has always been something more than a union. . . . The UFW was the beginning! We attacked that historical source of shame and infamy that our people in this country lived with. We attacked this injustice, not by complaining, not by seeking handouts, not by becoming soldiers in the War on Poverty.
>
> We organized! Farm workers acknowledged we had allowed ourselves to become victims in a democratic society—a society where majority rule and collective bargaining are supposed to be more than academic theories or political rhetoric. And by addressing this historical problem, we created confidence and pride and hope in an entire people's ability to create the future.[173]

The UFW gave farmworkers a sense of pride and dignity. It accorded them recognition of their civil rights for the first time. Chavez was always aware that the UFW was part of the larger civil rights movement epitomized by Martin Luther King Jr.

> The union's survival, its very existence, sent out a signal to all Hispanics that we were fighting for our dignity, that we were challenging and overcoming injustice, that we were empowering the least educated among us, the poorest among the poor. The message was clear; if it could happen in the fields, it could happen anywhere—in the cities, in the courts, in the city councils, in the state legislatures.[174]

The UFW was a popular movement that linked workers with fields and farms, economic justice with ecological justice, and the good of the union with the common good. Chavez spoke about the owners' use of pesticides and herbicides, the threat they posed to human health, and the harm they inflicted on the soil and aquifers. Chavez addressed the source of ecological injustice in his speech to the Commonwealth Club of California on November 9, 1984.

> The growers often try to blame the union for their problems—to lay their sins off on us, sins for which they only have themselves to blame. The growers have only themselves to blame as they begin to reap the harvest from decades of environmental damage they have brought upon the land—the pesticides, the herbicides, the soil fumigants, the fertilizers, the salt deposits from thoughtless irrigation—the ravages from years of unrestrained poisoning of our soil and water. Thousands of acres of land in California have already been irrevocably damaged by this wanton abuse of nature. Thousands more will be lost unless growers understand that dumping more poisons on the soil won't solve their problems—on the short term or the long term.[175]

In his speech at Pacific Lutheran University in Tacoma, Washington, in March 1989, Chavez spoke about the moral purpose of *la causa* and the union. He linked ecological justice with the common good.

> For one hundred years succeeding waves of immigrants have sweated and sacrificed to make this industry rich. And for their sweat and for their sacrifice, farm workers have been repaid with humiliation and contempt. With all these problems, why, then, do we dwell so on the perils of pesticides? Because there is something even more important to farm workers than the benefits unionization brings. Because there is something more important to the farm workers' union than winning better wages and working conditions. That is protecting farm workers and consumers from systematic poisoning through the reckless use of agricultural toxics. There is nothing we care more about than the lives and safety of our families. There is nothing we share more deeply in common with the consumers of North America than the safety of the food all of us rely upon.
>
> We are proud to be part of the House of Labor. Collective bargaining is the traditional way American workers have escaped poverty and improved their standard of living. It is the way farm workers will also empower themselves. But the UFW has always had to be something more than a union. . . . What good does it do to achieve the blessing of collective bargaining and make economic progress for people when their health is destroyed in the process? If we ignored pesticide poisoning, . . . then all the other injustices our people face would be compounded by an even more deadly tyranny.[176]

The Rhetoric of Cesar Chavez

Chavez succeeded in organizing farmworkers because his speech, vision, and style embodied Mexican American popular religion, culture, and tenacity. His speeches were simple and convincing. Chavez spoke comfortably in English and in Spanish. He sometimes asked permission from his audience to speak in both. His unassuming stature and appearance, simple farmworkers' clothing, and rhetorical style created empathy with his audiences. Listeners identified with him and with *la causa* because he spoke to their hearts. He used his speeches to educate rather than impress. He taught truth in the name of justice. He addressed farmworkers, students and other young people, activists, celebrities, politicians, clergy, and fellow unionists in the AFL-CIO. His speeches followed a pattern. He usually spoke for twenty to thirty minutes. After a brief introduction, he would quickly plunge into his subject matter. He would present information and persuade with facts. He reinforced his words with concrete, emotionally touching vignettes drawn from his own experience, from the suffering of farmworkers, and from the experience of their families. He concluded his speeches quickly and immediately engaged listeners in questions and answers. Chavez maintained intense eye contact with his listeners during all speeches, dialogues, and conversations. When he spoke in Spanish, he wove homespun proverbs and sayings (*dichos*), words of advice (*consejos*), and stories (*cuentas*) that contained a moral lesson.[177]

Communication and Practical Strategies

Chavez succeeded in communicating a millennial vision. *La causa* was a crusade that became a movement. *El movimiento* became a union. Chavez saw it all as part of God's plan. The plan acknowledged the injustice, poverty, and suffering of the past; but its thrust was directed to the future. Chavez was patient, and he taught that patience and nonviolence would triumph over injustice. Victory was inevitable because of the inherent truth and rightness of *la causa*. Workers had justice and time on their side.

Chavez advanced *la causa* in practical ways. He started an underground newspaper in December 1974. *El Macriado*—literally "the ill-bred one" or "children who speak back to their parents"—was dropped off at barrio grocery stores every two weeks. Editorials called for a living wage and took on owners who complained about losing the bracero program. The paper featured a hapless cartoon character, Don Sotaco, who taught workers about their rights. Chavez also used strikes (*huelgas*), picketing, and boycotts to educate farmworkers and their supporters. "Chavez emphasized the need for picketing because he believed that no experience promoted a keener sense of solidarity or afforded strikers a more graphic and compelling illustration of the struggle's essential character."[178] Boycotts required sacrifice, a value deeply rooted in the workers' religious imagination. Many sacrificed dearly by leaving their family and home in California to organize boycotts in the cities of the United States and Canada.

> While the boycott continued to serve as the union's most effective weapon, especially after employees persuaded compliant local judges to issue injunctions severely restricting picketing and other direct action in the strike region, the

> slowness with which it operated to prod recalcitrant growers toward the bargaining table produced in farmworkers and volunteers alike an impatience that reduced both morale and discipline. It also undermined *la causa*'s commitment to nonviolence. "There came a point in 1968," Chavez recalled, "when we were in danger of losing. . . . There were those who felt that the time had come to overcome violence with violence. . . . There was demoralization in the ranks, people becoming desperate, more and more talk about violence. People meant it, even when they talked to me."[179]

Chavez responded to this crisis with a risky, unusual, and radical tactic. In February 1968 he entered into a twenty-five-day fast. The fast was a personal, religious, and political act. It purified Chavez, unified the workers, and recommitted the union to its goals through nonviolence.[180] When Chavez ended the fast, Bobby Kennedy, his close friend and ally, and some eight thousand workers and supporters joined him in the celebration of the Eucharist.

> Those in the union who were closest to Chavez . . . found the fast's effect undeniably therapeutic . . . "Before the fast," [Jerry] Cohen noted, "there were nine ranch committees, . . . one for each winery. The fast . . . made a union out of those ranch committees. . . . Everybody worked together." Dolores Huerta also recognized the curative power of Chavez's ordeal. "Prior to the fast," she insisted, "there had been a lot of bickering and backbiting and fighting and little attempts at violence. But Cesar brought everybody together and established himself as a leader of the farm workers."[181]

Ethnic and Religious Symbolism

Chavez tapped into the ethnic and religious symbols of his culture. In 1962 Richard Chavez created a simple black Aztec eagle as the union's symbol. The eagle represented Mexican pride and dignity. It was stamped onto every box of produce that union workers picked. Many boycott participants questioned supermarket managers and quizzed restaurant owners about their grapes and lettuce. They refused to buy or to eat produce unless it came in boxes marked with the black eagle.

Chavez envisioned the need for a farmworkers' performing group to inform the farmworkers and the general public about the strike. El Teatro Campesino (ETC), a Mexican popular theater redolent of the tent show (*la carpa*), emerged out of the lifeworld of working-class experience. Founded by Luis Valdez and Augustin Lira in 1965, the ETC portrayed the plight of the farmworkers. It accompanied Chavez on the pilgrimage from Delano to Sacramento in March and April 1966.[182] The ETC attracted audiences with live music. It performed its plays on the back of flatbed trucks, in the village public squares, and on local stages. It performed locally and regionally, and it eventually nationally and in Europe. The ETC became an important instrument of social change. It was also excellent theater. Performances used mime, music, song, dance, dancelike movement and acrobatic motions, marionettes (*titeres*), stinging humor, satire, and the classic underdog comic figure. The ETC enacted the cultural memory of the farmworkers, fostered their solidarity, provided a welcome relief from backbreaking labor, and embodied the community's self-knowledge.[183]

The UFW tapped deeply into the popular religiosity of the workers and their families. Banners honoring Our Lady of Guadalupe accompanied the farmworkers at their meetings and on their marches. Chavez devoted himself to a life of sacrifice and penance, personal prayer, and participation in the liturgy of the Eucharist.

> Acting out what biographer Jacques Levy called his "quiet, unpretentious piety," Chavez often went "unnoticed into churches to pray or to receive Communion, alone." His deep religious faith formed the foundation for his determination in the farm workers' movement. As he confided: "Today I don't think that I could base my will to struggle on the cold economics or on some political doctrine. I don't think there would be enough to sustain me. For me, the base must be faith."
>
> Chavez's faith justified his actions. His "deepest belief . . . was that sacrifice and selfless service to others lead to the authentic life." As Chavez stated: "We are men locked in a death struggle against man's inhumanity to man." Chavez uncovered a spiritual basis for his militant crusade in the documents of the Second Vatican Council that emphasized justice and condemned the separation of the spiritual from the material. . . . Chavez said that he saw himself as "literally commanded to do something about people who were suffering"; he was convinced that "even in the face of the biggest disappointment there's always that faith, that tomorrow's gonna be different."[184]

Higgins and the Yardstick *Columns*

In the early years when Chavez was beginning the UFW, he was surprised that some Catholic priests and parishes remained aloof from the farmworkers and indifferent to their efforts to organize. He was bewildered when he encountered priests who openly supported the growers and the agribusiness' interests. This changed as the struggle continued and gained the support of individual bishops, priests, religious, and laity.[185] The National Conference of Catholic Bishops became directly involved with the farm-labor dispute at their November 1968 meeting. It issued a statement that encouraged reconciliation between the growers and the workers.

> Greater awareness on the part of the general public has resulted in some progress such as is mirrored in the Migrant Health Act. However, the workers' dramatic struggle to improve their lot has sometimes produced divisions and protracted conflict. . . . We, the Catholic bishops . . . , address ourselves to this problem with the high hope of assisting in a reconciliation between grower and worker.
>
> For 30 years the disadvantaged field workers of this nation have stood by helplessly and listened to other Americans debating the farm labor problem. Burdened by low wage scales, mounting health problems, inadequate educational opportunities, substandard housing and a lack of year-round employment, they have often been forced to live a life devoid of security, dignity and reasonable comfort. For the past three years, however, many of them have been attempting to take their destiny into their own hands. This is a very healthy development.[186]

The statement called for the legal protection of the farmworkers' rights.

> Farm workers are now very painfully aware that not only do they have to struggle against economic, educational and social inequities, but they have also been excluded from almost every piece of social legislation as well . . . Farm workers are demanding legislative protection for their natural rights to organize for the purpose of collective bargaining. They are demanding inclusion under a law which has protected the bargaining rights of other American workers for 33 years, namely the Nation Labor Relations Act.[187]

The statement acknowledged the obstacles facing small growers and family farms. It recommended that they "unite with . . . fellow farmers and growers in associations proper to themselves. This is their natural right and even their duty at this moment of our history."[188] It acknowledged that the government and legislation had thus far been biased in favor of the growers. In an effort to redress the situation, it proposed legislative remedies on behalf of "the men working in the fields."[189] It urged Congress to enact legislation

1. To include farm workers under the National Labor Relations Act
2. To include farm workers more effectively under a national minimum wage which will ensure them a decent standard of living
3. To include farm workers under the national employment insurance program[190]

Hugh A. Donohoe, bishop of Stockton, California, published an article in the September 24, 1970, issue of the *Catholic Voice*, the Oakland diocesan paper, in support of Chavez and the UFWOC's right to organize. Donohoe quoted *Rerum Novarum* and *Gaudium et Spes* (no. 68) and reaffirmed the right of both groups to organize: "The right to organize is as proper for farm owners as it is for farm laborers, or for any other group that wants to come together for a valid reason."[191] He indicated that the growers' decision not to exercise their right to organize did "not entitle them to deny it to others."[192] Donohoe endorsed secret-ballot elections and collective bargaining as a solution.

The bishops' pro-farmer initiatives were severely criticized by reactionary Catholics. The July 12, 1970, issue of *Twin Circle*, a notoriously reactionary Catholic paper, issued a vitriolic editorial written by Jesuit father Daniel Lyons.[193] Lyons stated that he and his fellow Jesuit father Cletus Healy had recently toured the Coachella valley, where they interviewed growers, workers, pastors, and others involved in the farm-labor disputes.[194] The editorial attacked Chavez, misrepresented the facts concerning the table-grape boycott, maligned the Bishops Committee on Farm Labor, and accused Higgins of forcing the union onto the workers. The U.S. bishops' ad hoc committee on farm labor responded on July 15, 1970. It lamented the "untruths, innuendoes, distortions and plain inaccuracies in interpreting the views and motives of ad hoc committee members, all of whom are bishops, speaking for and acting in the name of the entire American hierarchy."[195] It stated that the *Twin Circle* editorial was fraudulent, divisive, and harmful.

> At this very moment the ad hoc committee is meeting in Fresno at the *written invitation* of the Western Employers Council which speaks for growers with more than 50 per cent of the table grape acreage in California. We have been asked by these growers to try to get negotiations started in this major segment of the table-grape industry.[196]

It indicated that the U.S. bishops endorsed the work of the committee as a "ministry of service to growers and workers" through a process of collective bargaining.[197]

Higgins served as a consultant to the U.S. Bishops Committee on Farm Labor because of his knowledge of the facts of the farm-labor dispute, background in labor–management relations, and experience in collective-bargaining negotiations. Bishop Joseph F. Donnelly chaired the committee and Monsignor Roger Mahony of Fresno, California, was its secretary.[198] Donnelly was a seasoned veteran in labor–management negotiations. Donnelly and Higgins were tough, tireless, and tenacious at the bargaining table. Both were committed to a just and fair resolution to the dispute. Higgins commuted over a hundred times between Washington, DC, and California in the 1970s. Between 1970 and 1973, he spent half of his time working on behalf of the farmworkers in California, Arizona, and Florida.[199] He met with growers and workers and supervised union-certification voting. True to his style of placing principles before personalities, Higgins' commitment to *la causa* was not based on friendship with Chavez. He respected and admired Chavez, but, more important, he supported him because he believed in the objective truthfulness and rightness of the farmworkers' cause.[200] He continued to offer his support by attending rallies, meetings, and liturgies.[201]

The *Yardstick* columns demonstrated the depth of Higgins' feeling and compassion for the plight of the family farmers and the farmworkers. The former had to deal with unpredictable weather hazards, high interest rates, low commodity prices, and the rising cost of machinery and farm implements. Because the growers were unorganized themselves, they faced what Higgins termed "a money jungle."[202] The braceros, uneducated and unskilled, worked long hours for less pay than did domestic workers, were often exploited, and were afraid of being fired. Police verbally abused farmworkers, treated them and their families discourteously, and interfered with their efforts to organize.[203] Higgins wrote that the plight of the domestic worker was similar to that of African Americans. A job-caste system walled off white-collar workers from people of color.[204] Farmworkers lacked political clout and were seen as second-class citizens. Many of their children worked in the fields and faced health and safety hazards. Workers (and the UFW) represented David doing battle with Goliath (the Teamsters).[205] The Teamsters' mentality toward the UFW was clearly summed up in two comments made by the Teamster Frank Fitzsimmons.

> Chavez is not a trade unionist. I wouldn't even let him be a janitor in a trade union office. Chavez is leading a cause, not a trade union, and his cause has nothing to do with the welfare of the Mexican American worker. His cause, his teaching, and his ideals have all been taken from Saul Alinsky and his brand of Marxism. . . .
>
> Let the clergy worry about the Ten Commandments and we'll take care of the labor unions.[206]

To which Higgins replied, "That's what Chavez is afraid of; and, frankly, so am I."[207]

Higgins strongly condemned the Teamsters, not as an organization, but for their tactics and unethical chicanery. (In fact, he stated that he would rather work with them in social projects of mutual interest and concern.) But he bluntly told them that "they should have never gotten into it with the growers."[208] He told Jimmy Hoffa that his threat to destroy the UFW was "disgraceful from the point of view of trade-union ethics."[209] He called Hoffa a street-corner bully, told him that he was calling his bluff, and indicated that the AFL-CIO would give full support to the UFW. He called April 13, 1973, a dark, shameful day in U.S. labor history because, on this day, the Teamsters had signed contracts with thirty grape growers in the Coachella valley who had been under contract with the UFW for three years.[210] This violation of trade-union ethics, he predicted, would eventually bring the Teamsters to their knees.[211] The UFW, which represented the workers in the fields, epitomized trade-union democracy; and the Teamsters, which represented unscrupulous agribusiness interests, manifested trade-union paternalism.[212]

Ten years of struggle culminated in celebration and legislation. Farm Labor Week, May 1–10, 1975, celebrated deeply cherished national values, such as freedom of association, self-determination, and fair play. The UFW now asked society to live up to its professed values by guaranteeing workers the right to form and choose unions, to participate freely in their activities without risk of reprisal, and to participate in socioeconomic development and the attainment of the common good.[213] The time had come not only to celebrate but also to legislate on behalf of California's farm laborers and seasonal workers. Governor Jerry Brown singed the Agricultural Labor Relations Act into law on June 5, 1975. This was the first law in the nation's history that guaranteed farmworkers the right to determine, by secret-ballot elections, which union (if any) they wanted to designate as representation.[214] By February 6, 1976, over 350 secret-ballot elections had been held. While some politicians and growers tried to circumvent the law and to stymie the funding necessary for the functioning of the Agricultural Labor Relations Board, the victory had been won. Farmworkers had become first-class citizens. "The sour grapes of oppression tasted sweet again."[215] Higgins was optimistic and immediately began working on amnesty for undocumented workers.

> My hope is that the commission's recommendations will be as humane and compassionate as possible. Despite our own domestic problems, this is no time for the United States to reverse its long and honorable tradition in welcoming the poor, the needy, and the politically oppressed.[216]

Higgins' work was important. It resulted in greater cooperation between growers and workers and in a greater trust in the process of collective bargaining.[217] His contribution to improving the lot of the nation's agricultural workers and their quest for worker justice had been immense. His moral stature in the church and organized labor, spiritual presence as a priest and man of integrity, and practical skills in analysis and labor–management negotiations enabled him to collaborate with those who had been, for far too long, politically and economically unrepresented. Agricultural workers, the most marginalized and lowly, the least and the last, had finally achieved economic citizenship.

Advocacy for Worker Justice

The *Yardstick* columns during these years considered the steps that many workers were beginning to take in their quest for workplace justice and the response of the church's hierarchy to them. The columns reported on labor issues in the clothing and textile industries, the support of individual bishops for workers in their diocese or region, and the actions undertaken by the U.S. bishops' conference. Higgins first considered the labor relations' controversy between employees and the Farrar Manufacturing Company.[218] Farrar, the second-largest manufacturer of men's slacks in the country, had maintained a paternalistic labor relations policy. It underpaid its workers, denied them an opportunity to unionize, and refused to engage in collective bargaining. The workers' plight came to the attention of Bishop Sidney Metzger, ordinary of the El Paso diocese. He studied the situations and gave his support to the workers, many of whom were poor Mexican Americans. He then reported on their plight and his action on their behalf at the national meeting of the U.S. bishops. The bishops supported the strike and endorsed a boycott of all Farrar products. Higgins also supported the boycott. The church's efforts on behalf of Farrar workers and its strong stand with organized labor were essential to the success of the boycott. Farrar eventually dropped its paternalistic language when the boycott cut seriously into its profits. It consented to the workers' request to unionize. Workers voted in favor of the Amalgamated Clothing Workers (ACW). For the first time in the company's fifty-four-year existence, workers had representation, access to collective bargaining, and a sense of dignity.

Higgins reported that Ralph de Toledano, a nationally syndicated columnist, and Father Daniel Lyons, S.J., a reactionary columnist for *Twin Circle* and the *National Catholic Register*, were walking around "with egg on their faces" because both had made inaccurate and irresponsible statements against Higgins and the ACW. In fact, Higgins stated that the church was increasingly becoming an advocate willing to take bold steps on behalf of the human betterment of the poor.

> I also have the impression . . . that . . . the church can be expected to take a strong public stand in support of these disadvantaged workers in their

> struggle for recognition and equality. The efforts of the Church will probably be resented in some circles and may lead to the charge that the Church, which is supposed to exercise a ministry of reconciliation, is doing just the opposite.
>
> The bishops of Southeast Asia . . . faced up to this charge . . . and answered the charge by declaring that the Church must be on the side of the poor, even if this involves the risk of alienating itself from the powers that be. "Opting to be with the poor . . . involves risk, . . . the risk of conflict with vested interests of 'establishments,' religious, economic, social and political. It also involves, for leaders of the Church especially, loss of security, and that not only material but spiritual. For it means taking the unfamiliar course of looking for guidelines of policy and action, not to ready-make theological, legal and sociological systems . . . but to a discernment of the historical process taking place among our own people."[219]

Indeed, the bishops had provided the ACW with the same kind of strength to win as that given to the UFW.[220] Since the end of the boycott, Farrar had gone downhill and faced bankruptcy. Higgins suggested that the real reason for the company's undoing was poor management and anti-unionism.[221]

Higgins next turned his attention to the controversy between the Amalgamated Clothing and Textile Workers Union (ACTWU) workers and the J. P. Stevens Company.[222] Stevens, a New York–based textile manufacturer and the second-largest in the country after Burlington Industries, had consistently violated the National Labor Relations Act with impunity. Furthermore, the company had a reputation as being the most notorious antiunion company in the country.[223] In the spring of 1976, Bishops Michael Begley of Charlotte, North Carolina; F. Joseph Gossman of Raleigh, North Carolina; and Ernest Unterkoefler of Charleston, South Carolina, began studying the issues involved in the controversy. It was reported that these bishops and the United States Catholic Conference (USCC) were about to endorse a boycott of Stevens products, even though this boycott would be more difficult, prolonged, and expensive than the UFW and Farrar boycotts. Only 10 percent of the company's seven hundred thousand Southern workers were unionized, and Stevens refused to negotiate. It was learned that in the fall of 1976, Whitney Stevens, the company's president, visited Begley, Gossman, and Unterkeofler. In November 1976 the three bishops, with Bishops Joseph A. Donnellan of Atlanta and Raymond Lessard of Savannah, met with Howard Samuels, then an ACTWU vice president and later a deputy undersecretary of labor in the Carter administration. In early February 1977 Higgins and Monsignor Francis Lally, associate secretary for social development and world peace at USCC, visited Roanoke Rapids, North Carolina, the site of ACTWU's only election victory to represent workers in seven Stevens plants. Higgins and Lally sent their report to the bishops before they and Bishop Walter Sullivan of Richmond, Virginia, would issue any public statement or take any position. The bishops of the southeast made their public statement on June 6, 1977. They stopped short of endorsing the boycott already in effect and offered their services as mediators in what was a controversy that involved eighty-five plants in their respective dioceses. They urged Stevens to give positive signs of its willingness to bargain in good faith with workers. The bishops renewed their offer as mediators in November 1977. The National Labor Relations Board, in a 4–0 decision issued on November 17, 1978, stated that Stevens had bargained in bad faith for two years in its seven Roanoke Rapids plants.[224] Higgins supported the boycott and suggested that individual Catholics should make up their own minds regarding the boycott.[225] In 1979 the bishops of the southeast endorsed the boycott, and a growing, ecumenically based consensus supported it. The boycott succeeded. In October 1980 J. P. Stevens finally settled with ACTWU workers, despite the subsequent skepticism that Stevens would abide by the settlement.

The *Yardstick* columns kept readers informed about boycotts against the Nestle and Campbell companies. The former boycott, begun in 1977, hoped to thwart Nestle's attempts to market its infant formula in underdeveloped countries.

> The demands of the boycott, called for by Infant Formula Action Coalition (INFACT), are a model of moderation. . . . INFACT asks only that Nestle stop all direct consumer promotion: stop the use of company milk nurses; stop distribution of free samples to new mothers and health care institutions; stop promotion in the form of gifts to the medical profession; and inform health care personnel fully of the dangers inherent in the use of the product under poverty conditions.[226]

Nestle ignored the boycott and refused to sit down at the bargaining table. The latter boycott involved the church in a controversy between the migrant workers, the Campbell Soup Company, and Libby-McNeil-Libby products. Many in the church supported the boycott as an application of the principles of Catholic social teaching.

> The first principle involved concerns work and human dignity. Church teachings hold that through work, men and women must be able to achieve at least a minimum standard of living, allowing them to live in the divine image. . . . The wages and living conditions of these children of God represent a denial of his law. . . .

> The church teaches that, although each person has an individual relationship with God, relationships with others are also vital. People are responsible for the impact of their decisions on others . . . It is incorrect to conclude that the church is against the growers in this controversy. The church is not against anyone; she is for God's law and its application to human affairs.
>
> In fact, the church has long been concerned that small and medium-sized farmers will someday disappear from the American landscape and has urged these farmers to organize. Farmers have traditionally prided themselves on their independence, as evidenced by the fact that they negotiate individually with Campbell and Libby. Ironically, establishing farmers' organizations may be the only way left for farmers to preserve their independence in the face of the already organized agribusiness industry.[227]

The *Yardstick* columns supported the right of hospital workers, janitors, public employees, and teachers to form unions and to strike.[228] Higgins tackled the hospital and educational industries, those secular and Catholic. He supported the right of hospital workers to negotiate with their employers, preferably through a union of their own choice. He recommended that all labor–management agreements be put in writing. Hospital administrators practiced this policy with vendors who provided medical supplies, fuel, pharmaceutical medication, appliances, and insurance.[229] He maintained that Catholic hospitals were obligated to foster policies and advocate strategies that were faithful to the church's social teaching.[230] He encouraged administrators of Catholic institutions to

> take the lead in establishing progressive labor–management relations in their particular profession. . . . The administrators . . . can no longer ask for special treatment on the grounds that their institutions are serving society on a nonprofit basis and should therefore be exempt from the normal rules of labor-management relations.
>
> If Catholic administrators want to be real professionals today, they must operate according to the highest standards of the communities in which their institutions exist. In the field of labor-management relations, that means complete freedom for their professional and non-professional employees to exercise their right to organize and to carry on collective bargaining according to the procedures long since established, under the law of the land, in private industry.[231]

Higgins also supported the unionization of Catholic teachers. Teachers in Catholic schools, unlike teachers in other educational settings, were not covered under the National Labor Relations Act. Nevertheless, Higgins maintained that this did not vitiate their right. Catholic schools had a moral obligation to respond positively to Catholic teachers who sought to form associations or unions for the purpose of collective bargaining.[232]

The Renewal of the International Labor Movement and the Promotion of Human Rights

Higgins maintained a lively interest in the labor movement in Europe and South America. He encouraged reconciliation between the International Confederation of Free Trade Unions and the communist-dominated World Federation of Trade Unions.[233] He promoted unity and mutual understanding between the neutral secular labor movement in the United States and the Latin American Confederation of Christian Trade Unions.[234] He was invited to be a consultant to the U.S. delegation at the Conference on Security and Cooperation in Europe, commonly referred to as the Belgrade Conference on Human Rights, in late 1977 and early 1978.[235] The purpose of the conference was "to review the implementation of the provisions of the Helsinki Final Act on security, cooperation, and human rights and to consider new proposals, especially in the area of human rights."[236] Higgins admired and was inspired by the work of the U.S. delegates. They had held the Soviet Union and other communist states accountable, as forcibly and effectively as possible, for having violated the human rights provisions. They had planted seeds of justice, peace, and human rights, "which, please God, will in due time bear abundant fruit."[237] Higgins recommended patience because he believed that the spark of justice would not die and that the seeds would in time bear fruit.

> The real test of one's commitment to a worthwhile cause—and what cause . . . could be more important than that of peace and human rights—is a willingness to wait patiently, as the farmer does, for results and, hardest of all, to be resigned to the possibility that one may not live to see the full results of his or her efforts—the possibility that, in God's providence and in his own good time, others may reap where they have sown.[238]

During this period Higgins continued to support the International Labor Organization because, despite its limitations, it promoted and protected workers' rights and enabled the nations of the world to cooperate with one another on behalf of the international common good. He encouraged continued U.S. membership.[239]

Higgins published his first article on Solidarity, the Polish labor union, on September 8, 1980, which ironically coincided with his retirement from the bishops' conference on Labor Day 1980. His words were filled with emotion.

> Those who lived to see the rise of communism, Nazism and fascism, however, learned the hard way that they had been living in a dream world. They learned that when the freedom of labor organizations is not protected by political democracy, it is soon suppressed. . . .
>
> Professor Yves Simon . . . pointed out in his classic study of democratic government that there is no question for the working man of choosing between the autonomous action of labor and political democracy. Political democracy is the condition for the autonomous action of labor.
>
> Unless competing parties are interested in winning labor's vote, unions will soon disappear into a monopolistic organization dominated in all significant respects by whatever class or party controls the state.
>
> This is what happened in Poland. . . . The so-called unions (like the unions of Hitler's Labor Front) are unions in name only. They are really controlled by the party in power, . . . instruments of the state.
>
> The courageous strikers in Poland have challenged this totalitarian system at its roots. The historic significance of their demand for trade-union autonomy can hardly be exaggerated. This demand goes directly contrary to communist theory and cannot be resolved short of radical changes in the communist political system. . . .
>
> The Polish strikers, by their courage, have won the admiration of the entire non-communist world. They also have started a process which cannot be reversed.
>
> Their cause must and, please God, will prevail sooner or later.[240]

Allies and Adversaries

Higgins worked indefatigably during this period. It was for him a time of intense involvement, excitement, and newness. He was involved in the demanding yet energizing work of the Second Vatican Council in the first half of the 1960s. The council and the synod profoundly shaped his outlook, exposed him to a world church, and brought him to new commitments. He was involved in the farm-labor dispute in the first half of the 1970s, which put him into direct contact with farmworkers and positioned him on the side of the poor.

The *Yardstick* columns that Higgins wrote about individual people during this period revealed his depth of emotion, keen sense of history, and immense gratitude to those whose commitment to social justice put them "on the side of the angels."[241] In some instances Higgins was writing about people with whom he had deep, personal ties for many years. Some of these *Yardstick* columns were eulogies that Higgins delivered at funerals. Others were tributes written in memoriam. In other instances he was writing about people whom he admired and whom he respected as allies in the cause for social justice and the renewal of the church, the nation, and the labor movement. The

Yardstick columns introduced readers to a roster of diverse and significant people in the areas of intellectual scholarship, organized labor, the social apostolate, and public service. He considered church historian Monsignor John Tracy Ellis; the public intellectual Walter Lippman; and theologians John Courtney Murray, S.J., Pope Paul VI, Monsignor Pietro Pavan, and Paul Ramsey as allies shaping the public conscience. Higgins lauded Ellis' contribution at a celebration honoring his fortieth anniversary of ordination to the priesthood.

> Msgr. Ellis' professional work as an historian and as a scholarly journalist has been at all times a very priestly and pastoral work. What the Italian historian, Professor Giuseppe Alberigo, has said with reference to historians in general is eminently true of our jubilarian: All historical research conducted with scientific rigor is a spiritual adventure; and research into the history of the church is also a religious experience.[242]

Higgins also noted that both Pope John XXIII and Pope Paul VI had inaugurated a distinctive approach to social, economic, and political issues. Both wrote with modesty and awareness that all documents were historically conditioned and limited. Higgins noted in particular that Pope Paul VI invited fraternal dialogue with the world, a collegial style of learning, a spirit of optimism and hope, and a courteous regard for those involved in dialogue. Higgins esteemed these qualities and emulated them in his own way.[243]

The *Yardstick* columns praised those involved in organized labor. Higgins preached at the funeral of Joseph Beirne, the president of the Communications Workers of America. He mentioned Beirne's imaginative thinking, compassion for the ordinary rank-and-file worker, his understanding of human nature, and his tolerance for human foible.[244] He wrote in memoriam about John Brophy, the first general organizer of the CIO. He portrayed him as a man whose life was animated and sustained by deeply religious convictions. "He had a vocation in life—a calling to which he gave himself with boundless generosity. . . . He literally wore himself out in the service of his fellow man."[245] He wrote with respect and awe about the significance of Cesar Chavez for the farmworkers' cause. "We haven't seen anyone like him in the American labor movement in many a long day."[246] Higgins deeply esteemed A. Philip Randolph, whom he first met in the 1940s. "Mr. Randolph is one of the truly great Americans of this century and as fine a human being as anyone could ever hope to meet." Higgins lauded Randolph's charity, honesty, tolerance, and his lifelong commitment to African American workers in the labor movement.

> He, more than any other single individual, . . . has sold his own people and the liberal white community on the need for a strong labor–Civil Rights coalition. May God reward him, in the twilight of his remarkable life, for this and for all of his other contributions to the cause of social justice and human dignity.[247]

The *Yardstick* column for March 31, 1980, reported on a testimonial dinner that Higgins and several hundred others attended in celebration of Bayard Rustin's seventieth birthday. Higgins admired Rustin's lifelong commitments to nonviolence, the advancement of the poor and working people, and the labor movement. Rustin knew that the basis for economic citizenship for African American workers rested on their participation in bona fide labor unions and other coalitions. Having a job still gave workers a voice, a vote, and a place of recognition and dignity in the democratic process. Rustin understood that economic citizenship was the cornerstone for attaining civil rights.

Higgins singled out Joseph L. Rauh Jr., Walter Reuther, and George Meany for their contribution to organized labor. Rauh—a Washington, DC, lawyer; liberal activist; and key congressional lobbyist for Walter Reuther—devoted thirty years of his life to organized labor. Higgins' encomium for him was of the highest order.

> [Joseph Rauh served] with the social conscience of an Amos or an Isaiah and with the energy and drive of three men packed into one. . . . The labor movement never had a better friend than Joseph Rauh. . . . Whatever his faults and limitations . . . he is generally on the side of the angels. . . . I personally hold him in high esteem and consider it an honor and a privilege to have known him as a friend for twenty years or more.[248]

Walter Reuther, the president of the UAW for over a quarter century, "was literally born into the labor movement. . . . Devotion to the labor movement and the cause of the poor and the underprivileged came to him quite as naturally and instinctively as devotion to his family and his nation. He inherited the tradition from his father before him."[249] Higgins described Reuther's dedication to the cause of social justice as a "vocation—a calling to which he gave himself with eager generosity and with great imagination."[250] Reuther guided UAW workers to achieve self-governance in their professional lives. Millions of workers were able to stand on their own two feet as

> mature citizens of a developing economic democracy which, in turn, is an indispensable bulwark or support of political democracy. . . . The labor movement is a tremendous power for good in the life of our country. . . . But the labor movement is only what its members make it. May the sudden and

very tragic death of one of its most respected leaders remind us that the life of any one of us is very short. May it remind us . . . to put first things first. May it remind us that all our efforts and all our sacrifices will have lasting influence for good and lasting significance only to the extent that they are motivated by the love of God and the love of our fellowmen—only to the degree that our personal motives are pure and unselfish—to the degree that we "hunger and thirst after justice" and not after personal glory or gain. "Blessed are they who hunger and thirst after justice, for they shall be filled."[251]

Higgins also wrote that George Meany, the president of the AFL-CIO, was a man possessing "granite-like integrity, great sincerity and strength of character."[252] He wrote these words after attending Meany's retirement celebration at the end of 1979. This entire *Yardstick* column was filled with emotion. Higgins noted that Meany broke down in tears as he thanked God at the close of his address. Other delegates and observers, "including this one, reached for his handkerchief to wipe a tear away. This great outpouring of respect and affection . . . was richly deserved . . . because of his sterling personal qualities."[253] Respect for Meany and all that he had done on behalf of working people bordered on awe. In a very personal vein Higgins wrote:

> I owe him a great personal debt of gratitude for many favors over the past 40 years, but I would find it difficult to express my gratitude in words. In lieu of that, upon my retirement from the U.S. Catholic Conference staff, I will present my entire labor library, in his honor, to the George Meany Center for Labor Studies in suburban Maryland.[254]

Higgins preached the homily at Meany's funeral at St. Matthew's Cathedral in Washington, DC, on January 15, 1980. The *Yardstick* column for January 28, 1980, printed a portion of that homily.[255]

The *Yardstick* columns paid tribute to those who shared in the social apostolate and in public service. Higgins was always grateful for the innovative style of Monsignor Reynold Hillenbrand, his seminary rector. When Hillenbrand died, Higgins paid tribute to Hillenbrand's leadership.[256] Hillenbrand incorporated Catholic social teaching into the seminary curriculum, and he promoted the liturgical movement and various movements involving the laity. Higgins also wrote in memory of Father Raymond A. McGowan.[257] McGowan's quiet and unpretentious presence shaped Higgins' vision during his early years at SAD. He devoted a number of *Yardstick* columns to the devoted work of social action priests Raymond Clancy; Matthew F. Connolly; Bill Smith, S.J.; and Bishops Joseph F. Donnelly and Robert E. Lucey.[258]

Higgins was deeply moved by the deaths of John Cogley, Dorothy Day, and Hubert H. Humphrey. In a homily preached at a memorial Mass for John Cogley at St. Joseph's Church in Greenwich Village on May 14, 1976, Higgins praised his honesty, compassion, dignity, love for the poor, and respect for others' viewpoint. He said that Cogley had

> a deep sense of compassion for the frailty of human nature, a profound respect for the dignity of the human person and the sacredness and integrity of the human conscience, and a realistic insight into the ambiguity of the human experience and the ambivalence of human motivation.[259]

He then addressed Cogley's decision to change religious affiliation and his search for meaning. Higgins said, in words revealing his reverence for personal conscience, "That decision remains a mystery which none has any need or claim to question. It is far better, when confronted with a friend's decision on a matter of this kind, to honor the privacy of his conscience and to respond, if at all, in respectful silence."[260] Higgins, using a quote from Dom Aelred Graham, revealed his own religious magnanimity:

> Without prejudice to the traditional constitution of the Church, it may be suggested that what is now becoming apparent to all is the theological truism that any ecclesiastical system as such cannot fully meet the aspirations of those who desire to be authentically religious. . . . Spiritual renewal lies beyond the scope of administrative acts. The most these can do is point the way, help to provide the atmosphere in which each individual may undergo, by an actual experience as well as symbolically, a rebirth, lose his egocentricity and become an enlightened, free, and loving human being.[261]

His memorial column for Dorothy Day focused not on the chronology of her life but on a facet that he thought other columnists missed.

> As the British author, Muriel Trevor, put it some years ago: "Prophets and radicals easily become prigs, and a prophetic community, as we see from the history of the sects, is liable to develop into a closed circle of self-righteous moralists."
>
> Dorothy Day never fell into that trap. One would be hard put to find anything she ever wrote or said in public that was judgmental, moralistic or self-righteous. She taught by example more than word—although her output as a writer for more than 50 years was enormous. She lived a life of heroic poverty and service to the poor and was a prophetic Christian witness in many other

> areas as well; but she never sat in judgment of those whose lifestyles or views differed from her own. She was never a prig, and the Catholic Worker movement, which she and Peter Maurin started, never developed into a closed circle of self-righteous moralists.[262]

The *Yardstick* column for January 30, 1978, memorialized Hubert H. Humphrey. Higgins praised Humphrey's life of public service and his devotion to his wife and family. Most of all, he lauded the ways that Humphrey fought against political cynicism and promoted political idealism. "Finally, Hubert Humphrey taught us more about the art of dying than anyone in my memory, with the possible exception of John XXIII. . . . [He was] an exceptional human being. It will be a long time before we see anyone like him again. May he rest in peace."[263]

Higgins devoted several *Yardstick* columns to those who maligned or misrepresented the church, opposed its teachings on social justice, or acted unjustly toward the poor. The *Yardstick* column for February 11, 1980, was redolent of the post–Second World War era and the last vestiges of blatant anti-Catholicism. Higgins wrote this column in memory of Paul Blanshard. Once the general counsel of Protestants and Other Americans United for Separation of Church and State, Blanshard was a notoriously anti-Catholic critic and writer in the 1950s and 1960s. Blanshard died on January 27 in St. Petersburg, Florida, at the age of eighty-seven. Higgins wrote:

> I knew Blanshard fairly well and, while I frequently crossed swords with him, I liked him as a person. . . . In reading his autobiography, I sometimes felt that I owed him an apology for having been so severe in my criticism of his books on Catholic issues. But, though I respect the sincerity of his convictions, honesty compels me to say that apologies are not in order.[264]

Higgins attacked bigotry wherever he found it, and he was particularly offended by Blanshard's anti-Catholic animus. Blanshard had once described the Catholic Church as "the baldest, most unashamed, most absolute dictatorship in the world." Higgins wrote:

> I suppose it was this one statement more than anything else that made me change my mind about apologizing to Blanshard. I have already offered Mass for the repose of Blanshard's soul, fully confident that the God whom he said he didn't believe in will judge him mercifully. May he rest in peace.[265]

Far more difficult than the era and the writings of Paul Blanshard were the negativity and untruthfulness of Catholic papers such as *Twin Circle*,

National Catholic Register, and *The Wanderer*, as well as a trio of writers who misinformed the public about Cesar Chavez and the farmworkers' struggle. Higgins wrote several *Yardstick* columns to refute editorials or articles written by Dan Lyons, S.J., Cletus Healy, S.J., and Ralph de Toledano. He began the column for January 6, 1969, by reminding readers that several *Yardstick* columns in 1968 had supported Chavez and his efforts to unionize the farmworkers in California and Texas. He then proceeded to endorse the table-grape boycott as a legitimate last resort in the effort to persuade the growers to recognize the workers' right to organize. He supported this position with a quote from Monsignor John A. Ryan's article on labor unions in volume 8 of the 1910 *Catholic Encyclopedia*. Ryan stated that a boycott is legitimate

> when the injustice inflicted by the employer is grave, and when no milder method will be effective. To deny this would be to maintain that the employer has a right to pursue his advantage in an unreasonable way and immune from reasonable interference. The laborers are endowed with the same right of seeking material benefits on reasonable conditions and by reasonable methods; in this case the boycott is a reasonable method.[266]

The next section of the column commented on a series of anti-Chavez articles that appeared in *Twin Circle*. Higgins wrote that

> the author of these articles is strongly opposed to Cesar Chavez and his union and also, of course, to the California grape boycott. He takes the position that Chavez speaks only for a small minority of farm workers and . . . his efforts to force the growers to deal with his union are totally unjustified.
>
> The answer to this . . . is extremely simple. . . . All that the growers need to do . . . is to agree to impartially supervised elections. Their continued refusal to do so . . . can only question the integrity of the growers' contention and induce more and more people to support the boycott.
>
> The fact, however, that I happen to disagree with Twin Circle's correspondent regarding the merits of the boycott and of Cesar Chavez' organizing tactics is of secondary importance. I am much more concerned about his repeated attempts to undermine Chavez' reputation and to cast doubt on his personal integrity as a labor leader and a Catholic layman.[267]

Dan Lyons wrote more anti-Chavez articles than any other reporter or columnist in the country. One editorial told readers that he and Cletus Healy had visited the Coachella valley and interviewed various people about the farm-labor dispute. He said that the farmworkers were well-paid and content with things as they were. Lyons then accused Higgins of coercing workers into voting for the union. Higgins' response set the record straight. He said that the bishops had endorsed the boycott since 1975 and that their 1968 statement had supported an amendment that would have brought farmworkers under the coverage of the National Labor Relations Act and would have thus guaranteed their right to organize and bargain collectively.[268]

Higgins also set the record straight with Ralph de Tolendino, the Washington-based author and journalist. He wrote, "Ralph de Toledano . . . recently dashed off a nationally syndicated column on Cesar Chavez . . . which, in my judgment, deserves to be awarded first prize as the worst thing written about Chavez during the year 1970." De Toledano said that Chavez had faked his fasts, that there were few workers interested in unionizing, and that Chavez had offered the growers a sweetheart contract. On the last issue, Higgins wrote:

> I must report that I laughed out loud when I read this remarkable statement, knowing, as I do, on the basis of first-hand experience, how difficult it was for the parties to hammer out the terms of the collective bargaining agreements which eventually settled the grape dispute and the four or five contracts which have thus far been negotiated in the case of the lettuce dispute. Sweetheart contracts? Balderdash.[269]

Two *Yardstick* columns reviewed and refuted points that de Toledano made in *Little Cesar*. He described it as "a low-grade, mean-spirited hatchet job on Cesar Chavez [filled with] half-truths, sly innuendoes, irresponsible gossip, and out-right inaccuracies."[270] He attacked de Toledano's opposition to the closed shop and the open shop, his lack of objectivity as a reporter, and his disrespect for the U.S. Bishops Committee on Farm Labor. "[He looks] like an old-style Sunday supplement gossip monger and . . . a professional propagandist for the National Right to Work Committee."[271] Higgins lamented de Toledano's disdain for organized labor and his hatred for Cesar Chavez.

> Cesar Chavez is a great labor leader and a man of conscience and compassion. . . . Mr. de Toledano, incredibly enough, has never met the man. . . . [Chavez] is almost universally regarded, with deep respect and admiration, as being a very constructive figure in American society and a great credit not only to his own people but to the nation as a whole. He will be remembered long after Mr. de Toledano and his unscrupulous diatribe against him are forgotten.[272]

Conclusion

Higgins' social theology deepened, developed, and expanded during these years. He built on his theological anthropology in concrete ways. He enriched a theology that cherished the worth of each person, and he enhanced it with a theology of action and practical expressions of community. He applied theological principles about the human person and about human associations into specific and particular commitments. He wrote about racism and involved himself in working for civil and human rights. He looked at poverty and committed his time and energy to the nation's farmworkers. He supported their union; provided a rationale for boycotts and strikes; and joined them at rallies, meetings, liturgies, and negotiating sessions. He wrote about Catholic–Jewish relations and became a partner in dialogue and friendship. He wrote about the renewal of organized labor and attended local meetings and national conventions.

His theological method underwent a change. Higgins began to move away from a classical methodology that took principles and applied them to action. He allowed his experience, involvements, and actions to shape his thought; to teach him new insights; and to magnify the principles he held dear. His study of the papal encyclicals of Popes John XXIII and Paul VI made him more aware of historical contingency, the limits of language, and the need to engage in mutual conversation and dialogue with a wide circle of people. His involvement with a global church at the Second Vatican Council made him more aware of theological plurality and cultural diversity. His participation at the 1971 synod made him more aware of the significance of the ordained priesthood in a world church; the need for institutional self-criticism in the church; and the responsibility to do justice in Catholic institutions while promoting social, political, and economic justice in the world. His engagement with Catholic–Jewish conversations made him aware of the need for Catholics to be humble, as the church learned from Jews and Judaism. His commitment to the farmworkers' cause made him see the face of the suffering Christ in the poorest of the nation's poor.

The face of the suffering Christ has made him a passionate prophet. This was evident in the *Yardstick* columns. He was also a compassionate companion, as demonstrated in the ways in which he was a presence among the poor and the powerful. He was a man of gratitude, as evidenced in his friendships and in his funeral homilies. These were years in which he wed the words of the *Yardstick* columns with the practice of the apostolic life. He wrote about the indispensable role of the laity in the marketplace. He encouraged them to social action shaped by prayer, liturgy, and the insights of personal conscience. He promoted a spirit of trust, openness, and esteem for those who were partners in dialogue. His social theology—rooted in Catholic ecclesiology, social teaching, and the practice of the apostolic life—looked to the future and included religious freedom, human rights, an international labor movement, and global cooperation.

CHAPTER FIVE

~

Higgins' Later Years in the Social Apostolate: 1981–1994

Chapter five considers the development of Higgins' social theology in the years following his work at United States Catholic Conference, 1981–1994. First, it looks at the *Labor Day Statements* issued between 1981 and 2001. Second, it investigates the *Yardstick* columns that Higgins wrote between 1981 and 1994. Third, it summarizes the developments in his social theology during this time.

Higgins' retirement did not curtail his involvement in public life and in the social apostolate. People asked him to lecture and teach. He traveled, always inquiring into the well-being of workers and the labor movement. He maintained a lively interest in international labor, especially the birth and the development of the Solidarity labor union in Poland. He continued as chair and member of the UAW's PRB and as a member of the board of the UFW's Martin Luther King Jr. Fund. In many ways, his work for social and marketplace justice continued. His commitments and convictions did not change.

But something significant did change. Higgins became the elder statesman in the social apostolate. People called him for advice, asked his opinion, and sought his council. Having been priest and prophet for many years, he now came to be perceived as one who spoke wisdom. This was evident in his final *LDS*, written and issued in 1990. There he reiterated his lifelong conviction that a strong labor movement was necessary and essential for a vital democratic society. The 1993 *LDS*, a tribute to his person and his lifelong work, presented him in a role of wisdom. In the introduction Bishop John H. Ricard writes:

> We focus on Msgr. Higgins not simply to recognize a giant in our midst, but to recommit ourselves to the Catholic tradition of defending the dignity and rights of workers which has been the focus of his life.
>
> For more than a half a century, Msgr. Higgins has been the bridge between the Church and the labor movement and a pre-eminent analyst and articulator of Catholic social teaching. . . . He has challenged our Church to take our social tradition seriously. His powerful intellect, his respectful candor, his refreshing consistency, and his remarkable loyalty to both Church and labor, have made this Chicago priest a symbol of what is best in our social justice tradition.
>
> In this Labor Day Statement, we share a few of the insights contained in this very readable and challenging summary of the wisdom of the best known "labor priest."[1]

Quoting from *Organized Labor and the Church* in the 1993 *LDS*, Ricard related a conversation between Higgins and a woman who cleaned his room at a hotel in Disneyland. The story poignantly conveyed his respect for the individual, his empathy for the working poor, and his commitment to the labor movement.

> Several years ago I stayed in a hotel in Disneyland for a two-week conference. . . . I got to know some of the hotel workers, including the woman who cleaned my room. I asked her how long she had worked there. "Twenty years," she said. I asked her if she would mind telling me how much she earned. "Minimum wage," was her reply.
>
> I am often asked: Why are unions needed in this day and age? People should not ask me. They should ask the maid at Disneyland and other low-wage workers. If her situation was like that of other minimum-wage workers, she probably had no health insurance, in addition to no living wage. Health insurance, which originated at the bargaining table, represents one of organized labor's great contributions to the American worker. Without this coverage, people can run up bills for health care that would otherwise land them in the poorhouse. And yet, millions of non-union workers have no health insurance; as a result, more than thirty million Americans are not covered and several times as many are under-insured.[2]

The Labor Day Statements (1981–2001)

When Higgins concluded his work at United States Catholic Conference, the task for writing and producing the annual *LDS* was handed over to the Office for Social Development and World Peace. The *LDSs*, now parceled out to those responsible for the social apostolate, continued to reflect Higgins' agenda and mentality.[3] Each *LDS* in these two decades investigated some aspect of the issues that affected workers and workplace justice: What is the nature and meaning of work? What is the social position of workers? Who are the poor, and what does the "option for the poor" mean in a land of plenty? What legislative and policy reforms are necessary to ensure a living wage and a decent way of life for the nation's workers? What principles will guide the church, business, and government in addressing the needs of the working poor? The *LDS* and the *Yardstick* columns examined these issues.

The Social Situation

Several issues touched the lives of workers in new ways in the 1980s and the 1990s. First, the gap between the rich and the poor kept getting bigger. In fact, the gap in the United States was larger than anywhere else in the world.[4] Upper-income families experienced substantial income growth in the 1980s, and the bottom 40 percent experienced stagnation or a decline in wages. The disproportion between the earnings of CEOs and the salaries of ordinary workers was increasing. Younger people, especially those with a minimum amount of education, were more likely to be poor. Many of the new jobs in the 1990s were part-time, provided meager wages, and offered few benefits. People increasingly felt uneasy. Even with low employment, many workers felt insecure about their future.

Second, the country was becoming a single nation with three economies.[5] The first economy was prospering and moving ahead. People in this economy had the skills that enabled them to flourish in a global economy and in an information age. This economic class had power and prestige. The passage of the North American Free Trade Agreement and the ability of transnational corporations to transcend national borders suited many in this economy. The second economy was just getting by, but it was being squeezed by the decline in real incomes. People in this economy feared the loss of their jobs, their health care benefits, and their retirement pensions when companies downsized or relocated. They worried that they would be unable to educate their children. This economic class had limited power and prestige. Many in the middle were at a breaking point. Temporary illness or disability could plunge them into poverty. The third economy was losing ground. People in this economy were on the margins and not getting by. They worried about not having enough to pay the rent, buy food, and afford decent health care. Sometimes they had to settle for one over the other. This economic class had no power and prestige. Many, even those working full-time at the minimum wage, were unable to afford safe, quality child care, decent housing, and transportation to and from work.

> Common sense tells us that some things should be different. . . . The economy should be moving toward full employment with prosperity shared fairly and widely. We should be growing together not pulling apart.[6]

Third, the old verities, once so certain and sure, were shifting. Workers were no longer guaranteed stable, lifelong jobs with the same company. Their loyalty, honesty, productivity, experience, and concern for the company were not rewarded with pensions. Companies no longer counted on workers to give a fair day's work for a fair day's pay. Owners and managers did not assume the honesty and integrity of their workers. Employers and employees viewed each other suspiciously. In short, the so-called social contract between employers and employees was unraveling. New partnerships and forms of cooperation were needed.[7]

The Working Poor

The *LDSs* clearly identified the working poor in the United States.[8] They were those that the new economy had left behind or left out, such as older workers whose companies downsized or relocated elsewhere. They were considered too young to retire and too qualified to be rehired. Many took jobs that paid less than their former jobs or demanded less than their current skills. Some took part-time jobs that provided a salary but lacked health care and pension benefits. Younger workers were particularly vulnerable. Those with only a high school education were at a disadvantage. Their starting jobs in the mid-1990s paid 30 percent below what similar jobs had paid in the late 1970s. Many lacked the skills and the training to obtain a better job. They may have lived in the wrong place, lacked adequate housing and health care, and had no access to resources that would haved opened up opportunities for them. Frequently poverty had eroded their self-esteem and self-confidence. Low-wage families were among the working poor. More family members in these households worked longer hours just to keep pace. Real incomes had stagnated or fallen. Even with both parents working, their standard of living was lower than that of their own parents who had lived on just a father's income. Children in the United States were among the poor. One in four grew up in poverty. Women were poor, especially those that headed up households. They earned less than male coworkers. Seasonal agricultural workers, people of color, and newly arrived immigrants were among the poor. The number of poor people and the depth of their poverty were a surprise, a shock, and a scandal for a country that had so much abundance.

The Vocation of Work

What can be done to alleviate poverty? What can be done to protect and enhance the dignity and the rights of workers? What can responsible citizens do to effect significant change? The *LDSs* addressed these questions in two ways. First, they posited that communities of conscience can think differently. Catholics can look beyond their personal circumstances to consider the common good and the health of the entire economy. A willingness to think large is an important first step.

> Our union with Jesus Christ and our faith in him reminds us that it is not enough to focus simply on how we personally are faring. We cannot neglect the common good nor the economic health of the larger community we are part of. Despite the difficulties that we may face in life, we cannot become blind to the difficulties that are experienced by our neighbors.[9]

Second, we can invest work with a religious meaning, and we can envision economic life from a theological perspective. *Laborens Exercens*, issued by Pope John Paul II in 1981; *Economic Justice for All*, the pastoral letter of the U.S. bishops issued in 1986; and the *LDSs* from 1981 to 2001 are resources that enhance theological reflection and enable conversation about the meaning of work. Work is a duty, a right, and a responsibility. It reflects and expresses human dignity and imagination. It is the way that people actualize human potential and contribute to the community. Working people collaborate with God in fashioning creation. They are agents of God, not tools of production. Their work is not a penalty, a punishment, a way to reduce the welfare rolls or pay off welfare assistance. Work is something people do to secure decent lives for themselves and their families. This includes the important work of loving one's children. In short, work is a Christian vocation that strives to transform the world in the light of the Gospel.[10]

> Catholicism does not call us to abandon the world, but to help shape it. This does not mean leaving worldly tasks and responsibilities, but transforming them. . . . Our entire community of faith must help Catholics to be instruments of God's grace and creative power in business and politics, factories and offices, in homes and schools, and in all the events of daily life.[11]

Everyone has a right and a responsibility to work because working people collaborate with God in building the kingdom. This demands nothing less than full employment, a goal that Higgins had promoted from the very beginning of his work in the social apostolate. "Full employment remains the most fundamental economic and social objective for our society."[12]

Imagining the Future

The *LDSs* looked at two significant questions that regarded the future of economic life and the well-being of working people. First, how does the economy influence working people and their human dignity? The *LDSs* insisted that the economy was for people and human dignity. Therefore, work was for the person, not the person for work. People are more important than things.

People are more valuable for who they are than for what they have, for the work they do rather than for what they possess. "Human labor cannot be treated merely as a factor necessary for production. People are more than a 'human resource.' A person cannot be regarded as a tool of production."[13] Second, how does a global economy influence the people of the world? The economy is no longer simply local and personal. People do not live in isolation from one another or the systems that influence economic life. The global and international nature of work and finances requires that U.S. Catholics seriously consider the values that guide their thinking, decision making, and involvement in the new economy. We ask: How will the global economy affect people, especially the poor and vulnerable? Will it lift people up or push them down, bring people together or drive them apart, build new bridges or increase the gaps between the rich and the poor?

> The global economy exists to serve the human person, not the other way around. The moral measure of any economy is not simply the information shared, the wealth created, the trade encouraged, but how the lives and dignity of the poor and vulnerable, the hungry and destitute are protected and promoted.[14]

Will the economy foster human solidarity and reduce global xenophobia? Will it help people to see others as economic rivals, problems, or disposable parts or as members of one human family? "In a rapidly shrinking world 'loving our neighbor' takes on a new meaning and globalization redefines and enlarges the biblical question 'who is my neighbor?'"[15] Choices that U.S. Catholics make are made within a religious and humanitarian context. How will this choice promote human dignity? How will this structure affect the common good? How will this action lift up the poor, the weak, and the vulnerable? How will this stance strengthen solidarity? These questions are particularly germane to Catholics in the United States because of the nation's economic power and unique role in the world community.

> Catholicism does not call us to abandon the world, but to help shape it. This does not mean leaving worldly tasks and responsibilities, but transforming them. . . . Our entire community of faith must help Catholics to be instruments of God's grace and creative power in business and politics, factories and offices, in homes and schools, and in all the events of daily life.[16]

The *LDSs* offered suggestions for economic life and the well-being of working people. These suggestions involve the role of organized labor, the passage of new legislation and policy making, and a spirituality of partnership. First, "the best social program is still a decent job with decent pay and benefits."[17] Getting a decent job demands a strong labor movement.

> Unions never capitulated to the concept of "class" that found such fertile ground in the rest of the industrial world. Union leaders instead saw their organization as part of the American experiment in democracy and urged their membership to seek social justice for all instead of class struggle.[18]

The labor movement had been declining in numbers for decades. Only about 15 percent of the workforce is organized. Nevertheless, church support for organized labor is not based on statistics. Its support rests on the social nature of people and the principle that strong, democratic unions are indispensable and essential partners in society. Unions help people to obtain work with decent benefits, encourage participation in the wider society, and promote the common good. The labor movement in the mid-1990s began to take steps to revitalize itself by organizing the unorganized; by reaching out to newly arrived immigrants in the workforce; and by appealing to the needs of pink-, gray-, and white-collar workers and their families. The *LDS* encouraged the church to reevaluate its own commitment to organized labor. Values in the labor movement's search for social justice

> reflect our own faith values as we seek public policies that protect and promote strong families, expand a stable middle-class, create decent jobs, and reduce the level of poverty and need in our society. Unions seek such policies when their own members do not directly benefit from the legislation. An early example of this is the historic legislation that became the Social Security Program.[19]

A new church–labor alliance is necessary to protect the dignity and the rights of working people and to promote the common good. This alliance supports the values that working people have traditionally held dear. It reaffirms their right to organize and to bargain collectively for a living wage, health care insurance, safe and affordable child care, and a pension plan. Unions, in their best moments, promote excellence in production and service. They encourage the rank and file to participate in the life of the community.

Second, the *LDSs* encouraged the passage of new legislation to help families, the elderly, and the poor. Working people need help to balance their work and family responsibilities, correct disparities between men and women's wages, protect women from discrimination in hiring and promotions, and raise the minimum wage to a living wage. High on the legislative agenda are the protection of social security for the elderly, a review of the welfare system reform in the late 1960s, and programs to assist the poor. "As people of faith we are one family, not competing classes. We are sisters and brothers in Christ, not economic units or statistics."[20]

Third, the *LDSs* suggested partnership as the new social capital and the new spirituality for the future. People from varied backgrounds are involving themselves as partners to enhance life in the public square and to bring about economic justice and citizenship. Economic life is increasingly being carried out in marketplaces where investments are made, contracts are negotiated, products are created, workers are hired, and policies are set. Owners, investors, consumers, and workers are moral agents in economic life. They either build up or tear down justice and community. Dedicated laity leaven a society that espouses the value of work, the dignity of workers, fairness in wages and in hiring, social contracts, and the common good.[21] A spirituality of partnership is created in the town commons and in moments of recreation, leisure, conviviality, and prayer.

> This year, after the Labor Day picnic, take time to say a prayer for the low-wage workers who provide our food. Many of them work long hours, in horrible working conditions, for meager wages. Pray for the workers who still don't have a forty-hour week, safe and sanitary shops, or the chance to make a decent living for their families; remember the workers confronting firing, intimidation, delays, replacement, and bad faith when they try to organize to defend their right. But recognize the contributions of those employers whose initiative and investment create decent jobs at decent wages, who treat their workers as partners and who help them build the economic health and vitality of the community.[22]

The *Yardstick* Columns (1981–1994)

The *Yardstick* columns of this period considered the significant social and political changes that were taking place nationally and internationally, including the Reagan administration's impact on the labor movement, the decline of membership in organized labor, papal and U.S. social teaching on work and economic justice, and many of the practical issues associated with the unions and worker justice. In addition, the *Yardstick* columns investigated the issues that Higgins had remained committed to throughout his life.

The Shifting Social and Political Situation

The presidency of Ronald Reagan coincided with a major shift in the social and political life of the nation. The harmonious and cooperative relationship among labor, management, and government that had existed since the late 1940s began to unravel in the 1970s. The decline of union membership and the effects of concession bargaining and the so-called give-back contracts had weakened the institutional role of organized labor in the public square. The ascendance of big business in the 1980s—reinforced by an ideology of individualism, a limited role for the federal government, and an even more limited role for organized labor—ushered in a new social and political era. Though once embodied in its public institutions and enhanced by lively discourse, the nation's social capital diminished. Big business antagonized the rank-and-file worker when it ignored workers' needs and awarded top executives with so-called sweetheart bonus plans, stock options, and incentive programs. It promoted the all-powerful market and replaced other forms of public participation and social citizenship with consumerism. A mood of distrust and cynicism began to permeate the society. Henry A. Giroux explained the new era:

> Neoliberalism, associated with the rise of the Reagan and Thatcher governments in the early 1980s, refers . . . to those polices "that maximize the role of markets and profit-making and minimize the role of nonmarket institutions. . . . Neoliberalism . . . posits that society works best when business runs things and there is as little possibility of government interference with business as possible." Neoliberalism . . . refers to a political, economic, and cultural formation that construes profit making as the essence of democracy and consuming as the only operable form of citizenship and provides a rationale for a handful of private interests to control as much of social life as possible in order to maximize their personal gain and profit.[23]

Higgins addressed the new situation in the eleven *Yardstick* columns that looked at the policies of the Reagan administration.[24] The first of these column commented evenhandedly on Reagan's inaugural address. In particular, Higgins questioned Reagan's assertion that

> "in this present crisis, government is not the solution; it is the problem." . . . It is one thing, however, to argue that we need less federal intervention in today's economy, something else to say or imply that limited government has always worked to our advantage in the past.[25]

He then cited two historical examples: the McKinley robber-baron era, when the rich became richer and the poor became destitute; and the Harding-Coolidge-Hoover era and Great Depression that followed. Higgins pointed out that prosperity returned when the federal government was willing to spend and intervene during the Second World War. Higgins questioned the prudence of curbing the size and influence of the federal government because such a policy would hurt the poor.

> It is well to recall that when many of the states were flat broke during the Great Depression, they were only too happy to have the federal government bail them out. It is also well to recall that most civil rights legislation—which

> strangely enough the president didn't mention—was enacted precisely because the several states could not or would not protect the basic right of their black citizens. I raise these ungracious questions not to throw water on Reagan's overall economic program, but simply to express hope he will pursue it on its own merits and not try to rewrite economic history or get bogged down in a divisive ideological argument about states' rights. I am encouraged by Reagan's statement that "our objective must be a healthy, vigorous, growing economy that provides equal opportunities for all Americans with no barriers born of bigotry or discrimination." If he can do this with less government, more power to him. But if he finds more rather than less government is needed, I hope he will have the courage to revise the inaugural rhetoric and to act accordingly.[26]

Higgins was much more direct in his critique of the underlying assumptions of the so-called Reagonomics and its impact on the poor. First, he criticized the assumption that federal spending was out of control and had grown too large for the nation's economy. He pointed out that the United States ranked among the lowest of all Western industrialized nations in government spending as a percentage of its gross national product. Second, he objected to Reagan's assumption that the federal deficit had caused inflation and that the solution was a balanced budget. Higgins found no evidence to support this assumption.

> This is a pretty fuzzy basis for eliminating or severely cutting the social programs established during the last 25 years. If what we need is a dramatic show of government determination, why must it come at the expense of the poor?[27]

Third, Higgins indicated that Reagan's economic plan hurt the poor.

> There is simply no way to make severe cuts in food stamps, public-service jobs and low-income housing without hurting the poor. . . . Reagan claims the proposed budget cuts have been spread among all income groups. But why should the poor bear any of the burden when it means the loss of such basic necessities as food, housing, and employment? Unless some of these fundamental questions and assumptions are dealt with more directly, I'm afraid Reagan's rhetoric will soon begin to sound hollow.[28]

The *Yardstick* criticized the Reagan administration's position on Latin America in two instances. First, Higgins opposed the nomination of Ernest W. Lefever as assistant secretary of state for human rights and humanitarian affairs. His opposition was based on the record. Lefever had criticized priests and nuns in Latin America who had spoken out on behalf of human rights. Higgins stated bluntly that Lefever had spoken irresponsibly, especially in light of the death of three U.S. sisters and a laywoman in El Salvador.[29] Second, the *Yardstick* criticized Reagan for ignoring the recommendations of the U.S. Select Commission on Immigration and Refugee Policy. The commission had suggested that there be tighter boarder controls, penalties for employers who hire illegal aliens, and a more secure method of identifying eligible employees. Reagan had recommended an open border so that Mexican workers could enter the United States and take jobs that U.S. workers did not want. Higgins saw this recommendation as a thinly veiled return to the bracero program.

> There are few jobs that U.S. workers are unwilling to take if the wages and working conditions are reasonably satisfactory by American standards. Coal mining and garbage collecting are two of the most miserable jobs imaginable, yet there is no shortage of miners or sanitation workers. There would be . . . if mine operators and city administrators refused to pay decent wages.[30]

The *Yardstick* addressed the conflict between President Reagan and the air traffic controllers in 1981. When members of the Professional Air Traffic Controllers Organization (PATCO) went out on strike, Regan fired them, decertified their union, and hired replacement workers. Higgins felt that PATCO and the administration had seriously miscalculated each other. The controllers thought that they could shut down the airports. The administration thought that the president's threat to terminate strikers, as well as fire and jail a few union officers, would scare the controllers into going back to work. Neither side, as he viewed it, had sufficiently consulted labor–management relations experts. Higgins believed that the administration's action was repressive.

> The president may have felt he had no recourse but to terminate the strikers, yet he was under no compulsion to destroy their union. Nor was there any excuse for asking the courts to assess exorbitant fines against the union or for the shocking sight of a minor union official being led off to jail in handcuffs and leg irons. Not even Poland's communist regime has resorted to such measures in dealing with the leaders of Solidarity.[31]

He suggested that the government find a method that would allow public employees to address their legitimate collective-bargaining needs. "Any law which prohibits public employees from striking while denying them recourse to arbitration is not only grossly unfair, but unworkable. The administration ought to face that fact."[32]

The administration's decision to fire and replace PATCO workers became the defining yardstick for the kind of relationship that the government would have with organized labor in the 1980s. Its decision was ominous. It dealt organized labor its most lethal blow since the passage of the Taft-Hartley Act. As a result, four hundred thousand unionists rallied in Washington in 1981 to protest against the policies of the Reagan administration. A decade later, three hundred thousand unionists would march again on Washington to demand workplace fairness and health care reform.

Furthermore, strikes by the professional sports leagues were a sign of the times. The baseball players went out on strike in 1981 and in 1994. The latter strike resulted in the cancellation of the World Series; it seriously tarnished baseball's image and angered many of baseball's fans. In 1987 professional football players went out on strike. Labor–management strife continued into the 1990s.

The Work of Organized Labor

Higgins' concern for the survival of organized labor, his dedication to workplace justice, and his compassion for the poor are reflected in the almost one hundred *Yardstick* columns that he wrote in this period. Some columns focused on specific groups, such as the farmworkers and janitors and their efforts for economic citizenship. A few columns reflected on milestones in union history, such as the one-hundredth anniversary of the AFL-CIO and of the issuance of *Rerum Novarum*. Other columns spoke about union leadership and the spiritual and inspirational significance of Labor Day. Most of columns, however, revealed Higgins at his best as he treated the practical issues that formed the work of organized labor in the 1980s and 1990s. These included specific issues such as the wages earned by teenage workers, mothers and other women in the workplace, unemployment and the goal of full employment, the right of workers to organize and to strike, and attitudes toward collective bargaining. Other columns investigated more universal topics, such as the dignity of workers, union democracy and ethics, the role of the laity in the workplace, job satisfaction, the salaries of labor and management executives, and the role of organized labor in fostering democracy at home and abroad.[33] He suggested the use of outside experts to help organized labor solve its decline in membership and revitalize its contribution to the common good.

> Representative democracy is the very essence of a free labor movement. Despite its limitations, the American labor movement still fits this category. Its democratic procedures are admittedly imperfect and even sometimes violated, but it is still the most democratic of all our major institutions, including our educational institutions.[34]

Farmworkers

Higgins continued to support the working poor, especially the nation's agricultural workers and janitors. On February 5, 1986, he testified for the United States Catholic Conference before a congressional subcommittee investigating sanitation standards in the fields. The issue of drinking water and adequate sanitation facilities had been discussed and debated for fourteen years by officials in the federal government and in individual states. Finally, on February 8, 1987, a federal appeals court ordered labor secretary William E. Brock to issue federal standards requiring farmers to provide toilets and clean water for millions of farmworkers. This decision provided a just solution to the problem and a set of normative standards applicable in every state. Higgins used this occasion to reaffirm the rationale for the church's concern for the farmworker.

> [Our] concern . . . is rooted in pastoral experience. Many priests, sisters, and lay people live and work among farm laborers attesting that the work and living conditions are often grossly inadequate. I can substantiate their stories through the many visits I have made to labor camps and farms. The basis of our concern for farm laboers is our religious belief that every person is made in the image and likeness of God and endowed with a special dignity protected by a set of basic human rights.[35]

In 1987 he sent an encouraging message to Cesar Chavez on the twenty-fifth anniversary of the UFW. He remembered with bittersweet nostalgia being present in Delano when the collective-bargaining contracts in the table-grape industry had been signed in 1970. He recalled that many had thought then that the struggle for justice in the fields had been accomplished. However, as the *Yardstick* column pointed out, the UFW was "forced to struggle against seemingly impossible odds. But the UFW will prevail."[36] Chavez, his union associates, Higgins, and others maintained that time and public opinion were on the side of the farmworkers. They believed that they and the public still drew from a communal fund of social capital and still subscribed to the social values of freedom of association, self-determination, and fair play.

> The basic issue is that farm workers have a right to organize into a union of their choosing and that no other union and no group of growers should be permitted to interfere with this right. For 25 years the agricultural industry has been needlessly caught up in the most bitter kind of conflict. For what purpose? To avoid dealing with the UFW. . . . The time has come for the industry's leaders to admit their mistake and begin to develop a mature system of labor-management relations.[37]

The *Yardstick* fortified its position by quoting from *Laborens Exercens*:

> Even in developed countries, the pope noted, . . . "the right to work can be infringed" when farm workers are denied the possibility of sharing in decisions concerning their services or denied the right to free association with a view to their just advancement. He urged "radical and urgent changes " to "proclaim and promote the dignity of work, of all work, but especially of agricultural work." That describes the UFW's goals. May the Good Lord give it the strength and courage to continue struggling for these goals and to do so with confidence that justice will prevail.[38]

On August 21, 1988, Cesar Chavez ended his thirty-six-day fast at a Eucharistic liturgy that Higgins concelebrated. The fast had been a dramatic protest against the poisonous, cancer-inducing pesticides that were used in the fields. Chavez hoped that the owners would discontinue the practice. Higgins wrote movingly, "As I watched him from the altar I recalled a happier day some 15 years ago when Chavez and his wife, Helen, were received in a private audience at the Vatican by Pope Paul VI."[39] Also present were Bishop Donnelly, Monsignor Higgins, and two of Chavez's aides. The pope, the *Yardstick* recalled, spoke about the work of the UFW, Chavez's efforts to apply the principles of Christian social teaching, and the collaboration of the UFW with the U.S. bishops and their farm-labor committee. The pope closed by saying, "We renew the full measure of our solicitude for the human and Christian condition and for the genuine good of all those who lend support to this lofty vocation."[40] Higgins then passionately expressed the role and the relationship between the religious communities, the UFW, and the farm owners.

> The UFW . . . has always been and, please God, always will be, a movement of, by, and for the people it represents. Rank-and-file farm workers built the UFW, not clergymen. Churches and many other outside groups have assisted the movement at critical moments, but it is the farm workers' movement and they have every reason to be proud of it and of their leader, Cesar Chavez. . . . The charge is sometimes made that because of its support for the farm workers, the church is prejudiced against the growers. It is absolutely unfounded. The involvement of church groups in the farm labor dispute has only one purpose: helping farm workers achieve the right to organize into a union of their own choice, a right that has been legally guaranteed workers of every other major industry for several decades. Once it has been effectively granted, the religious bodies will do everything they possibly can to promote, in a spirit of reconciliation, a constructive working relationship between the union and the growers. The history of labor relations in the United States makes it clear, however, that this kind of relationship, so long overdue in the agricultural in-

dustry, cannot be established until the workers are granted the right to self-determination and have acquired enough economic power to bargain as equals with their employers.[41]

The *Yardstick* column for March 7, 1994, reported on the 1994 Combined Social Ministry Gathering in Washington, DC. During a plenary session Higgins preached a homily at a Mass celebrated in memory of Cesar Chavez. Higgins took his opening lines from the last paragraph of Chavez's autobiography:

"Fighting for social justice, it seems to me, is one of the profoundest ways in which man can say yes to man's dignity, and that really means sacrifice. There is no way on this earth in which you can say yes to man's dignity and know that you're going to be spared from sacrifice."[42]

Higgins considered Chavez's commitment to nonviolence a sign of the kind of sanctity that was needed to evangelize the world and effect social transformation.

The presence of individuals such as Cesar Chavez among us has been a sign that the human spirit still thirsts for a transcendent affirmation of the individual's worth and the right of the individual to live with a modicum of personal dignity and with some communal bond with others. The UFW . . . had much in common with the Polish labor movement, Solidarity, not least because of the UFW's commitment to non-violence. . . . *Centissimus Annus* says that the collapse of communism "began with the great upheavals which took place in Poland in the name of solidarity." The working people of Poland richly deserve this accolade. . . . But also worthy of special emphasis . . . is the fact that the fall of the communist bloc was "accomplished almost everywhere by means of peaceful protest using only the weapons of truth and justice." . . . The pope's tribute to Solidarity's commitment to non-violence applies in equal measure to Chavez and the UFW. In fact, it might even be said that Lech Walesa and Solidarity were following Chavez's example in this regard. . . . For Chavez non-violence did not mean inaction. Like his mentor, Mahatma Gandhi, he wasn't afraid to move and to make things happen, and he never asked people to do things he wouldn't do himself. We honor Chavez because he said yes to human dignity at great personal sacrifice.[43]

Justice for Janitors

The *Yardstick* informed its readers about the problems that service workers faced in cities where the new economy was developing. While executives, attorneys and financiers at the top did very well, people at the bottom did poorly in wages, benefits, and job security. The Service Employees International Union (SEIU) took the initiative to organize the custodial workers who cleaned and maintained the office buildings of the new and revitalized cities. SEIU called the campaign "Justice for Janitors." It was "making a major effort to help more this largely female, largely minority work force share in the economic miracle."[44] It sought to organize the more than one million custodial workers; improve their low-wage, no-benefits conditions; and help these workers and their families obtain health insurance. In addition, SEIU addressed the issue of job security.

> In recent years, janitorial work in large buildings has been almost totally subcontracted. Janitors no longer work directly for a building owner but instead for a contractor. These contractors, driven by fierce competition, frequently cut hours and increase workloads to bid successfully on contracts. Janitors are now frequently paid by how many floors they clean, not by the hour. This piecemeal approach has resulted in wages below the statutory hourly minimum and has reintroduced child labor in the work force as custodial workers are driven to use their children to try to make the grade.[45]

Higgins knew that janitors did not have to be poor, because many janitors in unionized cities worked for a living wage that supported their families and provided basic benefits such as health care. Through the SEIU, janitors brought their cause to the general population through public protest and information. The column concluded with Higgins' words of support. "The Justice for Janitors campaign is an exciting opportunity to assist America's working poor to win justice. I plan to support the campaign in every possible way and I urge others to do the same."[46]

Women in the Workforce and Working Mothers

Several *Yardstick* columns considered gender bias in the workplace and the role of working mothers. Higgins passionately stated his opinion about gender bias in one of his later *Yardstick* columns:

> Employment discrimination of any kind, whether based on gender, race, color, national origin, religion, age or disability is a menace to decent societies. It thwarts social and economic justice. However, the persistence of gender bias in the world of work around the globe—in industrial as well as developing countries—is depressing and unacceptable. Its cost to society is incalculable. . . . Throughout the world . . . women are concentrated in jobs with the least prospects of economic gain and self-esteem. . . . Working women [are confronted with the problem] of sexual harassment. [It] drives one in 12 women out of the work force in industrialized countries. . . . Some 15 to 30 percent of working women . . . were subjected to frequent and serious sexual harassment. Often these demeaning experiences led to stress and related ailments. Clearly, the community of nations must move in their own societies to eradicate all

> forms of discrimination. . . . "For women to be equal, they must have equal access to the economic resources of society. The equality of women begins with their ability to participate fully and on an equal basis with men in gainful activity which enables them to be economically independent." . . . We must act decisively to assure equality—and we must act now.[47]

Women scholars raised the issue at several conferences devoted to studying *Laborens Exercens*. Higgins responded carefully and commended the encyclical's balanced approach to the economic role of working mothers.

> [The encyclical] says women can work if they want. Mothers can work too, so long as they fulfill their irreplaceable role in raising their children. But if a mother chooses not to work, she shouldn't be forced to do so by financial necessity; nor should working women be discriminated against. In other words, there should be equal pay for equal or comparable work.[48]

He indicated that many mothers of young children have entered the workforce out of necessity to keep their families solvent during a period of inflation. He expressed his anger regarding the antifamily policy of the Reagan administration.

> Ironically, the pro-family Reagan administration now proposes to compound the problem by requiring all parents in the welfare program for mothers and children to search for a job outside the home, regardless of the age of their children. It seems safe to presume the pope would be appalled by this punitive, anti-family approach. Compelling mothers of young children to abandon their homes in order to take paid work outside the home is, he says, "wrong from the point of view of the good of society and of the family." In a country as wealthy as ours it is worse than wrong—it is barbaric. If feminists, especially those in religious orders, fail to protest this move and demand that the administration reverse itself, they will forfeit much of their hard-won credibility.[49]

Issues Facing Organized Labor

Higgins continued to write on topics that were familiar to readers of the *Yardstick* columns. But his focus was on the future, not the past. He returned to the essentials to envision a stronger, revitalized labor movement. He proposed steps that organized labor could take in its own behalf. The first step was fairly evident: organized labor should exercise greater self-criticism and greater self-correction to promote justice in the workplace. Higgins' years on the UAW's PRB gave him a unique perspective on union democracy and labor–management cooperation. He noted that, in the five hundred cases that the board had heard between 1957 and 1981, the UAW had cooperated fully. It had provided the board with relevant information in every case, and it had even reopened cases that the board believed had been incompletely litigated. Sometimes the board had called attention to instances of injustices to union members that the board had no power to correct. In a number of these cases, remedies were effected. The PRB provided a model for union democracy that other unions could use. The fact that other unions failed to adopt similar voluntary programs meant greater court intervention in union affairs before voluntary internal remedies had been even minimally exhausted. In the future, the unions would need to exercise greater responsibility through internal structures of self-review.[50]

The *Yardstick* suggested that labor and management had a responsibility to move beyond mutual suspicion and hostility caused by years of adversarial politics and concession bargaining. Each group needed to move beyond narrow self-interest. Higgins hoped that each group would raise the process of collective bargaining above the level of struggle between competing economic pressure groups and to a more cooperative, conciliatory, and constructive climate.

> Labor and management must subordinate their particular interests to the common good, not just because it is the right thing to do, but because it is the price of survival. It's a pity it has taken so long for labor and mangement to start acting on this principle.[51]

Higgins hoped for a new era of labor–management cooperation.

> [I do] not suggest that organized labor represents the "good guys" and management the "bad guys" in the American economy. Such invidious distinctions are reprehensible. The truth is that industry is a combined operation of management and labor. Labor officials should and . . . do realize that they have neither the right nor the technical knowledge to tell employers how to run businesses. . . . Business executives might just as well face the fact that they will never again enjoy the luxury of unilateral decision making. That day is gone forever.[52]

Higgins had studied labor history sufficiently to know the deleterious effects of the open shop. "The bad old days of the so-called union shop [pitted] labor and management against one another in the worst possible kind of class struggle, with disastrous results for all concerned."[53] He recognized the indispensable role that unions played in fostering economic citizenship.

> Even if most injustice and exploitation were removed, unions would still have a legitimate and necessary role to play. Unions are the normal choice of labor, necessary to organize social life for the common good. In other words, there is a positive need for such organizations.[54]

The only viable alternative to class struggle and antagonism was labor–management cooperation. The *Yardstick* pointed out the benefits of such cooperation. Cooperation could give organized labor a voice in the struggle for social justice, for the just rights of working people, and the common good of society. It could help overcome the prevailing ethos of individualism, build a spirit of community, and develop a climate of solidarity between those who work in an industry and those who manage an industry. Cooperation would encourage joint participation in planning for economic growth; decent wages, benefits, and profits; and the personal satisfaction of workers doing their jobs and of owners running their industries. Cooperation would allow both groups a stake in the future survival and vitality of a company.[55]

The *Yardstick* indicated that organized labor could not alone change the structural economic and political problems of the 1980s. The labor movement could not control inflation or unemployment in the United States, abate competition from companies in other countries, or influence the reform of antiunion labor legislation in the courts. However, there were some things that organized labor could do to revitalize the unions. The leaders could offer inspiration. Leaders such as Samuel Gompers, A. Philip Randolph, Cesar Chavez, and Dolores Huerta envisioned their unions as part of a universal movement on behalf of worker justice. The unions, as in the past, could organize the unorganized—especially the poor, the new immigrants, and the workers in the service sectors of the new economy.[56] They could also engage in grassroots negotiations that might prevent company and plant closings or relocation. They could promote the creation of jobs with adequate pay and decent working conditions, especially for hotel clerks, bank tellers, janitors, and workers in the expanding fast-food industry.[57] Higgins remained confident that organized labor would weather the storm of the hard times of the 1980s. He reaffirmed the principle that "we are not likely to have a free and democratic society without a free and democratic labor movement. Trying to have economic democracy without unions is like trying to have political democracy without political parties."[58]

Solidarity

Higgins lent his support to the birth and development of Solidarity, the Polish labor movement.[59] On October 1, 1981, Higgins addressed the First Congress of Solidarity in Gdansk. In his homily at the opening Mass, he offered greetings from the AFL-CIO and from the Catholic social movement in the United States. The *Yardstick* reported that the leaders of Solidarity, while aware that the union could be suppressed at any time, were cautiously optimistic for its future. They were determined to continue. Lech Walesa expressed this determination in his autobiography:

> If nothing is done to satisfy the basic needs and aspirations of our people, then, rather than resign themselves to inaction, they will fight, and whether it's in a day or whether it's in 10 years, Solidarity will be born again. . . . If government measures are too slow or too superficial and our country continues to stagnate, then there will be an outburst of legitimate protest along the lines of August 1980 and earlier.[60]

Higgins expressed his hope that Solidarity, struggling to rise Phoenix-like from the ashes, would succeed. He noted that "Polish workers are struggling for one goal: the right to contribute, in and through their own movement, to the common good of their beloved nation."[61] Solidarity was suppressed less than a year later. However, Higgins wrote that he had noticed the vitality of the movement in his subsequent visits to Poland and had found this encouraging. He ended the column on a triumphal note:

> As Walesa said the day he received the Nobel Peace Prize, "I still believe the day will come when we will sit together at the same table and come to an understanding about what is best for Poland, because whether we like it or not, we have no choice but to come to an understanding; there is no other solution."
>
> I share his hope and his dream. In the words of one of the oldest American labor songs: Solidarity Forever.[62]

The *Yardstick* reported on the kinds of moral support that Solidarity received. Rallies were held on January 30, 1982, in the United States in support of the movement. Higgins proudly noted the support of Lane Kirkland, president of the AFL-CIO; Pope John Paul II; and the U.S. labor movement in general.

> The pope gave support and encouragement to workers everywhere in his encyclical on human work. "In order to achieve social justice in the various parts of the world, in the various countries and in the relationships between them, there is need for ever new movements of solidarity of the workers and with the workers. . . . The church is firmly committed to this cause, which she considers her mission, her service, a proof of her fidelity to Christ, so that she can be truly the church of the poor." Despite the tragic events which have since overtaken his homeland, the pope has neither lost hope nor faltered in his support of Solidarity.[63]

Solidarity drew confidence from the international labor movement and from the church. The church and Solidarity, each following its own path, became two voices speaking on behalf of the dignity of working people.[64] Both were shaping a new and changed Poland. Higgins stated:

> Polish leaders stand in need of our prayers and support as they face this historic challenge. Both they and the leaders of Solidarity face hard days as they struggle against tremendous odds to nudge Poland toward a system of genuine economic and political democracy.[65]

Solidarity prevailed, and the Polish government recognized the union as a legal organization. Kirkland and Higgins traveled to Poland in late August 1990 to celebrate Solidarity's tenth anniversary. The opening ceremony was held in the conference room of the Gdansk shipyard, the room where the government had capitulated to striking workers' demands. Lech Walesa and Prime Minister Tadeusz Mazowiecki spoke. Lane Kirkland and several other international trade union leaders offered their greetings. On the second day a dozen Polish bishops celebrated a Mass at the foot of the monument that Solidarity had built to honor the workers whom security forces had killed during the first abortive uprising in 1970. In the *Yardstick* column of October 1, 1990, Higgins proudly reported on his participation on the second day:

> Before Mass I had the honor of blessing a commemorative plaque which Kirkland implanted in an adjacent wall as the American labor movement's tribute to the martyred workers. In his address Kirkland stressed Solidarity's beginnings as a trade union movement and its present responsibility . . . to represent the interests of Polish workers as their nation begins to dismantle the communist state-controlled economic system and moves toward a market-oriented system. This transition will bring great hardship to Polish workers—at least in the short run. In fact, it has already adversely affected their miserably low standard of living.[66]

Despite the hardships and the sacrifices that Polish workers had endured, the story of Solidarity's birth, development, and recognition was truly a historic witness to the power of truth and justice. The *Yardstick* column, quoting from Professor Roman Laba's book *The Roots of Solidarity*, commented on the role that nonviolence played in the Solidarity movement:

> Professor Laba is particularly eloquent . . . in his treatment of Solidarity's unswerving commitment to non-violence. "Solidarity . . . stands out in comparison with other political movements . . . by virtue of its symbolic disinterest in the enemy. No other characteristic shows as clearly the movement's moral renewal [and] concern. To hate the enemy, to vilify him, was to risk becoming like him. . . . The lack of aggression, the lack of a symbolic portrayal of the enemy is a remarkable aspect of the Solidarity movement. This apparently was an

> important part of Solidarity's political strategy. By ignoring its enemy, the party-state, it acted as if it were free rather than locked in a life-and-death struggle." . . . History will judge that Solidarity's deeply held commitment to non-violence, its foreswearing of vengeance of any kind, its openness to negotiation, dialogue, and witness to the truth, and its almost superhuman respect for the dignity even of the "enemy" constitute its most important and most enduring legacy. . . . The Solidarity movement is unique in this respect among all the revolutions of recent centuries.[67]

The Church and Social Justice

Higgins welcomed the publication of U.S. bishops' pastoral letters *The Challenge of Peace* (1983) and *Economic Justice for All* (1986) and the papal encyclicals issued between 1981 and 1991. The latter analyzed the social, political, and economic reality on the global level; it grounded Catholic social doctrine in an authentic anthropology; it offered a prophetic stance against unjust and oppressive economic and political systems; and it provided a theological vision for a new world order. *Laborens Exercens* (1981), the encyclical on human work, commemorated the ninetieth anniversary of *Rerum Novarum*.[68] Its publication coincided with the rise of Solidarity as the principal agent of social transformation in Poland. It influenced Catholic social teaching on the meaning of human work and the indispensable necessity of free democratic labor movements. *Solicitudo Rei Socialis* (1987) was written to commemorate the twentieth anniversary of *Populorum Progressio*, the encyclical that Pope Paul VI had issued on development. It treats the economic and social aspects of development, investigates international politics, and gives a critical examination of the economic structures of Western civilization. Pope John Paul II indicated that true development was a vocation, a process within the human being, and an expression of a moral dynamic. The document spoke about the human solidarity that bound all peoples together. It viewed the "other" not as a unit of work or as a threat but as a neighbor with whom one shares the banquet of life.[69] The encyclical combined ethics and spirituality. In defining how Christians should act in the world, it acknowledged the role of orthopraxis for the Christian life. This represented a significant paradigm shift in Catholic social teaching. The *Yardstick* discussed this shift in the column for May 18, 1991.

> Msgr. Pietro Pavan . . . describes Paul's style this way. "Nothing has changed except that we have moved from theory to practice, that is, we no longer make deductions from abstract principles, but we observe reality, for this is where we have discovered that the gospel potential is."
>
> Perhaps even closer to the mark is the observation of Father Marie Dominique Chenu: "Nothing has changed, and yet everything has changed. The pluralism that is henceforth to be regarded as the norm is not merely a conse-

> quence of the diverse situations in which Christians find themselves in the world. It is also a matter of principle, stemming from the very nature of the church which defines itself in terms of its presence in the world and not as an institution endowed with absolute reality. The world is the place where the Christian discerns the appeals of the Gospel."[70]

Centissimus Annus, issued on May 1, 1991, commemorated the one-hundredth anniversary of *Rerum Novarum*. It investigated the economic and political transformations that were sweeping Eastern Europe and other parts of the world in 1989. It offered a moral and theological reflection on capitalism and democracy and on socialism and totalitarianism. It also treated the role that the economy plays in a society and in the authority of the state. The three encyclicals are a papal rereading of Catholic social teaching in light of current events and a century's development of Catholic social doctrine.

The *Yardstick* columns did not attempt to give a complete analysis of these documents. Instead, Higgins picked salient points in the documents and related them to contemporary issues, which enabled him to give his readers a set of themes for contemporary Catholic socioeconomic life. First and foremost, he affirmed the primacy of the person over things. This criterion underlay every judgement that was made regarding the value of any economic system.[71] Second, he indicated that every economic structure, policy, and decision must manifest a preferential option for the poor. Higgins rooted this theme in a few of his favorite texts from the Old and New Testaments:

> It is recorded . . . that Moses told his followers on the threshold of their entry into the Promised Land that "there will be no lack of poor men in the land that is to be thy home; I must needs warn thee, then, to be open-handed towards thy brother, thy fellow-countryman, when he is poor and in want. . . . It may be that one of thy brothers . . . will fall on evil days. Do not steel thy heart and shut thy purse against him; be generous to his poverty."
>
> Christ came into the world not to destroy the law, . . . but to perfect and fulfill it. "By this," he said, "shall all men know that you are my disciples, that you have love one for another," adding very solemnly . . . that on the last day our love of God will be measured strictly by the degree to which we have ministered—or failed to minister—to the material as well as the spiritual needs of our neighbor. "Believe me," the Lord will say to each of us on the final day of judgment, "when you did it to one of the least of my brethren here, you did it to Me," or " . . . when you refused it to one of the least of my brethren here, you refused it to Me. And these shall pass on to eternal punishment, and the just to eternal life."[72]

Higgins was aware that the poor had drifted out of national consciousness. He wanted to make the poor visible again, and he hoped to place them before his readers.

> This lack of awareness has occurred not because Americans are cruel but because they are looking the other way. It is hoped that [*Centissimus Annus*] will bring the poor back into our consciousness . . . and will prompt our nation to show a preferential option for the poor in such a way as to empower them to take control of their own lives and to participate fully in the economic and political decisions which affect their economic welfare. This is demanded of all of us as a matter of strict justice, not merely as an expression of paternalistic charity.[73]

Third, work is an expression of the Christian vocation in the world. All work, including manual work, is an expression of human dignity and humanity's partnership with God the creator. The purpose of work and the goal of companies and unions are to give people better lives.[74] Fourth, the vocation of the worker and the authentic meaning of work are protected, preserved, and enhanced through the labor movement. Unions are places where people can express themselves, serve the development of an authentic culture of work, and help workers to share in the life of the workplace. Papal social teaching was calling for new experiments in comanagement and coownership and a role for unions that went beyond their limited position in traditional collective bargaining.

> Lip service in support of [a strong and effective labor movement] is not enough. The time has come for Catholic conservatives and neoconservatives to take the lead in persuading the rest of the conservative and neoconservative community . . . to change course and belatedly come out loud and clear in support of the legitimate goals of organized labor.[75]

The *Yardstick* columns addressed the relationship of spirituality to social action.[76] First, Higgins reminded his readers that the early pioneers in the labor movement had invested Labor Day with religious significance. "All things considered, however, these early labor leaders were on the side of the angels. They started a good tradition which, to their own disappointment, was slow in developing, but is now experiencing a revival."[77]

Higgins suggested that Catholic parishes needed to offer more than an annual Labor Day Mass. He proposed "a continuing program of religious education to convince workers and employers of the importance of communal worship in their daily lives and to show them the connection between the liturgy and social action."[78] A new social order depended on a genuine spiritual renewal. Higgins, like many of his mentors and contemporaries in the church, appreciated that liturgy and social action were two sides of the same coin, distinct but complementary aspects of the work and worship of the mystical body of Christ.

> It is the Mass that matters most even in the political order, for the Mass is the primary source of asceticism and penance, without which there can be no conversion from human selfishness or sin, and no redemption either of individuals or the temporal order.[79]

Economic Justice for All brought liturgy and social action together when it considered the Christian vocation in the world.

> When Christians come together in prayer, they make a commitment to carry God's love into all . . . areas of life.
>
> The unity of work and worship finds expression in a unique way in the Eucharist. As people of a new covenant, the faithful hear God's challenging word proclaimed to them—a message of hope to the poor and oppressed—and they call upon the Holy Spirit to unite all into the one body of Christ. For the Eucharist to be a living promise of the fullness of God's Kingdom, the faithful must commit themselves to living as redeemed people with the same care and love for all people that Jesus showed. The body of Christ which worshipers receive in Communion is also a reminder of the reconciling power of his death on the Cross. It empowers them to work to heal the brokenness of society and human relationships and to grow in a spirit of self-giving for others. . . .
>
> In worship and in deeds for justice, the Church becomes a "sacrament," a visible sign of that unity in justice and peace that God wills for the whole of humanity.[80]

Higgins wanted to keep the liturgy and social action together. The church had kept them together in the first half of the 20th century, especially between 1930 and 1950, when the church gave the labor problem special attention.[81] He also wanted to keep social action and the church's ministry and mission together. He feared that as the church concentrated on other social problems, it might lose its tradition as well as its deep sympathy for working people and their unions.[82] He hoped that the hierarchy would continue to act as political prophets and a voice for justice and that the priests would remain active in direct social action.[83] He thought that the social apostolate was a constitutive part of priestly life and ministry, especially in evangelizing and preaching and in helping the church remember the anguished cry of those who experienced injustice and suffering. He also thought that the clergy should work with the laity, encouraging its work in social action and education.[84] Quoting from the writing of Cardinal Joseph Bernardin, Higgins supported efforts to develop programs that would help the laity in carrying out its specific and indispensable ministry:

> Despite today's enormously increased interest in lay ministry, . . . we have scarcely begun to tap its rich potential. Bearing in mind that the primary field

for the exercise of lay ministry is in the workaday world, its possibilities within the church are vast. The laity's specific role is not to serve the church in an institutional sense, but the world. They share in Christ's priesthood and are charged with the responsibility of bringing the message of the Gospel to the world.[85]

Unions in Catholic Institutions

Is the church a just employer? Does it practice what it preaches? Does it honor workers' rights to organize in its own institutions? The answer to these questions would determine the credibility of the church and of Higgins, too. The *Yardstick* columns that addressed these questions were among the most direct and forceful columns that Higgins wrote. The *Yardstick* column for November 5, 1990, set the record straight:

> In the 45 years I have been writing this column I have received my fair share of letters saying I was dead wrong about some matter. While I can't say I enjoy receiving them, they are better than the ones that charge me with hypocrisy for writing about workers' rights while remaining silent about workers' rights to organize in Catholic institutions. These complaints are frustrating because I have, in fact, written many columns pointing out . . . that all the moral principles that govern the just operation of any economic endeavor apply to the church and its agencies and institutions. Indeed, the church should be exemplary.[86]

Higgins' record on this issue was unflinchingly consistent through the years. Early in his *Yardstick* career, he wrote in support of the fundamental human right of every worker to organize, if she or he so chooses, for the purpose of collective bargaining. His position, originally derived from *Rerum Novarum* and *Quadragesimo Anno*, was further amplified and reinforced at the 1971 Synod of Bishops. The synod's final document, *Justice in the World*, stated that the church would be credible in its proclamation of social justice to the degree that it practiced social justice in church-related institutions. This idea reaffirmed Higgins' own lifelong conviction. His position was consistently and unequivocally clear:

> Any attempt to circumvent or interfere with the free exercise of this right will predictably lead to serious trouble—the kind that could divide the Catholic community for years to come and neutralize the effectiveness of ongoing church-related programs of social justice both at home and abroad. One of the greatest mistakes made by American industry 50 years ago—when industrial unionism was coming into its own—was that it completely underestimated the intelligence, the determination, the skill, and the drive of the workers it was dealing with. Catholic institutions, for ethical as well as practical reasons, will want to avoid making the same mistake.[87]

During these years Higgins was sought out as a consultant by nurses and other employees of Catholic hospitals. In his correspondence with Catholic nurses, employees, and officials in Catholic chanceries, he pointed out that Catholic institutions had an obligation to follow the church's own social teaching. He denounced Catholic hospital administrators for hiring union-busting agencies that intimidated workers with antiunion memos, threatened their physical well-being and safety, and thwarted their efforts to form unions. Similarly, the *Yardstick* condemned efforts to eliminate or decertify existing unions or hire replacements for union nurses.

> These nurses have a right to feel insulted when they are told in a hospital bulletin that the hospital "would be better off without them" and are urged to go to work in a hospital already covered by a [union] contract. It is hard to square such rhetoric with the hospital's claim to be dedicated to compassion, hospitality, and commitment to service. It is also hard to square it with the U.S. bishops pastoral on the economy, which says: "All church institutions must . . . fully recognize the rights of employees to organize and bargain collectively with the institution in whatever association or organization they freely choose."[88]

His language was particularly critical of women's religious communities and nun-administrators who opposed Catholic laywomen who sought to unionize. He regretted the antipathy and hostility that was developing between religious women and laywomen. The *Yardstick* recommended that leaders of women's communities and the national leadership conferences discuss and resolve these issues quickly. "Isn't it time for the religious orders of women who own and operate the majority of Catholic hospitals to address this problem head-on and to get serious about resolving it?"[89] Higgins was equally supportive of Catholic teachers and their unions.

> In my view, strong teachers' unions, given a willingness on the part of school administrators to cooperate with them in good faith, can make a significant contribution to the betterment of the entire Catholic school system. Many of their officers, I know, are willing and anxious to do that. What I'd like to see are some interviews with the officers of the Catholic teachers' unions, affording them an opportunity to speak for themselves and for the teachers they have been elected to represent.[90]

Higgins' forthright and courageous support for workers and their unions in Catholic institutions was exemplary through the years. Sometimes his voice seemed to be the only voice. But his voice was effective in obtaining economic citizenship for Catholic employees, and he made the church credible in the workplace.

Catholic–Jewish Relations

Higgins continued to remain active in Catholic–Jewish relations through the 1980s and 1990s.[91] When he observed his fiftieth anniversary of ordination to the priesthood, he said:

> The occasion prompted me to recall some of the more important changes in the life of the church during the past half century and, more specifically, since Vatican Council II. I would put the improved relationship between the church and Judaism very near the top of the list. . . . [I] consider it a great grace to have had the opportunity to be involved in the post Vatican II Catholic-Jewish dialogue.[92]

Higgins hoped that the relationship between Catholics and Jews would continue to enrich the church in its self-understanding, that it would bless the world and serve as a model of collaboration.[93] The goal of Catholic–Jewish dialogue, according to Higgins, was "a common witness to the world, based on the vision we share of the kingdom of God."[94] Higgins remained committed to the dialogue despite the stridently anti-Semitic letters he received from some of his readers. In many ways, he continued to expose the dangers of anti-Semitism and to promote a positive appreciation of Jews and Judaism in Catholic preaching, drama, and religious education.[95]

Allies and Adversaries

Higgins wrote several *Yardstick* columns about people whose lives had intersected with his own and whose commitments had contributed to social justice.[96] Some of the columns were eulogies and memorial pieces; others were encomiums for people he admired. The *Yardstick* revealed Higgins' openness to people of diverse backgrounds and their insights. These included Arthur Goldberg and Rabbi Marc Tannenbaum, Bayard Rustin, Martin Luther King Jr., Roy Wilkins, Michael Harrington, and Charles Owen Rice. Higgins also wrote in memory of John A. Ryan, John Courtney Murray, Luigi Ligutti, Reinhold Niebuhr, Cesar Chavez, and Walter Reuther. Higgins held fellow labor priests and activists in great esteem. The *Yardstick* column for July 23, 1984, remembered the work of two Jesuits, John M. Corridon and Mortimer H. Gavin, who had died within days of each other. Corridon was described as "extremely affable, but fearless and tough as nails."[97] He had risked his life to bring about needed labor–management reforms in hiring on the New York docks. Gavin, a former truck driver and amateur boxer, was "a burly bear of a man with a heart of gold, a man of great good cheer and boundless compassion."[98] Higgins praised Gavin for his work with the Boston Labor Guild and with the Industrial Relations School, the last of its kind in the United States. The school still provides courses in labor history; economics; and social ethics for union officials, management representatives, lawyers, teachers, and government officials. Gavin served as a mediator and troubleshooter in several New England labor–management disputes. Higgins wrote:

> People took to him immediately and trusted him instinctively as a person of integrity and fairness. Commonly described as a "labor priest," Father Gavin preferred to be known as a labor-management priest. . . . Though different in some respects, these two priests were in many ways two of a kind. Unfortunately they were among the last of what appears to be a dying breed. We are all going to miss them very much. May they rest in peace.[99]

Higgins also lamented the death of Monsignor Geno Baroni, an innovative and effective social activist in Washington, DC. Baroni had a "genius for building community [and] . . . for getting people of different racial, ethnic, and religious background to recognize common interests and work together to solve common problems."[100] He had helped to effect change through an interracial program of political and social reform. Higgins was deeply moved by his funeral.

> His funeral Mass, held in a black Washington neighborhood, was symbolic evidence that both groups understood his message and appreciated his leadership. Never have I seen such a multiethnic, multiracial, multiple congregation in a church or anywhere else. The presence of so many people of such different backgrounds jointly and joyfully celebrating Geno's life and death—and their own unity of purpose—would have gladdened his heart.[101]

When Higgins preached at the memorial Mass for Dorothy Day in New York in January 1981, he was reticent to propose her for canonization as a saint. However, by 1983, Higgins had changed his mind. The *Yardstick* described her as a sacrament, a sign of mediating grace to those she served. Taking a frequently quoted text from Isaiah and the Gospel of Saint Luke, Higgins wrote:

> Miss Day was a true sign of God after the example of Christ himself, anointed . . . "to preach good news to the poor, to proclaim release to the captives and recovering of sight to the blind, to set at liberty those who were oppressed, to proclaim the acceptable year of the Lord."[102]

Day, Higgins acknowledged, had enabled the poor to see, know, and love God. "She was a pure gift to his church."[103] She persevered in her service to the poor because she had kept the failure of the cross in mind and followed Christ by serving the poor. "She did so heroically . . . 'with a joy that made her want to kiss the earth in worship, because his feet once trod the same earth.'"[104]

Higgins continued to critique interpretations of Catholic social teaching contained in *The Wanderer*. He seriously considered the work of conservative Catholic scholars, such as Richard John Neuhaus and Michael Novak.[105] The *Yardstick* column for December 10, 1984, reported on the scholarly letter on the U.S. economy written by Novak and William Simon: "Toward the Future: Catholic Social Thought and the U.S. Economy." Their letter proposed an alternative reading to the market capitalism of the U.S. economic system. Higgins complimented them for their section on unions. The letter affirmed the rights, legitimacy, and social role of labor unions and applauded labor's historic contribution to democracy's cause. It acknowledged the difficulties that the labor movement had faced in recent years, and it suggested a new era of labor–management cooperation.

> To the best of my knowledge no comparable new-conservative group has come out as explicitly as this letter in favor of labor-law reform. On this and on protecting legitimate interests of U.S. workers adversely affected by foreign competition, the Simon-Novak letter compares favorably with—in some respects I find it better than—sections of the pastoral dealing with the same issues.[106]

Higgins applauded Simon, Novak, and their committee for their positive treatment of the union question. He was critical, however, of another letter: "Roman Catholicism and American Capitalism: Friends or Foes?" The letter, written by Father Enrique Rueda, was uncritically and blatantly antiunion.

Higgins continued to monitor the situation in Catholic hospitals, especially when administrations denied employees the right to unionize or attempted to devalue or discredit unions already in existence. Higgins was genuinely surprised and scandalized that administrators in Catholic hospitals, especially nun-administrators, would act in such obvious opposition to Catholic social teaching. He unequivocally demanded that individual religious communities and the leadership conferences of religious women evaluate their position and, where necessary, change their practice. The credibility and integrity of Catholic health care and the church's mission for social justice were at stake.

Conclusion

Profound religious, social, economic, and political change occurred in the United States in the 1980s and 1990s. The American Catholic bishops studied, listened, and developed their social teachings on war, on nuclear arms and peace, and on the economic life of the nation. The *Labor Day Statements* and the *Yardstick* columns addressed the significance of work, the vocation of workers, the decline of union membership, downsizing, unemployment, workplace relocations, and the human and moral aspects of these issues. Higgins and the *LDSs* focused deeply on two concomitant movements: on one hand, the international nature of the economy and the globalization of industry and, on the other, the local economies that affected the lives of individuals and families in every region, nation, and neighborhood. As the bishops pointed out in the *LDSs*, the United States was increasingly becoming a nation with three classes: a small but powerful group of people with wealth, power, and prestige; a poor, powerless, and permanent underclass; and an anxious, overworked, and worried middle class. Furthermore, economic issues were increasingly becoming transnational and international due to technology and communications.

Higgins devoted his attention to issues that had been the warp and woof of his social theology. These included the continuing decline of union membership, the revitalization of the labor movement, the relationship of organized labor in the United States with other labor movements (such as Solidarity in Poland), and the need to strengthen collective bargaining as the best available pathway to worker justice. Higgins' social theology was deeply attentive to the cry of the poor, especially the nation's farmworkers; minority and marginal workers, such as janitors and other service employees; and the needs of women, especially mothers, in the workforce. While anchoring his social theology in foundational and classical social principles, such as the value of the human person and the common good, Higgins continued to turn more deeply toward a praxis methodology in the *Yardstick* columns. He was continually correlating principles and practice, social justice and social charity. This was especially evident in the columns he wrote about the unionization of Catholic institutions. His critique of Catholic institutions revealed his granite-like integrity, and it was the most significant development of his social theology in this period.

Higgins remained optimistic during these very difficult years. He firmly believed that Gospel values would prevail and that time was on the side of those who espoused justice and truth. In light of this spirit of hope and optimism, Higgins had applauded the efforts of the SEIU to organize new immigrants and obtain workplace justice for service employees. He was encouraged by the new initiatives of the AFL-CIO under the presidency of John Sweeney. Higgins firmly believed that the benefits that union workers won and the contributions that unions made to the common good redounded to the well-being of all working people. During these years his words and deeds encouraged members of the laity to carry out their mission in the marketplace and the public square. He continued to suggest and support programs that formed the laity and developed their skills in public ministry. His notion of partnership, as noted in the conclusion of chapter four, expanded into a sense of solidarity. Solidarity, with its roots in the political sphere, gradually became the new cardinal virtue for the spirituality of the 21st century.

The Contribution of George G. Higgins

Soon after his ordination in 1940, Father George Gilmary Higgins set out for Washington, DC. He began graduate studies at the Catholic University of America. After he was awarded the doctoral degree, he fully expected to return to an assignment in the archdiocese of Chicago. This never happened. Higgins remained in Washington and became a so-called bureaucrat in the church's social apostolate. In many ways, he was a link between a storied past, extending back to the pioneers in the social apostolate, and a complex, ever-changing future. What were his contributions as a public intellectual to the social mission of the church and the social capital of the country? What significance did his social teaching have? What will remain as his legacy for the world in the 21st century? This conclusion elucidates Monsignor Higgins' contribution in three areas. First, it considers his work in Catholic journalism and his role in informing, educating, and promoting the church's social teaching for several generations of Catholic activists. Second, it summarizes the salient themes of his social teaching and its relevance for the workplace and the public square. Third, it addresses the personal witness that Higgins gave to the church and the country, as well as its meaning for the Catholic priesthood and its pastoral mission.

Higgins the Journalist

Higgins wrote a weekly *Yardstick* column for fifty-six years. In itself, this was a remarkable contribution to Catholic journalism. The column educated his readers about the social order and their place in it. Higgins drew from many perspectives and diverse intellectual disciplines. Each *Yardstick* column aimed at objectivity and fairness. Many columns offered information and insights drawn from Catholic social teaching. He gave his readers principles to reflect on and then showed them how to apply them practically. He attempted to persuade with the beauty and the cogency of truth. Known as the labor priest, Higgins suggested ways in which his readers could participate in the social mission of the church according to their own personal charism and vocation. In many ways, the *Yardstick* built bridges between sociology, economics, labor history, labor–management studies, and allied fields on the one hand and the church's magisterium on the other. In his early columns Higgins manifested an ability to move from theory to practice, from principles to applications. He manifested this ability throughout his entire writing career. But as his horizons broadened and his insights deepened, he moved toward an action-based thought, an American-styled orthopraxis. The narratives of working people, the poor, and the marginalized became as normative for his social theology as the principles of Catholic social teaching and the themes of the inherited tradition. Higgins moved back and forth from the world of labor leaders, the rank and file, and the poor to the world of politics, analysis, and thought. The *Yardstick* columns built bridges between the church and the world, between the sanctuary and the marketplace. All of the *Yardstick* columns were public documents for a public church involved in the public square. Their goal and purpose were more than education and information. The *Yardstick* intended to foster in its readers a conversion of mind and heart. Higgins the journalist wanted to motivate others to an orthopathy through lives committed to social and worker justice and the creation of a just and compassionate world.

It is difficult to estimate the impact that the *Yardstick* columns have had on the Catholic community. The Catholic News Service did not keep records or conduct surveys to determine the effectiveness of the column. But, if one can judge its effectiveness from the lives and involvements of Catholic activists over several generations, and if one can gauge its value on the accolades that Higgins has received and the esteem in which he was held, then it can be said that the *Yardstick* columns have influenced its readers significantly. The column's longevity also suggests that it is a legitimate *locus theologicus*. While not offering the space for depth and the methodological discipline required in writing a scholarly book, the newspaper column does require a robust intellectual life and a professional discipline. It allows public intellectuals, theologians, and serious thinkers the opportunity to present theological themes and to relate them to diverse narratives, cultures, and social settings. In addition, the *Yardstick* kept the church from social amnesia. Columns on organized labor, poverty, unemployment, Catholic–Jewish relations, racism, and the plight of working people forced readers to address economic injustice, anti-Semitism, racism, and xenophobia in society.

Higgins the Social Teacher

The *Yardstick* columns present Higgins' contribution to Catholic social teaching, which consists of four interlocking ideas: the dignity of the human person, the common good, the desire to build community, and participation in decision making. The starting point is the dignity and value, the worth and human rights of the person. Every person bears the imprint of the divine image. Every person desires her or his own good and the common good. As a naturally social being, every person wants a voice in one's job, community, and country. Every person wants to form associations that will enhance their voice and empower them in decision making. Higgins called this empowerment *economic citizenship*. Having a job is a sign of personal dignity, and it gives a voice in the other spheres of society. In the workplace, economic citizenship is protected by strong, free, and democratic unions. Unions help their members to acquire a voice, and they teach them the values and the virtues that are necessary for public life. They equip their members with the skills necessary for a just and harmonious society. Therefore, labor–management relations, the process of collective bargaining, and other forms of dialogue and negotiation are not ends in themselves but the means that move people beyond antagonism and competition. Styles of cooperation and collaboration in labor–management relations can give union members alternative models for a healthy democracy. Ultimately, the goal of Higgins' social teaching was to restore all things in Christ and to create a just, happy, and wholesome social order.

Higgins built on a traditional theological anthropology of sin and grace and on a classical, albeit Biblically rooted ecclesiology. The human person must freely choose either to build community, encourage participation, and create structures of cooperation or turn the other way, retreat into self-serving individualism, and cultivate greed and self-interest. Persons in communities can refuse to build bonds with others and can remain apathetic, indifferent, and uninvolved. Organizations such as unions and the church can be weakened by corruption and dishonesty. Negative and destructive attitudes, actions, and structures are examples of personal and systemic sins. The way to overcome systems and circles of sin is to belong to a redemptive community. For Christians, the redemptive community is the church. Higgins' ecclesiology, rooted in the Pauline metaphor of the body of Christ, is the mystical body. Each part of the body has a role to play and a function to perform for the good of the whole. The church sees the pathos of God in the parts of the body that are poor and downtrodden. Its social apostolate reaches out to working women, farmworkers, racial minorities, and the marginalized to invite their participation in building the kingdom of God. The necessary spiritual nourishment is provided at the Lord's table. Higgins kept liturgy and social action together.

Similarly, he did not buttress his social teaching with scriptural prooftexts. Biblical stories and images were presented more by innuendo than explicit quotation. In fact, the *Yardstick* columns employed language taken from the natural law tradition and the common sense tradition of religion as it was actually lived in America. Higgins, in the tradition of Thomas J. Bouquillon, William J. Kerby, and John A. Ryan, looked to the empirical sciences and to the testimony of individuals and redemptive communities who engaged the powers and the principalities in the struggle for social and workers' justice.

Higgins the Priest

Higgins did not live the life of a parish priest. He was a bureaucrat, a professional churchman. He was loyal to the institutional church and appreciated its power for change and human betterment. His participation at the Second Vatican Council and at the Synod of Bishops broadened his horizons, expanded his social theology, and brought him to new commitments. This was evident in his *Yardstick* columns on racism, poverty, Catholic–Jewish relations, the role of the laity, and the application of the principles of social justice to the church's own institutional structures. His involvement with African Americans in the labor movement enabled him to appreciate the impact of racism on the working poor. His social teaching promoted racial equality and cooperation between ethnic whites and African Americans in Washington, DC, and in other cities. His work with Cesar Chavez, Dolores Huerta, and the UFW helped him become a prophetic voice for justice on behalf of the nation's farmworkers. He called for labor–management cooperation in California, Arizona, Texas, and Florida; the support of UFW boycotts; the end of the bracero program; and the passage of legislation to provide healthy working and sanitation conditions for farmworkers. His life in Washington, DC, his contact with minority workers at the United States Catholic Conference, and his presence among the rank and file at labor meetings and conventions taught him that the church and organized labor provided religious and social capital for the nation's well-being. His social teaching envisioned a new alliance between church and labor. His support for the workers in Catholic hospitals and schools, as well as his involvement with Solidarity, strengthened his courage and kindled his hope. His social thinking reflected the conviction that the credibility of the church rested on its ability to practice what it preached. Higgins maintained an optimism, even when organized labor had reached its nadir and others had written its obituary. His support for organized labor was never based on the number of people who belonged to unions. It was based on his theological conviction that unions were indispensable for a democratic society.

Higgins' life and ministry were spent in the marketplace and the public square. He served at the Lord's table and at the negotiation table. He devoted years to the UAW's PRB and the UFW's Martin Luther King Jr. board. He was a witness of Gospel values and an advocate for social justice. He often said that he tried to be a presence. His presence manifested his integrity and fairness, his honesty and truthfulness. Higgins modeled the qualities that priests of the present and future church need. These include:

- a dedication to a life of serious study in theological and related sciences;
- a commitment to encouraging the ministry of the laity and to supporting their formation and education;
- a dedication to the social apostolate through presence, preaching, and prayer so that the church will not forget its social mission;
- a willingness to provide pastoral care for all people, especially the new immigrants, working people, business people, and the poor;
- a lived experience of a liturgical spirituality, especially manifested in a love for the Eucharist, and the courage to keep liturgy and social action together; and
- an optimism and a hope, combined with a sense of humility, that the Spirit of God is still making a new heaven and a new earth.

Higgins stood on the side of the poor. The words of Barbara Ehrenreich could easily have appeared in a *Yardstick* column.

> The working poor, as they are approvingly termed, are in fact the major philanthropists of our society. They neglect their own children so that the children of others will be cared for; they live in substandard housing so that other

> homes will be shiny and perfect; they endure privation so that inflation will be low and stock prices high. To be a member of the working poor is to be an anonymous donor, a nameless benefactor, to everyone else. As Gail, one of my restaurant coworkers puts it, "You give and you give."[1]

Higgins spent his entire life on the side of the working poor. He was a man of granite-like integrity. He was on the side of the angels. May his tribe increase! May God invite him to come up higher at the heavenly table! Someday we shall see him again when we all shall meet merrily in paradise!

APPENDIX A

The Literature on Civil Religion

The literature on civil religion began with a seminal article by Robert N. Bellah, a sociologist at the University of California. "Civil Religion in America" (*Daedalus* 96 [1967]: 1–21) kindled discussion about the religious and mythic origins of the United States. His *The Broken Covenant, American Civil Religion in Time of Trial* (New York: Seabury Press, 1975) addressed the crisis that civil religion faced at the time of the nation's bicentennial and in the wake of the Vietnam War and the Watergate scandal. The inquiry continued in "Religion and the Legitimation of the American Republic" (in *Varieties of Civil Religion*, edited by Robert N. Bellah and Philip E. Hammond [San Francisco: Harper and Row, 1980]); "The Quest for the Self" (*Philosophy and Theology* 2 [1988]: 374–86); "Religion and the Shape of National Culture" (*America* 181 [August 7, 1999]: 9–14); and "Is There a Common American Culture? Diversity, Identity and Morality in American Public Life" (in *The Power of Religious Publics, Staking Claims in American Society*, ed. William H. Swatos and James K. Wellman [Westport, Conn.: Praeger, 1999], 53–67). Two books brought the discussion further onto center stage, both by Robert N. Bellah, Richard Madsen, William M. Sullivan, Ann Swidler, and Steven M. Tipton: *Habits of the Heart: Individualism and Commitment in American Life* ([Berkeley: University of California Press, 1985], 27–51 and 275–96); and *The Good Society* ([New York: Alfred A. Knopf, 1991], 179–253).

A number of scholars investigated the issue of civil religion vis-à-vis contemporary U.S. culture, such as Philip E. Hammond, "Constitutional Faith, Legitimating Myth, Civil Religion" (*Law and Social Inquiry* 44 [1989]: 377–91); and Brian O'Connor, *Civil Religion: The Underpinnings of American*

Democracy (Hanover, N.H.: Tufts University Press, 1999). See also Ronald E. Richey and Donald G. Jones, *American Civil Religion* (New York: Harper and Row, 1974); and Leroy S. Rouner, "To Be at Home: Civil Religion as Common Bond" (in *Civil Religion and Political Theology*, ed. Leroy S. Rouner [Notre Dame, Ind.: University of Notre Dame Press, 1986], 125–37). Two recent encyclopedia entries, though brief, are helpful: Ronald C. Wimberley and William H. Swatos Jr., "Civil Religion" (in *Encyclopedia of Religion and Society*, ed. William H. Swatos Jr. [Walnut Creek, Calif.: AltaMira Press, 1998], 94–960); and Robert Wuthnow, "Civil Religion" (in *The Encyclopedia of Politics and Religion*, ed. Robert Wuthnow [Washington, DC: Congressional Quarterly, 1998], 153–57). Also insightful and valuable is the work by James E. Wood Jr., "Public Religion vis-à-vis the Prophetic Role in Religion" (in *The Power of Religious Publics, Striking Claims in American Society*, ed. William H. Swatos and James K. Wellman [Westport, Conn.: Praeger, 1999], 33–51); and Robert Wuthnow, *Christianity and Civil Society: The Contemporary Debate* (Valley Forge, Penn.: Trinity Press International, 1997).

APPENDIX B

The Literature on Public Religion

Martin E. Marty, the distinguished church historian at the University of Chicago, popularized the idea of public church and public theology. He defined the concept and indicated its interdenominational constituency in *The Public Church* (New York: Crossroad, 1981). He continued the discussion in his book *The One and the Many: America's Struggle with the Common Good* (Cambridge, Mass.: Harvard University Press, 1997); and in his contribution "Public Religion" in *Encyclopedia of Religion and Society* (ed. William H. Swatos Jr. [Walnut Creek, Calif.: AltaMira Press, 1998], 393–94). He expanded his interest in this topic through his involvement with the public religion project.

Other scholars have contributed to the discussion about public religion, public theology, and public church. These include Jose Casanova, *Public Religion in the Modern World* (Chicago: University of Chicago, 1994); and Linell E. Cady, "H. Richard Niebuhr and the Task of a Public Theology" (in *The Legacy of H. Richard Niebuhr*, ed. Ronald E. Thiemann [Minneapolis, Minn.: Fortress Press, 1991], 107–29). See also the work of J. Bryan Hehir: "The Public Church: The Implications of Structural Pluralism" (*Origins* 14 [May 31, 1984]: 40–43); "The Discipline and Dynamic of a Public Church" (*Social Thought* 11 [1985]: 4–8); and "Forum: Public Theology in Contemporary America" (*Religion and American Culture* 10 [2000]: 20–27).

Philip E. Hammond, *With Liberty for All: Freedom of Religion in the United States* ([Louisville, Ky.: Westminster / John Knox Press, 1998], 96–111), is very helpful. Richard John Neuhaus first investigated the role of religion in the public square in *Time toward Home: The American Experiment in Revela-*

tion (New York: Seabury Press, 1975). He then developed his thought in *The Naked Public Square: Religion and Democracy in America* (2nd ed., [Grand Rapids, Mich.: Eerdmans, 1995]). Three essays by two contemporary Catholic moral theologians are helpful: John Pawlikowski, "The American Catholic Church as a Public Church" (*New Theology Review* 1 [1988]: 7–29); David Hollenbach, "Public Theology in America: Some Questions for Catholicism after John Courtney Murray" (*Theological Studies* 37 [1976]: 290–303); and Hollenbach, "Catholics as Citizens: Pastoral Challenges and Opportunities" (*Logos* 3 [2000]: 57–69).

The finest treatment of public theology is contained in Michael J. Himes and Kenneth R. Himes, *Fullness of Faith: The Public Significance of Theology* (New York: Paulist Press, 1993); Ronald E. Thiemann, *Constructing a Public Theology: The Church in a Pluralistic Culture* (Louisville, Ky.: Westminster / John Knox Press, 1991); Thiemann, *Religion in Public Life* (Washington, DC: Georgetown University Press, 1996); and Thiemann, "Public Religion: Bane or Blessing for Democracy?" (in *Obligations of Citizenship and Demands of Faith, Religious Accommodation in Pluralist Democracies*, ed. Nancy L. Rosenblum [Princeton, N.J.: Princeton University Press, 2000], 73–89).

Finally, two works relate public religion and public theology to the U.S. context: John F. Wilson, *Public Religion in American Culture* (Philadelphia: Temple University Press, 1979); and Steven M. Tipton, "Public Theology" (in *The Encyclopedia of Politics and Religion*, ed. Robert Wuthnow [Washington, DC: Congressional Quarterly, 1998], 624–28).

APPENDIX C

Cardinal Gibbons' Defense of the Knights of Labor, February 20, 1887

Your Eminence:

In submitting to the Holy See the conclusion which after several months of attentive observation and reflection, seem to me to sum up the truth concerning the association of the Knights of Labor, I feel profoundly convinced of the vast importance of the consequences attaching to this question, which forms but a link in the great chain of the social problem of our day, and especially of our country.

In weighing [treating—*jugeant*] this question I have been very careful to follow as my constant guide the spirit of the Encyclicals in which our Holy Father, Leo XIII, has so admirably set forth the dangers of our time and their remedies, as well as the principles by which we are to recognize association condemned by the Holy See. Such was also the guide of the Third Plenary Council of Baltimore in its teaching concerning the principles to be followed and the dangers to be shunned by the faithful either in the choice or in the establishment of those associations toward which the spirit of our popular institutions so strongly impels them. And considering the dire consequences that might result from a mistake in the treatment of organizations which often count their numbers by the thousands and hundred of thousands, the council wisely ordained (n. 225) that when an association is spread over several dioceses, not even the bishop of one of these dioceses shall condemn it, but shall refer the case to a standing committee of all the archbishops of the United States; and even these are not authorized to condemn unless their sentences be unanimous; and in case they fail to agree unanimously, then only the supreme tribunal of the Holy See can impose a condemnation, all this in order to avoid error and confusion of discipline.

This committee of archbishops held a meeting, in fact, toward the end of last October, especially to consider the association of the Knights of Labor. We were not persuaded to hold this meeting because of any request on the part of our bishops for some of them had asked for it; and it should also be said that, among all the bishops we know, only two or three desire the condemnation. But the importance of the question in itself, and in the estimation of the Holy See led us to examine it with greatest attention. After our discussion, the results of which have already been communicated to the Sacred Congregation of the Propaganda, only two out of the twelve archbishops voted for condemnation, and their reasons were powerless to convince the others of either the justice or the prudence of such a condemnation.

In the following consideration I wish to state in detail the reasons which determined the vote of the great majority of the committee—reasons whose truth and force seem to me all the more evident today; I shall try at the same time to do justice to the segments advanced by the opposition.

1. In the first place, in the constitution, laws and official declarations of the Knights of Labor, there can clearly be found assertions and rules which we would not approve; but we have not found in them those elements so clearly pointed out by the Holy See, which places them among condemned association.
   (a) In their form of initiation there is no oath.
   (b) The obligation to secrecy by which they keep the knowledge of their business from strangers or enemies, in no wise prevents Catholics from manifesting everything to competent authority, even outside of confusion. This has been positively declared to us by their president.
   (c) They make no promise of blind obedience. The object and laws of the association are distinctly declared, and the obligation of obedience does not go beyond these limits.
   (d) They not only profess no hostility against religion or the Church, but their declarations are quite to the contrary. The Third Plenary Council commands that we should not condemn as association without giving a hearing to its officers or representatives: "auditis ducibus, corypheis vel sociis praecipuis" (n.254). Now, their president is sending me a copy of their constitution, says that he is a Catholic from the bottom of his

heart; that he practices his religion faithfully and receives the sacraments regularly; that he belongs to no Masonic or other society condemned by the Church; that he knows of nothing in the association of the Knights of Labor contrary to the laws of the Church; that, with filial submission he begs the Fathers of the Church to examine all the details of their organization, and if they find anything worthy of condemnation, they should indicate it, and he promises its correction. Assuredly one does not perceive in all this any hostility to the authority of the Church, but on the contrary a spirit, in every way praiseworthy. After their convention last year at Richmond, he and several of the offices and members, devout Catholics made similar declarations concerning their feeling and the action of that convention, the document of which we are expecting to receive.

(e) Nor do we find in this organization any hostility to the authority and laws of our country. Not only does nothing of this kind appear in their constitution and laws, but the heads of our civil government treat with the greatest respect the cause which they represent. The President of the United States told me personally, a month ago that he was then examining a law for the amelioration of certain social grievances and that he had just had a long conference on the subject with Mr. Powderly, president of the Knights of Labor. The Congress of the United States, following the advice of President Cleveland is busying itself at the present time with the amelioration of the working classes, in whose complaints they acknowledge openly there is a great deal of truth. And our political parties, far from regarding them as enemies of the country, vie with each other in championing the evident rights of the poor workmen, who seek not to resist the laws but only to obtain just legislation by constitutional and legitimate means.

These considerations, which show that in this association these elements are not to be found which the Holy See condemns, lead us to study, in the second place, the evils which the associations contend against, and the nature of the conflict.

2. That there exist, among us, as in the other countries of the world, grave and threatening social evils, public injustices, which call for strong resistance and legal remedy, is a fact which no one dares to deny, and the truth of which has been already acknowledged by the Congress and the President of the United States. Without entering into the sad details of these wrongs—which does not seem

necessary here—it may suffice to mention only that monopolies on the part of both individuals and of corporations, have already called forth not only the complaints of our working classes, but also the opposition of our public men and legislators; that the efforts of these monopolies, not always without success, to control legislation to their own profit, cause serious apprehension among the disinterested friends of liberty; that the heartless avarice which, through greed of gain, pitilessly grinds not only the men, but particularly the women and children in various employments, makes it clear to all who love humanity and justice that it is not only the right of the laboring classes to protect themselves, but the duty of the whole people to aid them in finding a remedy against the dangers with which both civilization and the social order are menaced by avarice, oppression and corruption.

It would be vain to deny either the existence of the evils, the right of legitimate resistance, or the necessity of a remedy. At most doubt might be raised about the legitimacy of the form of resistance and the remedy employed by the Knights of Labor. This then ought to be the next point of our examination.

3. It can hardly be doubted that for the attainment of any public end, association—the organization of all interested persons—is the most efficacious means, a means altogether natural and just. This is so evident, and besides so conformable to the genius of our country, of our essentially popular social conditions, that it is unnecessary to insist upon it. It is almost the only means to invite public attention, to give force to the most legitimate resistance, to add weight to the most just demands.

   Now there already exists an organization which presents a thousand attractions and advantages, but which our Catholic workingmen, with filial obedience to the Holy See, refuse to join; this is the *Masonic* organization, which exists everywhere in our country, and which, as Mr. Powderly has expressly pointed out to us, unites employer and worker in a brotherhood very advantageous for the latter, but which numbers in its ranks hardly a single Catholic. Freely renouncing the advantages which the Church and their consciences forbid, workingmen form association, having nothing in common with the deadly designs of the enemies of religion and seeking only mutual protection and help, and the legitimate assertion of their rights. But here they also find themselves threatened with condemnation, and so deprived of their only means of defense. Is it surprising that they should be astonished at this and that they ask *Why?*

4. Let us now consider the objections made against this sort of organization.
   (a) It is objected that in these organizations Catholics are mixed with Protestants, to the peril of their faith. Naturally, yes, they are mixed with Protestants in the workers' associations, precisely as they are in their work; for in a mixed people like ours, the separation of religion in social affairs is not possible. But to suppose that the faith of our Catholics suffers thereby is not to know the Catholic workers of America who are not like the workingmen of so many European countries—misguided and perverted children, looking on their Mother the Church as a hostile stepmother—but they are intelligent, well instructed and devoted children ready to give their blood, as they continually give their means (although small and hard-earned) for her support and protection. And in fact it is not in the present case that Catholics are mixed with Protestants, but rather that Protestants are admitted to the advantages of an association, two-thirds of whose members and the principal officers are Catholics; and in a country like ours their exclusion would be simple impossible.
   (b) But, it is said, could there not be substituted for such an organization confraternities which would unite the workingmen under the direction of the priests and the direct influence of religion? I answer frankly that I do not believe that either possible or necessary in our country. I sincerely admire the efforts of this sort which are made in countries where the workers are led astray by the enemies of religion; but thanks be to God, that is not our condition. We find that in our country the presence and explicit influence of the clergy would not be advisable where our citizens, without distinction of religious belief, come together in regard to their industrial interests alone. Without going so far, we have abundant means of making our working people faithful Catholics, and simple good sense advises us not to go to extremes.
   (c) Again, it is objected that the liberty of such an organization exposes Catholics to the evil influences of the most dangerous associates, even of atheists, communists, and anarchists. That is true, but is one of the trials of faith which our brave American Catholics are accustomed to meet almost daily, and which they know how to disregard with good sense and firmness. The press of our country tells us and the president of the Knights of Labor has related to us, how these violent

and aggressive elements have endeavored to seize authority in their councils, or to inject their poison into the principles of the association; but they also verify with what determination these evil spirits have been repulsed and defeated. The presence among our citizens of this destructive element, which has come for the most part from certain nations of Europe, is assuredly for us an occasion of lively regrets and careful precautions; it is an inevitable fact, however, but one which the union between the Church and her children in our country renders comparatively free from danger. In truth, the only grave danger would come from an alienation between the Church and her children, which nothing would more certainly occasion than imprudent condemnations.

(d) An especial charge is drawn from the outbursts of violence, even to bloodshed, which have characterized several of the strikes inaugurated by labor organizations. Concerning this, three things are to be remarked: first, strikes are not an invention of the Knights of Labor, but a means almost everywhere and always resorted to by employees in our land and elsewhere to protest against what they consider unjust and to demand their rights; secondly in such a struggle of the poor and indignant multitudes against hard and obstinate monopoly, anger and violence are often as inevitable as they are regrettable; thirdly, the laws and chief authorities of the Knights of Labor, far from encouraging violence or the occasions of it, exercise a powerful influence to hinder it, and to keep strikes within the limits of good order and legitimate action. A careful examination of the acts of violence which have marked the struggle between capital and labor during the past year, leaves us convinced that it would be unjust to attribute them to the association of the Knights of Labor. This was one of several associations of workers that took part in the strikes, and their chief officers, according to disinterested witnesses, used every possible effort to appease the anger of the crowds and to prevent the excesses which, in my judgment, could not justly be attributed to them. Doubtless among the Knights of Labor as among thousands of other workingmen, there are violent, or even wicked and criminal men, who have committed inexcusable deeds of violence, and have urged their associates to do the same; but to attribute this to the organization, it seems to me, would be as unreasonable as to attribute to the Church the follies and crimes of her children against which she protests. I repeat that in such a struggle of the great masses of the people against the mail-clad power, which, as it is acknowledged, often refuses them the simple rights of humanity and justice, it is vain to expect that every error and every act of violence can be avoided; and to dream that this struggle can be prevented, or that we can deter the multitudes from organizing, which is their only practical means [hope—*moyen pratique*] of success, would be to ignore the nature and forces of human society in times like ours. The part of Christian prudence is evidently to try to hold the hearts of the multitude by the bonds of love, in order to deter them from what would be false and criminal, and thus to turn into a legitimate, peaceable and beneficent contest what could easily become for the masses of our people a volcanic abyss, like that which society fears and the Church deplores in Europe.

Upon this point I insist strongly, because, from an intimate acquaintance with the social conditions of our country I am profoundly convinced that here we are touching upon a subject which not only concerns the rights of the working classes, who ought to be especially dear to the Church which our Divine Lord sent to evangelize the poor, but with which are bound up the fundamental interests of the Church and of human society for the future. This is a point which I desire, in a few additional words to develop more clearly.

5. Whoever meditates upon the ways in which divine Providence is guiding contemporary history cannot fail to remark how important is the part which the power of the people taken therein at present and must take in the future. We behold, with profound sadness, the efforts of the prince of darkness to make this power dangerous to the social weal by withdrawing the masses of the people from the influence of religion, and impelling them towards the ruinous paths of license and anarchy. Until now our country presents a picture of altogether different character—that of a popular power regulated by love of good order, by respect for religion, by obedience to the authority of the laws, not a democracy of license and violence, but that true democracy which aims at the general prosperity through the means of sound principles and good social order.

In order to preserve so desirable a state of things, it is absolutely necessary that religion should continue to hold the affections, and thus rule the conduct of the multitudes. As Cardinal Manning has so well written, "In the future era the Church has no longer to deal with princes and parliaments, but with the masses, with the people. Whether we will or no this is our work; we need a new spirit, a new direction of our life and activity." To lose influence over the people would be to lose the future altogether; and it is by the heart, far more than by the understanding, that we must hold and guide this immense power, so mighty either for good or for evil. Among all the glorious titles of the Church which her history has merited for her, there is not one which at present gives her so great influence as that of *Friend of the People*. Assuredly, in our democratic country, it is this title which wins for the Catholic Church not only the enthusiastic devotedness of the millions of her children, but also the respect and admiration of all our citizens, whatever be their religious belief. It is the power of precisely this title which renders persecution almost an impossibility, and which draws toward our holy Church the great heart of the American people.

And since it is acknowledged by all that the great questions of the future are not those of war, of commerce or finance, but the social questions, the questions which concern the improvement of the condition of the great masses of the people, and especially of the working people, it is evidently of supreme importance that the Church should always be found on the side of humanity, of justice toward the multitudes who compose the body of the human family. As the same Cardinal Manning very wisely wrote, "We must admit and accept calmly and with good will that industries and profits must be considered in second place; the moral state and domestic condition of the whole working population must be considered first. I will not venture to formulate the acts of parliament, but here is precisely their fundamental principle for the future. The condition of the lower classes as are found at present among our people, can not and must not continue. On such a basis no social edifice can stand." In our country, especially, this is the inevitable program of the future, and the position which the Church must hold toward the solution is sufficiently obvious. She must certainly not favor the extremes to which the poor multitudes are naturally inclined, but, I repeat, she must without them from these extremes by the bond of affection, by the maternal desire which she will manifest for the concession of all that is just and reasonable in their demands, and by the maternal blessing which she will bestow upon every legitimate means of improving the condition of the people.

6. Now let us consider for a moment the consequences which would inevitably follow from a contrary course, from a lack of sympathy for the working class, from a suspicion of their aims, from a hasty condemnation of their methods.
   (a) First, there is the evident danger of the Church's losing in popular estimation her right to be considered the friend of the people. The logic of men's hearts goes swiftly to its conclusions, and this conclusion would be a pernicious one for the people and for the Church. To lose the heart of the people would be a misfortune for which the friendship of the few rich and powerful would be no compensation.
   (b) There is a great danger of rendering hostile to the Church the political power of our country, which openly takes sides with the millions who are demanding justice and the improvement of their condition. The accusation of being "un-American," that is to say, alien to our national spirit, is the most powerful weapon which the enemies of the Church know how to employ against her. It was this cry which aroused the Know-Nothing persecution thirty years ago, and the same would be quickly used again if the opportunity offered itself. To appreciate the gravity of this danger it is well to remark that not only are the rights of the working classes loudly proclaimed by each of our two great political parties, but is very probably that, in our approaching national elections, there will be a candidate for the office of President of the United States as the special representative of these complaints and demands of the masses. Now, to seek to crush by an ecclesiastical condemnation an organization which represents nearly 500,000 votes, and which has already so respectable and as universally recognized a place in the political arena, would to speak frankly, be considered by the American people as not less ridiculous as it is rash. To alienate from ourselves the friendship of the people would be to run great risk of losing the respect which the Church has won in the estimation of the American nation, and of destroying the state of peace and prosperity which form so admirable a contrast with her condition in some so-called Catholic countries. Already in these months past, a murmur of popular anger and of threats against the Church has made itself heard, and it is necessary that we should move with much precaution.
   (c) A third danger, and one which touches our hearts the most, is the risk of losing the love of the children of the Church, and of pushing them into an attitude of resistance against their

Mother. The whole world presents no more beautiful spectacle than that of their filial devotion and obedience. But it is necessary to recognize that, in our age and in our country, obedience cannot be blind. We would greatly deceive ourselves if we expected it. Our Catholic working men sincerely believe that they are only seeking justice, and seeking it by legitimate means. A condemnation would be considered both false and unjust, and would not be accepted. We might indeed preach to them submission and confidence in the Church, but these good dispositions could hardly go so far. They love the Church, and they wish to save their souls, but they must also earn their living, and labor is now so organized that without belonging to the organization there is little chance to earn one's living.

Behold, then, the consequences to be feared. Thousands of the most devoted children of the Church would believe themselves repulsed by their Mother and would live without practicing their religion. The revenues of the Church, which come entirely from the free offerings of the people, would suffer immensely, and it would be the same with Peter's pence. The ranks of the secret societies would be filled with Catholics, who had been up to now faithful. The Holy See, which has constantly received from the Catholics of America proofs of almost unparalleled devotedness, would be considered not as a paternal authority, but as a harsh and unjust power. Here are assuredly effects, the occasion of which wisdom and prudence must avoid.

In a word, we have seen quite recently the sad and threatening confusion caused by the condemnation inflicted by an Archbishop upon a single priest in vindication of discipline—a condemnation which the Archbishop believed to be just and necessary, but which fell upon a priest who was regarded as the friend of the people. Now, if the consequences have been so deplorable for the peace of the Church from the condemnation of only one priest, because he was considered to be the friend of the people, what will not be the consequences to be feared from a condemnation which would fall directly upon the people themselves in the exercise of what they consider their legitimate right?

7. But besides the danger which would result from such a condemnation and the impossibility of having it respected and observed, one should note that the form of this organization is so little permanent, as the press indicates nearly every day, that in the estimation of practical men in our country, it cannot last very many

years. Whence it follows that it is not necessary, even if it were just and prudent, to level the solemn condemnations of the Church against something which will vanish of itself. The social agitation will, indeed, last as long as there are social evils to be remedied, but the form of organization and procedure meant for the attainment of this end are necessarily provisional and transient. They are also very numerous, for I have already remarked that the Knights of Labor is only one among several forms of labor organizations. To strike, then, at one of these forms would be to commence a war without system and without end; it would be to exhaust the forces of the Church in chasing a crowd of changing and uncertain phantasms. The American people behold with perfect composure and confidence the progress of our social contest, and have not the least fear of not being able to protect themselves against any excesses or dangers that may occasionally arise. And, to speak with the most profound respect, but also with the frankness which duty requires of me, it seems to me that prudence suggests, and that even the dignity of the Church demands that we should not offer to America an ecclesiastical protection for which she does not ask, and of which she believes she has no need.

8. In all this discussion I have not at all spoken of Canada, nor of the condemnation concerning the Knights of Labor in Canada. For we would consider it an impertinence to involve ourselves in the ecclesiastical affairs of another country which has a hierarchy of its own, and with whose needs and social conditions we do not pretend to be acquainted. We believe, however, that the circumstances of a people almost entirely Catholic, as in lower Canada, must be very different from those of a mixed population like ours; moreover, that the document submitted to the Holy Office is not the present constitution of the organization in our country, and that we, therefore, ask nothing involving an inconsistency on the part of the Holy See, which passed sentence *juxta exposita*. It is of the condition of things in the United States that we speak, and we treat that in these matters we are not presumptuous in believing that we are competent to judge. Now, as I have already indicated, out of the seventy-five archbishops and bishops of the United States, there are about five who would desire a condemnation of the Knights of Labor, such as we know them in our country; so that our hierarchy are almost unanimous in protesting against such a condemnation. Surely, such a fact ought to have great weight in deciding the question. If there are difficulties in the case, it seems to me that the prudence and experience

of our bishops and the wise rules of the Third Plenary Council ought to suffice for their solution.

9. Finally, to sum it all up, it seems clear to me that the Holy See should not entertain the idea of condemning an association:
    1. When the condemnation does not seem to be justified either by the letter or the spirit of its constitution, its law and the declaration of its leaders.
    2. When the condemnation does not seem *necessary*, in view of the transient form of the organization and the social condition of the United States.
    3. When it does not seem to be *prudent*, because of the reality of the grievances of the workers, and the admission of them made by the American people.
    4. When it would be *dangerous*, for the reputation of the Church in our democratic country, and possibly even arouse persecution.
    5. When it would be *ineffectual*, in compelling the obedience of our Catholic workers, who would regard it as false and unjust.
    6. When it would be *destructive* instead of beneficial in its effects, impelling the children of the Church to disobey their Mother, and even to join condemned societies, which they have thus far shunned.
    7. When it would be almost *ruinous*, for the financial maintenance of the Church in our country, and for the Peter's pence.
    8. When it would turn into suspicion and hostility the outstanding devotedness of our Catholic people toward the Holy See.
    9. When it would be regarded as a cruel blow to the authority of bishops in the United States, who, it is well known, protest against such a condemnation.

Now, I hope the considerations here presented have shown with sufficient clearness that such would be the condemnation of the Knights of Labor in the United States.

Therefore, with complete confidence, I leave the case to the wisdom and prudence of your eminence and the Holy See.

Rome, February 20, 1887
J. Cardinal Gibbons
Archbishop of Baltimore

Source: "27. Cardinal Gibbons' Defense of the Knights of Labor, February 20, 1887," in *Documents of American Catholic History*, vol. 2, *1866–1966*, ed. John Tracy Ellis (Wilmington, Del.: Glazier, 1987), 444–57.

APPENDIX D

Letter of Cardinal Gibbons to Cardinal Simeoni, February 25, 1887

Your Eminence:

I have already had the honor of presenting to your Eminence my views on the social questions which agitate America, especially with regard to their bearing on the association of the Knights of Labor. But recently another form of social debate has developed relating to the doctrines of Mr. Henry George, an American author identified with the working classes. And since my arrival in Rome I have heard the idea discussed that the writings of Henry George should be put on the Index. After having fully thought over the subject I believe it my duty to submit to your Eminence the reasons which seem to me to demonstrate that a formal condemnation of the works of Henry George would be neither opportune nor useful.

1. Henry George is in no way the originator of the theory which he advocates concerning the right of ownership of land. In his principal book, "Progress and Poverty," he cites precisely the teaching of Herbert Spencer and John Stuart Mill, two of England's chief authors. And in the English periodical, the "Contemporary Review," of November 1886, a distinguished Professor quotes them more fully to prove, as he says, that Mr. George is only a plagiarist of these celebrated authors. Now it seems to me that the world will judge it a bit singular if the Holy See attacks the work of a humble American artisan instead of attacking his great masters. And if there are some who, therefore, think that it is the

duty of the Holy See to pronounce judgment on Spencer and Mill, perhaps it would be prudent first to take counsel with their Eminences Cardinals Manning and Newman on the opportunness of such actions.

2. It is well to remark that the theory of Henry George differs from that which is ordinarily called Communism and Socialism. Because as Father Valentine Steccanella shows very well in his work on Communism, published by the Propaganda Press in 1882, this implies the abolition of private property and the collectivization of all goods in the hands of the State. Now anyone who has read the books of Henry George ought to recognize that he neither teaches this nor does he at all wish it. On the contrary, he maintains the absolute ownership of all the fruits of human energy and industry, even when they amount to great riches acquired either by labor or heredity. It is only with regard to land itself that he would wish to limit the ownership of individuals by an extension of the *supremum dominum* of the state, and on this point he has expressly stated that he would in no way dispossess the actual owners; but he would desire simply that our system of taxation be changed in such a way that only the land would provide taxes and not the fruits of human industry. One can see, therefore, that in the practical form in which the controversy presents itself to the American public it is simply a question of the government's power over individual ownership of land. And on that there is this to be noted:
   (a) Anyone who studies properly the question of the relations of the State to the right of ownership of land, as it is treated by Father Steccanella and by other Catholic writers, or as it is regulated by the laws of taxation and the care of the poor in some countries, and especially in England, cannot help but understand that it is a very complex question, very much subject to the diverse circumstances of time and place, and not yet ready to be resolved by a decisive judgment;
   (b) The question is already before the American public as a political issue, and in so practical an arena it will soon find its end;
   (c) As Mr. George himself realizes, it is only the legislative power of the country which could bring about such a disposition of affairs; and it is quite certain that neither a Congress nor a legislature will ever be found that would vote for such a profound change in social relations, nor a President who would approve it.

(d) In a country such as ours, which is by no means a country of doctrinaires and visionaries, speculative theory will not be dangerous, nor will it live long after its practical application will have been rejected; one may, therefore, in all certainty, let it die by itself.

3. Certain recent events in our country have occasioned a profound and widespread popular excitement having an intimate relation to this question. Therefore, your Eminence understands better than I how necessary it is for us to have care not only to speak the truth, but also to choose well the time and the circumstances to say it, so that our action may produce salutary and not fatal results. It seems evident, therefore that even if there is certainly a need for condemnation, now is not the right time to speak out.
4. Finally, it would be prudent to apply here the principle of morality which counsels one not to pronounce a sentence the consequences of which will probably be adverse rather than favorable to the good end proposed. Now I am sure that such would result of a condemnation of the works of Mr. George. It would give them a popular importance that they would not ever otherwise have, and would excite an appetite of curiosity that would make them sell by the thousands of copies, and would thus extend immensely the influences that the condemnation sought to restrain and prevent.

Once again, in dealing with so practicable a people as the Americans in whose genius bizarre and impractical ideas quickly find their grave, it seems to me that prudence suggests that absurdities and fallacies be allowed to perish by themselves, and not run the risk of giving them an importance, a life and an artificial force by the intervention of the tribunals of the Church.

Source: "26. Cardinal James Gibbons to Cardinal Simeoni. 25 February 1887," in *Public Voices, Catholics in the American Context*, ed. Steven M. Avella and Elizabeth McKeown (Maryknoll, N.Y.: Orbis Press, 1999), 80–83.

APPENDIX E

~

Social Action Series Pamphlets

Archives of the Catholic University of America (ACUA)

Social Action Department (SAD):
National Catholic Welfare Conference (NCWC) / United States Catholic Conference (USCC)

Collection 10, box 68

1. Raymond A. McGowan. *New Guilds: A Conversation*. New York: Paulist, 1937.
2. John F. Cronin. *Rugged Individualism*. New York: Paulist, 1937.
3. Francis J. Haas. *The Wages and Hours of American Labor*. New York: Paulist, 1937.
4. Elizabeth Morrissy. *What Laws Must We Have?* New York: Paulist, 1937.
5. Edgar Schmiedeler. *Consumers' Cooperatives*. New York: Paulist, 1937.
6. Francis J. Haas. *The American Labor Movement*. New York: Paulist, 1937.
7. Frank O'Hara. *Credit Unions*. New York: Paulist, 1937.
8. John A. Ryan. *The Constitution and Catholic Industrial Teaching*. New York: Paulist, 1937.
9. John F. Cronin. *Prices in the United States*. New York: Paulist Press, 1937.
10. George T. Brown. *Economic Power in the United States*. New York: Paulist, 1937.

11. Edgar Schmiedeler. *Our Rural Proletariat*. New York: Paulist, 1937.
12. Richard Dana Skinner. *Debt System or Property System?* New York: Paulist, 1937.
13. Henry Somerville. *Why the Guilds Decayed*. New York: Paulist, 1938.
14. Members of the NCWC, Social Action Department. *Women in Industry*. New York: Paulist, 1938.
15. Edgar Schmiedeler. *Balanced Abundance*. New York: Paulist, 1938.
16. Matthew Clancy. *Sound Old Guilds*. New York: Paulist, 1939.
17. Francis J. Gilligan. *The Negro Worker in Free America*. New York: Paulist, 1939.
18. Edgar Schmiedeler. *The Rural South: Problem or Prospect?* New York: Paulist, 1940.
19. Francis J. Haas. *Jobs, Prices, and Unions*. New York: Paulist, 1941.
20. John M. Hayes. *Designs for Social Action*. New York: Paulist, 1941.
21. Edgar Schmiedeler. *Vanishing Homesteads*. New York: Paulist, 1941.
22. Martin E. Scherber. *Inflation and the Common Man*. New York: Paulist, 1941.
23. Joseph B. Kenkel. *Sharing Profits with Employees*. New York: Paulist, 1943.

APPENDIX F

~

Christian Democracy Series

Archives of the Catholic University of America (ACUA)

Social Action Department (SAD):

National Catholic Welfare Conference (NCWC) / United States Catholic Conference (USCC)

Collection 10, box 68

1. John A. Ryan. *The Citizen, the Church, and the State*. New York: Paulist, 1939.
2. John A. Ryan. *American Democracy vs. Racism, Communism*. New York: Paulist, 1939.
3. Jerome G. Kerwin. *Making Democracy Work*. New York: Paulist, 1930.
4. James M. Eagan. *The Pope's Peace Program and the U.S.* New York: Paulist, 1941.
5. Francis J. Boland. *The Popes and Christian Citizenship*. New York: Paulist, 1941.

APPENDIX G

Higgins Documents

A Selection of Yardstick Columns

1. A Leap Forward in the Agricultural Industry: *August 24, 1970*
2. A Tribute to the Memory of Father Raymond A. McGowan: *November 24, 1975*
3. Hope for the Resolution of the California Farm Labor Dispute: *January 31, 1977*
4. National Labor Relations Board Invocation: *March 21, 1977*
5. Tribute to Bishop Joseph F. Donnelly: *July 25, 1977*
6. A Labor Day Prayer: *September 5, 1977*
7. George Meany's Creed: *January 28, 1980*
8. A Time to Say Good-Bye: *September 25, 2001 (written September 10, 2001)*

1. A Leap Forward in the Agricultural Industry

August 24, 1970

The U.S. Catholic Bishops' Committee on Farm Labor became involved in the California table grape dispute several months ago in an effort to bring the parties together and to persuade them to settle their differences peacefully and equitably through the normal processes of collective bargaining. Partly because of the Committee's efforts in this regard, the grape dispute has now been substantially resolved, but no sooner had the decisive Delano contracts been negotiated when, quite unexpectedly, a potentially more troublesome problem arose in the form of a jurisdictional dispute between the United Farm Workers Organizing Committee and the Western Conference of Teamsters. In response to this worrisome development, the Bishops' Committee, acting through its Chairman, Bishop Joseph F. Donnelly, Auxiliary Bishop of Hartford, Connecticut, addressed an urgent appeal to the United Farm Workers Organizing Committee and the Western Conference of Teamsters to meet with representatives of the Committee in a sincere effort to resolve their jurisdictional dispute. Bishop Donnelly's appeal to the parties reads, in substance, as follows:

> There is, in our mind, no question that the farm workers want union recognition. We are also convinced that the grower employers are willing to recognize such a union. The only question remaining is which union do the workers want. In order to safeguard the newly-won peace in the agricultural industry, and to avoid the possibility of another prolonged struggle, we, the members of the U.S. Catholic Bishops' Committee on Farm Labor, appeal to all the parties concerned to come together to seek a resolution to this problem. As Chairman of that committee, I specifically call upon the United Farm Workers Organizing Committee, AFL-CIO, the Western Conference of Teamsters, and the growers involved to meet with our committee to attempt to resolve and settle this dispute. Because the current harvest is underway, it is urgent that a meeting be scheduled immediately. Therefore, I am calling for such a meeting to be held early this week.

Both parties responded immediately and very favorably to the Committee's appeal and agreed to hold a series of meetings with representatives of the Committee in Salinas, California on Tuesday, August 11. In the absence of the Chairman, Bishop Donnelly, who was unavoidably detained in Connecticut, I was privileged to chair those meetings, with the able assistance of Monsignor Roger Mahony of Fresno, California, who was serving in his capacity as Secretary of the Committee. Beginning early Tuesday morning, August 11, Monsignor Mahony and I met with the parities separately over a period of several hours and at 10:30 P.M. called them together for what turned out to be a non-stop all-night session which, happily, resulted at 6:00 A.M., Wednesday, August 12, in a formal pact between the United Farm Workers Organizing Committee and the Western Conference of Teamsters.

As I told the media at a joint peace conference at noon that day, I look upon this mutual assistance pact as being a truly historic document in the annals of farm labor, and I am fully confident that it will work to the mutual benefit of all concerned, workers and growers alike. In the name of the Bishops' Committee, I should like to congratulate both parties very sincerely for the statesmanlike and highly constructive manner in which they have resolved their jurisdictional dispute, and Monsignor Mahony and I, speaking in a more personal vein, wish to comment them for the maturity, the good judgment, the good will, and the unfailing courtesy which they brought to their difficult assignment.

We told the parties when we first met with them on the morning of August 11 that we were hoping for and would do our best to help them hammer out a document which would be more than an armistice, more than a legalistic non-aggression pact. In short, we urged them to try to come up with an agreement which would be thoroughly positive in tone and would be calculated not so much to defend or protest their separate interests as to promote their mutual interests and the general interest of the entire agricultural industry. We think they have done just that and have done it very well.

The growers in the Salinas Valley are also to be congratulated for their willingness to recognize the collective bargaining rights of their workers and to help develop a sound system of labor-management relations in their crucially important industry. On Thursday morning, August 18, they started negotiating with the United Farm Workers Organizing Committee. I was asked by the parties to sit in on these negotiations as a representative of the Bishops Committee on Farm Labor. Speaking in that capacity, I fully expect to be able to announce—even before this column appears in print—that the parties have settled their differences and have signed collective bargaining contracts covering a variety of crops in the Salinas Valley. In fact, I am absolutely certain that this is going to happen. I am equally certain, however, that it couldn't have happened—possibly for several years—if the Teamsters and the Farm Workers had failed to settle their jurisdictional dispute on August 12. When I arrived in Salinas on August 11, I was frankly pessimistic about their ability or their willingness to do so. In fact, I was reasonably certain in my own mind that if they didn't settle the dispute by Wednesday morning, August 12, they were headed inevitably for a civil war which might have dragged on indefinitely. It was for this reason that I decided to keep them in session all night without so much as a coffee break. Fortunately this emergency strategy was successful and, by noon the following day, with the formal announcement of their mutual assistance pact, we had moved into a new era in the annals of farm labor not only in the State of California but throughout the rest of the nation as well.

From here on there can no longer be any doubt that collective bargaining will eventually become the standard method of handling labor-management relations in the entire agricultural industry. The question is no longer "if" but "when" this will happen. For my own part, I am optimistic enough to think that it won't take very long. That's why I said at the press conference in Salinas on August 12—and wish to repeat at this time—that the Teamster-UFWOC mutual assistance pact was a truly historic document in the annals of the farm labor movement in this country. Again, sincere congratulations to both unions.

2. A Tribute to the Memory of Father Raymond A. McGowan

November 24, 1975

Father John Sheerin, C.S.P., former editor of "The Catholic World" and currently a consultant to the NCCB Secretariat for Catholic-Jewish Relations, is the author of a new biography of the late Msgr. John J. Burke, first general secretary of the original national Catholic Welfare Conference (now the U.S. Catholic Conference). The book is entitled "Never Look Back: The Career and Concerns of John J. Burke" (Paulist Press, New York, N.Y.-Paramus, N.J. $7.95). I recommend it highly.

In reading Father Sheerin's book, I was reminded of how quickly we tend to forget our forebears in the faith. Msgr. Burke died in 1936. When I joined the NCWC staff in 1940, his memory was still very much alive in the Conference. In the beginning I heard much about him from some of the old-timers on the staff, but after a few years I hardly ever heard his name mentioned. Moreover, I have the impression that the present members of the Conference staff knew practically nothing about him until Father Sheerin's biography brought his name alive again.

One of Msgr. Burke's closest collaborators in the original NCWC—Father Raymond A. McGowan, long-time assistant director and director of the Social Action Department—has suffered a similar fate. Though he died less than 15 years ago, one hardly ever hears his name mentioned any more, even among professional Catholic social activists, who owe so much to his innovative leadership in their own field from 1919 until his retirement in 1954. This column, adapted from an earlier column printed at the time of his retirement, is intended to keep his name alive and to pay tribute to his memory.

Many years ago—in the early winter of 1923—a young priest just beginning a distinguished career in the field of Catholic social action was invited to consult with a grand old man who was rapidly approaching the end of his own distinguished career as the dean of the American labor movement. The young priest was Father Raymond A. McGowan, who had only recently been appointed assistant director of the Social Action Department of the National Catholic Welfare Conference. The illustrious old man who had summoned Father McGowan to meet with his Executive Council at the American Federation of Labor headquarters—then, as now, only four blocks from the NCWC headquarters on Massachusetts Avenue in Washington—was Samuel Gompers, founder and first president of the Federation.

Father McGowan had just established the Catholic Conference on Industrial Problems. A garbled news release on the proceedings of the first meeting of this new organization in Chicago was a little disturbing to Mr. Gompers. He was under the mistaken impression that the CCIP was to be a separate Catholic action or federation of Catholic unions which would compete with the affiliates of the AFL for the loyalty of Catholic workers. After Father McGowan had cleared up the unfortunate misunderstanding, he went on to explain that the long-range program of the CCIP was an organized system of labor-management-government cooperation in American economic life. In other words, almost 10 years before the publication of Pope Pius XI's encyclical, *Quadragesimo Anno*, he was advocating the encyclical program, which has since come to be known as the Industry Council Plan. Gompers was sympathetic to the idea, but unfortunately he died before he was able to do anything about it in a practical way.

Within the limits of this column it is impossible even to list the many contributions which Father McGowan had made to the cause of social justice, at home and abroad, during his lifetime association with NCWC. We can only hope that the previous unpublicized story of his first meeting with the great Samuel Gompers will serve to illustrate a few of the distinctive qualities which have consistently characterized his work in the important field of social action.

From the very beginning Father McGowan proved himself to be a man of extraordinary vision. Surely it required unusual vision to establish a Catholic Conference on Industrial Problems in the "golden" 1920s and even greater vision to establish, a few years later, a Catholic Association for International Peace. Both of these organizations and several others which owed their existence to his initiative were started at a time when few Americans were even remotely interested in the application of moral principles to domestic economic life and international relations. It is doubtful if any of them would have been established at such an early date except for the initiative and the vision of Father McGowan.

But if Father McGowan was a pioneer organizationally speaking, he was even further ahead of his time in the realm of Catholic social theory. Few, if any, of his contemporaries were as quick to see the logical necessity of an organized system of labor-management-government cooperation in American economic life. . . . As we have already seen, he was advocating the industry council idea long before *Quadragesimo Anno*. After *Quadragesimo Anno* he was one of the first Americans to grasp the full significance of the encyclical program of social reconstruction and one of the first to begin to think realistically about its application to the American economy. Two or three of his publications stand up as being among the most valuable commentaries on the papal program.

Father McGowan during his years at NCWC was interested in social legislation, but only as a secondary method of social reform. Temperamentally, as well as intellectually, he was primarily interested in organization. And thus it was very appropriate that, even as a very young priest, he should have been consulted by the elders of the AFL. His meeting with Gompers in the early 1920s was to be the first of literally thousands of formal and informal conversations with representatives not only of labor organizations but employers' associations as well. The greater part of his time and energy was to be devoted over a period of 35 years to a patient effort to persuade these organizations of the importance and the necessity of their working together for the solution of their common problems. There is reason to believe that his efforts are now beginning to bear substantial fruit.

Father McGowan's countless friends will want to remember him in their prayers.

3. Hope for the Resolution of the California Farm Labor Dispute

January 31, 1977

The California farm labor dispute has been with us so long, has been so bitter on both sides, and has generated so many scare headlines that the outside observer may despair of its ever being peacefully resolved. However, I have always been optimistic about the outcome of the unfortunate—and, in many respects, unnecessary—dispute. As one who has met with the parties frequently over seven or eight years, I have felt that they would bury the hatchet eventually and settle their differences in an orderly fashion through collective bargaining.

While it would be overly optimistic to say this has already happened, I don't doubt that a satisfactory settlement is in the offing, at least in California. And the terms agreed to in California will almost inevitably set a pattern for the rest of the country.

What reason is there for saying a settlement is in the offing?

For one thing, it seems almost certain that the United Farm Workers of America (UFWA) and the Teamsters will, before long, resolve their own differences and sign a permanent jurisdictional pact. Some observers are of the opinion that, even if such an agreement is signed, sealed and delivered, the parties will, sooner or later, repudiate it and be back where they started. I don't expect this to happen. It is my impression that both parties mean business this time and that many growers who previously tried to pit the two unions against one another realize that that was a costly mistake and are prepared, willy nilly, to deal with the UFWA as the exclusive bargaining agent for their field workers. Hopefully, the UFWA and the Teamsters will look for ways to join forces for the good of all instead of fighting one another as they have, to no one's advantage, for the past several years. If this occurs, you can take it for granted that in all future representation elections the UFWA will sweep the field.

In fact—and this is my reason for optimism—the UFWA has already won a sizeable number of secret ballot elections and has negotiated reasonably good collective bargaining contracts with the growers involved in these elections. The record will show that, by and large, these contracts are being well administered and the parties are developing a new spirit of mutual trust and confidence and, in some cases, have become good friends.

I saw encouraging evidence of this during a recent visit to Calexico, California, on the Mexican border. Following a regularly scheduled meeting in Calexico of the Martin Luther King Farm Workers Fund—a social welfare and educational fund financed by employer contributions and jointly administered by the two parties, with the present writer serving as chairman of the Board of Trustees—the UFWA hosted a public labor-management reception at a restaurant in Mexicali, across the boarder. This was a historic gathering, for it brought together for the first time a large number of growers, UFWA officials, and the rank and file farm workers (plus a number of invited guests) in an extremely cordial atmosphere. I talked to all of the growers who attended. To a man, they said they were more than satisfied with their relationship with UFWA and were determined to cooperate with the union in an effort to achieve a satisfactory solution to the labor-management problem in their important industry—the largest single industry in California.

The union officials and workers who attended the reception indicated that they, too, are happy about recent developments and are eager to make collective bargaining work for the good of the entire industry.

When I first head the UFWA was planning to host this reception, I kept my fingers crossed. Given the sad history of labor-management relations in the agricultural industry, I was afraid the growers would not shop up or that, at best, the atmosphere would be strained and the parties ill at ease with one another. I was wrong. It was enjoyable.

The fact that similar labor-management receptions are being planned for other sections of California does not mean that the labor-management dispute in that state has been settled once and for all or that the atmosphere between the parties is one of permanent sweetness and light. I think it does mean that this long-standing dispute, despite the residue of bitterness which still exists in some segments of the industry, is on the way to a satisfactory solution.

Praise the Lord! Alleluia.

4. National Labor Relations Board Invocation

March 21, 1977

On March 21 the National Labor Relations Board hosted a public dinner in Washington to celebrate the thirty million votes that had been cast in union representation elections conducted by the board since the National Labor Relations Act was passed in 1935. Higgins reiterated Monsignor John A. Ryan's laudatory description of the Wagner Act as "probably the most just, beneficent, and far-reaching piece of labor legislation ever enacted in the United States." To this Higgins added, "American history turned a corner—perhaps one of the most important since the Emancipation Proclamation." The following is an abbreviated version of the invocation that Monsignor Higgins delivered on that occasion.

The prophet Isaiah, a man sent by God to reach and guide his people, has warned us: Woe to those who enact unjust statutes and who write oppressive decrees, / Depriving the needy of judgment and robbing my people's / poor of their rights.

Isaiah's words of warning, first spoken several thousand years ago, are still as timely as the latest television newscast. In many countries throughout the world, including some that once enjoyed a measure of political freedom, unjust statutes and oppressive decrees are now the order of the day. Woe to those responsible for this tragic turn of events.

But if Isaiah's dire warning is still to be taken seriously, there is no reason to despair. Scripture also tells us that the just man shall flourish like a tree planted by the water. Reversing the Prophet's warning, then, surely we can say with due propriety: Blessed are those who enact just statutes and write fair and equitable decrees, and blessed are they who provide judgment for the needy and protect the rights of the poor.

We have gathered here this evening to honor the memory of men and women who merit this blessing, men and women who, more than 40 years ago, enacted into law a statute which, whatever its limitations—and these can and must be changed—was surely just and fair. The purpose of the law which they sponsored and enacted was to extend the blessings of freedom and democracy to the field of labor-management relations, to guarantee to the working people of this country the free exercise of the right to organize for the purpose of collective bargaining, to enable them, by means of secret ballot elections, to choose, as free men and women in a free society, the organization they want to represent them.

During the past four decades 30 million votes have been cast in such elections—a remarkable exercise of freedom and democracy in action. Our nation as a whole has benefited greatly from this process, and the cause of freedom is the more secure because of it.

O God our Father, as we gather to celebrate this landmark in the history of labor-management relations, we thank You for these and all the other blessings You have bestowed upon our nation and its people. We give You thanks and praise You for our 200 years as a nation, for the vision of its founders, a vision which, under Your providential care, has made it possible for immigrants from many different parts of the world to create here a new nation with liberty and justice for all, a nation dedicated but not yet fully committed to the proposition that all men and women are created free and equal.

Let Your spirit purify our love of country that it may be true to its principles and faithful to its ideals. Help us to safeguard all that is good in our common heritage and to strive for even greater progress in the future. Heal the wounds that injustice has inflicted on our people, break down the barriers that divide us.

Blessed be Your name, our God and our provider, for the food that we are about to receive from Your gracious bounty. Bring us together in this sharing. Let this occasion nourish us with faith in Your providence and with care for one another, especially for those less fortunate than ourselves. We know that we can only thank You with a great conscience if our sharing reaches out to all who are in need.

5. Tribute to Bishop Joseph F. Donnelly

July 25, 1977

Bishop Joseph F. Donnelly, Auxiliary of Hartford and Chairman of the Bishops Committee on Farm Labor, died suddenly at his residence in New Haven, Connecticut on June 30. His death is a great loss not only to his own archdiocese, but also to the Catholic social action movement from one end of the United States to the other.

Few bishops in recent American history have come to the episcopate so well prepared to promote the Church's apostolate in the social order. Appropriately, Bishop Donnelly's episcopal motto and the details of his episcopal coat of arms reflected his long-standing and effective involvement in this phase of the priestly ministry. His coat of arms featured two clasped hands, symbolizing his 20 years of service on the Connecticut Board of Mediation and Arbitration and his 15 years of service as chairman. During those years, in mediating more than 2,000 labor-management disputes, he joined the hands of labor and management in peaceful and equitable solutions to their problems. Those years of service were under the patronage of St. Joseph the Worker, Bishop Donnelly's baptismal patron. The lily, symbolic of St. Joseph, was represented by the fleur de lis, the French form of the lily, in the clasped hands.

The bishop's episcopal motto expressed the guiding principle of his many years of devoted public service. "Peace, the Work of Justice" signified his dedication to the principle that peace can only come from the application of justice. His service in the field of Catholic social action, labor education, labor-management relations, interracial justice, housing and urban renewal, were inspired by the conviction that only when the rights of all are respected will it be possible for men and women to live together in happiness and peace.

During the last 10 years of his life, Bishop Donnelly made perhaps his greatest single contribution to the cause of social reform by the effective manner in which he carried out his arduous duties as chairman of the Bishops Committee on Farm Labor. As his staff assistant, I was in contact with him at least once or twice a week and traveled with him to the West Coast on countless occasions as he worked tirelessly—occasionally, for weeks at a time—to mediate the California farm labor dispute. On the basis of that experience, I think I can say, without fear of contradiction, that no single individual outside their own ranks did more than Bishop Donnelly, to assist the farm workers in their courageous struggle for self-determination. It was fitting and proper, then, that Cesar Chavez, the extraordinary leader of the United Farm Workers, should have been invited to do one of the Scriptural readings at the bishop's funeral Mass in Hartford, Connecticut on July 6. They were the closest of friends and had profound admiration and respect for one another.

Let me say a word about the priestly spirit which characterized Bishop Donnelly's tireless efforts on behalf of social justice. He was precisely the type of apostle Pope Pius XI had in mind when, towards the end of his encyclical "On Reconstructing the Social Order," he instructed the bishops of the world to assign specially qualified priests to the social apostolate. "All those who are candidates for the Church's ministry," Pius XI wrote, "must be prepared for (the social apostolate) by an intense study of the social question. It is essential that those whom you (bishops) propose to assign specially to this ministry should manifest a delicate sense of justice, and be prepared to oppose all unjust demands and actions with manly firmness; they should excel in prudence and in the discretion which avoids extremes; above all, they should be thoroughly imbued with the charity of Christ which alone has the power, acting at once with firmness and gentleness, to make men submit their hearts and wills to the laws of justice and equity."

That's an accurate profile of the Bishop Donnelly I knew and admired and cherished as a friend—first as a priest and later as a bishop—for more than 30 years. He was a good priest and a good bishop—a man of sound judgment, courageous initiative, and deep pastoral compassion, especially for the poor and underprivileged. We are going to miss him very much. May he rest in peace.

6. A Labor Day Prayer

September 5, 1977

O God our Father we thank You for our nation's 200 years of life and growth and for the Founding Fathers' inspired vision of liberty and justice for all. Make this our vision, too, and our constant goal. Out of many nations, many people, You have made us one, though we are not yet fully one in heart and mind. May Your spirit heal our divisions and disunity. Help us to respect and prize and share with glad acceptance the rich and various gifts of this great people, that we may work together for the common good.

We thank You in particular for the contribution which the working people of this nation, whom we honor symbolically on Labor Day, have made to the welfare of all their fellow citizens. The nation as a whole has been the beneficiary of their labor and their extraordinary skill. And the cause of freedom everywhere, both home and abroad, has been continually enhanced and, in these troubled times, is now the more secure because of their ongoing struggle to achieve their own basic human rights. We commend them especially for having struggled to secure that most fundamental of all rights, the right to organize and, through their own union, to bargain collectively with their employers for justice in the economic order and freely to petition their government for those reforms that only government can provide.

Many years ago the American labor movement, in one of its earliest statements of policy, fixed as its goal "nothing less than the complete richness of life, without limitation of any kind, the attainment of the complete human ideal, in all its economic, ethical and spiritual implications." May the memory of the men and women whose achievements we honor on Labor Day and the example of their dedicated lives of service in the interest of justice and human dignity inspire us to be faithful to these high ideals in the years that lie ahead.

We ask You to bless our Chief Executive, the members of his Cabinet, our legislators, our judges and administrative officers. Theirs is a noble calling. May they exercise their constitutional authority with diligence, honor, and unimpeachable integrity and may we, the American people, accord them in turn our full cooperation.

Almighty God, our Father, You have charged us with the task of building on this earth a home where all nations may dwell in unity, with liberty and justice for all. We pray for peace and all that makes for peace, for the humility to see that there are ways other than our own, for the generosity to share the goods of this earth with those less privileged than ourselves, and for the steadfast courage to overcome the barriers that stand in the way of peace and human solidarity.

7. George Meany's Creed

January 28, 1980

This week's column was excerpted from Monsignor Higgins' homily at the funeral Mass of AFL-CIO president George Meany, at St. Matthew's Cathedral, Washington, DC, January 15, 1980.

George Meany was instinctively diffident, in a manly sort of way, about parading or publicizing his deeply held religious faith. By contrast, however, he wore his patriotism on his sleeves, and unashamedly so. The quality of his patriotism was misunderstood by some of his critics. Mainly because they thought he was too inflexibly anti-communist, they wrote him off—sometimes rather disdainfully—as a myopic and narrow-minded chauvinist. They were wrong about that—completely wrong, in my opinion. In standing up consistently not only against communism but against any and all forms of totalitarianism George Meany was not defending the so-called American way of life as such, however devoted he was to his own country. He was defending the cause of human rights which, for him, were indivisible and were meant to be universal in their application.

Meany's anti-communism derived directly and, from his point of view, very logically from his unshakable commitment to the cause of freedom and, more specifically, the freedom of workers to organize into autonomous trade unions of their own choice. In his 1979 Labor Day Statement, the last of 25 statements he had written as president of the AFL-CIO, he succinctly stated his position as follows: "One cannot have a trade union or a democratic election" without freedom of speech, freedom of association and assembly. "Without a democratic election, whereby the people choose and remove their rulers, there is no method of securing human rights against the state. No democracy without human rights, no human rights without democracy, and no trade union rights without either. That is our belief; that is our creed."

Throughout his entire lifetime, Meany never deviated from this belief or this creed and was prepared at all times to do battle with any form of political tyranny, whether fascist or communist, which denied or unjustly restricted the right of workers to organize.

In large measure, then, Meany's anti-communism grew out of his life-long commitment to the cause of organized labor which, next to his family, was his greatest love: "I have no other interest in life outside my family and the federation," he said when he was first elected president of the old American Federation of Labor. "To me this is the greatest honor that could possibly come to me in my lifetime. I do not relish the work in the sense of the time which it will take, but I am prepared to give it all of my time and give it the very best that I have in me. . . There is a job to be done. I hope to be able to do that job."

We honor him this morning, with sincere gratitude and affection, for having done that job so diligently and with such great integrity in the service of the working people of the nation and to the great benefit of the nation as a whole. The cause of freedom everywhere, both at home and abroad, has been greatly enhanced and, in these dangerously troubled times, is now the more secure because he did his job so well.

8. A Time to Say Good-Bye

September 21, 2001 (written September 10, 2001)

I began writing the Yardstick in 1945—56 years ago. In 1970, in a retrospective column marking my 25th anniversary, I said that, while a weekly deadline was a bit of a chore, I planned to continue writing The Yardstick for the indefinite future. I realize now that I spoke too soon. I failed to anticipate that the time might eventually come when, for reasons of age and health, I might have to resign voluntarily. That time has now arrived. Here is why.

In my 25th anniversary column referred to above, I said that not the least of the fringe benefits of writing a column is that anyone who does so over an extended period of time is almost compelled, in spite of himself, to do more serious reading than he might otherwise be prompted to do. Not that reading doth a columnist make, but other things being equal, it helps to prime the pump and, once it has been primed, helps to keep the well from going dry.

I still subscribe to that notion but, unfortunately, macular degeneration has severely impaired my vision and has made it impossible for me to do any sustained and serious reading. I can barely cope with newspaper headlines and can hardly read my own notoriously illegible handwriting. This means that even dictating a column is no longer possible.

To make a long story short, I have reluctantly decided to retire—effective immediately. This Labor Day column will be the last of some 3,000 columns I have written since I first inherited The Yardstick in 1945 from its originator, the late Father Raymond A. McGowan, my "boss" for many years in the Social Action Department of the old National Catholic Welfare Conference (now the United States Conference of Catholic Bishops).

Passionist Father John O'Brien, a doctoral student at the Weston Jesuit School of Theology who has been dipping into my accumulated papers in The Catholic University of America Archives, has done me the invaluable service of cataloging almost all of these 3,000 columns. Scanning his catalog has been a rewarding but also a very chastening experience. It reminded me that on many controversial issues I was wide of the mark, if not completely wrong. Father O'Brien's catalog shows that while I covered a lot of ground in my 3,000 disparate columns, I wrote more columns about labor issues than about any other subject. For this reason, I thought it would be appropriate to sign off after 56 years with this farewell Labor Day column.

The message of my scores of columns on labor issues and the message of this, the last of my 3,000 columns, can be succinctly summarized in the words of the late Msgr. John A. Ryan, first director of the old NCWC Social Action Department and a revered mentor of several generations of American Catholics in the field of Catholic social reform. At the height of the great Depression in the thirties, Msgr. Ryan wrote as follows: "Effective labor unions are still by far the most powerful force for the protection of the laborer's rights and the improvement of his or her condition. No amount of employer benevolence, no diffusion of a sympathetic attitude on the part of the public, no increase of beneficial legislation, can adequately supply for the lack of organization among the workers themselves."

Some readers of The Yardstick probably feel that I have emphasized this point too often—even ad nauseam—during the past 56 years. I respectfully disagree, but there is no point in saying exactly why now that I am retiring from the fray. My views on this issue are on the record and it's too late to withdraw them.

Thirty years ago, the late Louis Kronenberger, a well-known literary critic who wrote a column for six months for a New York daily newspaper, said in his autobiography, "a column is something everyone at some time wants to try his hand at, and should—if only to have done so and know better." I disagree. I feel privileged to have been able to write The Yardstick for 56 years and, health permitting, would be glad to keep at it for many more years to come. But, alas, that is not to be.

As I say farewell, let me close with a word of sincere thanks to my many editors during the past 56 years. They have been helpful to me beyond the call of duty. And last, but not least, let me add a word of thanks to my readers. I will miss hearing from them—including those who were honest enough to tell me that I never should have begun to write in the first place, and should have retired years ago.

Best wishes to my unnamed successor. I hope that he or she will enjoy writing the column as much as I have enjoyed it for so many years.

Good-bye to all—and thanks for a wonderful 56 years.

APPENDIX H

A Catholic Framework for Economic Life

A Statement of the U.S. Bishops, United States Catholic Conference, 1996

As followers of Jesus Christ and participants in a powerful economy, Catholics in the United States are called to work for greater economic justice in the face of persistent poverty, growing income gaps, and increasing discussion of economic issues in the United States and around the world. We urge Catholics to use the following ethical framework for economic life as principles for reflection, criteria for judgment, and directions for action. These principles are drawn directly from Catholic teaching on economic life:

1. The economy exists for the person, not the person for the economy.
2. All economic life should be shaped by moral principles. Economic ethics and institutions must be judged by how they protect or undermine the life and dignity of the human person, support the family, and serve the common good.
3. A fundamental moral measure of any economy is how the poor and vulnerable are faring.
4. All people have a right to life and to secure the basic necessities of life (e.g., food, clothing, shelter, education, health care, safe environment, economic security).
5. All people have the right to economic initiative, to productive work, to just wages and benefits, to decent working conditions, as well as to organize and join unions or other associations.

6. All people, to the extent they are able, have a corresponding duty to work, a responsibility to provide for the needs of their families, and an obligation to contribute to the broader society.
7. In economic life, free markets have both clear advantages and limits; government has essential responsibilities and limitations; voluntary groups have irreplaceable roles, but cannot substitute for the proper working of the market and the just policies of the state.
8. Society has a moral obligation, including governmental action where necessary, to assure opportunity, meet basic human needs, and pursue justice in economic life.
9. Workers, owners, managers, stockholders, and consumers are moral agents in economic life. By our choices, initiative, creativity, and investment, we enhance or diminish economic opportunity, community life, and social justice.
10. The global economy has moral dimensions and human consequences. Decisions on investment, trade, aid, and development should protect human life and promote human rights, especially for those most in need wherever they might live on this globe.

According to Pope John Paul II, the Catholic tradition calls for a "society of work, enterprise and participation" which "is not directed against the market, but demands that the market be appropriately controlled by the forces of society and by the state to assure that the basic needs of the whole society are satisfied" (*Centesimus Annus*, 35). All of economic life should recognize the fact that we are all God's children and members of one human family, called to exercise a clear priority for "the least among us."

The sources for this framework include the *Catechism of the Catholic Church*, recent papal encyclicals, the pastoral letter *Economic Justice for All*, and other statements of the U.S. Catholic bishops. They reflect the Church's teaching on the dignity, rights, and duties of the human person: the option for the poor; the common good; subsidiarity and solidarity.

APPENDIX I

The *Yardstick* Columns of Monsignor George G. Higgins (1945–1994)

The *Yardstick*: Catholic Tests of a Social Order
Department of Archives: Catholic University of America (ACUA)

ACUA: George G. Higgins Papers, series 4

A. The Yardstick Chronological

2. The Higgins Years (1945–1994)
ACUA 129, box 57: 1945–1952
ACUA 129, box 58: 1953–1964
ACUA 129, box 59: 1965–1973
ACUA 129, box 60: 1974–June 27, 1983
ACUA 129, box 61: July 4, 1983–1986
ACUA 129, box 62: 1987–1990
ACUA 129, box 63: 1991–1994

1945

January 8	We Can No Longer Tolerate Discrimination
January 15	Unionism for "White-Collar" Workers
February 19	Labor Leads the "Chase"
February 26	Wild Charges by the Automotive Council
August 27	[Untitled]
September 3	Super-Seniority and the Veteran
September 17	Preface to the Agenda

December 17	Less Rhetoric, More Common Sense
December 31	Natural Rights Are Not for Hire
1946	
January 7	The Over-all Economic Philosophy
January 14	Rally Round a Righteous Leader
January 21	Consolidating Communist Strength
January 28	Who Is More Subversive?
February 4	Academic Authoritarianism
February 11	Speaking of Labor Unions
February 25	A Friendly Warning
March 4	Week-end Jitters
March 11	Ignorance Is No Excuse
March 18	Counter-irritant to Hayck
March 25	We Can't Afford Complacency
May 27	Regarding Legitimate Social Reform
June 3	Legislation Not Enough
June 10	Organized Cooperation in Economic Life
June 17	Labor and Economic Objectives
June 24	Meaning of Europe's Objectives
July 1	A Truly Classless Society
July 8	Competition or Cooperation
July 15	Public Health Insurance
July 22	A Tribute to Sidney Hillman
July 29	Misinterpreting Catholic Teaching
August 5	The Problem of Our Day
August 12	A Common Fallacy Today
August 19	Organized Labor Yesterday and Today
August 26	"Company Unions" and Collective Bargaining
September 2	Economics and Social Work
September 9	The Communists and Mr. Green
September 16	He Who Proves Too Much
September 23	Light on Labor–Management Relations
September 30	Industrial Leaders Complain
October 7	Communist Problem in the CIO
October 28	Australian Catholic Social Action
November 4	Strengthening Organized Labor
November 11	Revival of Belloc
November 18	The Industry Council Program
November 25	Communism and the CIO Convention
December 9	The Side of the Angels

December 16	The Nathan Report
December 23	Industry-wide Collective Bargaining
1947	
January 20	Americans for Democratic Action
January 27	A Classroom Project for Catholics
February 3	An Almost Revolutionary Innovation
February 10	Morals in Management
February 17	The Closed Shop
February 24	Un-American Affairs and Angles
March 10	Democratic Experiments versus Totalitarian Collectivism
March 17	Public Relations in Reverse
March 24	Equilibrium or Crisis?
March 31	The Really Important Problem
April 7	[Untitled]
April 14	A French Lesson in Communism
April 21	The Problem of Lowering Prices
April 28	Should Teachers Unionize?
May 5	What Is Social Justice?
May 12	The Bible of Individualism
May 19	Ethics and Economics
May 26	The State and Labor
June 2	A Hopeful Beginning
June 9	Scholarly Restatement of Principles
June 23	Inconsistent Philosophy
July 14	The Freedom Road
July 21	Billboard Rhymes, Economics Made Easy
July 28	The Law of the Land
August 4	Our Common Responsibility
August 11	Still Time to Choose
August 18	Private Little Heresy
August 25	Christ the Worker
September 1	Search for an Honest Solution
September 8	The Urgency of Social Action
September 29	Shall We Forfeit Freedom?
October 6	A New South
October 13	An Obligation in Social Justice
October 20	Economic Slavery and Freedom
October 27	History Is Made
November 3	Left of the Kremlin
November 10	Social and Economic Justice

November 17	Let Us Be Frank
November 24	Encouraging Labor to Organize
December 1	Taking Stock
December 8	Freedom as Defined
December 15	More Plagiarism Desired
December 22	Public Relations, Prices, Wage Increases

1948

January 12	Our National Economy
January 19	Who's Hysterical Now?
January 26	Baruch Talks Turkey
February 2	Restrictive Covenants
February 9	"Caste, Class, and Race"
February 16	A Great Man's Library
February 23	Industry Councils
March 1	Some Things in Glocco Mora
March 8	"Double-Talk"
March 15	Fiddlers Other Than Nero
March 22	Differences of Opinion
April 5	Our Failure as Christians
April 12	Security versus Respectability
April 19	A Home Needs a House
April 26	Good, as Far as It Goes
May 3	Yes, or No?
May 17	Our Serious Disadvantage
May 31	A Challenge to Businessmen
June 7	Headed in the Right Direction
June 14	Anybody's Guess
June 28	Life Embarrasses Protestants
July 5	Laski's Approach
July 19	"Low-Down Expediency"
July 26	Reform from Within
August 2	A Form of Apostasy
August 9	When Is There a Crisis?
August 16	A Feeling of Frustration
August 23	"Imbedded Individualism," Virtue or Vice?
August 30	Taking Stock on Labor Day
September 6	Keyserling Analysis of Inflation
September 13	The Amsterdam Report
September 20	They Do Get Along
September 27	GM and Norman Thomas

October 11	The Social Message of Christ
October 18	Our Ailing Economy
October 25	Trickery on the Waterfront
November 1	Congressman Hartley Owns Up
November 8	Is a Labor Party Desirable?
November 15	Dr. Taylor Prescribes
November 22	The Real Worry
November 29	A Very Mixed Economy
December 6	An Old "Fascist" Custom
December 13	A Question of Literacy
December 20	Industry Council Truly Radical Plan
December 27	Out-of-Date and Anti-social

1949

January 3	Diplomatic Servants
January 10	More Than a Mote
January 17	Problems Down in Dixie
January 24	Alternative to Two Extremes
January 31	No Friend of Labor?
February 7	Fundamental Scheme for Reconstruction
February 14	All for a Good Cause
February 21	Correct, Mr. Eby?
February 28	Something to Think About
October 3	Veiled Indictments
October 10	The Record Speaks
October 17	Cause for Amazement
October 24	"Man on Horseback"
October 31	What's the Use?
November 7	Advance Notice?
November 14	Candid Opinion
November 21	A Lot More Sensible
November 28	ACTU
December 5	ACTU's Program
December 12	Beside the Point
December 19	NAM Wailing Wall
December 26	Man with a Panacea

1950

January 2	On Samuel Gompers
January 9	Interdependence of Interests
January 23	A Wholesome Development

January 30	Ask the Experts
February 6	A Case for Freedom
February 13	Danger! Words at Work
February 20	Two Pronged Definition
February 27	Abolish Hostility, Promote Cooperation
March 6	Coal Trouble Bigger Than John L.
March 13	Prevailing Philosophy
March 20	U.S. Workers Not Marxists
March 27	The Sixth Stage
April 3	Three Documents
April 10	The End Result
April 17	A Choice of "Modern Classics"
April 24	An Organized Economic Society
May 1	"Voluntary Adjustments"
May 8	A Lack of "Conscience"
May 15	Another Labor–Management Conference
May 22	Economic Individualism No "Dead-Horse"
May 29	For Right and Justice
June 5	Let's Not Be "Used"
June 12	The Time Has Come
June 19	Taft-Hartley versus Unions
June 26	The "Watchdog" Takes a Nap
July 3	Our Holy Father Warns
July 10	Cause for Optimism
July 17	A Long Step Forward
July 24	Trend in the Right Direction
July 31	No News Is Harmony
August 7	Reuther's Four Points
August 14	Mid-century Legal Status of Labor
August 21	[Untitled]
August 28	"Instead of a Fanciful Dream"
September 4	Union Security
September 11	"Let's Look at the Record"
September 18	The Underlying Philosophy
September 25	Neither Letter nor Spirit
October 2	Jurist Seeks a Middle Way
October 9	Back Where We Started
October 16	Responsible Behavior
October 23	In Separate Categories
October 30	Neither Yea nor Nay
November 6	A Disease Called Proletariat

November 27	An "Independent" Analysis
December 4	Catholic–Socialist Split in CIO
December 11	False Anti-Communism
December 18	Shake-up on the Waterfront
December 25	A Triple Sequence

1951

January 1	Socialist–Christian Controversy
January 8	Required Reading
January 15	Voluntarism
January 22	Antitrust Laws
January 29	Subsidiarity
February 5	"Americanism"
February 5	The Bishops' Program 1919
February 12	Superficial Book
February 19	Catholic Union Theory
February 26	Co-determination
March 5	Co-determinism
March 12	"A Socialist's Faith"
March 19	The Welfare State
March 26	Worker Security
April 2	Laissez-Faire No Great Idea
April 9	Social Action's Saleslady (Linna E. Bresette)
April 16	No TV, No Tears
April 23	"The Socialist Tragedy"
April 30	When and Where of Revolution
May 7	Divinity Student Considers Plan for New Social Order
May 14	A Major Social Heresy
May 21	Literally, on Record
May 28	Blanshard on Social Encyclicals
June 4	Slogans of the Past
June 11	How D'Ya Mean Tolerance
June 18	Easy-to-Swallow Principle
June 25	Loose Talk by a Great Soldier
July 2	Time for Moral Suasion
July 9	The Next "Investigation"
July 16	Socialist–Communist Economics
July 23	Take It Away . . .
July 30	Battle for Men's Souls
August 6	Georgia Goes "Nature"
August 13	The "Consultative" Approach

August 20	Industrial Democracy
August 27	Christian Meaning on Labor Day
September 3	Theology and Politics
September 10	The Mote and the Beam
September 17	Who's a Socialist
September 24	Dr. Clark Prescribes
October 1	Prophets of New Economic Order
October 15	Wanted: A Via Media
October 22	Lobbying No Phenomenon
October 29	Lay Spirituality
November 5	Labor in Spain
November 12	GE's White Head
November 19	Buckley's Social Philosophy Not That of the Catholic Church
November 26	Freedom of Education
December 3	Something New
December 10	Our Commonweal
December 17	Time Overlooks Two Sources
December 24	Collective Bargaining in Action
December 31	Plight of Farm Worker

1952

January 7	We Hold to This Opinion
January 14	The Working Rank and File
January 21	A God Given Faculty
January 28	Socialist System
February 4	A Century of Charity
February 11	Capitalism in USA
February 18	Neutrality of American Unions
February 25	ILO Employer Delegations
March 3	Trick of the Trade
March 10	Man and Society
March 17	Something Wrong Somewhere
March 24	Catholicism and American Freedom
March 31	Pegler's Pique
April 7	Skeleton Belongs in Closet
April 14	Is Anybody Listening?
April 21	What Is Capitalism?
April 28	Timely Little Book
May 5	A Natural Myth Questioned
May 12	Union Shop Has to Stay

May 19	Why Catholic Social Action
May 26	Hope of the Future
June 2	Our Choice, Monsignor Ryan
June 9	A Minor Classic, at Least
June 16	"Fundamental, Permanent Mission"
June 23	Honeymoon Is Over
August 11	Germany's New Labor Law
August 18	An Empty Slogan
August 25	The Spiritual Meaning of Trade Unionism
September 1	Anti-clericalism Sounding Board
September 8	Socialists Begin to Understand
September 15	Rank-and-File Conviction
September 22	Contra Catholic Social Philosophy
October 6	Catholic Social Education
October 27	[Untitled]
November 10	Vocational Organization of Economy
November 17	In Memoriam
November 24	The Cardinal Paved the Way
December 1	Business Unionism
December 8	Discussion, Speculation: AF of L, CIO
December 15	Reuther's Underlying Philosophy
December 22	Proper Balance the Problem
December 29	Essential Function of Industry Council

1953

January 5	Word to the Wise Timely
January 12	A New "Labor Law"
January 19	Labor Statement
January 26	Neither Self-Righteous nor Patronizing
February 2	Labor and Foreign Aid
February 9	Family Allowances—Pro and Con
February 16	Future of Family Allowances
February 23	Dr. Morrison's Prescription
March 2	New Look at Old Theories
March 9	Status of Socialism in USA
March 16	The Big Change
March 23	Bureaucracy—Inevitable?
March 30	Authority Indispensable
April 6	The Quest for Community
April 13	The UAW and Women in Industry
April 20	"Tolerance" a Big Word

April 27	Family Allowances
May 4	Wanted: Economic Advisors
May 11	Contemporary Socialism
May 18	Industry-wide Bargaining
May 25	De Toledano Hurts Himself
June 1	Practical Applications of a Theory
June 8	Father Dietz—Social Pioneer
June 15	A Living Document
June 22	The Problem of Monopoly
June 29	Ethics of Private Property
July 6	"The Conservative Mind"
July 13	Labor Union the Basic Unit
July 20	Reuther Entitled to Hearing
August 24	A Master of Conjecture
August 31	The Adjectives Are Important
September 7	ICFTU Notes MRA Move
September 14	One Feasible Alternative
September 21	"Let's Look at the Record"
September 28	"Priest-Workers of France"
October 5	A Right to Be Proud
October 12	Limitless Future for AFL
October 19	The ICFTU—a Propaganda Mill?
October 26	Catholic Proponents of ILO
November 2	A Wholesome Contribution
November 9	In Behalf of Peace
November 23	Guaranteed Annual Wage
November 30	Industry Council Plan
December 7	Working for Peace—John F. Cronin, S.S.
December 14	The Attacks on the UN
December 21	[Untitled]
December 28	The Assembly Line

1954

January 4	Labor's Rights
January 11	Religious Prejudice
January 18	Guaranteed Annual Wage
January 25	Democratic Socialism
February 1	Freedom of the Press
February 8	Kerosene on the Fire
February 15	[Untitled]
February 22	The United Nations Charter

March 8	A Matter of Lexicography
March 22	Ambiguous Terminology
March 29	Sauce for the Gander
April 5	Catholics and the United Nations
April 12	Spirit of Christian Optimism
April 19	Priest-Worker Controversy
April 26	Difference of Opinion
May 3	"Liberal" Anti-Catholicism
May 10	Economic Co-determinism
May 17	A Sense of Balance
May 24	The Malins Declaration
May 31	Unwarranted Political Regulation
June 7	The "Theology" of Work
June 14	Others Have a Word for It
June 21	International Labor Relations
June 28	Running the Country?
July 12	The Pot and the Kettle
July 19	Catholic Education and Unionism
July 26	Not Limited to Bargaining
August 2	Principles at Stake
August 9	ICP Here to Stay
August 16	Conditions Rather Than Abstractions
August 30	Labor Day and Religion
October 4	Tarnished Maybe, Still the Ideal
October 11	The Tax Controversy
November 15	"A Program for Conservatives"
November 22	"Specifically on Moral Aspects"
November 29	Priest of Great Vision
December 6	The American Myth—at Home and Abroad
December 20	No "Labor Party" Envisioned
December 27	Guaranteed Annual Wage

1955

January 3	On the Waterfront
January 10	Rights of Federal Employees
January 24	"Number One" Objective
January 31	Curtailing the Unions
February 7	Passivism No Alternative to Excessive Individualism
February 21	Reconstruction of the Social Order
February 28	Unfinished Business
March 14	The Tried and Tested American Way

March 21	Industry-wide Collective Bargaining
March 28	Labor Movement—Pro and Con
April 4	American Catholics—Conservatives?
April 11	Guaranteed Annual Wage
April 18	The U.S.A. and ILO
April 25	The President's Moderate Proposal
May 2	Sin on the Waterfront
May 9	Inadequate Alternative
May 30	Political Action, a Natural Right
June 6	The Heart of the Matter
July 4	Americans Speak Up at Vienna
July 11	Louder, Please!
July 18	Out of Context
July 25	No Pro-labor "Bias"
August 1	Hot Weather Comments
August 8	Simple Standard of Ethics
August 15	Already the Shouting Begins
August 22	Who's Gouging Whom?
August 29	Religious Significance of Labor Day
September 5	The Moral Rearmament Movement
September 12	More about Duties, Less about Rights
September 19	A Question Still Unanswered
October 3	Fraternal Charity, Yes; Also, a Sense of Humor
October 10	Labor Leader Receives Lay Leadership Award!
October 24	On to Greater Heights
October 31	Hew to the Line
November 7	Philanthropy Purely
November 14	Whistling in the Dark
November 21	Those So-Called "Neutral" Unions
November 28	Truth More Convincing Than Fiction
December 5	The Advent of Labor Unity
December 12	Liberal Arts and Labor Leaders
December 26	Meany Lowers the Boom

1956

January 2	'Tain't Funny, No More
January 9	Our Hopes for 1956
January 16	Uncle Sam's Employees
January 23	Not an Adequate Solution to Serious ILO Problem
January 30	The NEA and Teachers' Unions
March 26	Social Apostolate in the Americas

April 2	Fortune Takes Some Pot Shots
April 9	No Time for Exaggeration
April 16	Too Much Winking at Labor Racketeering
April 23	Feast of St. Joseph the Workman Observed in USA on Labor Day
April 30	"Rider" Approach All Wrong
May 7	Hands across the Border
May 14	ILO Convention Banning Forced Labor
May 21	Crystal Ball, Factual Predictions
May 28	Who Speaks for the Church?
June 4	Unions and the Bar
June 25	Unions and Political Action
July 2	A Particularly Distasteful Combination
July 9	Heading for a Showdown
July 16	Labor's Biggest Current Problem
July 23	Refutation of Certain Unions Rests on Acts of Individuals
July 30	Public Prayer Symbolically Important
August 6	Beware the "Socialist" Ideal
August 13	Morality of the Living Wage
August 20	Like-to-Like Apostolate in the Field of Social Reform
August 27	In Terms of Social Justice
September 3	A Place of Pilgrimage
September 10	Three Score Years and Ten Finds Labor Moving in Right Direction
September 17	That Christ's Ideals May Prevail
September 24	Education and Service
October 1	First Things First
October 8	An Association and the Natural Law
October 15	First Things First
October 29	Mutual Understanding, Good Will
November 5	Moral Aspects of Safety Problem
November 12	Labor and Political Action
November 19	The Practice of Unionism
November 26	Ever-Changing Problems Require New Approaches
December 3	Neither Timely Nor Right
December 10	Function, Authority of Catholic Press
December 17	An Investigation Is Asked
December 24	The Laity and Social Action
December 31	Reception to Column on NAACP

1957

January 7	Investigation of Racketeering in Labor Movement
January 14	The International Labor Organization
January 21	U.S. Participation in the ILO
January 28	Social Apostolate and the Press
February 4	Two Things Are Needed for Practical Effects
February 11	ILO Methods and Goals Too Little Known
February 18	No Bill of Divorcement—Yet
February 25	Proof in the Press
March 4	Why, Oh Why?
March 25	Extension Fair Labor Standards' Coverage Considered by Congress
April 1	"Social Gospel"—1957
April 8	Effect of Senate Investigation
April 15	Moral and Spiritual Crisis Confronting Labor Movement
April 22	What Price Economy and Efficiency
April 29	Authority of Automotive Workers' "Watchdog" Committee
May 6	NAM's Opposition to Douglas-Ives Bills
May 13	Pegler's Smear of Durkin
May 20	North Africa Convention of ICFTU
June 3	Quebec Pastoral and "Right to Work" Laws
June 10	NAM Protests
June 17	Decline of Interest in Industry Council Plan
June 24	The Liturgy and Social Action
July 1	Labor Relations in Spain
July 8	European Socialism and the ICFTU
July 15	The Problem of Inflation
July 22	Chase-War Cartoons
July 29	Social Justice Loses a Champion
August 5	Inflation Solution Possible
August 12	The McClellan Committee's Function
August 19	Concerns for Human Values
August 26	The Spiritual Meaning of Labor Day
September 2	Walter Reuther's Proposal
September 9	Crying Need Fulfilled
September 16	What Is the YCW?
November 18	Labor Movement Crisis Is Moral and Religious Movement
November 25	The Industry Council Plan and Dr. Ropke
December 2	CAIP Is Small but Articulate

December 9	Asks Divine Guidance for Labor Movement
December 16	AFL-CIO Convention Marks Turning Point in Labor's History
December 23	Are Neutral Unions Morally Harmful?
December 30	NEA Considered as "Company Union"

1958

January 6	European Religion–Labor Outlook Hopeful
January 13	NAM and Ethical Practice Codes
January 20	Advantage of Collective Bargaining over Legislation
January 27	Labor–Management Committees and the Spirit of Partnership
February 3	Unions and Freedom of the Worker
February 10	Catholic Press Grows and Improves
February 17	Reliable Secular Reporting in Social Action Field
February 24	Are Labor Unions Too Powerful?
March 3	How Popular Is Organized Labor?
March 10	Mid-Twentieth-Century American Capitalism
March 17	Catholic Scholarship and Industrial Relations Research
March 4	"Words at Work"
March 31	Are So-Called "Labor Priests" Too Kind to Labor?
April 7	Rank and File Apathy in Unions
April 14	Reuther and the Industry Council Plan
April 21	Unusual Conference at Maryknoll
April 28	Integration of the Liturgy and Social Justice
May 5	Labor and the Churches
May 12	Rending Labor Legislation
May 26	Should Fund for Republic Pay Taxes?
June 2	Religious Tensions Aired at Seminar
June 9	"Blessed Are the Peacemakers . . ." [Cardinal Stritch]
June 16	Too Much Preoccupation with Production
June 23	UAW Anti-clerical?
June 30	The Wage–Price Question
July 7	Is There a Jewish Labor Movement?
July 14	Is Inflation Just a Conversation Piece?
July 21	The Closed Shop and Rights of the Worker
July 28	A Labor–Management "Summit-Conference"
August 4	Wage Rates and Inflation
August 11	Labor—between the Devil and the Deep
August 18	Work and the Individual Soul
August 28	Future of the Labor Movement

September 1	End of Summer Postscripts
September 8	"Confessional" Union—Undemocratic?
September 15	Criticisms of Labor Day Statement
September 22	The New Bakers' Union
September 29	The Future of Catholic Social Action
October 6	Race News Not All Bad
October 13	The Soviet Threat to America's Steel Supremacy
October 20	Pope Pius XII on Social Problem
October 27	"Right-to-Work" and Canadian Labor
November 3	Cardinal Mooney and the Labor Movement
November 17	Arthur Goldberg's Proposal
November 24	Ill-Advised Attack on George Meany
December 1	Golden Opportunity for the Building and Construction Industry
December 8	Mr. Ascolis Challenge to "Liberals"
December 15	Church's Influence on Labor
December 22	Salazar and the Teaching Mission of the Church
December 29	First Year of UAW's "Watch-Dog Committee"

1959

January 5	Hopes and Resolutions for 1959
January 12	Who Was to Blame for the Newspaper Strike?
January 19	The Wage-Price Spiral
January 26	Millinery Workers Salvage Hat Company
February 2	The President's Economic Report to Congress
February 9	The Press and the Social Order
February 16	Our Not Quite Affluent Society
February 23	Who Is to Blame for Unemployment?
March 2	How Serious Is the "Right-to-Work" Problem?
March 9	Canadian Cardinal on Unemployment
March 23	The Problem of "Administered" Prices
March 30	Press Coverage of Labor News
April 20	Economic Statesmanship
April 27	Organization of Government Employees
May 4	The Ethics of Catholic Press Controversy
May 18	"News Magazine" or Journal of Opinion
May 25	Are Modern Theologians Missing the Boat?
June 1	Class Conflict Still Has Champions
June 8	Priests in the Social Action Field
June 15	Citizens of Two Worlds
June 22	Some Employers Still Avoid Unions

June 29 An Effective Instrument for Peace
July 6 The Plight of the Migratory Worker
July 13 Dedicated Civil Servants
July 20 New Christian Unions—a Matter of Judgment
July 27 New Hope for Farm Workers
August 3 [Untitled]
August 10 Catholic Teaching on the Market Economy
August 17 Catholics on Matters of Public Policy
August 24 Invitation to Class Warfare
August 31 Don't Forget the First Beatitude
September 7 Progress in the Moral Sphere
September 14 Labor–Management Outlook Gloomy
September 21 Predictions on New Labor Reform Law
September 28 Khrushchev Missed a Lesson on Freedom
October 5 The Church and Temporal Order
October 12 The Truth about Financial Power in the U.S.
October 19 Is the Family Farmer "The Forgotten Man?"
October 26 The Steel Strike and the Taft-Hartley Act
November 2 The Plight of American Migrant Farm Workers
November 9 Hail to the Kaisers
November 16 On Airing Differences
November 23 Class War Over—Name Calling Continues
November 30 The German Social Democrats' New Manifesto
December 7 Support Mounts for Labor–Management Meet
December 14 Power in the New Society
December 21 Cradle-to-Grave Security
December 28 New Millinery Contract Important

1960

January 18 Social Action Looks to the Future: City Problem
January 25 On Definitions of Democracy
February 1 Discredited Principles Restated
February 8 Blanshard Back at Old Stand
February 15 Labor Schools Still Vital
February 22 Treatment of Labor in Catholic Press
February 29 Hutchins—the Boat Rocker
March 7 "The Enemy Within" a Wonderful Book
March 14 Blanshard Losing Ground
March 21 Strikes Still Necessary
March 28 Amendment of Mexican Farm Labor Movement
April 4 Real Issue Obscured in Controversy over National Council of Churches

April 18	Mr. Schlesinger Oversimplifies
April 25	Democracy in Labor and Business
May 2	Moral Values in Economic Field
May 9	Who Caused the Steel Strike?
May 16	NAM Bucks the President's Proposal
May 23	Hope for Minimum Wage for Farm Workers
May 30	Featherbedding at the Top
June 6	"Clarification" of Wagner-Peyser Act
June 13	America's Working Women
June 20	Real Estate Myth Exploded
June 27	Child Labor in Agriculture
July 11	Public versus Private Spending
July 18	The Federal Pay Increase
July 25	Credit Unions and Catholic Social Teaching
August 1	Commercial Farm Bloc's Lobby
August 8	The Church and Secular Unions
August 22	"A Second Thought" on the Union Shop
August 29	More Than Justice
November 21	Why CTCC "Deconfessionalized"
November 28	Course in Communism
December 5	History of Catholic Social Action
December 12	Our National Purpose
December 19	ILO Report on U.S. Labor Unions
December 26	Politics in Washington

1961

January 2	Farm Labor Still Gets Short End
January 9	Report on National Goals
January 16	Minimum Wage Legislation
January 23	"The Forgotten American"
January 30	Trade Unions in Russia
February 13	World Refugee Year Evaluated
February 20	A National Council of Labor–Management Advisors
February 27	The Livernash Report
March 6	Experts Speak on Communism and the Churches
March 13	Is Labor Seeking Co-management?
March 20	A New Look at Anti-trust Laws
March 27	Diffusion of Political and Economic Power
April 3	Extremists Hinder Anti-Red Cause
April 10	Formal Recognition of Federal Unions
April 17	Two Important Anniversaries
April 24	Economic Life—the Christian View

May 1	Reconstruction through Industry Councils
May 8	"First and Foremost Remedy"
May 15	Opportunity for U.S. Catholics
May 22	Foreign Aid and Christian Principles
May 29	Unionists Support Peace Corps
June 5	The Church and Economic Advancement
June 12	The Wage-Price Spiral
June 19	A Step Forward
June 26	Massive Foreign Aid
July 3	The Looper Case
July 10	Looper Decision and "Right-to-Work"
July 17	Automation Committee Report
July 24	Detroit—1961
July 31	Wives as Breadwinners
August 7	New Encyclical Breaks New Ground (*Mater et Magistra)*
August 14	A Fortunate Coincidence
August 21	New Encyclical and Trade Unionism
August 28	"Rendering of a Service"
September 4	Controversy over a Word
September 11	Government's Role in Social Progress
September 18	Wages, Prices and the Common Good
September 25	The Optimism of Pope John XXIII
October 2	Labor in the Doldrums
October 9	Reagan and Labor
October 17	Clergy and Laity in Social Action
October 23	NAIA's Boycott of ILO
October 30	ILO—Instrument of Social Progress
November 6	ILO's Technical Assistance Widespread
November 13	ILO's Battle against Slave Labor
November 20	[Untitled; concludes series in defense of ILO]
November 27	The Future of Christian Social Action
December 4	National Health Insurance
December 11	Decline in Union Membership
December 18	Campaign to Bring Unions under Sherman Act
December 25	Interpretation of New Social Encyclical

1962

January 1	Turn of the Screw in TV Commercials
January 8	Radical Right vs. True Conservatives
January 15	Pope John and the Industry Council Plan
January 22	Would Labor–Management Conferences Work?

February 19	"Guideposts" for Wage-Price Behavior
February 26	Today's Social Problems
March 5	TV's Good Programs
March 12	Lobbyists in Washington
March 19	Railroad Commission's Report Lambasted
March 26	Dual Unionism
April 2	Catholic Social Action
April 9	[Untitled]
May 14	Labor, Management Have Opportunity
May 21	Do They Really Want Them Back?
May 28	A Critic Is Answered
June 4	Need to Study Economic Goals
June 11	The Government's Role
June 18	Ford on Business Ethics
June 25	The Strikes in Spain
July 2	End to Eight-Year Strike
July 9	U.S. Economists in an Ivory Tower
July 16	Criticism about Washington Politics
July 23	Is American Labor "Bourgeois"?
July 30	Work and Leisure
August 6	Rights of Union Members
August 13	The Laity and Social Action
August 20	Are Catholics Isolationists?
August 27	Labor Day—1962
September 3	Union Rank and File Rebellion
September 10	NAM on Union Power
September 17	NFO's "Withholding Action"
September 24	Credit Union Founder
October 1	Realistic View of Automation
December 31	Ultraconservatists Echo Red Opinion

1963

January 7	The Council and Social Reform
January 14	Strikers and Employers Living in Past
January 21	Labor, Management and the Public Interest
January 28	Catholic Employers and Managers Organize
February 4	Conference on Religion and Race
February 11	Controversy between Trade Union Internationals
February 18	TRB on Federal Aid
February 25	The Churches and Race Relations
March 4	Implementing Conference on Religion and Race

March 11	Definition of American Economic System
March 18	Briton Critical of American Catholicism
March 24	A Great Labor Leader [John Brophy]
April 1	Time's Attack on Church in Chicago
April 8	Unconscious Marxists
April 15	Is the "Union Shop" Immoral?
April 22	U.S. Unions Guided by Christian Principles
April 29	"Pacem in Terris"—a Step Forward
May 6	False Analysis of Catholicism
May 13	Labor Unions Worth "the Price"
May 20	The Poorest Work Group
May 27	Unions Necessary
June 3	NBC's "The Quiet Revolution"
June 10	Pope John's Impact in Socio-economic Field
June 17	Racial Discrimination in Unions
June 24	Labor Unions Have One Purpose
July 1	U.S. Steel and the Unions—1963
July 8	Catholic Teaching and Medicare
July 15	Right to Decent Housing
July 22	Something New to Argue About
July 29	Interest in Business Ethics on Increase
August 5	One-Sided Wall of Separation
August 12	New Farm Labor Bill
August 19	Early Days of Organized Labor
August 26	Big Labor and the Race Question
September 2	Best Answer to Red Propaganda
September 9	Self-Appointed Friends Insult Businessmen
September 17	Do Social Encyclicals Still Apply?
September 23	Have Christian Churches Failed the Negro?
September 20	Strange Agreement

1964

January 20	Schema 17
January 27	"Baneful Heritage of the 18th Century"
February 3	Seminar on "Poverty in Plenty"
February 10	A Durable Modern Fallacy
February 17	Two Types of Unions
February 24	National Study Conference on Church and State
March 2	Government and Social Welfare
March 9	"Holy Liberty"
March 16	The Real Enemy

March 23	Economic Anarchy
March 30	Lay Apostolate in the Secular World
April 6	Collective Bargaining and the Common Good
April 13	Now Who's Silent on Civil Rights?
April 20	Labor's Disenchanted Friends
April 27	Social Encyclicals and Contemporary Problems
May 4	The Anti-poverty Bill
May 11	The Council and the Lay Apostolate
May 18	Profile of a "Liberal"—by a "Conservative"
May 25	Liturgy, Properly Explained, Spurs Social Consciousness
June 8	Interpreting Social Encyclicals
June 15	Research in Social Sciences
June 22	"A Funny Thing Happened"
June 29	Face to Face, Hand in Hand
July 6	Unionization of Hospital Employers
July 13	Understanding Capitalism
July 20	[Untitled]
July 27	A Cause for Rejoicing
August 3	Social Justice Is "Christian Sentimentalism"?
August 10	A Practical Example
August 17	Pope Paul's First Encyclical
August 24	Analyzing "His Church"
August 31	The Clergy and Politics
September 7	General Economic Welfare
September 14	Labor on the Spot?
September 21	On Automation
November 23	In the Temporal Order

1965

January 18	Letter from Latin America
January 25	Christian–Jewish Relations
February 1	Tribute to Cardinal Cardijn
February 8	Migratory Workers: The Poorest of the Poor
February 15	European Controversy: Schema 13
February 22	Pacifist Attack
March 1	Role of Clergy and Laity in Socio-economic Reform
March 8	Poverty, the Poor, and Low Wages
March 15	On Sociology—and Jews and Catholics
March 22	Common Sense and Zeal
March 29	A Statesmanlike Decision
April 5	The Church's Role in Interracial Justice

April 12	Mr. Buckley on Brutality
April 19	Clerical Critics of U.S. Foreign Policy
April 26	Rules of Evidence—and Courtesy
May 3	National Policy and the Clergy
May 10	Second Time Around
May 17	Helping the Truly Poor
May 24	Right-to-Work Legislation and the Catholic Community
May 31	Public Prayer at Civic Events
June 7	May Religious Objection to Labor Union Membership Be Valid?
June 14	Destructive Criticism
June 21	Should the Council Support Conscientious Objectors?
June 28	Telling Us Who Our Friends Are
July 5	Lack of Labor Relations Knowledge
July 12	Oversimplifying Vietnam
July 19	Whirling in His Grave
July 26	Council Interlopers
August 2	The Moon, the Earth, the Cities
August 9	Who Makes U.S. Foreign Policy?
August 16	Church Groups and Section 14 (b)
August 23	Work Still Needed in Civil Rights
August 30	Why Socialism Didn't Catch On
September 6	Aids in Teaching Catholic Social Doctrine
September 13	"In the Name of Common Decency"
September 20	Birth Control and Anti-poverty Campaigns
September 27	Why Use Half-Measures? Let's Sterilize Them!
October 4	A Friendly Criticism
October 11	Gauging the Mood of the Council
October 18	Making a Scapegoat of American Bishops
October 25	Celibacy of the Clergy
November 1	A Guide in Brotherhood
November 8	Twilight Shadows of Vatican Council II
November 15	Church and Press
November 22	Religious Liberty from Gibbons to Murray
November 29	Unity, Freedom, Charity
December 20	Dialogue and Freedom
December 27	Moynihan a Racist?

1966

January 3	Priests and Laymen: Roles in the Temporal Order
January 10	Labels Don't Mean Much

January 17	Transit Tie-Up
January 24	The Right to Strike
January 31	Opus Dei
February 7	[Untitled]
February 14	Blueprint for the Future
February 21	National Economic Planning
February 28	Clergy on Vietnam Debate Continued
March 7	Can We Settle for Affluence Based on "Poverty" Wages?
March 14	Toward Fruitful Jewish–Christian Dialogue?
March 21	Scholarly Basis for Jewish–Christian Dialogue
March 28	The Church in the Modern World
April 4	"The Greatest of These Is Charity"
April 11	The Age of Dialogue—and Christian Optimism
April 18	Cesar Chavez: "New Breed" Labor Leader?
April 25	Post-conciliar Problems
May 2	A Lonely Voice
May 9	A Form of Sick Humor
May 16	War and Peace
May 23	Freedom of Association
May 30	Threat to the Religious Press
June 6	The "New" NAM
June 13	U.S. Labor and the ILO
June 20	About Anti-Semitism Study
June 27	[Untitled]
July 4	From Midnight to Dawn
July 11	Preaching, Columning and Civil Rights
July 18	Organization and Cooperation: Only Hope of Workers and Growers Alike
July 25	Minimum Wage for Farm Workers
August 1	Catholic Action
August 8	Strikes and Compulsory Arbitration
August 15	Hemisphere Labor Cooperation
August 22	The Price of Freedom
August 29	The Right to Strike
September 5	"Rewrite" the New Testament?
September 12	"Black Power" and the "White Problem"
September 19	The Nurses' Revolution
September 26	Guaranteed Annual Income
October 3	Organized Labor in 1966 and Beyond
October 10	Fair Labor Standards
October 17	Paul Blanshard on Vatican II

October 24	Freedom of the Catholic Press
October 31	"Give Me Your Poor . . ."
November 7	For Those Who Can*not* Work—or Should Not Work
November 14	Latin American Trade Unions
November 21	"A Providential Opportunity"
November 28	Messengers of Peace
December 5	A Union or an Association?
December 12	Post-conciliar Zeal
December 19	Workers All: Blue and White Collars
December 26	Selective Service and the Conscientious Objector

1967

January 2	Maritain's New Book
January 9	U.S. Chamber of Commerce Looks at Socio-economic Reform
January 16	Stormy Weather for Labor Unions?
January 23	Regarding HUAC
January 30	Unrest in Churches—Lay and Clerical
February 6	Guidelines or Not—Profits Rise Faster Than Wages
February 13	The Labor Revolution
February 20	Seen a Social Action Heretic Lately?
February 27	A Breakdown in Christian–Jewish Relations
March 6	Would You Believe?
March 13	"Open Letter on Vietnam"
March 20	Family Allowances in Our Future?
March 27	"Word and Worship"—Teaching What the Church Teaches
April 3	George K. Hunton—Interracial Lay Leader
April 10	The Farmer Still Needs Help
April 17	Pope Paul on Capitalism
April 24	What Is It? [U.S. Economic System]
May 1	The Secular and the Sacred
May 8	Organized Labor's Problems
May 15	The Death of "Widget"
May 22	History Made in Catholic Action
May 29	Two Views of Conscientious Objection
June 5	Angry Young Men
June 12	Expo '67
June 19	A Smorgasbord of Comment
June 26	The Israeli–Arab War
July 3	The Church's Social Teaching: An Anti-Catholic View

July 10	Compulsory Arbitration
July 17	Labor Leaders and Union Members
July 24	The Public Policy Role of the Church and the Synagogue
August 7	Violence—No; Government Assistance—Yes!
August 14	A Monumental Task: Laity's Opportunity
August 21	Adult Education Needed
August 28	Father John Courtney Murray
September 4	Two Great National Problems: Race Relations and Justice for Farm Workers
September 11	Up with Collective Bargaining
September 18	Warner and Sway's Enlightened Policies
September 25	Perhaps Unintentionally
October 2	About the "Catechism Controversy"
October 9	Should Teachers Organize, Strike?
November 13	About Selective Conscientious Objection
November 20	Refreshing Example
November 27	The Church and Society: To Act or Not to Act
December 4	Jewish–Christian Dialogue
December 11	When Civil Disobedience Becomes Anarchy
December 18	The Council on Labor's Rights
December 25	Labor's Leadership and Membership

1968

January 1	Farm Bureau Federation Wastes Its Time
January 8	Hope for the Future
January 15	Labor School Pioneer
January 22	Public Prayer at Civic Gatherings
January 29	Laymen and Temporal Affairs
February 5	Sociological Methodology: Where Angels Should Fear to Tread
February 12	"Green Card" Commuters
February 19	Cool Heads Needed for Civil Rights Progress
February 26	The Clergy in Politics?
March 4	When May Public Employees Strike?
March 11	Politics and the Clergy
March 18	Examination of Conscience
March 25	Collective Bargaining in Church-Related Institutions
April 1	Protection for Fifty Million Workers
April 8	A Summary of the Synod
April 15	Beyond and After Memphis: A Major Turning-Point?
April 22	Do Men Really Listen to Women?

April 29	"Now Is the Time for All Good Men . . ."
May 6	Safety Act Attacked by Chamber of Commerce
May 13	Democracy in Action in UAW's Public Review Board
May 20	The National Catholic Reporter and the Bishops
May 27	Federal Case or Local Crisis?
June 3	Straightening Out the Record
June 10	Crisis in Public Transportation
June 17	The Future of Organized Labor
June 24	To Be Generous and Open-Handed
July 1	Simplifying the Complex
July 8	Real Heroes of Peace Movement
July 15	Comparing Immigrant and Negro Experience in the U.S.
July 22	Who's "Clerical" Now?
July 29	Criticizing the "Institutional Church"
August 5	Some Labor and Political Notes
August 12	The Clergy and Political Campaigns
August 19	Future Dialog on the Church's Social Doctrine
August 26	Social Action Leaders
September 2	A Second Look at Chicago
September 9	A Sense of Perspective
September 16	Deprecates Attack on Cesar Chavez
September 23	"Children," My Eye!
September 30	If Life Were Only Simple Again
October 7	Our Future Race Relations
October 14	A Critique on the "Council and the Jews"
October 21	"World Federation of Labor"
October 28	A Pretty Broad Statement
November 4	Dialogue between Catholics and Jews
November 11	Organized Labor Should Be "Conscience of the Nation"
November 18	A Note of Hope
November 25	The Rest Is up to Us
December 2	The Laity's Role in Economic and Political Action
December 9	Let's Be Glad Press and Public Are Interested in Church
December 16	Rewarding Public Service
December 23	Young Turks of the New Left
December 30	Norman Thomas

1969

January 6	The Grape Boycott and the Right to Organize
January 13	Government's Obligation in Social Welfare Reform
January 20	Crime: What Do We Know about It?

January 27	"Stop Shouting . . . Speak Quietly . . ."
February 3	Prayer at Public Evens—Including Presidential Inaugurations
February 10	Black Militants and Anti-Semitism
February 17	A Threat to Genuine Collective Bargaining
February 24	Clergy and Laymen in a Time of Social Change
March 3	Public Service Employees and the "Public Interest"
March 10	The Pharisee in All of Us
March 17	Suburbia and the Social Revolution—I
March 24	Suburbia and the Social Revolution—II
March 31	Freedom in the Church
April 7	A Letter from a Reader
April 14	Browsing
April 21	In Rome Rain Falls Mostly on the "American Dream"
April 28	Scraggly Haircuts and Scraggly Thinking
May 5	The Dutch in Dialogue: Ferment but No Solution
May 19	A. Philip Randolf at Eighty
May 26	Voluntaryism
June 9	Libel in Law, Slander in Theology
June 16	Tomorrow's Christian
June 23	A Fragmented Society: How Can All Our People Share in It?
June 30	Pope Paul in Geneva
July 7	A Toast to Miss Delvin
July 14	Trade Union Freedom in Spain
July 21	The Angriest Book of the Year
July 28	Various Establishments and Their Critics
August 4	The Price of Being an Editor
August 11	Mary McGrory Referees Fulbright-Meany Bout
August 18	Government Employees Expense Allowance Is Miserly Sum
August 25	Moynihan Has Edited Constructive Study of the War on Poverty
September 1	"Conservative to the Core"
September 8	Liberal-Labor-Negro Alliance
September 15	Farm Workers' Right to Organize and Bargain Collectively
September 22	Construction Industry and Housing Crisis
September 29	Religious Freedom in Oak Park
October 6	Kinds of Socialism
October 13	The More the Merrier

October 20	Democratic Rules of Union Procedure
October 27	A Glance at the Past and a Look at the Future
November 3	The Press and the Synod
November 10	Grape Workers: For or against Cesar Chavez?
November 17	Wasn't That Settled in the 1880s?
November 24	In Defense of Bayard Rustin
December 29	Innocent Abroad

1970

January 5	Alan in Wonderland!
January 12	First Things First
January 19	Are You Harried, Uptight, Lacking Leisure?
January 26	Plea for Good Listeners in Christian–Jewish Dialogue
February 2	Revisionist History: Labor and U.S. Foreign Policy
February 9	Initiative and Leadership Proper to All Levels of the Church
February 16	Respect and Love: Guides to Truth and Goodness
February 23	U.S. Policy and Latin America
March 2	Labor Leaders and the Rank-and-File
March 9	Is Twin-Circle Anti-Semitic?
March 16	Seeking Justice and Peace in Vineyards
March 23	The Kerner Report and the Silent Majority
April 13	"As I Was Saying"
April 20	On the Administration's Family Income Plan
April 27	Farm Labor Breakthrough
May 4	The American Labor Movement—Dead or Alive?
May 11	Civil Rights in the Southwest
May 18	Walter Reuther—in Memoriam
May 25	On the Sidewalks of New York . . .
June 1	Enemies of the Poor . . . ?
June 8	Cities Disproportionate Attention to Minorities
June 15	On Writing a Column
June 22	Tempering Criticism with Charity
June 29	Advertising "Mindhinders" and Their Critics
August 24	A Leap Forward in the Agricultural Industry
November 9	The Traveling American
November 16	The Church and Secular Affairs
November 23	A Fair Hearing
November 30	Attacking the Scandal of Day Labor Hiring
December 7	Pope Paul Admires Youth's Idealism
December 14	Toward Coalition of Blacks and White Ethnics

December 21	When the Oppressed Unite . . .
December 28	Desk Clearing
1971	
January 4	Elitist Snobbery
January 11	Differing Points of View
January 18	Abolish the Old-Fashioned Wake?
January 25	A "Liberal" Par Excellence
February 1	On Second Reading . . .
February 8	New Style Liberal
February 15	At This Late Date . . . ?
February 22	Bernadette and American Problems
March 1	Christian Ecumenism a Threat to the Jews?
March 8	Prayer and Social Action
March 15	The Church and Political Action
March 22	Your Right to Privacy
March 29	Spain and Its Trade Unions
April 5	Renewed Pact in California Farm Labor Dispute
April 12	Ralph De Toledano on Cesar Chavez
April 19	De Toledano Visits Chavez—Part II
April 26	"Honest Discussion . . . Mutual Charity . . . Common Good . . ."
May 3	Harsh Judgments: Naming "Villains," Then Reading Their Minds
May 10	About That Book
May 17	May Day Aftermath
May 24	New Hopes for the City
May 31	Progress in the Lay Apostolate
June 7	The Church and Communications
June 14	To Analyze "with Objectivity" . . .
June 21	The American Catholic Church in Social Action and Reform
June 28	Peonage in America?
July 5	A Time for Good Will, Not Recrimination
July 12	Are We Being Fair to ILO?
July 19	Middle Americans
July 26	The Trouble with Broad Statements
August 2	Berkeley and Anti-Semitism: Enough Is Enough
August 9	"Some Arguments Used by Slave Owners One Hundred Years Ago"
August 16	The Jesus People

August 23	Socialism and Christianity
August 30	Working-Class Leaders and Followers
September 6	Reform in the Church
September 13	Labor Day an Anachronism?
September 20	Church Influences on Legislative Process
September 27	Social and Political Issues—Instructing the Faithful
October 4	The Name of the Game in Social Action Is Controversy
October 11	Putting the Synod in Perspective
October 18	The Synod Gets Underway
October 25	Report on the Synod
November 1	Who Should Do What?
November 8	The Synod Comes to a Close
November 15	Report on the Synod
November 22	Church in Spain Holds Great Promise for the Future
November 29	Respect for the President
December 6	Criticism of the Press
December 13	Football Games Redeem Television's Image
December 20	The Synod Analysis of Father Greeley
December 27	Judge Not That You Not Be Judged

1972

January 3	Charity Begins at Home
January 10	Taking Issues with a Synod Critic
January 17	[Untitled]
January 24	The Church and Social Justice
January 31	Opinions about the Synod's Document on World Justice
February 7	Christian–Jewish Relations
February 14	The Catholic Position on War
February 21	Problem Is Greatest for the Parents
February 28	Religious Liberty and the Government
March 6	The Role of Intellectuals
March 13	The Evils of Professional Football
March 20	Women and the Equal Rights Amendments
March 27	Labor Relations and the Automobile Industry
April 3	Israel's Claim to National Survival
April 10	Criticism of Chavez and His Union Tactics
April 17	Report on Sweden's Middle Way
April 24	Opening the Bishops' Meeting to the Press
May 1	[Untitled]
May 8	Criticism of the NFPC
May 15	More Criticism of the NFPC

May 22	Employment of Handicapped and Mentally Retarded
May 29	Catholic Membership in the World Council of Churches
June 5	The Criticism of Father John Courtney Murray, S.J.
June 12	The Arizona Farm Labor Bill
June 19	Farewell to a Friend [Saul Alinsky]
June 26	"Porkchoppers" in the Labor Movement
July 3	The Future of Socialism
July 10	Religion and Politics
July 17	Politics in the Public?
July 24	Tolerance of Diversity
July 31	The Farm Labor Union Crisis
August 7	The Farm Labor Union Crisis
August 14	Solving the Farm Labor Crisis through Collective Bargaining
August 21	The Influence of Labor in the Political Arena
August 28	Some Liberals and Labor Union History
September 4	The Catholic Vote
September 11	[Untitled]
September 18	Setting the Record Straight
September 25	Using the Pulpit for Political Purposes
October 2	The Work of the Local and Regional Church
October 9	Spiritual Renewal the Real Need
October 16	Calling Attention to the War
October 23	The Phenomenon of Change in the Church
October 30	The Role of the Intellectuals
November 6	Some Thoughts on "Bare Ruined Choirs"
November 13	Intellectuals and the Labor Movement
November 20	Strikes and Compulsory Arbitration
December 4	Speaking Out on Abortion
December 11	Catholic–Jewish Relations in the United States
December 18	Who Is Xavier Rynne?
December 24	Labor Unions and Joseph Rauh

1973

January 1	Happy in Your Work?
January 8	Taking a Look at America
January 15	Attack on Daniel P. Moynihan
January 22	The Administration and Welfare Reform
January 29	Too Much of a Good Thing
February 5	Farm Workers Legislation and the Farm Bureau Federation

February 12	Proposed Merger of Teamsters and Farm Bureau
February 19	Defending the Right to Criticize
February 26	Farm Labor Legislation
March 5	Hoffa and the Teamsters Union
March 12	Criticism of the National Federation of Priests Councils
March 19	Role of Religious in the Political and Social Order
March 26	William Serrin and the Labor Movement
April 2	Abolition of the Death Penalty
April 9	The Influence of the Labor Movement
April 16	An Attack on Catholicism and Christianity
April 23	Teamsters versus Farm Workers
April 30	Writing about the Farm Labor Problem
May 7	The Farm Labor Dispute
May 14	Newspapers—Good and Bad
May 21	More on the Farm Labor Crisis
May 28	Time and Public Opinion Favor Farm Workers
June 4	Open Letter to American Labor
June 11	Unionism, American Plan
June 18	Criticism of the Labor Movement
June 25	Looking at the Ecology Crisis
July 2	Setting the Facts Straight
July 9	Why Revive the Old Bracero Program?
July 16	The Teamsters Are Learning?
July 23	The Clergy and the Farm Labor Crisis
July 30	The Public Image of the Teamsters
August 6	Watergate and Key 73
August 13	Social Involvement of the Church
August 20	Social Justice for All?
August 27	Father Munzing's Report on Farm Report
September 3	Cooperation between Religious and Lay Leaders
September 10	"Multiple-Job, Multiple-Pay" Trend
September 17	[Untitled]
September 24	The Minimum Wage Bill Veto
October 1	Playing Politics with Farm Workers' Issue
October 8	The Teamsters-United Farm Workers Treaty
October 15	Newspapers, Women's Lib, and Such
October 22	Chilean Crisis: Vatican Diplomacy Attacked
October 29	Institute of Continuing Theological Education Offers Excellent Program for Clergy
November 5	Italian Outlook on Watergate
November 12	Attack on Theologians and Biblical Scholars

November 19	Buckley, the Bishops and the Farah Controversy
November 26	American Bishops Consider the Farm Labor Problem
December 3	Developing a Conscience
December 10	Pro Civitate Christiana
December 17	Unjust Criticism of Leading Scripture Scholar Continues
December 24	Catholic Social Teaching and the Farah Controversy
December 31	Political Message of the Nativity Story?

1974

January 7	The Middle East Crisis and Anti-Semitic Propaganda
January 14	Let's Look at the Farm Labor Research Committee
January 21	The Logic of Moynihan's Law
January 28	Women and Equality
February 4	More on the Farah Controversy
February 11	Let's Think about Sin
February 18	Notes on Father Berrigan's Speech
February 25	Turn Back the Clock
March 4	Paternalism
March 11	Union against Union
March 18	California Farm Labor Dispute: The Teamsters
March 25	Free Election Bill: The Burton-Alsatorre
April 1	Mary in the Modern Church
April 8	Will Pride Keep a Low-Wage Earner Quiet?
April 15	Are the Teamsters Trying to Destroy the UFW?
April 22	Charges Infuriate Spanish-Speaking Leaders
April 29	Farm Workers Victimized by Teamsters and Growers
May 6	Reconciliation Is Not a Syndrome for Appeasement
May 13	Women Set Example
May 20	Two Men Practiced Social Justice
May 27	Criticism Calls for First-Hand Knowledge
June 3	Turn Back the Clock?
June 10	"My Friends . . . Keep Me Walking the Floor Nights"
June 17	The Abortion Issue and Cesar Chavez
June 24	Will We Allow "Commonweal" to Die?
July 1	More on Labor Unions
July 8	Can the Republic Survive?
July 15	The Press and Freedom
July 22	The Ethnics and Politics
July 29	Vic Gold and the Farm Labor Dispute
August 5	Status and the Wages of Streetcleaning
August 12	Father Humphreys Neutral?

August 19	More about Father Humphreys
August 26	What Are Our Goals?
September 2	More about Big Unions and Big Corporations
September 9	Tribute to Joseph Beirne
September 16	Dale Francis and Questions He Raised
September 23	Is Chavez Beaten?
September 30	Comments on Father Andrew Greeley's Views of Catholic Social Activists
October 7	Comments on Father Lawlor's Letter to the Archbishop of Chicago
October 14	Labor Union Criticized
October 21	Let's Look at the Bracero Program
October 28	Social Activism and the Clergy
November 4	Observation of Father Drinan's Political Responsibility Views
November 11	Three Items for Discussion
November 18	We Need Good Catholic Publications
November 25	More about Father Virgil Blum's Statement on the Democratic Party and the AFL-CIO
December 2	Anti-Semitism Attitudes
December 9	Special Immigrants
December 16	Ambassador Scali Criticizes the United Nations
December 23	Chavez Still Under Attack
December 30	Where Does the Future Lead?

1975

January 6	The Church Must Keep Alive the Spirit of Hope
January 13	The Vatican's Guidelines on Catholic–Jewish Relations
January 20	Says Bishops Position on Farm Labor Misrepresented
January 27	"Teach Me, O My God, to Look upon Humanity as You Yourself Behold It . . ."
February 3	Let's Look at the Right-to-Life Groups Honestly . . .
February 10	What Is the Position of Organized Labor?
February 17	What about Alien Workers?
February 24	Catholic–Jewish Relations Given a Boast
March 3	What Is Discrimination?
March 10	Finding the Brotherly Community We Seek
March 17	Barnet and Muller Respond on Criticism
March 24	A Special Commemorative Stamp
March 31	The "Illegal" Alien Problem: Msgr. Higgins Testifies
April 7	Perspectives on Archbishop Dwyer's Attack on USCC
April 14	Comments on Father Andrew Greeley's Views

April 21	Editor Critical of Support for United Farm Workers
April 28	Will We Permit Child Labor?
May 5	Farm Workers Seek Justice
May 12	Farm Labor Legislation
May 19	AFL-CIO Anti-Fascist and Anti-Communist Policy
May 26	A Reason for Uneasiness
June 2	Call for Texas Legislation
June 9	Political Matters: Lay Responsibility and "Prophetic Witness"
June 16	Federal Farm Legislation Needed
June 23	Amnesty for Aliens
June 30	Drinan Has Done It Again
July 7	About the Media . . .
July 14	Commentary on Father Lyons' Views
July 21	What Is the Future of the United Nations?
July 28	Senator Packwood's Bill
August 4	Landmark in the History of Interreligious Dialogue
August 11	Is Organized Labor Responsible for New York's Crisis?
August 18	Father Drinan Responds
August 25	Msgr. Higgins Answers Father Drinan
September 1	Police Strikes Put in Perspective
September 8	Comments on "Liberation Theology": Detroit Conference
September 15	Do Public Employees Have the Right to Strike?
September 22	Signs of Hope for the World
September 29	Growers Reaction to the California Farm Labor Law
October 6	Professional Sports: Combat Units?
October 13	Church History: Relevance for Today
October 20	Cynicism and the Bicentennial
October 27	Collective Bargaining Disputes
November 3	Vatican Council's Declaration on Catholic–Jewish Relations Only a Beginning
November 10	Threat to Our System of Justice in the Field of Labor Relations
November 17	New Anti-union Book Is Off Base
November 24	Tribute to the Memory of Father Raymond A. McGowan
December 1	Is Anti-Semitism Still Alive?
December 8	Father Robert Bosc, S.J., Asks "Why Is the Marxist Line . . . So Weak in the American Labor Movement?"
December 15	Meeting Human Needs: Social Responsibility and State Implementation

December 22	In Defense of Daniel P. Moynihan
December 29	National Economic Planning with a Capital "P"

1976

January 5	How Should the Churches Address Themselves Specific Socioeconomic Problems
January 12	"Cross Currents" a Valuable Journal
January 19	Hispanic Americans and Civil Rights
January 26	The Church and Women's Lib
February 2	What's Wrong with Women's Lib
February 9	"Simple Justice": A Perceptive Study
February 16	Power Struggle Continues
February 23	The Tripoli Fiasco
March 1	More on Women's Lib
March 8	Putting Things into Perspective
March 15	Construction Workers and the Recession
March 22	Comments on Coverage of the International Catholic–Jewish Liaison Committee Meeting
March 29	A Call for Broader Dialogue: Islam, Judaism, Christianity
April 5	The Eastland Bill
April 12	"If You Don't Come in Sunday . . . Don't Come in Monday"
April 19	Law Enforcement for All . . .
April 26	The California Farm Labor Dispute Goes On
May 3	Where Does Solzhenitsyn Stand on Authoritarianism?
May 10	Rising Health Care Costs Call for Action
May 17	For the Sake of Truth and Justice
May 24	On Paying Our Dues to the ILO
May 31	In Memory of John Cogley
June 7	An Abuse of Religious Freedom
June 14	"Action Is Where You Make It" . . .
June 21	The Labor Movement and the Black Working Class
June 28	Indians Criticize the Gandhi Regime Too . . .
July 5	Anti-busing Plan—"Misguided, Mischievous"
July 12	The Principle of Subsidiarity
July 19	Father Murray and Religious Freedom
July 26	"Trusting the People: Opportunity in Detroit"
August 2	Is Capital Punishment Really Necessary?
August 9	Let's Not Play One Ethnic Group Off against Another
August 17	The Hispanic Side of the Illegal Alien Controversy
August 23	A Bad Year for Seers and Prophets

August 30	What Is the Ethnic Stand on Race?
September 6	Mr. President, Attorney General Lei—Won't You Listen and Act?
September 13	A Call for Justice to Farm Workers
September 20	Is the Labor Movement Dead, or Too Powerful?
September 27	Who Is a Liberal? Who Is a Conservative?
October 4	"No Offense to Movement, but Tactics"
October 11	Organized Labor and Profit Sharing
October 18	Catholic Teachers and Collective Bargaining
October 25	A More Humane Economic Order
November 1	Are Catholic Schools Open to Collective Bargaining?
November 8	"Call to Action" Conference Historic and Successful
November 15	A Few Non-partisan Observations
November 22	The "Catholic Vote"
November 29	As We Approach the Inauguration
December 6	John Carroll: A Spokesman for Freedom
December 13	The Church's Historic Confrontation of American Society
December 20	The Presence of the Church in America Today
December 27	The Institutional Church in the United States Today

1977

January 3	The Place of Religion in Coping with Society's Problems
January 10	On Day Care Centers
January 17	More on Day-Care Center Needs
January 24	United Auto Workers Win Significant Victory in the South
January 31	Hope for Resolution of the California Farm Labor Dispute
February 7	More Study Needed on the Illegal Alien Problem
February 14	A Look at the Outside Interference in Recent United Steelworkers of America Union Elections
February 21	The Bullock Report
February 28	How Can We Meet Day-Care Needs
March 7	A Celebration Well Deserved
March 14	What about the Status of Illegal Aliens?
March 21	National Labor Relations Board Invocation
March 28	Justice Delayed Is Justice Denied
April 4	Bishop Rausch Has Prepared the Way
April 11	Destructive Criticism Is Unfortunate
April 18	Democracy in the Church

April 25	Right to Work Laws
May 2	United Auto Workers and General Motors Celebrate Fortieth Anniversary
May 9	Catholic–Jewish Relations on Theological Matters
May 16	What's Eating Labor Critic?
May 23	We Must Always Look Forward
May 30	Zero Population Growth Foundation and Legal and Illegal Immigration
June 6	A Texas Business Man Opposes Minimum Wage
June 13	How Will 1977 Be Remembered?
June 20	Future of the International Labor Organization Shaky
June 27	Human Rights and International Action
July 4	International Labor Organization Conventions
July 11	Basic Needs, the United States and the International Labor Organization
July 18	The ILO and Vocational and Management Training
July 25	Tribute to Bishop Joseph F. Donnelly
August 1	White House Rules Out Bracero Type Program
August 15	Who Has the Right to Organize for the Purpose of Collective Bargaining?
August 22	Comments on President Carter's Proposed Illegal Aliens Program
August 29	Teachers in Catholic Schools: Unions and Collective Bargaining
September 5	A Labor Day Prayer
September 12	U.S. Withdrawal from ILO Would Encourage Political Manipulation
September 29	Pompous Pronouncements about the Labor Scene
October 3	Is the Church Blindly and Uncritically Pro-Labor and Hypercritical of Management
October 10	Why Is the Farah Company Nearly Bankrupt?
October 17	Questions about Full Employment: Part I
October 24	Questions about Full Employment: Part II
October 31	Full Employment Week: Part III
November 7	Christianity and the Future of Israel
December 26	Human Rights: The U.S. Delegation to the Belgrade Conference

1978

January 2	Starting Dialogue about Lay Leadership
January 9	Is a Dialogue about the Roles of Church Leaders and Laity on Social Reform in Order?

January 16	Undocumented Aliens: Who Are They?
January 23	The Belgrade Conference
January 30	[Untitled; eulogy for Hubert H. Humphrey]
February 6	The Poor and American Politics
February 13	Should There Be an Amendment to the Taft-Hartley Act?
February 20	National Health Insurance
February 27	Looking Back at Support for the ILO
March 6	"Declaration of Christian Concern"
March 13	Bishops' Group Tackles Crime Problem
March 20	The Belgrade Conference
March 27	The Coal Strike
April 3	A Lesson in Pastoral Style: French Bishops on Death Penalty
April 10	Government Has "No Catholic Problem"
April 17	A Bizarre Scenario
April 24	Commentators Uninformed on Belgrade Meeting
May 1	"Holocaust"—TV at Its Best
May 8	Catholics in Government
May 15	Capital Punishment Revisited
May 22	The Labor Law Reform Bill
May 29	Cracking Down on Executive "Perks"
June 5	Playing Politics with Explosive Issue
June 12	Was the Holocaust a Hoax?
June 19	Msgr. Ellis Contribution to American Catholicism
June 26	Solzhenitsyn's Address Raises Questions
July 3	Labor Law Reform Bill
July 10	Criticisms of the Belgrade Conference Continue
July 17	Our Right to Collective Bargaining Threatened
July 24	Proselytism and the Jews
July 31	For Christians and Jews: A Golden Anniversary
August 7	Let's Watch the Texas Farm Workers Union Meeting in October
August 14	More on the Illegal Alien Problem
August 21	Pope Paul VI
August 28	The Meaning of Labor Day
September 4	More on NAM's Council on Union Free Environment
September 11	More on the International Conference on Undocumented Aliens
September 18	Does Israel Discriminate against Arab Citizens?
September 25	Prejudice against Illegal Aliens
October 2	When a Journalist Predicts . . . Well . . .

October 9	What about Anti-Catholicism in America?
October 16	More about Anti-Catholicism in the United States
October 23	Where Do Hispanics Stand in the United States?
October 30	What Do Laws Making the Union Shop Illegal Mean?—Part I
November 6	What Do Laws Making the Union Shop Illegal Mean?—Part II
November 13	Is the Church Blindly and Uncritically Pro-Labor and Hypercritical of Management?
November 20	Election Reflection
November 27	Blacks and Hispanics Beginning to Work Together
December 4	A Public Debate on Right-to-Work Laws
December 11	Reaction to Undocumented Workers Strong on Emotion, Weak on Facts
December 18	Msgr. Thomas J. Tobin
December 25	Pax Christi and SALT II Treaty

1979

January 1	The J. P. Stevens Company Controversy
January 8	Anti-Zionist Books Fails to Convince
January 15	Will the Black-Hispanic Coalition Be Short-Lived?
January 22	The Labor Movement and Aid to Private Schools
January 29	Catholic Tests of a Social Order
February 5	The Labor Movement Still an Active, Growing Force
February 12	Farm Spokesman Attacks Churches
February 19	U.S. Church Looks to the Future
February 26	Tensions Threaten Jewish–Black Coalition
March 5	The Bracero Program
March 12	More Views on the J. P. Stevens Company Dispute
March 19	Public Law 95-250: A Landmark
March 26	Domestic Violence
April 2	More on the Proposed Bracero Program
April 9	Collective Bargaining Rights of Teachers in Church-Related Schools
April 16	The Case of Norma Rae
April 23	The Church and Social Concerns
April 30	Msgr. Matthew F. Connolly
May 7	Seeking Justice for the Agricultural Industry
May 14	Should Bishops Speak Out on Socio-political Issues?
May 21	Should Bishops Speak on Socio-economic Issues?
May 28	Liberals

June 4	Tribute to A. Philip Randolph
June 11	Human Rights and Palestinians Conference Biased?
June 18	Religion and the Unions
June 25	Do Blacks Need Unions?
July 2	Cool Reception Due for CHA Lobbyists
July 9	Answers for Palestine Human Rights Campaign
July 16	Journalists Debate Weber Ruling
July 23	Criticizing Unionism
July 30	Busing Amendment Would Strike at Civil Rights
August 6	Pope Paul VI
August 13	The Tradition of the Family Farm
August 20	The Time Bomb of Youth Unemployment
August 27	Black–Jewish Alliance in Trouble Again
September 3	Tribute to a Great Priest [Reynold Hillenbrand]
September 10	Why Don't Americans Vote?
September 17	Patterns of Prejudice
September 24	A Call for Andrew Young to Speak Out
October 1	More on Black–Jewish Relations
October 8	Campaign for Human Development
October 15	Tribute to George Meany
October 22	American Journalists and Pope John Paul II
October 29	Pressures in the Modern Workplace
November 5	Jewish–Christian–Moslem Trialogue
November 12	Two Bishops Issue Pastoral Letters on Racism
November 19	The Nestle Solution: Are We Nearing Solution?
November 26	Nobel Peace Prize Controversy
December 3	Tribute to George Meany
December 10	Socialism Is No Longer a Dirty Word in the Church
December 17	We Can't Afford Tunnel Vision
December 24	The Chrysler-Friseur Experiment
December 31	Martin Luther King Day

1980

January 7	Farm Labor Contractors
January 14	Let Us Not Be Judges
January 21	The Church and Labor Unions
January 28	George Meany's Creed
February 4	Islam and Israel: Learning the Lessons of Iran
February 11	Paul Blanshard
February 18	NBC and the United Farm Workers
February 25	The UFW, Agribusinesses and the Media

March 3	The United States and the ILO
March 10	Women and the Labor Movement
March 17	Reflections on the Abortion Issue
March 24	Illegal Aliens: A Realistic View
March 31	Bayard Rustin on His Seventieth Birthday
April 7	The Power of the Press
April 14	Budget-Cutting Fever
April 21	Spare the Children
April 28	The Bishops and the Boycott
May 5	The Human Terms of Unemployment
May 12	The New Right Connection
May 19	The Church and the Campbell Boycott
May 26	Archbishop Hilarion Capucci
June 2	The Church and Energy Policy
June 9	Regulating the Infant-Formula Industry
June 16	A Crucial Turning Point
June 23	A New Maturity in Christian–Jewish Relations
June 30	Love Canal: A Glimpse of the Future
July 7	Human Rights in Zaire
July 14	The Campaign for Human Development: Action on Poverty
July 21	Immigration Policy: A Status Report
July 28	A Step in the Right Direction?
August 4	The Pope's Traveling Encyclical
August 11	An Unfortunate Reassessment
August 18	A Dire Warning
August 25	The Image Television Projects of Laborers
September 1	The World's Huddled Masses
September 8	Courage in Poland
September 15	The Moral Majority
September 22	A New Coalition of Blacks and Hispanics
September 29	The Union Question in Catholic Hospitals
October 6	Our Jobless Breadwinners
October 13	A Measured, Forthright Address on Contraception
October 20	Religion and Politics
October 27	Free Speech, the Media, and the Churches
November 3	The Truce Between J. P. Stevens and the ACTWU
November 10	Fighting Poverty in the Eighties
November 17	Airport Solicitors and the First Amendment
November 24	The Biblical School of Economics
December 1	What's Ahead for Labor in the New Administration?

December 8	Anti-Semitism and Anti-Zionism
December 15	Dorothy Day
December 22	Who Should Pay at the Inaugural?

1981

January 5	The Image of America
January 12	Response to an Attack
January 19	A Subminimum Wage for Teen-agers?
January 26	The Search for Justice in the Middle East
February 2	Reagan's Inaugural Address
February 9	The Nixon-Reagan Letters
February 16	Can Psychohistorians Be Taken Seriously?
February 23	Will the UAW-Chrysler Pact Set a Trend?
March 2	The Myth of "Reagonomics"
March 9	The Resurgence of the Ku Klux Klan
March 16	Reagan's Controversial Human Rights Appointment
March 23	Closing the Door on Illegal Immigration
March 30	Reagan's Open Boarder
April 6	El Salvador: Who Speaks for the U.S. Bishops
April 13	What Services Must Government Provide?
April 20	The Israeli-Christian Right Alliance
April 27	Confusing Political Protest with Political Terrorism
May 4	The Worker-Pope and His Employees
May 11	Israeli's Witness to Hope
May 18	Are the Social Encyclicals Outdated?
June 1	Making Sense of the Riddles of Death and Sorrow
June 8	Rhetoric Won't Solve Economic Woes
June 15	Why Have a Dialogue with the Jews?
June 22	The Clergy and Partisan Politics: What Is the Influence?
June 29	The Vindication of Teilhard De Chardin
July 6	What William Buckley Doesn't Know about Maryknoll
July 13	Illiberal Liberals
July 20	Toward a Liberal-Conservative Dialogue on Abortion
July 27	What's in a Name
August 3	Social Welfare: What Partnership of Church and Government?
August 10	Mrs. O'Connor's Fitness for the Court
August 17	Reagan's Immigration Plan Looks Like a Loser
August 24	The Lessons of the Air Traffic Controller's Strike
August 31	Collective Bargaining for Federal Employees?
September 7	A Cheerless Labor Day

September 14	A Potentially Bitter Harvest
September 21	Economic Culture Shock
September 28	The New Encyclical (*Laborem Exercens*)
October 5	New Encyclical No Instant Cure All
October 12	Dignity in the Workplace
October 19	Solidarity
November 9	The Jewishness of Jesus
November 16	The Truth about Solidarity
November 23	Working Mothers
November 30	The AFL-CIO's 100th Birthday
December 21	A Little Compassion, Lots of Common Sense
1982	
January 4	Developing a Dialogue on Liberation Theology
January 11	Operation Whitewash
January 18	The Jews in Poland
February 1	"Man of Iron"
February 8	Twenty Years after the Council
February 15	Hope for Poland
February 22	CRS under Attack
March 1	Union Democracy
March 8	Poland's Plan to Re-organize Its Unions
March 15	Signs of the Times
March 22	The Spirit of '82
March 29	Priests and Politics
April 5	A Double Standard
April 12	Central America: Have the Bishops Done Their Homework?
April 19	Using Tax Dollars against Labor Unions
April 26	Good Samaritans Aren't Enough
May 3	A Stab in the Back
May 10	The New Right: A Lesson for Liberals
May 17	The Return of the Sinai
May 24	GM's Wakeup Alarm
May 31	Working for the Church
June 7	Executive Pay: How High Can It Go?
June 14	Human Rights and the ILO: A Problem of Enforcement
June 21	Truth in Advertising
June 28	Equal Opportunity in the NFL
July 5	The U.S. Bishops and Their National Staff
July 12	Do We Really Need Unions?

July 19	Holy Terror
July 26	The Impending National Crisis
August 2	Questions on Our Economic System
August 9	The Mondregon Experiment
August 16	The Gap in the Women's Network
August 23	Two Great Americans [Martin Luther King Jr. and Roy Wilkins]
August 30	Of Abortion and Nuclear Weapons
September 6	A Moment of Truth
September 13	Rigidly Defining the Church's Political Role
September 20	What's in a Name?
September 27	Role Playing
October 4	Let's Be Realistic about Labor
October 11	Dissent and the Debate over Nuclear Weapons
October 18	New Troubles in the Control Towers
October 25	The Press and the Council
November 1	Assessing the American Economy
November 8	Cardinal Benelli, Farm Workers' Friend
November 15	People for the American Way
November 22	Syndicated Hysteria
November 29	The Bishops and the Social Order
December 6	The Ombudsman We Need
December 13	Has the Laity's Role Been Usurped?
December 20	The Church and Solidarity
December 27	Latin American Unions: "New Solidarity"

1983

January 3	How Divided Is the Nicaraguan Church?
January 10	Who Really Is Drafting the Bishops' War and Peace Pastoral?
January 17	Social Ethics in the American Context
January 24	The CIA and Latin America
January 31	Canadian Controversy
February 7	Japanese Lessons
February 14	Priest-Politicians in the Revised Code
February 21	Catholics, Jews and Lebanon
February 28	Israel's Accountability
March 7	Religious Oppression in the Soviet Union
March 14	Children's TV Ads: A Question of Ethics
March 21	The Final Solution
March 28	Do We Need the ILO?

April 4	A Remembrance of Cardinal Mooney
April 11	Giants to Remember
April 18	Family Protection
April 25	In Praise of Public Servants
May 2	Does Religion Contribute Anything to Social Reform?
May 9	The Church, Solidarity, and the Government in Poland
May 16	Now That the War and Peace Pastoral Is Completed
May 23	Maintaining U.S. Credibility
May 30	Rehabilitating the U.S. Economy
June 6	Hard Times, Easy Answers
June 13	Religious Freedom and Bob Jones University
June 20	Random Thoughts
June 27	The Laity and the Bishops' Pastoral
July 4	Blacklisted
July 11	The Vatican and the Bishops' Pastoral
July 18	Drawing the Line
July 25	The Other Side of the Coin
August 1	A Stingy Magnanimity
August 8	Staying Alive
August 15	Practicing What We Preach
August 22	Putting America Back to Work
August 29	Detroit's Saint of the Slums [Monsignor Clement Kern]
September 5	A Fishing Expedition
September 12	Socialist Bias
September 19	I Take It All Back: Canonize Dorothy Day
September 26	Religion and Labor: New Life in an Old Relationship
October 3	Work and Worship
October 10	Unions Are Here to Stay
October 17	Influencing Public Policy
October 24	Central America: The Second Enemy
October 31	In Defense of Cardinal Spellman
November 7	Grenada
November 14	Taking Issue
November 21	Mrs. Luce and the Bishops' Economic Views
November 28	Promoting the Rights of Unions
December 5	The Right of Workers to Organize
December 12	In Defense of Human Life
December 19	An Emerging Anti-religious Bias
December 26	Women Workers

1984

January 2	Success Story through Bargaining
January 9	Democratic Values and the WCC
January 16	Is the Future Already in View?
January 23	One in a Million [Monsignor Luigi Ligutti]
January 30	Foreign Aid: Penny Wise and Pound Foolish
February 6	Lobbyists
February 13	Beyond Our Own Mythology
February 20	Mulling over Social Teachings
February 27	Whose Ox Is Being Gored?
March 5	The Wise Man Stays Home
March 26	Clerical Politics
April 2	Union Ethics
April 9	Pro-Life Strategy
April 16	A Marvelous Human Being
April 23	Reading Matters
April 30	What Do Unions Do?
May 7	Critics of the Church and Solidarity
May 14	Politicizing History
May 21	Farm Labor: A Costly Import
May 28	A Bizarre Biography
June 4	The High Costs of the Enterprise
June 11	Executive Sweets
June 18	Distinctions with a Difference
June 25	Immigration Reform in Focus
July 2	The Italian Solution?
July 9	Passion Plays
July 16	Should We Go to Oberammergau?
July 23	Two of a Kind: Distinguished Jesuits [John M. Corridon and Mortimer H. Gavin]
July 30	The Shape-Up
August 6	Do Nurses Have a Right to Unionize?
August 13	Mixing Religion and Politics
August 20	In Changed Times, Changed Needs
August 27	The Spiritual Meaning of Labor Day
September 3	A Matter of Education
September 10	How to Criticize Unions
September 17	Making National Economic Planning Respectable
September 24	A Master Builder [Monsignor Geno Baroni]
October 1	Passion Plays Revisited
October 8	Liberation Theology

October 15	Analyzing Marxism
October 22	Why the Double Standard on Abortion?
October 29	Helping Women
November 5	Promoters of a Union-Free Environment
November 12	Class Struggle in a New Key
November 19	A Proposal for Fewer Prayers at Public Ceremonies
November 26	Stalin's Daughter Goes Home
December 3	An Antidote for Anti-American European Snobbery
December 10	Credit Where Credit Is Due
December 17	What the Bishops Didn't Say
December 24	Religion Measured by a Socialist
December 31	The Aftermath of Bhopal

1985

January 7	Who's Qualified to Discuss the Economy
January 14	Good News for Book Readers
January 21	Some Thoughts on St. Dorothy Day
January 28	A Baneful Heritage
February 4	Recurrent Attitudes on Collective Bargaining
February 11	Providing for the Common Good
February 18	Is the Least Government the Best Government?
February 25	The Clergy's Role in Social Action
March 4	Worship and Work
March 11	Hymns of Praise
March 18	Families: Looking for a Home
March 25	The Bishops' Dilemma
April 1	Crossing the Line
April 8	Selective Indignation
April 15	An Unobjectionable Solidarity
April 22	Unions and Politics
April 29	The Good Life
May 6	Bedevilment
May 13	Capitalism in the Rest of the World
July 1	In the First-Person Singular
July 8	Our Pope's "Marxist Ideology"
July 15	A Preferential Option for the Poor
July 22	Are the Bishops Captives of Their Staff?
July 29	Open Season on the Bishops' Conference
August 5	Six Years after the Revolution [Nicaragua]
August 12	Should Labor Drop the Act?
August 19	Who Speaks for the Laity?

August 26	War of Words
September 2	The Church and Labor: An Endangered Tradition?
September 9	On the Salaries of Labor and Business Leaders
September 16	Inner Workshop
September 23	Breaking Ranks
September 30	How the Council Changed Us
October 7	Getting the Laity Involved
October 14	Pluralism and Sectarianism
October 21	No Joking Matter
October 28	Guessing Game
November 4	That Final Trip
November 11	An Unequalled Record
November 18	The Next Step in Church Renewal
November 25	A Tribute to Father John Courtney Murray, S.J.
December 2	Current Resources on Catholic Social Teaching
December 9	On Complimentary Letters—and Some Others
December 16	The Christmas Message: A Political Manifesto?
December 23	The Use of Leisure

1986

January 6	The Church's Internal Variety
January 13	A Universal Catechism?
January 20	Niebuhr's Legacy
January 27	How God Speaks to Us Today
February 3	More Vatican "Secrets"
February 10	Toward Better Vatican Press Relations
February 17	The American Family's Worthy Champion
February 24	What Makes a Job Adequate?
March 3	What the Philippine Bishops' Stance Means for the Church
April 7	Why Not Open the Synod to the Media?
April 14	Eyewash
April 21	Do Bishops' Conferences Have Any Real Authority?
April 28	Is Mary a Woman for Our Times?
May 12	A "Treasure" Unmasked
May 19	What's Faith Got to Do with It?
June 2	Sauce for the Goose, and the Gander
June 23	What Ever Became of Whatshisname?
June 30	A Heritage Worth Knowing
July 7	The Women's Liberation Movement Needs a Change of Focus

July 14 — Religious Convictions and Union Membership
July 21 — Anti-Semitism: Getting to the Issue at Hand
July 28 — On Being Pro-Jewish
August 4 — What the Church Teaches about Jews
August 11 — What about "Love Is Always"?
August 18 — A Sociologist's View of Capitalism
August 25 — Learning to Live with Change
September 1 — Who Are the Rich?
September 8 — Catholic Schools and Teaching about the Jews?
September 15 — The State of the Unions: A Review of the Views
September 22 — Public Dissent and the Church's Social Teaching
October 6 — A Unique Experiment in Democracy
October 13 — Do Business and Labor Owe the Public?
October 20 — Why Get to Know the Global Village?
October 27 — Father Hesburgh: Priest, President, Public Servant
November 3 — Cardinal [Michele] Pellegrino's Vision
November 10 — The Uncertain Future of U.S. Industrial Relations
November 17 — Research Gone Awry
November 24 — Is This the Catholic Moment?
December 1 — Sticking to One's Own Last
December 8 — Laity Issues Past and Present
December 15 — Labor and Management: The Cooperative Route
December 22 — Oxtail Soup
December 29 — On Overlooking the Goodness of This Age

1987

January 6 — Perspectives on Television from a Hospital Bed
January 12 — Dialogue within the Church
January 26 — The Impact of Vatican Policy on Israel
February 2 — When Monopoly Stops Being a Game and Becomes a Way of Life
February 9 — The Proper Balance
February 16 — Why Unions Can't Be Relegated to the History Books
February 23 — Action for Farm Workers
March 2 — The Case of Michael Miles
March 9 — Lay Leaders: A Lost Generation?
March 16 — The Mass and the Political Order
March 23 — The Secretary Surrounding the Synod
March 30 — Protecting the Right to Strike
April 6 — The Rare Spectacle of Civil Debate
April 13 — Catholic University Remembered

April 20	Consistency Counts
April 27	How Bad Is the Press?
May 4	Nurses Have Rights Too
May 11	Does It Pay to Travel?
May 18	Worker Rights, the ILO and International Trade
May 25	Using Trade to Promote Worker Rights
June 8	A Disservice to Dialogue
June 15	Father Flannery's Anguish
June 22	The United Farmworkers at Twenty-five
June 29	The Pope, Politics, and Unions
July 6	Trying to Keep Up with the Pope in Poland
July 13	The Waldheim Affaire: What Happens Now?
July 20	Confessions of a Newspaper Junkie
July 27	The Church Should Set an Example
August 3	French Lessons
August 10	What the Laity Want
August 17	Is the Pope's Retreat Master a Marxist?
August 24	A Distinguished Foursome
August 31	Loaded Words
September 7	Mirror Images Reflect Little Light
September 14	Good News for the Labor Movement
September 21	Bayard Rustin
September 28	A Historic Meeting in Miami
October 5	Two Ways to Finance the Church
October 12	Double-Standard Criticism
October 19	Union Busters Challenge Church's Credibility
October 26	What Makes the Holocaust Uniquely Jewish?
November 2	The Repentance Factor in Capital Punishment
November 9	Sustaining Capitalism
November 16	The Teamsters Return to the House of Labor
November 23	The Cost of Football—and the Papal Trip
November 30	Training Clergy and Laity for Social Action Roles
December 7	What Makes a Church Popular?
December 14	Is There a Real American Labor Movement?
December 28	What about the Jews for Jesus?

1988

January 4	Justice for Janitors
January 11	Playing the Rank and File Off against Their Leaders
January 18	No Easy Cure-All for Unions Where Most Members Do Not Participate

February 1	Football Fever
February 8	The Right to Speak against Abortion
February 15	Is There Socialism of a Non-totalitarian Kind?
February 22	More on Jews for Jesus
February 29	Promoting Human Rights
March 7	Time to Meet a U.S. Obligation
March 14	Setting the Record Straight
March 21	A Outrageous Contradiction in Terms
March 28	Time to Reregulate the Airlines?
April 4	Educating the Clergy
April 11	The Passing of Paul Ramsey
April 18	Chains of Command
April 25	On Christian Criticism of the Israelis
May 2	Nostalgia on the Potomac
May 9	Notes on Giving Back a Bit of What Workers Earn
May 16	Maryknoll Revisited
May 23	The Re-emergence of Solidarity
May 30	The Never-Ending Battle for Human Rights
June 6	Day Care and the Baby Jesus
June 13	Gentleman and Scholar, Priest above All [John Tracy Ellis]
June 20	Life in the Country
June 27	Is NOW Anti-Catholic?
July 4	Golfing in Red Square
July 11	A Word to the Wise
July 18	Honoring Michael Harrington
July 25	The Religious Right on Balance
August 1	Praying in Public
August 8	Just One Prayer at Civic Gatherings
August 15	Liturgy and Social Justice
August 22	Some Thoughts about National Health Insurance
August 29	Summer Musings about the Heat
September 5	The "Baptism" of Labor Day
September 12	What America Stands For
September 19	The Farm Workers' Courageous Struggle
September 26	The Good, the Bad, and the Cynical
October 3	Serious Reading
October 10	Unions in Catholic Schools: Bane or Blessing?
October 24	The Lessons of Asian Capitalism
October 31	A Civil Tongue and a Heart of Charity
November 7	Unions and Anti-trust Laws Revisited

November 14	The Bully Pulpit
November 21	Another Look at JFK's 1960 Houston Speech
November 28	Pertinent Questions about Religion and Politics
December 5	Double Standards on Church and Politics
December 12	Religion and the Presidency
December 19	Catholic Institutions: Afraid of the "U" Word?
December 27	Selective Compassion

1989

January 2	Paying Tribute to A. Philip Randolph
January 9	1988 and Catholic–Jewish Relations
January 16	Guidelines for Homilists on Catholic–Jewish Relations
January 23	The Real Story on Jewish–Christian Relations
January 30	The Terms of Debate
February 6	A Partnership Worth Keeping
February 13	Martin Luther King Jr., Witness to Faith
February 20	Television and Labor
February 27	Suggestions for Church–Labor Organizations
March 6	An Older, Wiser Nation?
March 20	The International War against Drugs
March 27	Hope for the Future
April 3	Putting the World to Work
April 10	Muzzling the Voice of the Voiceless
April 17	Eastern Airlines: What Kind of Omen for Labor
April 24	The Health Care Crisis
May 1	Breakthrough in Poland
May 8	How Much Is a CEO Worth?
May 15	Solidarity and the Church in Poland
May 22	When a Two-Way Street Becomes One-Way
May 29	An Admittedly Complicated Man [Msgr. Charles Owen Rice]
June 5	A Marriage Made in Heaven?
June 12	God's Faithfulness
June 19	The Undivided Road: Father Philip Carey
June 26	Is Social Justice Utopian?
July 3	Going Back to Work: The Penalties
July 10	Executing Minors and the Retarded
July 17	The UAW's Thirty-Two-Year-Old Experiment
July 24	Lunar Landings
July 31	Confused Standard of Union Loyalty
August 7	The Sorry State of the U.S. Health-Care System

August 14	Do Labor Unions Have a Future?
August 21	On the Decentralization of Government
August 28	Summer of Discontent
September 11	The Auschwitz Controversy Continues
September 18	Solidarity and the Church
September 25	Overwhelmed
October 2	Hope for the Future of Planet Earth
October 9	A Christian Response to Mean City Streets
October 16	It's Not My Fault
October 23	Unions Aid Democracy Here and Abroad
October 30	A Hero's Welcome
November 6	Confessions of a Public Prayer Monger
November 13	The Man Who Turned Poland Right Side Up
November 20	A Courageous Polish Priest [Father Henryk Jankowski]
November 27	An Invocation
December 11	Living Faith and Work
December 18	Implications of the Eastern Bloc's Collapse
December 25	The Church's "Silence" and the Environment

1990

January 1	Family Planning and the Government's Place
January 8	Is There Still a Working Class?
January 15	Are Unions in a Crisis?
January 22	The Church and the Intellectual Life
January 29	The Church, the Council and Social Change
February 5	A Warning for the CIO-AFL on Abortion
February 12	Secrecy Ill Suits a Church in the Modern World
February 19	Social Criticism at Its Best
February 26	Assessing the Pittston Strike
March 5	Controlling the Workplace
March 12	The Undivided Road: Faith and Justice
March 19	A Double Standard on First Amendment Issues
March 26	America and Catholicism—One Hundred Years of Growth
April 2	Helping Eastern Europe
April 9	Individualism Confronts American Labor
April 16	In Memory of Arthur Goldberg
April 23	On Replacing Strikers Permanently
April 30	Striking: Jobs and Dignity on Line
May 7	Supporting Moral Courage in Poland
May 14	Walter Reuther's Vocation

May 21	The War and the Council Shaped Fifty Years of Priesthood
June 4	My Hope Is in the Lord
June 11	A Life of Distinction [Father George H. Dunne, S.J.]
June 18	On Conscientious Objection to Union Fees
June 25	A Prayer for Our Unfinished Task
July 1	Eastern Europe after Communism
July 9	Christian–Jewish Relations Much Improved
July 16	My Washington Beginnings
July 23	Democracy in the Church
July 30	Anti-union Tactics in Church-Related Institutions
August 6	The Underside of East Asia's Economic Miracle
August 13	The AFL-CIO's Decision on Abortion
August 20	Labor Day: The Road Ahead
August 27	Book of the Year (Decade, Too)
September 3	Dirty Tricks
September 10	An Issue Personalized: National Health Insurance
September 17	Spiritual Balm for Social Ills?
September 24	To Love Justice
October 1	Solidarity's Second Decade
October 8	A Tradition of Public Service and Social Reform
October 15	A Saint of Our Time [Dorothy Day]
October 22	The Poverty of Uniqueness and Superiority [Dorothy Day]
October 29	Is Socialism an Alternative to Unions?
November 5	The Church: A Just Employer?
November 12	Pulpit Politics
November 19	Who Will Fight in a U.S. War?
November 26	In Defense of Archbishop Weakland
December 3	The Essential Difference Unions Make
December 10	The Basic Issue in Poland's Election
December 17	The Parish of My Youth
December 31	Employment Inequality in America

1991

January 7	Cardinal O'Connor: Friend to Labor
January 14	A Down-to-Earth Imitation of Mary
January 21	A Contemporary Martyr [Michael P. Hammer]
January 28	The Centenary of "Rerum Novarum"
February 4	Leo XIII's Prophetic Vision and Courageous Action
February 11	Toward a More Modest Patriotism

February 18	An Intriguing Double Standard
February 25	Don't Sell the Laity Short
March 4	Archie Bunker: The Good and the Bad
March 11	Justice Has No Borders
March 18	The Scandal of the Maquiladoras
March 25	When Paradigms Collide
April 1	Replacement Workers and the Balance of Bargaining Power
April 8	Religion and Media: Biased or Just Ignorant?
April 15	Individualism Confronts American Labor
April 22	Opportune Moment for the Health Care Debate
April 29	The Vatican and the Local Church
May 6	Keeper of the Flame
May 13	The New Encyclical's Time Message (*Centissimus Annus*)
May 20	What the New Encyclical Says about Unions
May 27	A Quick Study
June 3	Capitalism, the Pope, and the U.S. Bishops
June 10	Solidarity in the U.S. Economy
June 17	We Are What We Buy—and Eat
June 24	Memory Is Merciful
July 1	Outdated Anti-papal Rhetoric
July 8	Solidarity's Legacy
July 15	Giving Nuns Their Due
July 22	Spin Doctors Won't Cure What Ails the U.S. Economy
July 29	The Church and Politics

1992

February 10	The Media's Super Bowl Mania
February 24	Irish-American Catholics and Today's New Immigrants
March 9	What the "Holy Alliance" Showed
March 23	Catholic Hospitals' Labor Record
April 6	Compare Today's Labor Leaders with Their Predecessors
April 20	History of the National Catholic Welfare Council
May 4	Media's Benign Neglect of Organized Labor
May 18	A More Public Role for Religion?
June 1	Working for a Living
June 15	New Life for an Old Bigotry?
June 29	It's an Old Refrain: Religion, the Enemy of Democracy
July 13	In the Supreme Court's Wake: A Dialogue of the Deaf
July 27	An American Pioneer [Marc Tannenbaum]
August 10	A Worthy Program

August 24	Traveling through Time
October 5	Looking More Deeply into the Role of Unions
October 19	Unions Are More Than "Management's Failure"
November 17	Is Human Labor Just Another Commodity?
November 30	Father Coughlin and the Right to Strike
December 14	A Page from History
December 28	What the Church Says about Workers in a Free Market

1993

January 11	"Hoffa," the Movie: It's All Very Sad
January 25	Facing the Health Care Crisis in a New World Context
March 8	Labor's Prospects in the Clinton Administration
March 22	Slavery and Forced Labor
April 5	Gender Bias in the Workplace
April 19	Toward Sensible Limits on Public Prayer
May 3	The Holocaust Did Occur
May 17	The Unsung Accomplishments of Paul VI
May 31	A Few Words on "The Longest Hatred"
June 14	Does the UFW Have a Future?
July 12	New Twist in Polish Drama: Walesa Splits the Union
July 26	Understanding with the Heart as Well as the Head
August 9	Religion and Politics: Beyond JFK
September 6	The Catholic Contribution to Health Care Reform
October 4	Prayer at Public Functions
October 18	How It's Done: Prayer at Public Events
November 15	The Church in Labor in Today's Poland
November 29	Honest Differences about NAFTA

1994

January 10	A Masterpiece about Unspeakable Evil
January 24	Mexico Peasant Uprising
February 7	The Commonweal Catholic
February 21	The Struggle for Human Rights in the Workplace
March 7	The Sacrifice Commitment to Human Dignity Entails
March 21	A Model of Self-Discipline
April 4	Valuing Unions for Their Own Sake
April 18	A Global Economy Demands a Global Labor Movement
May 2	The Pope's Call for a Family Wage
May 16	Needed: Plain Talk about Real Problems
May 30	Shepherd Gazing
June 13	CHD: Adding Justice to Charity

June 27	The New Serenity in Christian–Jewish Relations
July 11	A Newer, Even Better "Catholicism"
July 25	On the Beach: Labor–Management Cooperation
August 1	[Untitled]
August 15	[Untitled]
August 29	[Untitled]
September 5	[Untitled]
September 26	[Untitled]
October 17	[Untitled]
November 14	[Untitled]
November 28	[Untitled]
December 12	[Untitled]
December 26	[Untitled]

B. The Yardstick Columns by Guest Columnists (1949–1977)

1949		
March 7	Smith, William	[Untitled]
March 14	[Unnamed]	Not Enough Light
	Tobin, Thomas	Aid and Comfort to Communists
March 21	Dobson, Philip	Duties of the Rank and File
March 28	O'Connell, Vincent J.	The American "USSR"
April 4	McColgan, Daniel T.	Housing—Scarcity or Sufficiency?
April 11	Brock, Edmund	Pegler Points at Providence
April 18	Kern, Clement H.	Workers' Centers in Mexico City
April 25	Wilken, Robert	Less Talk, More Practice
May 2	Munier, Joseph F.	Progressive Employers
May 9	Donnelly, Joseph F.	"Go to the Workingman"
May 23	Donnelly, Joseph F.	"Saints . . . to Do Away with Slavery"
May 30	Kenney, Philip J.	Social Action Practitioners
June 6	McGowan, R. A.	A New International
June 13	Cronin, John F.	The Pope Speaks to Employers
June 20	Winkler, Augustine L.	The Right to Profit
June 27	Smith, William J.	Spotlight on Social Reform
July 4	McGowan, R. A.	A Bill of Divorcement
July 11	Corriden, John M.	Longshoremen's Problem
July 18	Gelineau, Edward J.	America's Foremost Monstrosities

July 25	Hubble, Karl	Making Principles Work
August 1	Drolet, Jerome A.	Good News for White Collar Workers
August 8	Marciniak, Ed	The Real Danger
August 15	Gillis, James M.	If You Mean It, Say It
August 22	O'Connell, Vincent J.	Our Economic Expendables
August 29	McGowan, R. A.	Hard Decisions
1950		
November 13	McGowan, R. A.	Catholics of the Americas
November 20	McGowan, R. A.	Will the World . . . ?
1952		
June 30	McGowan, R. A.	Strange, Turbulent Time
July 7	McGowan, R. A.	Make Ownership Responsible
July 14	McGowan, R. A.	A Working Goal, at Least
July 21	McGowan, R. A.	A Big Stick Gently Waves
July 28	Kelly, Katherine B.	No Vacation for Tenants
August 4	McGowan, R. A.	For Ready Reference
1953		
August 3	Carney, Francis	A Social, Civic, Personal Need
August 10	Carney, Francis	That the World Be Restored to Providential Order
August 17	Carney, Francis	Von Papen's Memoirs
November 16	Boland, John P.	Social Justice, Whole and Entire
1954		
March 1	Cronin, John F.	Anti-anti-Communist
October 25	Cronin, John F.	Why Catholic Social Action
1955		
May 23	Cronin, John F.	Holiness and Social Action
June 13	Sensor, Bob	What Can I Do?
June 20	Marciniak, Ed	Sunday Shopping
December 19	Kelly, Katherine B.	A Puzzlement
1956		
February 6	McGowan, R. A.	Inter-American Social Action
February 13	Synon, Mary	Johnny Can Read . . . and Think!

February 20	Synon, Mary	For God and Country
February 27	Synon, Mary	Area of Conflicts
March 5	Synon, Mary	Field for Exploration
March 12	Synon, Mary	Geography Becomes a Social Study
March 19	Kelly, Katherine B.	Bi-partisan Support

1957

March 11	Theisen, Sylvester P.	American Labor Unions Want No "Co-determination" Laws
March 18	Theisen, Sylvester P.	Man, Freedom and Fulfillment
May 27	Vanistendael, Austin	Relationship of IFCTU and ICFTU
September 23	Geaney, Denis J.	The Nation's Conscience
September 30	Geaney, Denis J.	The Golf Course, an Island of Paradoxes
October 7	Geaney, Denis J.	Public Wants to Keep the Baby
October 14	Geaney, Denis J.	More Culture with the Shorter Work Week
October 21	Geaney, Denis J.	Priests and Laity—a Missionary Team
October 28	Geaney, Denis J.	Decisions for Integration
November 4	Geaney, Denis J.	Federal Government Sets Employment Example
November 11	Geaney, Denis J.	Industry Council Plan Still Needed

1958

May 19	Waters, Eleanor	Social Justice and Foreign Aid
November 10	Waters, Eleanor	CAIP 31st Conference: "Peace the Work of Justice"

1960

Guests wrote the *Yardstick* columns from September 5 to November 14. There is no listing of authors or articles in the archive's holdings.

1962

January 29	McGuire, Frederick A.	Laity's World-Wide Mission
February 5	McGuire, Frederick A.	Future of Education in Latin America

February 12	McGuire, Frederick A.	Challenge to North American Catholics
April 16	Vizzard, James L.	Rural–Urban Relations
April 23	Vizzard, James L.	Our Responsibility to the Needy
April 30	Vizzard, James L.	On Behalf of Farmers
May 7	Vizzard, James L.	A Century of Great Progress
October 8	Greeley, Andrew M.	[Untitled]
October 15	Greeley, Andrew M.	The Scapegoats
October 23	Greeley, Andrew M.	[Untitled]
October 29	Greeley, Andrew M.	[Untitled]
November 5	Greeley, Andrew M.	The Black Muslims
November 12	Greeley, Andrew M.	Dangerous Game
November 19	Greeley, Andrew M.	"Needs" of American Catholicism
November 26	Greeley, Andrew M.	Need for Research and Planning in U.S. Church
December 3	Greeley, Andrew M.	Communication—but the Wrong Kind
December 10	Greeley, Andrew M.	Golden Opportunity for Church in U.S.
December 17	Greeley, Andrew M.	Idealists without a Cause
December 24	Greeley, Andrew M.	Controversy over Birth Control as Public Policy
1963		
October 7	Greeley, Andrew M.	A Notable Twelve Months
October 14	Greeley, Andrew M.	Are Catholic Schools Really Inferior?
October 21	Greeley, Andrew M.	[Untitled]
October 28	Greeley, Andrew M.	"Revolution" Is Not Dead
November 4	Greeley, Andrew M.	Race Question Latent Issue in Next Elections
November 11	Greeley, Andrew M.	Freedom on the Catholic Campus
November 18	Greeley, Andrew M.	The Chicago Area Lay Movement
November 25	Greeley, Andrew M.	American Bishops and Theology
December 2	Greeley, Andrew M.	Death of a Magazine
December 9	Greeley, Andrew M.	A National "Revulsion" against Hate Groups?

December 16	Greeley, Andrew M.	Research on Race Question
December 23	Greeley, Andrew M.	The First of a New Breed
December 30	Greeley, Andrew M.	Kennedy's Contribution to American Catholicism
1964		
January 13	Greeley, Andrew M.	Transitional State of Church
1977		
November 14	Kistler, Alan	The Church and Labor: Part I
November 21	Kistler, Alan	The Church and Labor: Part II
November 28	Kistler, Alan	The Church and Labor: Part III
December 5	Kistler, Alan	The Church and Labor
December 12	McRaith, John J.	"Strike by Farmers—Could They, Would They, Should They?" Part I
December 19	McRaith, John J.	"A Look at the Goals of American Agriculture and Possible Alternatives to a Strike by Farmers"

~

Notes

Introduction

1. The University of Notre Dame awards the Laetare Medal to Catholics whose contribution to society is motivated by church ideals. The university awarded the first Laetare Medal in 1872 to John Gilmary Shea, the preeminent American Catholic Church historian of the 19th century. Higgins took Gilmary as his confirmation name in memory of John Gilmary Shea. Notre Dame also honored Higgins by naming its labor and social relations study center after Higgins in 1991.

2. *National Catholic Reporter* 27, no. 14 (April 13, 2001): 7.

3. George G. Higgins, "Laetare Medal Ceremony" (unpublished manuscript), 1–2. Cardinal Gibbons' letter in defense of the Knights of Labor appears in appendix C.

4. Ibid., 2–3.

5. The creation of the PRB was a unique step in labor history in the United States. The UAW established the board during a period of intense national anger against the labor movement because of Communist influence in some unions and reports of union racketeering. Higgins himself recognized the unique contribution that the PRB made on behalf of working people: "Msgr. George Higgins praised the UAW Public Relations Board . . . as an 'absolutely unique experiment in democracy.' . . . The Public Review Board, composed of seven impartial citizens including many well-known professors, provides UAW members with a final court of appeals to protect their rights to fair and ethical treatment. Higgins noted that the PRB does not have the power to pass judgments on the economic decisions of the union. 'It would have been totally unrealistic for this board to have anything to do with policy making,' Higgins said. . . . 'It will be hard to imagine the PRB without Msgr. Higgins,' said UAW President Stephen P. Yokich, who described him as 'a priest, a scholar, a trade unionist, and a social activist.' 'The union movement is about human dignity, and that is what you taught us,' Yokich told Higgins.'" This quotation is taken from the April 2001 issue of *Solidarity*, the UAW magazine (no page given). Pamela M. Klingbeil, executive secretary to the PRB, provided this information in her April 27, 2001, letter to the present writer.

6. Jerry Fiteau, "Revive Unions, Priest Says: Higgins, 'Labor Priest,' Says U.S. Workers Undervalued," *National Catholic Reporter* 36, no. 40 (September 14, 2000): 9.

7. *Origins* 30, no. 12 (August 24, 2000): 178. President Truman inaugurated the Presidential Medal of Freedom in 1945 to honor those who gave notable service in the Second World War. In 1963 President Kennedy amended the award for distinguished civilian service in peacetime. The ceremony was held at the White House for the first time in December 1963. President Johnson awarded labor leader George Meany in 1963, and President Clinton awarded Lane Kirkland and Cesar Chavez in 1994 (the latter posthumously).

8. SAD was a department of the NCWC (1922–1967). Monsignor John A. Ryan served as its first director from its inception to his retirement and death in 1945. His assistant director was Father Raymond A. McGowan. Ryan esteemed him personally and professionally. McGowan succeeded Ryan as director in 1945 and remained in this post until his retirement in 1954. Monsignor George G. Higgins began work full-time at SAD in 1944 and served in the church's social apostolate in Washington for the next thirty-six years. He served at SAD from 1944 to 1967. He was assistant director from 1944 to 1954 and director from 1954 to 1967. After the Second Vatican Council the Bishops' Conference restructured its offices, and Higgins became director for urban life in the Social Development Department, USCC, from 1968 to 1971. He then served as secretary for research, USCC, from 1972–1978 and as secretary for special concerns, USCC, from 1979 to 1980. After his retirement, the social apostolate became the Department of Social Development and World Peace.

9. Peter Matthiesen, *Sal Si Puedes: Cesar Chavez and the New American Revolution* (Berkeley: University of California Press, 2000), 335.

Chapter 1

1. See appendix A for a survey of the literature on civil religion.

2. See appendix B for a survey of the literature on public theology.

3. Ellen Skerrett, "The Irish in Chicago: The Catholic Dimension," in *Catholicism: Chicago Style*, ed. Ellen Skerrett, Edward R. Kantowicz, and Steven M. Avella (Chicago: Loyola University Press, 1993), 35. See also Bradford Verter, "Nativism," in *The Encyclopedia of Politics and Religion*, ed. Robert Wuthnow (Washington, DC: Congressional Quarterly, 1998), 557–61.

4. Andre Jardin, *Tocqueville: A Biography* (Baltimore: Johns Hopkins Press, 1998), 111–12.

5. Bernard E. Brown, "Tocqueville and Publius," in *Reconsidering Tocqueville's Democracy in America*, ed. Abraham S. Eisenstadt (New Brunswick, N.J.: Rutgers University Press, 1988), 42. The second part of *Democracy in America* was published in 1840.

6. Alexis de Tocqueville, *Democracy in America* (New York: Harper Collins, 1988), 9. Tocqueville did not exhibit a deterministic philosophy of history. However, he did think that the providence of God and the historical evolution of the nations were ineluctably leading 19th-century nations in the direction of democracy. For Tocqueville's philosophy of history see James T. Schleifer, "Tocqueville as Historian: Philosophy and Methodology in the *Democracy*," in Eisenstadt, *Reconsidering Tocqueville's Democracy in America*, 155–58; and Albert Solomon, "Tocqueville's Philosophy of Freedom" *Review of Politics* 1 (1939): 400–431.

7. Brown, "Tocqueville and Publius," 55.

8. Jardin, *Tocqueville: A Biography*, 194–223.

9. Tocqueville, *Democracy in America*, 295.

10. Ibid., 291. For a description of family life, see Kirk Jeffrey, "The Family as Utopian Retreat from the City: The Nineteenth-Century Contribution," in *The Family, Communes and Utopian Societies*, ed. Sallie TeSelle (New York: Harper and Row, 1972), 21–41.

11. G. K. Chesterton coined this phrase in 1922. Quoted in James H. Hutsen, *Religion and the Founding of the American Republic* (Washington, DC: Library of Congress, 1998), 3.

12. Nathan O. Hatch, "The Democratization of Christianity and the Character of American Politics," *Religion and American Politics: From the Colonial Period to the 1980s*, ed. Mark A. Noll (New York: Oxford University Press, 1990), 101.

13. For the impact of republicanism in the Roman Catholic Church in the United States see Patrick W. Carey, "Republicanism within American Catholicism, 1785–1860," *Journal of the Early Republic* 3 (1983): 413–37.

14. Stephen A. Marini, "Religion, Politics, and Ratification," in *Religion in a Revolutionary Age*, ed. Ronald Hoffman and Peter J. Albert (Charlottesville: University Press of Virginia, 1884), 188.

15. Robert N. Bellah, "Civil Religion in America," *Daedalus* 96 (1967): 1, 4, 12.

16. Robert Wuthnow, "Civil Religion," in *The Encyclopedia of Politics and Religion*, ed. Robert Wuthnow (Washington, DC: Congressional Quarterly, 1998), 153.

17. Ronald C. Wimberley and William H. Swatos Jr., "Civil Religion," in *Encyclopedia of Religion and Society*, ed. William H. Swatos Jr. (Walnut Creek, Calif.: AltaMira Press, 1998), 94.

18. Wuthnow, "Civil Religion," 153–54.

19. Ibid., 154.

20. Bellah, "Civil Religion in America," 5.

21. Wuthnow, "Civil Religion," 154.

22. Kenneth D. Wald, "American Presidents," in Wuthnow, *Public Religion in American Culture*, 620. See John F. Wilson, *Public Religion in American Culture* (Philadelphia: Temple University Press, 1979), 45–66; and Martin E. Marty, *Religion and Republic: The American Circumstance* (Boston: Beacon Press, 1987), 77–94.

23. Wald, "American Presidents," 20.

24. Wilson, *Public Religion in American Culture*, 29.

25. Wald, "American Presidents," 620.

26. Marty, *Religion and Republic*, 82. Civil religion borrows from Judaism when it speaks of the high priestly and prophetic roles. Wald and Marty do not investigate a wisdom role. However, U.S. presidents have exercised a wisdom role and made it part of the high priestly or the prophetic role.

27. George Washington, "The First Inaugural Speech," in *George Washington: A Collection*, ed. W. B. Allen (Indianapolis, Ind.: Liberty Fund, 1988), 460–62.

28. Matthew Spalding and Patrick J. Garrity, *A Sacred Union of Citizens: George Washington's Farewell Address and the American Character* (Lanham, Md.: Rowman and Littlefield, 1996), 2–44.

29. Spalding and Garrity, "Farewell Address," in *A Sacred Union of Citizens*, 183.

30. Ibid., 184.

31. Bellah, "Civil Religion in America," 7.

32. Ibid., 7–8.

33. Ibid., 8.

34. Later on such other texts as Washington's farewell address, *The Federalist Papers*, and the inaugural and Thanksgiving speeches were added to the canon of sacred texts.

35. Spalding and Garrity, *A Sacred Union of Citizens*, 1.

36. Gary Laderman, *The Sacred Remains* (New Haven, Conn.: Yale University Press, 1996), 17–18.

37. C. C. Goen, *Broken Churches, Broken Nation: Denominational Schisms and the Coming of the Civil War* (Macon, Ga.: Mercer University Press, 1985), 141. See Ronald C. White Jr., "Lincoln's Sermon on the Mount, The Second Inaugural," in *Religion and the American Civil War*,

ed. Randall M. Miller, Harry S. Stout, and Charles Reagan Wilson (New York: Oxford University Press, 1998), 208–25.

38. Bellah, "Civil Religion in America," 11.

39. Michael Kammen, *Mystic Chords of Memory: The Transformation of Tradition in American Culture* (New York: Vintage, 1991), 202.

40. Gregory S. Butler, "Visions of a Nation Transformed: Modernity and Ideology in Wilson's Political Thought," *Journal of Church and State* 39 (1997): 41–42.

41. Ibid., 42.

42. William E. Leuchtenburg, *The FDR Years: On Roosevelt and His Legacy* (New York: Columbia University Press, 1995), 11.

43. Patrick Henry, "'And I Don't Care What It Is': The Tradition-History of a Civil Religion Proof-Text," *Journal of the American Academy of Religion* 49 (1981): 35–36.

44. Richard Lischer, *The Preacher King: Martin Luther King Jr. and the Word That Moved America* (New York: Oxford University Press, 1995), 86–88, 148–53, 178–81.

45. Manning Marable, "The Rainbow Coalition: Jesse Jackson and the Politics of Ethnicity," *Cross Currents* 34 (1984): 21–42.

46. Robert D. Linder, "Universal Pastor: President Bill Clinton's Civil Religion," *Journal of Church and State* 38 (1996): 733–49.

47. Robert N. Bellah, *The Broken Covenant: American Civil Religion in Time of Trial* (New York: Seabury Press, 1975), 142.

48. Robert N. Bellah, "Is There a Common American Culture? Diversity, Identity, and Morality in American Public Life," in *The Power of Religious Publics: Staking Claims in American Society*, ed. William H. Swatos Jr. and James K. Wellman Jr. (Westport, Conn.: Praeger, 1999), 54.

49. Robert N. Bellah et al., *Habits of the Heart: Individualism and Commitment in American Life* (Berkeley: University of California Press, 1985), 41–44.

50. Tocqueville, *Democracy in America*, 535–38.

51. Ibid., 506–8. Individualism, according to Barry Alan Shain, "is the belief that every human being is a unique, rights-bearing moral entity and the final arbiter of the moral and religious truths that he or she believes and chooses to put into practice. Furthermore, this classical understanding requires that the political system be designed to protect . . . each fully rational adult from inappropriate public or private intrusion into his or her protected sphere of choice, especially in matters of religious or moral conscience. . . . The well-being of each decision-making individual is the most important social goal, with the meaning of well-being defined by each individual" ("Individualism," in Wuthnow, *The Encyclopedia of Politics and Religion*, 366). Michael Chevalier was the first to use the term in *Society, Manners, and Politics in the United States* in 1839. A year later Henry Reeve used it in his translation of the second volume of *Democracy in America*. Both use the term negatively. Later in the 19th century it will be synonymous with liberalism and its claims regarding the human person.

52. Tocqueville, *Democracy in America*, 506.

53. Bellah et al., *Habits of the Heart*, 45. For a critique of the present role of education and the corporation see Thomas Berry, *The Great Work: Our Way into the Future* (New York: Bell Tower, 1999), 72–85 and 117–35.

54. Robert D. Putnam, "Democracy in America at Century's End," in *Democracy's Victory and Crisis*, ed. Axel Hadenius (New York: Cambridge University Press, 1997), 56–59.

55. "Social capital refers to features of social organization, such as networks, norms, and social trust, that facilitate coordination and cooperation for mutual benefit" (ibid., 31). Putnam indicates that Jane Jacobs coined the phrase in 1961 (ibid., 63n7).

56. Richard John Neuhaus, *The Naked Public Square: Religion and Democracy in America*, 2nd ed. (Grand Rapids, Mich.: Eerdmans, 1995), 79–93.

57. Phillip E. Hammond, *With Liberty for All: Freedom of Religion in the United States* (Louisville, Ky.: Westminster John Knox Press, 1998), 106–7.

58. Anthony Delbanco, *The Real American Dream: A Meditation on Hope* (Cambridge, Mass.: Harvard University Press, 1999), 90–91.

59. Robert N. Bellah, "Religion and the Shape of National Culture," *America* 181 (July 31–August 7, 1999): 13–14.

60. James E. Wood Jr., "Public Religion vis-à-vis the Prophetic Role of Religion," in Swatos and Wellman, *The Power of Religious Publics*, 48–49.

61. Martin E. Marty, *The Public Church* (New York: Crossroad, 1981), 16.

62. Ibid., 57.

63. Linell E. Cady, "H. Richard Niebuhr and the Task of a Public Theology," in *The Legacy of H. Richard Niebuhr*, ed. Ronald F. Thiemann (Minneapolis, Minn.: Fortress Press, 1991), 119–26.

64. For Benjamin Franklin, see William Breitenbach, "Religious Affections and Religious Affectations: Antinomianism and Hypocrisy in the Writings of Edwards and Franklin," in *Benjamin Franklin, Jonathan Edwards, and the Representation of American Culture*, ed. Barbara B. Berg and Harry S. Stout (New York: Oxford University Press, 1993), 13–26. For Jonathan Edwards, see Gerald R. McDermott, *One Holy and Happy Society: The Public Theology of Jonathan Edwards* (University Park: Penn State Press, 1992), 93–116 and 137–84. For Reinhold Niebuhr, see his *Moral Man and Immoral Society* (New York: Charles Scribner's Sons, 1960); Langdon Gilkey, *On Niebuhr* (Chicago: University of Chicago Press, 2001); and Robert W. Lovin, *Reinhold Niebuhr and Christian Realism* (New York: Cambridge University Press, 1995), 158–90. For H. Richard Niebuhr, see his *The Responsible Self* (New York: Harper and Row, 1963). For Abraham Joshua Heschel, see his *The Insecurity of Freedom: Essays on Human Existence* (New York: Schoken Books, 66). For John A. Ryan, see Harlan R. Beckley, ed., *Economic Justice: Selections from Distributive Justice and a Living Wage* (Louisville, Ky.: Westminster John Knox Press, 1996). For John Courtney Murray, see his *We Hold These Truths, Catholic Reflections on the American Proposition* (Kansas City, Mo.: Sheed and Ward, 1988).

65. Christopher F. Mooney, *Public Virtue: Law and the Social Character of Religion* (Notre Dame, Ind.: University of Notre Dame Press, 1986), 18–20.

66. Robert W. McElroy, *The Search for an American Public Theology: The Contribution of John Courtney Murray* (New York: Paulist Press, 1989), 4–5. See John Courtney Murray, "Revising the Secularist Drift," *Thought* 24 (1949): 36–46; and "The Return to Tribalism," *Catholic Mind* 60 (1962): 5–12.

67. Rembert Weakland, "The Urban Poor and the Churches," *Origins* 26 (November 14, 1996): 360–61. Higgins presented the Henry Kaiser Memorial Lecture at the Georgetown University Law Center on October 2, 1996. See George G. Higgins, "Organized Labor and Collective Bargaining at the Crossroads," *Blueprint for Social Justice* 51 (April–May 1998): 1–10.

68. Judith N. Shklar, *American Citizenship: The Quest for Inclusion* (Cambridge, Mass.: Harvard University Press, 1991), 1–2.

69. Ibid., 3.

Chapter 2

1. George G. Higgins, *Organized Labor and the Church: Reflections of a "Labor Priest,"* with William Bole (New York: Paulist, 1993), 64. Keith F. Pecklers discusses the connection be-

tween the liturgical movement and social action in *The Unread Vision: The Liturgical Movement in the United States of America, 1926–1944* (Collegeville, Minn.: Liturgical Press, 1998).

2. Gerald M. Costello, *Without Fear or Favor: George Higgins on the Record* (Mystic, Conn.: Twenty-third Publications, 1984), 7.

3. Margery Frisbie, *An Alley in Chicago: The Ministry of a City Priest* (Kansas City, Mo.: Sheed and Ward, 1991), 286. Msgr. Egan died on May 19, 2001.

4. Costello, *Without Fear or Favor*, 8.

5. Cardinal Mundelein wanted to make Saint Mary's University the Catholic University of the West. Therefore, he refused to send his priests to Washington for study. When Stritch became the ordinary, he broke with Mundelein's tradition. He was unable to send any of his priests to Europe for study because of the Second World War. Therefore, he sent the twelve priests from the 1940 ordination class to Washington.

6. George G. Higgins, "The Under Consumption Theory in the Writings of Monsignor John A. Ryan," (unpublished master's dissertation, Catholic University of America, 1942), 59.

7. See chap. 1, n. 11.

8. Higgins frequently and good-naturedly called himself a church bureaucrat. However, SAD was hardly a bureaucracy. Its staff was small during these years. McGowan, Higgins, and Sulpician Father John F. Cronin divided up departmental tasks and chose their areas of responsibility according to their personal interests, training, and talents. Linna E. Bresette, SAD's field representative, ably assisted them with dedicated secretaries.

9. "The phrase 'Catholic Social Teaching' is perhaps the closest equivalent to public theology in the Catholic tradition. . . . This phrase also is of relatively recent coinage; strictly speaking, it refers to a series of documents of papal and conciliar origin in the last one hundred years of the life of the church. The 'social teaching,' therefore, is but one moment in the longer Catholic social tradition. . . . The 'social teaching' is primarily the creation of the twentieth-century papacy from Leo XIII (d. 1903) through John Paul II (1978–). Its sources lie in the biblical, theological, and philosophical heritage of the social tradition. Its purpose has been to bring that tradition to bear upon the distinctively new forms of 'The Social Question' generated by the Industrial Revolution, the rise of democratic polity, the consequence of two world wars and the cold war, and the wholly new phenomenon of globalization." J. Bryan Hehir, "Forum: Public Theology in Contemporary America," *Religion and American Culture* 10 (2000): 21.

10. Bruce Laurie, *Artisans into Workers: Labor in Nineteenth-Century America* (Urbana: University of Illinois Press, 1997), 16–17. Walter Licht, *Industrial America: The Nineteenth Century* (Baltimore: Johns Hopkins Press, 1995), 102–66.

11. Foster Rhea Dulles and Melvyn Dubofsky, *Labor in America: A History*, 5th ed. (Wheeling, Ill.: Harlan Davidson, 1993), 21–34.

12. David Montgomery, "The Working Classes of the Pre-industrial American City, 1780–1830," *Labor History* 9 (1968): 16.

13. Charles Sellers, *The Market Revolution: Jacksonian America, 1815–1846* (New York: Oxford University Press, 1991), 137–71.

14. T. J. Jackson Lears, *No Place of Grace: Antimodernism and the Transformation of American Culture, 1880–1920* (Chicago: University of Chicago Press, 1994), 59–96; and "From Salvation to Self-Realization: Advertising and the Therapeutic Roots of the Consumer Culture, 1880–1930," in *The Culture of Consumption: Critical Essays in American History, 1880–1980*, ed. Richard Wightman Fox and T. J. Jackson Lears (New York: Pantheon, 1983), 1–38.

15. The Gilded Age is a term used to describe the years 1875–1901 in U.S. history. The term was taken from *The Gilded Age: A Tale for Today*, a novel written by Mark Twain and Charles Dudley Warren in 1893. The novel satirizes the golden road to fortune. The term summed up

the greed and opulence of industrialists and financiers, an unregulated laissez-faire economy, and the political corruption that existed vis-à-vis the horrible squalor of urban tenements and the oppressive treatment of working people and the poor. *Sister Carrie*, a novel by Theodore Dreiser, aptly describes the plight of urban working people in this era. Some historians have recently suggested that the Gilded Age be considered as more than gilt, tawdriness, and corruption. They point out the accomplishments of this period. These include the industrialization of the country, the influence of railroads in creating national markets, the development of a two-party political system, and the growth of the great modern cities. The telephone, the automobile, and the motion picture were invented during this time as well. Museums, literature, and art flourished. In short, the period is much more than an interim between Reconstruction (1865–1877) and the Progressive Era (1893–1920). Louis L. Gould, "The Gilded Age," in *The Oxford Companion to U.S. History*, ed. Paul S. Boyer (New York: Oxford University Press, 2001), 308–10.

16. For a thorough treatment of how NAM and other national business associations transformed the country into a land of consumers in the 1890s, see William Leach, *Land of Desire: Merchants, Power, and the Rise of a New American Culture* (New York: Vintage, 1993).

17. Dulles and Dubofsky, *Labor in America: A History*, 97.

18. David Montgomery, "William H. Sylvis and the Search for Working-Class Citizenship," in *Labor Leaders in America*, ed. Melvyn Dubofsky and Warren Van Tine (Urbana: University of Illinois Press, 1987), 8.

19. Ibid., 9.

20. Ibid., 14.

21. The eight-hour workday became law on May 1, 1867. Between five thousand and six thousand marchers from forty-four local unions in Chicago staged a festive parade to celebrate the event. Ibid., 15.

22. Ibid., 14–15 and 25–26.

23. Ibid., 24. In 1869 Myers gathered labor leaders, preachers, and politicians into the Colored National Labor Congress. Its purpose was public education, apprentice training for blacks, black unionism, mutual understanding between labor and capital, and support for the Republican Party. The second congress in 1870 was its last. Bruce Laurie, *Artisans into Workers*, 159.

24. Jeremy Brecher, *Strike!* rev. and upd. ed. (Boston: South End Press, 1997), 39–68. Henry J. Browne, *The Catholic Church and The Knights of Labor* (Washington, DC: Catholic University of America, 1949), 182–275. Robert H. Craig, *Religion and Radical Politics: An Alternative Christian Tradition in the United States* (Philadelphia: Temple University Press, 1992), 6–45. Jay P. Dolan, *The American Catholic Experience: From Colonial Times to the Present* (Garden City, N.Y.: Doubleday, 1985), 329–40. Dulles and Dubofsky, *Labor in America*, 120–41. James Hennesey, *American Catholics: A History of the Roman Catholic Community in the United States* (New York: Oxford University Press, 1981), 172–203. Bruce Laurie, *Artisans into Workers: Labor in Nineteenth-Century America* (Urbana: University of Illinois Press, 1997), 141–75. David J. O'Brien, *Public Catholicism*, 2nd ed. (Maryknoll, N.Y.: Orbis, 1996), 131–51. Robert E. Weir, *Beyond Labor's Veil: The Culture of the Knights of Labor* (University Park: Pennsylvania State University Press, 1996). Michael Zoller, *Washington and Rome: Catholicism in American Culture* (Notre Dame, Ind.: University of Notre Dame Press, 1999), 114–17.

25. Sandra Yocum Mize, "Terence V. Powderly (1878–1924)," in *The Encyclopedia of American Catholic History*, ed. Michael Glazier and Thomas J. Shelley (Collegeville, Minn.: Liturgical Press, 1997), 1162–64; Richard Oestreicher, "Terence V. Powderly, the Knights of Labor, and Artisnal Republicanism," in Dubofsky and Van Tine, *Labor Leaders in America*, 30–61.

26. Dulles and Dubofsky, *Labor in America*, 120–21.

27. Robert E. Weir, *Beyond Labor's Veil*, 11–12.

28. Jeremy Brecher, *Strike!* 40.

29. Weir, *Beyond Labor's Veil*, 12.

30. Many Irish Catholics, thinking that intemperance caused poverty, wholeheartedly supported the temperance movement and made it part of 19th-century spirituality. The Catholic Total Abstinence Union of America was founded in 1872. Powderly was a strong advocate for temperance among the Knights. Dolan, *The American Catholic Experience*, 326; and Samuel Walker, "Terence V. Powderly, the Knights of Labor, and the Temperance Issue," *Societas* 5 (1975): 279–93.

31. Robert E. Weir, *Beyond Labor's Veil*, 117. Also Philip S. Foner, "Songs of the Eight-Hour Movement," *Labor History* 13 (1972): 571–88.

32. Archie Green chronicles how the oral tradition preserved and handed down labor music. "The Death of Mother Jones," *Labor History* 1 (1960): 60–80.

33. Aaron I. Abell, "Origins of Catholic Social Reform in the United States: Ideological Aspects," *Review of Politics* 11 (1949): 294–309; "The Catholic Factor in Urban Welfare: The Early Period, 1850–1880," *Review of Politics* 14 (1952): 289–324.

34. For the history of Freemasonry in the United States see Steven C. Bullock, *Revolutionary Brotherhood: Freemasonry and the Transformation of the American Social Order, 1730–1840* (Chapel Hill: University of North Carolina, 1996); Robert S. Ellwood, "Occult Movements in America," in *Encyclopedia of the American Religious Experience, Studies of Traditions and Movements*, ed. Charles H. Lippy and Peter W. Williams (New York: Charles Scribner's Sons, 1988), 2:711–22, especially 714–15; and Leo P. Ribuffo, "Religious Prejudice and Nativism," in Lippy and Williams, *Encyclopedia of the American Religious Experience*, 3:1525–46, especially 1530–31. Men in the Victorian period had a penchant for proving their "manhood" by participating in sports and by joining organizations and secret orders. The last third of the 19th century was a golden age of fraternity. See Mark C. Carnes, *Secret Ritual and Manhood in Victorian America* (New Haven, Conn.: Yale University Press, 1989), 1–14; Michael S. Kimmel, "Baseball and the Reconstitution of American Masculinity, 1880–1920," in *Baseball History from Outside the Lines: A Reader*, ed. John E. Dreifort (Lincoln: University of Nebraska Press, 2001), 47–61; and Woody Register, *The Kid of Coney Island: Fred Thompson and the Rise of American Amusements* (New York: Oxford University Press, 2001), 33–43.

35. William Barnaby Faherty, "The Clergyman and Labor Progress: Cornelius O'Leary and the Knights of Labor," *Labor History* 11 (1970): 175–89.

36. Henry J. Browne, "Terence V. Powderly and Church-Labor Difficulties of the Early 1880s," *Catholic Historical Review* 52 (1946): 1–27.

37. J. H. M. Laslett, "Haymarket, Henry George, and the Labor Upsurge in Britain and America during the Late 1880s," *International Labor and Working-Class History* 29 (1986): 62–82.

38. Dolan, *The American Catholic Experience*, 331; see also Robert L. Heilbroner, *The Worldly Philosophers: The Lives, Times, and Ideas of the Great Economic Thinkers* (New York: Simon and Schuster, 1953), 175–83.

39. Robert Emmett Curran, "Confronting 'The Social Question': American Catholic Thought and the Socio-Economic Thought in the Nineteenth Century," *U.S. Catholic Historian* 5 (1986): 186–94.

40. Robert Emmett Curran, "Prelude to 'Americanism': The New York Academia and Clericalism in the Late Nineteenth Century," *Church History* 47 (1978): 48–65.

41. Dominic P. Scibilia, "Edward McGlynn, Thomas McGrady, and Peter C. Yorke: Prophets of American Social Catholicism" (unpublished doctoral dissertation, Marquette University, 1990), 106–7.

42. Dominic P. Scibilia, "Edward McGlynn: American Social Catholic," *Records of the American Catholic Historical Society of Philadelphia* 101 (1990): 11.

43. Robert Emmett Curran, "The McGlynn Affair and the Shaping of the New Conservatism in American Catholicism, 1886–1894," *Catholic Historical Review* 66 (1980): 48–65. Gerald P. Fogarty, *The Vatican and the American Hierarchy from 1870 to 1965* (Collegeville, Minn.: Liturgical Press, 1982), 86–114. Alfred Isacsson, *Edward McGlynn: Studies Marking the Centenary of His Death* (Tarrytown, N.Y.: Vestigium, 1999); and *The Determined Doctor: The Story of Edward McGlynn* (Tarrytown, N.Y.: Vestigium 1998). Manuel S. "Jeff" Shanaberger, "A Missionary Priest and His Social Gospel," *U.S. Catholic Historian* 13 (1995): 23–47.

44. Alfred Isacsson, "Edward McGlynn (1837–1900)," in Glazier and Shelley, *The Encyclopedia of American Catholic History*, 885.

45. Charles R. Morris, *American Catholic: The Saints and Sinners Who Built America's Most Powerful Church* (New York: Vintage, 1997), 87.

46. Cardinal James Gibbons, "Defense of the Knights of Labor, February 20, 1887," in Glazier and Shelley, *The Encyclopedia of American Catholic History*, 772. The full text of this document appears in appendix C.

47. Morris states that Gibbons carried "only six of the nine archbishops. . . . Two voted for outright condemnation, and Corrigan abstained, although he would almost certainly have voted with a majority to condemn." Morris, *American Catholic*, 87. Gibbons stated that "only two of the twelve archbishops voted for condemnation, and their reasons were powerless to convince the others of either the justice or the prudence of such a condemnation." Gibbons, "Defense of the Knights of Labor," 772.

48. Gibbons, "Defense of the Knights of Labor," 776.

49. Ibid., 777.

50. "The Yardstick," *Catholic Observer* 47, no. 3 (February 4, 2000): 9.

51. Peter Steinfels contrasts two descriptions of liberalism. In the first instance, Owen Chadwick describes liberalism in this way: "Confused, vague, contradictory, the idea of liberalism dominated the nineteenth century, more a motto than a word, more a programme of what might be than a description of what was; a protean word, which some claimed to rest upon coherent philosophies and economic theory and others saw as the destruction of the stable structure of a reasonable society." Irene Collins, another historian, is more encouraging. " '[Liberals] held at heart a simple faith: a belief that progress, leading to final perfection, could be achieved by means of free institutions,' such as freely elected parliaments, accountable ministers, independent judiciaries, freedom of speech, press, religion, assembly, careers open to talent, the protection of property, and due process before the law." Peter Steinfels, "The Failed Encounter: The Catholic Church and Liberalism in the Nineteenth Century," in *Catholicism and Liberalsim, Contributions to American Public Philosophy*, ed. R. Bruce Douglass and David Hollenbach (New York: Cambridge University Press, 1994), 23.

52. Mary Elsbernd, "Papal Statements on Rights: A Historical Contextual Study of Encyclical Teaching from Pius VI–Pius XI (1791–1939)" (unpublished doctoral dissertation, Catholic University of Louvain, 1985), 237.

53. Ibid., 237–38.

54. Thomas Bokenkotter, *Church and Revolution: Catholics in the Struggle for Democracy and Social Justice* (New York: Image Books Doubleday, 1998) 209.

55. Elsbernd, "Papal Statements on Rights," 228.

56. Ibid., 229.

57. Paul Misner, "Wilhelm Emmanuel von Ketteler," in *New Dictionary of Catholic Social Thought*, ed. Judith A. Dwyer (Collegeville, Minn.: Liturgical Press, 1994), 503–6; Paul Mis-

ner, *Social Catholicism in Europe: From the Onset of Industrialization to the First World War* (New York: Crossroad, 1991), 136–44.

58. Elsbernd, "Papal Statements on Rights," 232.

59. Normand Paulhus, "Fribourg Union," in Dwyer, *New Dictionary of Catholic Social Thought*, 404–5.

60. Elsbernd, "Papal Statements on Rights," 234.

61. Bokenkotter, *Church and Revolution*, 192–204; David Newsome, *The Convert Cardinals: John Henry Newman and Henry Edward Manning* (London: John Murray, 1993), 327–42.

62. Bokenkotter, *Church and Revolution*, 192–204.

63. Ibid., 195.

64. Ibid., 204.

65. Ibid., 111–32.

66. Ibid., 245.

67. Matteo Liberatone was an important figure in the Scholastic renewal and in moral theology. He had recently published *Principles of Political Economy*.

68. Cardinal Camillo Mazella had taught in the United States and was deeply aware of the significance of the church's positive stance toward the labor unions. John Ciani, "Cardinal Camillo Mazzella, S.J.," in *The Varieties of Ultramontanism*, ed. Jeffrey von Arx (Washington, DC: Catholic University of America Press, 1998), 103–17.

69. Elsbernd, "Papal Statements on Rights," 246–47.

70. *Rerum Novarum* (hereafter *RN*) in *Catholic Social Thought: The Documentary Heritage*, ed. David J. O'Brien and Thomas A. Shannon (Maryknoll, N.Y.: Orbis, 1992), 7–10.

71. Stephen J. Pope, "*Rerum Novarum*," in Dwyer, *New Dictionary of Catholic Social Thought*, 832–33.

72. *RN*, 15.

73. *RN*, 16.

74. *RN*, 17.

75. Pope, "*Rerum Novarum*," 833.

76. *RN*, 24.

77. *RN*, 26.

78. *RN*, 27.

79. *RN*, 29.

80. *RN*, 36–43.

81. Pope, "*Rerum Novarum*," 837.

82. George E. McCarthy and Royal W. Rhodes, *Eclipse of Justice, Ethics, Economics, and the Lost Traditions of American Catholicism* (Maryknoll, N.Y.: Orbis Books, 1992), 157–58.

83. Elsbernd, "Papal Statements on Rights," 247–48.

84. Dolan, *The American Catholic Experience*, 335.

85. Joseph Chinicci, *Living Stones: The History and Structure of Catholic Spiritual Life in the United States* (New York: Macmillan, 1989), 119–45; Anne Taves, *The Household of Faith: Roman Catholic Devotions in Mid-Nineteenth-Century America* (Notre Dame: University of Notre Dame Press, 1986), 71–88 and 113–33.

86. Susan Hill Lindley, *You Have Stept Out of Your Place: A History of Women and Religion in America* (Louisville, Ky.: Westminster John Knox Press, 1996), 197–206; Colleen McDannell, *The Christian Home in Victorian America, 1840–1900* (Bloomington: Indiana University Press, 1986), 52–76.

87. Mary Jo Oates, *The Catholic Philanthropic Tradition in America* (Bloomington: Indiana University Press, 1995), 119–41 and 165–75.

88. Dolan, *The American Catholic Experience*, 335.

89. The National Catholic War Council, the first corporate structure for the Catholic Church in the United States, began during the First World War. It later became the NCWC.

90. Dolan, *The American Catholic Experience*, 336. For an excellent treatment of the Central-Verein, see Philip Gleason, *The Conservative Reformers: German-American Catholics and the Social Order* (Notre Dame, Ind.: University of Notre Dame Press, 1968).

91. David J. O'Brien, *Public Catholicism* (Maryknoll, N.Y.: Orbis, 1996), 138; Robert E. Doherty, "Thomas J. Hagerty, the Church, and Socialism," *Labor History* 3 (1962): 39–56; James Hennesey, *American Catholics: A History of the Roman Catholic Community in the United States* (New York: Oxford University Press, 1981), 214.

92. Toby Terrar, "Catholic Socialism: The Reverend Thomas McGrady," *Dialectical Anthropology* 7 (1983): 209–35; Scibilia, "Edward McGlynn, Thomas McGrady, and Peter C. Yorke," 209–10n112.

93. "David Goldstein and Martha Moore Avery, both of whom would shortly abandon socialism, disliked McGrady's rejection of religious myth and prejudice and attempts to use it in place of science. Foner summarizes Goldstein and Avery's socialism: 'The Karl Marx Club, established by Goldstein, Avery and other Boston socialists in 1899 sought to teach Marxian economics minus Marxist philosophy, whatever that meant.' . . . Goldstein and Avery sought to undermine McGrady by accusing him of charging excessive lecture fees" (Terrar, "Catholic Socialism," 218). Both Goldstein and Avery became significant Catholic apologists. Debra Campbell, "A Catholic Salvation Army: David Goldstein, Pioneer Lay Evangelist," *Church History* 52 (1983): 322–32; "David Goldstein and the Rise of the Catholic Campaigners for Christ," *Catholic Historical Review* 72 (1986): 33–50; Paula M. Kane, *Separatism and Subculture: Boston Catholicism, 1900–1920* (Chapel Hill: University of North Carolina Press, 1994), 182–86.

94. Joseph Quinn, "Thomas McGrady," in Glazier and Shelley, *The Encyclopedia of American Catholic History*, 885.

95. Terrar, "Catholic Socialism," 219–23.

96. Scibilia, "Edward McGlynn, Thomas McGrady, and Peter C. Yorke," 196.

97. Ibid., 197.

98. Dominic P. Scibilia, "Thomas McGrady: American Catholic Millennialist Millennial Social Catholic," *Records of the American Catholic Historical Society* 104 (1994): 45.

99. Dolan, *The American Catholic Experience*, 338.

100. Scibilia, "Edward McGlynn, Thomas McGrady, and Peter C. Yorke," 214.

101. Richard Gribble, *Catholicism and the San Francisco Labor Movement, 1896–1921* (Lewiston, N.Y.: Edwin Mellen Press, 1993), 25; see also Joseph Brusher, "Peter C. Yorke and the A.P.A. in San Francisco," *Catholic Historical Review* 51 (1951): 129–50 and "*Rerum Novarum* in the San Francisco Strike of 1901," *American Ecclesiastical Review* 141 (1959): 103–16.

102. Gribble, *Catholicism and the San Francisco Labor Movement*, 43.

103. Ibid., 54.

104. Ibid., 84.

105. Scibilia, "Edward McGlynn, Thomas McGrady, and Peter C. Yorke," 215–16.

106. Dolan, *The American Catholic Experience*, 341.

107. Aaron I. Abell, "The Reception of Leo XIII's Labor Encyclical in America, 1891–1919," *Review of Politics* 7 (1945): 479–80; Dolan, *The American Catholic Experience*, 341.

108. Sandra Yocum Mize, "Peter E. Dietz (1978–1947)," in Glazier and Shelley, *The Encyclopedia of American Church History*, 434.

109. Abell, "The Reception of Leo XIII's Labor Encyclical," 486–87; Gleason, *The Conservative Reformers*, 91–144.

110. Mary Harrita Fox, *Peter E. Dietz: Labor Priest* (Notre Dame, Ind.: University of Notre Dame Press, 1953), 43–68.

111. Sandra Yocum Mize, "Peter E. Dietz," in Dwyer, *New Dictionary of Catholic Social Thought*, 284.

112. Paul Stroh, "The Catholic Clergy and American Labor Disputes, 1900–1939" (unpublished doctoral dissertation, Catholic University of America, 1939), 33. See also Catherine Ann Cline, "Priest in the Coal Fields: The Story of Father Curran," *Records of the American Catholic Historical Society* 68 (1952): 67–84; Craig Phelan, *Divided Loyalties: The Public and Private Life of Labor Leader John Mitchell* (Albany: State University of New York Press, 1994), 154–90.

113. Stroh, "The Catholic Clergy and American Labor Disputes," 34.

114. Ibid., 42–48. This was the first time in the nation's history that the federal government had intervened in a labor dispute on the workers' behalf. Hyman Berman, "Labor," in *Dictionary of American History*, rev. ed., ed. Louise Bilebof Ketz (New York: Charles Scribner's Sons, 1976), 4:67.

115. Berman, "Labor," 52–53.

116. Ibid., 55–63.

117. Ibid., 66.

118. Ibid., 67–70.

119. Ibid., 70–71.

120. Ibid., 74.

121. Archives of the Archdiocese of Boston; Kane, *Separatism and Subculture*, 13–21.

122. Kane, *Separatism and Subculture*, 5.

123. Ibid., 6–7.

124. Stroh, "The Catholic Clergy and American Labor Disputes," 80–84.

125. Ibid., 84.

126. Melvyn Dubofsky, *Industrialism and the American Worker, 1865–1920*, 3rd ed. (Wheeling, Ill.: Harlan Davidson, 1996), 146; David Brody, *Workers in Industrial America, Essays on the 20th Century Struggle*, 2nd ed. (New York: Oxford University Press, 1993), 3–47.

127. Dubofsky, *Industrialism and the American Worker*, 146–54.

128. NAM was organized in Cincinnati in 1895. It encouraged laissez-faire, antiunion sentiment and protectionism. Its vigorous lobby on behalf of the open shop and its numerous publications were weapons in a frontal attack on unionism. By the 1920s, NAM and the U.S. Chamber of Commerce (founded in 1912) spoke for business interests. Thomas V. DiBacco, "National Association of Manufacturers," in Ketz, *Dictionary of American History*, 4:461; Allen M. Wakestein, "The National Association of Manufacturers and Labor Relations in the 1920s," *Labor History* 10 (1969): 163–76.

129. The Sherman Antitrust Act, enacted July 2, 1890, was the first federal law directed against industrial combination and monopoly. The key provision of the act declared that "every contract, combination in the form of trust or otherwise, or conspiracy, in restraint of trade or commerce among the several states, or with foreign nations, is hereby declared to be illegal." According to Richard E. Welch Jr., "The act was noteworthy as a pioneer measure in the field of federal regulatory legislation." Welch, "Sherman Antitrust Act," in Ketz, *Dictionary of American History*, 6:26–27.

130. Dubofsky and Van Tine, *Labor Leaders in America*, 82–87. Woodrow Wilson pledged to check monopoly and restore free competition in his 1912 election campaign. The Clayton Antitrust Act was a significant piece of that reform legislation in Wilson's New Freedom. "The 'rule of reason' promulgated by the Supreme Court in the Standard Oil case of 1911 had cre-

ated uncertainty about explicit standards of 'reasonable' and 'unreasonable' trade restraints and had left to the courts sweeping powers of interpretation in applying the rule. Accordingly, businessmen favoring suppression of unfair control of trade joined with Progressive advocates of stronger antitrust legislation in supporting a clarifying measure to outlaw certain monopolistic or restrictive trade practices not specifically covered by the Sherman Antitrust Act (1890). The omnibus bill, introduced in 1914 by Rep. Henry D. Clayton, . . . was . . . linked to companion legislation creating the Federal Trade Commission." The act prohibited monopolies and promoted competition. It allowed trade unions and farm organizations to function freely. However, further Supreme Court rulings in the 1920s thwarted the purpose of the act and weakened its value as a tool in preventing the buildup of monopoly power through merger. William Greenleaf, "Clayton Antitrust Act," in Ketz, *Dictionary of American History*, 2:71–72.

131. William B. Wilson was born in Scotland in 1862. His family emigrated to Arnot, Pennsylvania, in 1870. Wilson went to work in the mines at age nine. His experiences as a labor leader intensified his devotion to labor unionism and the desire to improve working-class conditions. He was connected with the coal strikes of 1899 and 1902. He was elected to Congress from 1907 to 1913 and was chair for the House committee on labor. He sponsored an investigation of safety conditions in mines and had much to do with the subsequent organization of the federal Bureau of Mines in 1910. He helped in the creation of the Department of Labor and became its first head. He served as secretary of labor from 1913 to 1921. He helped develop agencies for the mediation and adjustment of industrial disputes and took measures that ameliorated organized labor. Witt Bowden, "William Bauchop Wilson," in *Dictionary of American Biography*, vol. 10, ed. Dumas Malone (New York: Charles Scribner's Sons, 1936), 348–49.

132. John Milton Cooper Jr., *Pivotal Decades: The United States, 1900–1920* (New York: W. W. Norton, 1990), 324; Sean Dennis Cashman, *America in the Age of the Titans: The Progressive Era and World War I* (New York: New York University Press, 1988), 107–143; Kendrick A. Clements, *The Presidency of Woodrow Wilson* (Lawrence: University of Kansas, 1992), 73–91; Dulles and Dubofsky, *Labor in America: A History*, 175–232; Julie Greene, "Dinner-Pail Politics: Employers, Workers, and Partisan Culture in the Progressive Era," in *Labor Histories: Class, Politics, and the Working-Class Experience*, ed. Eric Arnesen, Julie Greene, and Bruce Laurie (Urbana: University of Illinois Press, 1998), 71–96; Julie Greene, "Negotiating the State: Frank Walsh and the Transformation of Labor's Political Culture in Progressive America," in *Organized Labor and American Politics, 1894–1994: The Labor-Liberal Alliance*, ed. Kevin Boyle (Albany: State University of New York, 1998), 71–102; Joseph Slater, "Public Workers: Labor and the Boston Police Strike of 1919," *Labor History* 38 (1997): 7–27; John S. Smith, "Organized Labor and Government in the Wilson Era, 1913–1921: Some Conclusions," *Labor History* 3 (1962): 265–86; Shelton Stromquist, "Class Wars: Frank Walsh, the Reformers, and the Crisis of Progressivism," in Arnesen, Greene, and Laurie, *Labor Histories*, 97–124.

133. Cooper, *Pivotal Decades*, 322–24.

134. Stroh, "The Catholic Clergy and American Labor Disputes," 104.

135. Ibid., 104–12.

136. Dubofsky, *Industrialism and the American Worker*, 151.

137. Lindley, *You Have Stept Out of Your Place*, 207.

138. Dominic Scibilia, "The Christological Character of Labor: The Theology of Mary Harris ('Mother') Jones," *U.S. Catholic Historian* 13 (1995): 49.

139. Mari Boor Tonn, "The Rhetorical Personae of Mary Harris "Mother" Jones: Industrial Labor's Maternal Prophet" (unpublished doctoral dissertation, University of Kansas, 1987), 40.

140. Tonn, *The Rhetorical Personae of Mary Harris "Mother" Jones*, 41.

141. Ibid., 49.

142. Scibilia, "The Christological Character of Labor," 56.

143. Tonn, *The Rhetorical Personae of Mary Harris "Mother" Jones*, 8–69.

144. Lindley, *You Have Stept Out of Your Place*, 207–8.

145. Patricia A. Lamoureux, "Irish Catholic Women and the Labor Movement," *U.S. Catholic Historian* 16 (1998): 33. See also Allen F. Davis, "The Women's Trade Union League: Origins and Organization," *Labor History* 5 (1064): 3–17; Robin Miller Jacoby, *The British and American Women's Trade Union Leagues, 1890–1925* (Brooklyn, N.Y.: Carlson, 1994), 19–35 and 119–47.

146. Lamoureux, "Irish Catholic Women and the Labor Movement," 34–38.

147. Ibid., 40.

148. Ibid., 40.

149. Ibid., 41–42.

150. Ibid., 44.

151. Ilia Delio, "The First Catholic Social Gospelers: Women Religious in the Nineteenth Century," *U.S. Catholic Historian* 13 (1995): 13.

152. Carol K. Coburn and Martha Smith, *Spirited Lives: How Nuns Shaped Catholic Culture and American Life, 1836–1920* (Chapel Hill: University of North Carolina Press, 1999), 203–25.

153. U.S. Bishops, "Letter of the Hierarchy to President Woodrow Wilson regarding the Establishment of the National Catholic War Council and Pledge of Catholic Loyalty," in *Our Bishops Speak*, ed. Raphael M. Huber (Milwaukee, Wisc.: Bruce, 1952), 173–74.

154. Quoted in Douglas J. Slawson, "National Catholic Welfare Conference," in Glazier and Shelley, *The Encyclopedia of American Catholic History*, 1005.

155. Douglas Slawson, "John J. Burke CSP: The Vision and Character of a Public Churchman," *Journal of Paulist Studies* 4 (1995–1996): 92.

156. The members of the committee were Bishops Peter J. Muldoon of Rockford, Joseph Schrembs of Toledo, William T. Russell of Charleston, and Patrick J. Hayes, who would become the cardinal archbishop of New York.

157. Toward the end of his career Ryan searched for a label that might best describe his public position. According to Francis L. Broderick, some characterized him as progressive because of his "forward-looking optimism that characterized most of his public statements from 1894 to 1945. Yet he settled finally on 'papalist.' The tag . . . was apt both because of the use he made of the encyclicals to promote Catholic concurrence in American social reform and because of the period in which he worked." Broderick, "The Encyclicals and Social Action: Is John A. Ryan Typical?" *Catholic Historical Review* 55 (1969): 1. Paula M. Kane states similarly that "biographers of Ryan have strenuously tried to claim him as a Catholic liberal, and in doing so have overlooked or minimized the less attractive features of his extreme conservatism, epitomized in his publication *The State and the Church* (1912). A recent appraiser of his career acknowledges, however, that 'the terms liberal and conservative might not be revealing when applied to the career of John A. Ryan, for he combined something from both agendas to create his own view,'" Kane, *Separatism and Subculture*, 330n57. Ryan's economic vision of the relationship of work and leisure was rooted in a natural law, understanding of the larger, visionary issues of his systematic, religious approach to social and cultural reconstruction. His approach to a shorter workweek, "underconsumption," unemployment, and wealth maldistribution was intended to counteract the incipient tendency toward a culture of abundance and unnecessary luxury. Benjamin K. Hunnicutt, "Monsignor John A. Ryan and the Shorter Hours of Labor: A Forgotten Vision of 'Genuine' Progress," *Catholic Historical Review* 69 (1983): 399–401.

158. Patrick W. Gearty, *The Economic Thought of Monsignor John A. Ryan* (Washington, DC: Catholic University of America Press, 1953), 39.

159. Jeffry Marlett, "Harvesting an Overlooked Freedom: The Anti-urban Vision of American Catholic Agrarianism, 1920–1950," *U.S. Catholic Historian* 16 (1998): 98; see also Robert D. Cross, "The Changing Image of the City among American Catholics," *Catholic Historical Review* 48 (1962): 33–52; Jacob H. Dorn, "The Rural Ideal and Agrarian Realities: Arthur E. Holt and the Vision of a Decentralized America in the Interwar Years," *Church History* 52 (1983): 50–65; R. W. Franklin and Robert L. Spaeth, *Virgil Michel: American Catholic* (Collegeville, Minn.: Liturgical Press, 1988), 105–20; Peter A. Huff, *Allen Tate and the Catholic Revival: Trace of the Fugitive Gods* (New York: Paulist, 1996), 50–71; Anthony Novitsky, "Peter Maurin's Green Revolution: The Radical Implications of Reactionary Social Catholicism," *Review of Politics* 37 (1975): 83–103; Edward S. Shapiro, "Catholic Agrarian Thought and the New Deal," *Catholic Historical Review* 65 (1979): 583–99 and Marvin Swanson, "The 'Country Life Movement' and the American Churches," *Church History* 46 (1977): 358–73. A return to the land is still evident in U.S. religion. See Rebecca Kneale Gould, "Getting (Not Too Close) to Nature: Modern Homesteading as Lived Religion in America," in *Lived Religion in America: Toward a History of Practice*, ed. David D. Hall (Princeton, N.J.: Princeton University Press, 1997), 217–42.

160. David J. O'Brien, *Public Catholicism*, 2nd ed. (Maryknoll, N.Y.: Orbis Books, 1996), 156–57.

161. O'Brien, *Public Catholicism*, 155. The 1919 pastoral letter is the first extensive treatment of work and working conditions by the U.S. Hierarchy. Mary Elsbernd, "Work and Workers in the Pastoral Letters of the United States Conference of Bishops," *Louvain Studies* 19 (1994): 222–24.

162. Peter Guilday, *The National Pastorals of the American Hierarchy (1792–1919)* (Washington, DC: National Catholic Welfare Council, 1923), 318.

163. Ibid., 319.

164. Ibid., 320–21.

165. Ibid., 321.

166. Ibid.

167. Lawrence B. Glickman, *A Living Wage: American Workers and the Making of Consumer Society* (Ithaca, N.Y.: Cornell University Press, 1997), 61–91 and 147–62.

168. Guilday, *The National Pastorals of the American Hierarchy*, 322.

169. Ibid.

170. Ibid., 322–33.

171. Ibid., 323.

172. Ibid., 323–24.

173. Higgins explored the purpose and goal of the SAD in the *Yardstick* columns for September 17 and 24, 1956. Bishop Austin Dowling states that the SAD "endeavors to make known and have more effectively applied the principles of Christian justice to the practical affairs of life. It has done so by special publications, by lectures, by a weekly news-sheet. It has undertaken the work of survey in many dioceses. To it we are indebted for the citizenship programme, the Catholic Conference on Industrial Problems, the Catholic Rural Life Bureau, and the Catholic Association for International Peace." Dowling, "The National Catholic Welfare Conference," *Ecclesiastical Review* 9 (1928): 348.

174. Karl H. Cerny, "Monsignor John A. Ryan and the Social Action Department: An Analysis of a Leading School of Catholic Social Thought" (unpublished doctoral dissertation, Yale University, 1955), 106–7.

175. Charles E. Curran, *The Origins of Moral Theology in the United States: Three Different Approaches* (Washington, DC: Georgetown University Press, 1997), 171–254; C. Joseph Nuesse, "Thomas Joseph Bouquillon (1840–1902): Moral Theologian and Precursor of the So-

cial Sciences in The Catholic University of America," *Catholic Historical Review* 72 (1986): 606–11.

176. For a careful analysis of the role social action in the spirituality of Father William J. Kerby, see Bruce Lescher, "The Spiritual Life and Social Action in American Catholic Spirituality" (unpublished doctoral dissertation, Graduate Theological Union, 1990), 142–94.

177. David J. O'Brien, *American Catholics and Social Reform: The New Deal Years* (New York: Oxford University Press, 1968), 144; see also William J. Lee, "The Work in Industrial Relations of the Social Action Department of the National Catholic Welfare Conference, 1933–1945" (unpublished master's dissertation, Catholic University of America, 1946), 5–14.

178. Bresette, a Kansas native, helped write the minimum-wage laws for women and the child labor laws for the state of Kansas. She was the first secretary for the Industrial Welfare Commission in Kansas. She came to Washington to work for the passage of minimum-wage and maximum-hour laws for women. She began work at the SAD in 1921. She conducted the first Catholic social study of Mexican workers in the United States. She organized Councils of Catholic Women; conducted conferences on the "negro in industry"; and organized and directed the Institute on Industry, the first Catholic summer schools for women in the United States. Bresette was instrumental in creating the Priests' Institutes on the Encyclicals and collaborated closely with Raymond A. McGowan. In her nearly thirty years as field secretary of SAD and CCIP, she organized over one hundred meetings and conferences in over one hundred cities in thirty-three states. "A Biographical Sketch," files of the Social Action Department, box 25, file 1, 1–5.

179. Sylvia M. Batdorf, "The Work of the Social Action Department of the National Catholic Welfare Conference in All Phases of Industrial Relations" (unpublished master's dissertation, Catholic University of America, 1933), 43.

180. James Myers was one of a number of Protestant clergy in the Federal Council of Churches who, during the 1930s, became involved in direct action on behalf of labor unions. Elizabeth Fones-Wolf and Ken Fones-Wolf, "Lending a Hand to Labor: James Myers and the Federal Council of Churches, 1926–1947," *Church History* 68 (1999): 71–82.

181. Cerny, "Monsignor John A. Ryan and the Social Action Department," 190–91.

182. Colin J. Davis, "'Launch Out into the Deep and Let Down Your Nets': Father John Corridan, S.J., and New York Longshoremen in the Post–World War II Era," *Catholic Historical Review* 86 (2000): 66–84; James T. Fisher, "John M. Corridan, S.J., and the Battle for the Soul of the Waterfront, 1948–1954," *U.S. Catholic Historian* 16 (1998): 71–87; Joseph M. McShane, "'The Church Is Not for the Cells and the Cave': The Working-Class Spirituality of the Jesuit Labor Priests," *U.S. Catholic Historian* 9 (1990): 289–304.

Chapter 3

1. Wakefield, *Under the Apple Tree: A Novel of the Home Front* (Bloomington: Indiana University Press, 1982), 189–90.

2. 1949 *Labor Day Statement* (hereafter abbreviated *LDS*), 1.

3. Ibid.

4. 1951 *LDS*, 1.

5. 1954 *LDS*, 5–6. Here McGowan quotes from the address of Pope Pius XII to a group of workers.

6. 1947 *LDS*, 2. McGowan is again quoting from Pope Pius XII.

7. 1946 *LDS*, 2.

8. See the *LDSs* from 1946, 1947, 1948, 1950, 1951, 1952, and 1953. The *Yardstick* columns frequently promote the establishment of industry councils.
9. 1946 *LDS*, 3.
10. Ibid., 3–4.
11. Ibid., 4.
12. Ibid.
13. 1947 *LDS*, 6.
14. 1952 *LDS*, 3–4.
15. 1947 *LDS*, 1.
16. 1948 *LDS*, 1.
17. Ibid., 3.
18. Ibid.
19. 1949 *LDS*, 4.
20. 1947 *LDS*, 6.
21. 1956 *LDS*, 1.
22. Ibid., 2.
23. Ibid., 3.
24. 1957 *LDS*, 4–5.
25. Ibid., 5; see also 1958 *LDS*, 5.
26. 1959 *LDS*, 3.
27. 1960 *LDS*, 4.
28. Ibid.
29. Appendix I, section A (p. 246) lists the titles of the *Yardstick* columns between 1945 and 1994.
30. Appendix I, section B (p. 304) lists the guest columnists and their columns (1949–1977).
31. The *Yardstick* column for December 10, 1956 (hereafter the *Yardstick* columns will be listed as Y plus the date). There is no way to estimate how many people read the *Yardstick* column. The Catholic Press Association and the Catholic News Service did not keep statistics regarding readership, nor did they know the reader's educational background, their occupations, or political affiliation. Conversations between people at the association and the present writer yield the following conjectures. First, the diocesan papers that subscribed to the news service's news package and used the *Yardstick* were generally in areas where some or all of the following factors obtained: either there was a strong union presence in the diocese; the Ordinary of the diocese or the editor of the Catholic paper supported organized labor; or the laity and the clergy of the local church were committed to social justice and the social apostolate of the church. Second, in light of Higgins' comment about twenty-odd newspapers carrying the column regularly, it can be assumed that the readership was a few million. Third, chances are that its readers were either people in organized labor or educated Catholics who also read Catholic magazines that featured Catholic social teaching and the social apostolate. These would include *America*, *Commonweal*, *Ave Maria*, *The Sign*, and *Orate Fratres / Worship*. Fourth, there is no way to gauge the transformative influence of the column. However, one can assume that Catholics who read the column regularly over the years were probably bringing the social dimension of the Gospel into their practice of Christianity in the workplace and in society.
32. The *Yardstick* columns model a clear and cogent method of intellectual balance and an analysis of social issues. Those who read the columns regularly learned how to think critically. In Y March 10, 1947, Higgins wrote, "The facts are public property, and it now becomes our common privilege—and, perhaps our common duty—to try to decide what they actually mean

and what they have to teach us here at home." In addition, he praised those who took this thought and concretely promoted and enacted justice. He said that they were "on the side of the angels," in *Y* January 5, 1950; May 1, 1950; March 5, 1951; December 23, 1951; November 24, 1958; December 15, 1958; May 18 and 25, 1953; October 26, 1953; August 6, 1956; February 23, 1959; May 29, 1959; May 23, 1960; and October 1, 1962. This did not mean that others were on the side of the devils or the demons. Higgins respected those who, in his opinion, were mistaken or wrong. He neither dehumanized nor demonized his adversaries.

33. David Hollenbach, "Contexts of the Political Role of Religion: Civil Society and Culture," *San Diego Law Review* 30 (1993): 892. John Courtney Murray considers education to be "the great 'affair' of the commonwealth. . . . It concerns the constitutional consensus whereby the people acquires its identity as a people and the society is endowed with its vital form, its entelechy, its sense of purpose as a collectivity organized for action in history. . . . [This consensus] is an ensemble of substantive truths, a structure of basic knowledge, an order of elementary affirmations that reflect realities inherent in the order of existence. It occupies an established position in society and excludes opinions alien or contrary to itself. . . . The whole premise of the public argument is that the consensus is real, that among the people everything is not in doubt, but that there is a core of agreement, accord, concurrence, acquiescence. We hold certain truths; therefore we can argue about them." Murray, *We Hold These Truths* (Kansas City, Mo.: Sheed and Ward, 1988), 9–10. See also Ronald F. Thiemann's *Religion in Public Life* (Washington, DC: Georgetown University Press, 1996), 135–41. He proposes three criteria for public discourse: public accessibility, mutual respect, and moral integrity. Douglas A. Hicks expands on these criteria in *Inequality and Christian Ethics* (New York: Cambridge University Press, 2000), 85–113.

34. Higgins read extensively in the field of labor relations, labor history, and labor economics. In addition, his work at SAD required that he read numerous Catholic and secular journals, newspapers, and editorials. The *Yardstick* columns frequently referred to current works in theology, spirituality, and pastoral thought. These served as a basis for reflection. In a bit of ironic wit, Higgins indicated (*Y* June 16, 1958) that the column was more than a book review column.

35. George G. Higgins, *Organized Labor and the Church: Reflections of a "Labor Priest,"* with William Bole (New York: Paulist, 1993), 78.

36. *Y* January 8, 1945.

37. Ibid. Higgins returned to both topics in future *Yardstick* columns.

38. Ibid.

39. *Y* January 15, 1945.

40. Ibid.

41. Ibid. This was the first time Higgins mentioned the "Industries and Professions" system. Labor–management cooperation, as envisioned in *Quadragesimo Anno*, appeared again and again in later *Yardstick* columns.

42. *Y* February 12, 1945. *Fortune* magazine indicated that 75 percent of U.S. workers wanted four things: security, a chance to advance, to be treated as human beings, and to feel important.

43. *Y* February 26, 1945.

44. *Y* August 27, 1945.

45. *Y* September 3, 1945.

46. *Y* September 17, 1945.

47. Ibid. It was fitting that Bishop Haas was the homilist for the Labor Day Mass. Haas was a noted scholar and labor expert who worked in social research at the Catholic University of America. After his ordination as bishop, Haas returned to Wisconsin. Governor Philip LaFollette appointed him to the Wisconsin Labor Relations Board in 1937.

48. Y December 17, 1945.

49. Ibid.

50. Y December 31, 1945.

51. Ibid.

52. David Brody, *Workers in Industrial America: Essays on the Twentieth Century Struggle* (New York: Oxford University Press, 1983), 159–60.

53. Y February 3, 1947, promoted the gradual establishment of a new economic system in which labor, management, and the public would have a voice in the establishing prices and in making other important economic decisions. See also Y March 27, 1947, and April 27, 1947.

54. *Quadragesimo Anno*, no. 88. Y January 7, 1946, and August 7, 1950.

55. *Yardstick* columns investigated full employment, permanent industrial peace, price controls, and the role of government. Y August 27, 1945; September 3, 1945; September 17, 1945; January 26, 1946; February 28, 1946; January 1, 1947; February 3, 1947; March 24, 1947; April 21, 1947; September 8, 1947; January 1, 1951; July 2, 1951; and June 30, 1952. Higgins was clear in Y May 15, 1950 that the alternative to self-governance through industry councils would not be a return to economic individualism but a gradual, inevitable trend toward government intervention and eventual control of economic life.

56. Y July 15, 1946, supported the National Health Act of 1945 and the right and the duty of the state to establish a system of public health insurance when it serves the common good or the interests of individual groups. Other *Yardstick* columns returned to the issue of health care insurance and benefit plans: May 9, 1949; May 6, 1957; and June 10, 1957.

57. Y July 15, 1946, 160–172. During the war CIO president Phil Murray proposed the industry council plan for business–labor–government cooperation. Organized labor wanted "a voice in the production goals, investment decisions, and employment patterns of the nation's core industries." The industry council plan, writes Phil Murray, was "a program for democratic economic planning and for participation by the people in the key decisions of the big corporations." Such important elements of the union movement's wartime agenda as the guaranteed annual wage, industry-wide bargaining, and rationalization of the wage structure could be won only through this initiative. See Nelson Lictenstein, "From Corporatism to Collective Bargaining: Organized Labor and the Eclipse of Social Democracy in the Postwar Era," in *The Rise and Fall of the New Deal Order, 1930–1980*, ed. Steve Fraser and Gary Gerstle (Princeton, N.J.: Princeton University Press, 1989), 125–26. Father Raymond A. McGowan, director of SAD, advocated the development of industry councils in Y February 5, 1945. One element in a program of postwar reconstruction would be "guidance of production, prices and income in each major industry by Industry Councils made up of the organized business associations and the labor unions in each industry and of organized farmers in agriculture under the chairmanship of a federal official; a national economic board similarly constituted; the rapid extension of this principle to other national industries and services; and comparable councils in the states for local industries and services for the purposes of getting full output and a high standard of living for all." Higgins also commented on the CIO's industry council plan in Y February 15, 1945; May 12, 1947; and April 14, 1958.

58. Brody, *Workers in Industrial America*, 157–58.

59. Lictenstein, "From Corporatism to Collective Bargaining," 122–23.

60. The Taft-Hartley Act allowed individual states to enact right-to-work laws. These laws were presented as the epitome of an authentic American spirit enabling each worker the freedom to bargain with management. In fact, right-to-work laws thwarted the ability of organized labor to engage management in collective bargaining.

61. Y February 11, 1946.

62. *Y* December 9, 1946. Regarding the "closed shop": "The closed shop is a union security clause in labor–management contracts that stipulates that all persons who are to be employed must be members of a specified union as a precondition for such employment." Paul E. Sultan, "Closed Shop," in *The Dictionary of American History*, vol. 2, rev. ed. (New York: Charles Scribner's Sons, 1976), 80. See *Y* December 9, 1946; February 17, 1947; September 4, 1950; May 12, 1952; June 2, 1952; January 24, 1955; July 18, 1955; January 9, 1956; June 4, 1956; October 1, 1956; July 21, 1958; October 17, 1958; March 2, 1959; January 4, 1960; August 22, 1960; and August 6, 1962.

63. *Y* June 10, 1946. See also *Y* March 6, 1950. A labor movement from below required the active involvement and participation of the rank and file. "The fact is that in far too many good, bad and indifferent unions the rank-and-file are perfectly willing to 'let George do it.'" *Y* April 25, 1960.

64. *Y* July 1, 1946.

65. *Y* October 12, 1955.

66. *Y* July 25, 1960, investigates how credit unions are an application of Catholic social teaching and a concrete example of the practicality of the "brotherhood of man."

67. *Y* December 19, 1960.

68. *Y* April 15, 1957.

69. *Y* May 15, 1961.

70. *Y* March 14, 1955. The U.S. labor movement did not want co-determination or co-management, as in the German system. The U.S. labor movement sought "a voice in determining all matters directly affecting the interests of the workers. This form of co-determination (if it can properly be designated by that term) American labor will continue to press for through the medium of collective bargaining. . . . Collective bargaining, entered into by labor and management in good faith and with an open mind—and with an eye to the common good—is the best means of forestalling or avoiding this kind of legislation in the field of labor-management relations in the United States."

71. "Collective bargaining is a two-party, rule-making process important in relationships between employers, or their associations, and workers represented by their unions. It is institutionalized in the United States, where it is widely practiced and highly sophisticated, as an alternative to rulemaking by employers alone or by government through legislation, compulsory arbitration, or edict. Although this two-party process is private rather than governmental, government does exert an influence. Collective bargaining in the United States arose out of the need felt by workers for a voice in, and some control of, the determination of wages, hours, and conditions of employment. In the United States such a role was originally denied to workers or was beyond their reach. As individuals they had no power, and the burgeoning power of employers was favored by the one-sidedness of the contracts of employment and by court rulings that were unfriendly to concerted action by workers. . . . Collective bargaining fits the values and needs of an enterprise society, and contrary to appearances under some circumstances and the use of the work stoppage to help effectuate agreements, it is a very sane, rational process. It is to be evaluated against the alternative rulemaking possibilities—unilateral decision by management or action by government through legislation, compulsory arbitration, or edict. Historically, employers have not refrained from abusing workers when they did not have power, through their unions, to resist. Government . . . has been notoriously inept whenever it has intervened in the labor and management world, and it is doubtful whether legislators can develop the expertise required to be effective in making rules for the workplace and setting remuneration. Compulsory arbitration requires a 'judiciary' and an entirely different forum, when . . . denigrates freedom and undercuts negotiation. Hence, collective bargaining is the most viable

and useful procedure for making rules for the workplace in a free enterprise society." Vernon H. Jensen, "Collective Bargaining," in *The Dictionary of American History*, vol. 2, rev. ed. (New York: Charles Scribner's Sons, 1976), 110–13. Higgins investigated the role of collective bargaining in over thirty Y columns: February 15, 1945; February 25, 1946; December 9, 1946; December 23, 1946; August 11, 1947; February 23, 1948; October 1, 1951; December 1, 1952; December 22, 1952; February 28, 1954; June 14, 1954; March 14, 1955; March 21, 1955; August 22, 1955; April 9, 1956; May 21, 1956; March 11 and 18, 1957; September 2, 1957; January 13, 20, and 27, 1958; August 24, 1959; September 14 and 21, 1959; November 23, 1959; January 11, 1960; February 1, 1960; March 21, 1960; February 20, 1961; February 19, 1962; March 19, 1962; and June 11, 1962.

72. Y August 11, 1947. See also March 28, 1955.

73. Y February 23, 1948. Two major issues that emerged in the 1950s were inflation (Y February 4, 1957; April 29, 1957; July 15, 1957; August 5, 1957; September 2, 1957; June 30, 1958; July 14, 1958; August 4, 1958; January 19, 1959; and February 2, 1959) and the impact of automation on job security (Y September 2, 1957; January 27, 1958; and September 14, 1959).

74. Y June 14, 1954.

75. Labor and management would need to "subordinate their particular interests to the common good, not only because this is the right thing to do in itself, but also because it is the price of freedom" (Y September 2, 1957). *Gaudium et Spes* describes the common good as the "sum of those conditions of social life which allow social groups and their individual members relatively thorough and ready access to their own fulfillment" (no. 74). Higgins highlights the role of the common good in over twenty columns: Y February 19, 1945; December 17, 1945; January 28, 1946; May 12, 1947; January 24, 1949; December 5, 1949; May 22, 1950; August 21, 1950; September 11, 1950; May 19 and 26, 1952; February 7, 1955; April 25, 1955; May 9, 1955; October 24, 1955; September 2, 1957; April 23, 1959; August 10, 1959; December 21, 1959; March 13, 1961; April 24, 1961; and July 3 and 10, 1961.

76. Longshoremen unions: Y July 11, 1949; December 18, 1950; January 3, 1955; May 2, 1955; and September 19, 1955. Teacher unions: Y March 3, 1947; April 28, 1947; February 21, 1949; January 30, 1956; and December 30, 1957. Transport workers: Y February 11, 1946. Farmworkers: Y November 4, 1946; December 31, 1951; January 21, 1952; November 2, 1953; October 1, 1956; February 16, 1959; July 27, 1959; October 19, 1959; May 23, 1960; January 2, 1961; and September 17, 1962.

77. Migrant workers: Y April 16, 1951; February 16, 1959; July 6, 1959; October 19, 1959; June 6, 1960; August 8, 1960. Women: Y June 13, 1960. Police, postal, and federal employees: Y January 10, 1955; January 24, 1955; January 16, 1956; April 22, 1957; April 27, 1959; July 13, 1959; July 18, 1960; April 10, 1961.

78. The "shape-up" is "the semi-circle of men gathered in front of the pier at the various hiring times when the foreman calls out the names of those who are to work" (Y July 11, 1949).

79. Y January 3, 1955.

80. Ibid.

81. Y September 9, 1955.

82. Y March 3, 1947. Here Higgins addressed teachers in the public school system. He did not consider the unionization of Catholic school teachers, because Catholic schools are primarily staffed by religious sisters, brothers, and priests. The lay teacher in the Catholic school system is still an exception. Higgins returned to this issue and addressed the right of lay teachers to organize in Catholic schools in the *Yardstick* columns of the 1970s. The National Labor Relations Act does not apply to Catholic school teachers, because of the separation of church

and state. Catholic schools are church institutions carrying out a religious mission. Nonetheless, Higgins encouraged the unionization of Catholic school teachers as a way of being faithful to Catholic social teaching.

83. Ibid.

84. Ibid.

85. Ibid.

86. Y February 11, 1946.

87. Y November 4, 1946; April 16, 1951; December 31, 1951; January 21, 1952; November 2, 1953; October 1, 1956; February 16, 1959; July 6 and 27, 1959; October 19, 1959; May 23, 1960; June 6, 1960; August 8, 1960; January 2, 1961; September 17, 1962.

88. Y June 13, 1960.

89. Ibid.

90. Ibid.

91. Ibid.

92. Ibid.

93. This topic was dear to Higgins' heart because his own father, C. V. Higgins, had been a postal worker.

94. Y April 10, 1961.

95. The CIO industry council plan was presented in Y February 15, 1945; May 12, 1947; and April 14, 1958.

96. The industry council plan was mentioned in over seventy-five *Yardstick* columns. Y 1945: January 15, February 19. 1946: January 7, January 28, June 3, September 23, November 18 and 25, December 9 and 23. 1947: January 27, February 3, May 12, December 22. 1948: February 23, March 1 and 22, June 7. 1949: January 10, February 7 and 14, June 13, November 14, December 5. 1950: January 23; February 27; March 6 and 13; April 24; May 1 and 15; July 3, 10, 17, and 31; October 30; November 6; and December 25. 1951: March 19, May 7, August 13 and 20, September 24, October 1 and 22. 1952: January 7, March 10, April 7 and 28, May 5, August 4, September 22, November 10, December 1 and 29. 1953: March 30, April 6, May 18 and 25, June 8 and 22, September 14, October 5, December 21. 1954: March 22, May 10 and 24. 1955: August 29. 1957: June 17, November 25. 1958: September 29, October 13. 1961: March 20, May 1. 1962: January 15. For the historical roots of the vocational groups and the industry council program see Jean Yves Calvez and Jacques Perrin, *The Church and Social Justice* (Chicago: Regnery, 1961), 403–37.

97. Y April 24, 1950.

98. Joseph A. Komonchak, "Subsidiarity in the Church: The State of the Question," in the *Nature and Future of Episcopal Conferences*, ed. Herve Legrand, Julio Manzanares, and Antonio Garcia y Garcia (Washington, DC: Catholic University of America Press, 1988), 298–349. See Y December 17, 1945; November 18, 1946; July 17 and 24, 1950; January 29, 1951; May 7, 1951; September 24, 1951; September 8, 1952; April 6, 1953; March 20, 1961; and George G. Higgins. *Subsidiarity in the Catholic Social Tradition: Yesterday, Today, and Tomorrow: The Annual Cardinal Meyer Lectures* (Mundelein, Ill.: Seminary/University of St. Mary of the Lake, 1994), 8–23.

99. Y November 18, 1946.

100. Y October 24, 1955.

101. Ibid.

102. Y December 5, 1955.

103. Y December 9, 1957.

104. Y 1946: October 28. 1950: January 23 and 30, February 6, June 19, September 4, October 16, November 13 and 20. 1951: January 1, March 5 and 19, July 2, October 15, Novem-

ber 5. 1952: January 28, June 23, September 1 and 15. 1953: January 5, September 7 and 22, October 19. 1954: January 11 and 25, July 4, November 21. 1956: May 7, October 29. 1957: May 20 and 27, June 3, July 1 and 8, September 9. 1958: January 6 and 20, October 17, December 8. 1959: March 9, May 18, July 20, November 30. 1960: November 21. 1961: January 30. 1962: March 26.

105. "The ILO is an intergovernmental agency established by the 1919 peace treaty, on recommendation of the Commission on International Labor Legislation chaired by Samuel Gompers. Since 1945–46 the ILO has been a specialized agency of the United Nations, although still governed under the terms of its own constitution and financed independently by annual assessments on its member states. Under the principle of tripartism, representatives of member governments share decisionmaking authority in the ILO annual conference and in the governing body with representatives of employers and workers; the ratio is 2:1:1. The permanent secretariat is the International Labor Office in Geneva. At the end of 1972, a total of 133 countries representing a wide range of social and political systems belonged to the ILO. Continuous U.S. membership goes back to 1934, when President Franklin D. Roosevelt and Secretary of Labor Frances Perkins gave strong support to a joint congressional resolution authorizing U.S. accession. . . . To its traditional tasks of setting international labor standards through conventions and recommendations and preparing factual studies and reports, the ILO added a broad range of technical assistance programs to help less-developed countries improve their services in the labor field." John P. Windmuller, "International Labor Organization," in *The Dictionary of American History*, vol. 3, rev. ed., ed. Louise Bilebof Ketz (New York: Charles Scribner's Sons, 1976), 454–55. Higgins devoted over twenty columns to the ILO. Y February 25, 1952; June 16, 1952; December 8, 1952; October 26, 1953; December 14, 1953; June 21, 1954; April 18, 1955; October 31, 1955; January 23, 1956; April 30, 1956; May 14, 1956; January 14 and 21, 1957; February 11, 1957; June 22 and 29, 1959; October 23 and 30, 1961; November 6, 13, and 20, 1961.

106. The basis for this recommendation was twofold. First, membership in the ILO allowed the United States to keep an eye on the Communists during the Cold War era. Second, membership allowed the United States to thwart the Communist agenda.

107. Y May 5, 1947.

108. Marie J. Giblin, "*Quadragesimo Anno*," in *The New Dictionary of Catholic Social Thought*, ed. Judith Dwyer (Collegeville, Minn.: Liturgical Press, 1994), 805.

109. Y July 30, 1951.

110. "Social justice is not enough . . . the virtue of social charity is also indispensable" (Y March 4, 1957).

111. Y May 8, 1961.

112. Ibid.

113. The communist threat, anti-communist fervor, and Cold War rhetoric reached its climax in the 1950s and the McCarthy hearings. At SAD, Father John F. Cronin was primarily responsible for overseeing the church's anti-communist activity. Higgins warned *Yardstick* readers about the menace and evil of communism, as well as the need to extirpate communist influence from the unions. His treatment of communism was reasonable and evenhanded. Higgins and the editors of *America* and *commonweal* did not identify the social mission of the church with fervent McCarthyism, nor did they indulge in the apocalyptic rhetoric found in some diocesan newspapers. Over thirty *Yardstick* columns were devoted to communism: October 7, 1946; November 25, 1946; March 31, 1947; April 7, 1947; October 20, 1947; January 24, 1949; August 8, 1949; October 31, 1949; November 28, 1949; March 20, 1950; April 3 and 17, 1950; June 5, 1950; October 23, 1950; December 11, 1950; May 14, 1951; July 16, 1951;

November 12, 1951; June 9, 1952; March 8, 1954; May 17, 1954; July 11, 1955; November 14, 1955; December 26, 1955; April 9, 1956; October 13, 1958; May 9, 1960; April 3, 1961; August 14, 1961; and January 8, 1962. See David F. Crosby, *God, the Church and the Flag: Senator Joseph E. McCarthy and the Catholic Church, 1950–1957* (Chapel Hill: University of North Carolina Press, 1978); Charles Owen Rice, "Confessions of an Anti-Communist," *Labor History* 30 (1989): 449–62; Steve Rosswurm, "The Catholic Church and Left-Led Unions," in *The CIO's Left-Led Unions*, ed. Steve Rosswurm (New Brunswick, N.J.: Rutgers University Press, 1992), 119–37; and Ellen M. Schrecker, "McCarthyism and the Labor Movement: The Role of the Church," in Rosswurm, *The CIO's Left-Led Unions*, 139–57. *Y* columns regarding xenophobia: January 8, 1945; November 3, 1947; March 15, 1948; May 14, 1951; August 6, 1951; March 17, 1952; October 8, 1956; December 31, 1956; September 6, 1958. *Y* columns regarding racketeering: *Y* April 16 1956; July 23, 1956; January 7, 1957.

114. He devoted twenty-nine *Yardstick* columns to NAM.

115. He devoted twelve columns to the Taft-Hartley Act.

116. *Y* October 29, 1951. Yves de Montcheuil belonged to a group of French theologians who were developing the *nouvelle theologie*. Yves de Montcheuil, M-D Chenu, and others were working to build bridges between the workplace and daily life, between church and society, Catholic action and the liturgy.

Chapter 4

1. Schmiedeler, *Our Rural Proletariat*, Social Action Series 11 (New York: Paulist, 1937); and *The Rural South: Problem or Prospect*, Social Action Series 18 (New York: Paulist, 1941). From the 1930s into the early 1940s, SAD and Paulist Press collaborated in publishing a series of twenty-three pamphlets on the social question and a series of five pamphlets on citizenship and democracy. See appendix E for the list of Social Action Series pamphlets, and appendix F for the list of the Christian Democracy pamphlets. Gilligan, *Negro Workers in Free America*, Social Action Series 17 (New York: Paulist, 1939).

2. Participants represented a wide spectrum of clergy and laity involved in the social apostolate, health, housing, social work, the Catholic press, and local neighborhood citizen-action groups.

3. *Seminar on the Negro Problem in the Field of Social Action* (Washington, DC: Nation Catholic Welfare Conference, 1946).

4. Linna E. Bresette, the department's field secretary, conducted oral histories of Mexican American women and did extensive research on workplace conditions that affected their health.

5. *LDS*s 1963, 1964, 1965, 1966, 1971.

6. Higgins frequently admitted that the labor movement did not have a good record on racism. He constantly reminded organized labor that it had to change by extirpating every aspect of racism in its halls. See also Bruce Nelson, *Divided We Stand: American Workers and the Struggle for Black Equality* (Princeton, N.J.: Princeton University Press, 2001); and Heather Thompson, "Another War at Home: Reexamining Working Class Politics in the 1960s," *Mid America* 81 (1999): 297–318.

7. 1964 *LDS*, 4.

8. 1965 *LDS*, 4.

9. 1971 *LDS*, 1.

10. 1966 *LDS*, 7.

11. Poverty is a complex reality and takes on many faces. People who are destitute, homeless, and jobless live in poverty; so, too, do people with full-time jobs that pay insufficiently.

Poverty also affects people who are paid substandard wages and who are victimized by unjust practices (such as the nation's agricultural workers and immigrants in the service industries). Finally, poverty extends to other currencies and contexts of inequality. See Douglas A. Hicks, *Inequality and Christian Ethics* (New York: Cambridge University Press, 2000), 17–42.

12. 1965 *LDS*, 1. The 1976 *LDS* also begins with the example of Moses.

13. 1965 *LDS*, 2.

14. 1964 *LDS*, 2. Here Higgins addressed the issue of the unemployed able-bodied worker. The able-bodied worker was considered the norm in the workplace. Workers with disabilities remained invisible. A significant number were unemployed because of their disabilities and were among the poorest of the poor. Pubic transportation and access to buildings still catered to the fully able-bodied population. Change in consciousness in church and society was slowly developing. Transformative change for the disabled was a fruitful consequence of the civil rights legislation of the 1960s. Years of advocacy, public protests, and legislative initiatives, especially in the 1970s, finally produced human and civil rights for those living with disabilities. Higgins, a member of the President's Committee on Employment of the Handicapped for two decades, was deeply sensitive to issues faced by persons with disabilities. He expressed his views about workers with disabilities in his Y column "Employment of Handicapped and Mentally Retarded," May 22, 1972. He wrote: "For the past 25 years the President's Committee on Employment of the Handicapped has been attempting the almost superhuman task of changing America's image of the handicapped from objects of pity and charity to human beings of dignity and independence. Moreover, the Committee is succeeding. Thanks to its efforts, the American people are undergoing a significant change for the better in their thinking about the handicapped. Increasingly they have come to think of the handicapped not as useless members of society, but rather as full-fledged citizens of very great courage—men and women who have risen above almost insurmountable obstacles." He noted that the public image of the mentally retarded and of those experiencing mental and emotional illness was changing. He indicated the two most pressing challenges in 1972: the continued integration of mentally retarded persons in the workforce and the "stream of disabled veterans returning from Vietnam." He concluded the column by saying, "The moral of all this is that the Committee's work is not yet done. It probably never will be done in our free society which moves to the best of many drums, including that of conscience—the Committee's chief weapon in its crusade of moral suasion."

15. 1975 *LDS*.

16. Higgins invited the esteemed Monsignor Geno C. Baroni, the director of program development for the Task Force on Urban Problems, USCC, to write the 1970 *LDS*. Higgins cosigned the text that Baroni prepared.

17. See *LDS*s 1963, 1964, 1970, 1972, and 1976.

18. See *LDS*s 1965, 1975, and 1977.

19. See *LDS*s 1976 and 1978.

20. See *LDS*s 1971, 1972, 1973, 1974, 1975, and 1978.

21. 1977 *LDS*, 3–4, 10.

22. Ibid., 5–6.

23. Ibid., 7–8.

24. Ibid., 9.

25. 1964 *LDS*, 56.

26. 1972 *LDS*, 4.

27. 1980 *LDS*, 4.

28. 1971 *LDS*.

29. 1972 *LDS*.

30. 1979 *LDS*, 5.
31. Ibid., 7.
32. 1965 and 1976 *LDSs*.
33. 1966 *LDS*, 9.
34. 1965 *LDS*, 1.
35. 1976 *LDS*, 5.
36. 1972 *LDS*, 4.
37. 1965 *LDS*.
38. 1970 *LDS*, 7.
39. The 1979 *LDS* addresses the right of teachers in Catholic schools to unionize.
40. *Y* August 28, 1978.
41. Fourteen columns are devoted to *Mater et Magistra*. 1963: January 7; April 8, 15, 22; September 30. 1964: February 17, April 6 and 27, June 8, August 3 and 17. 1968: August 19. 1976: July 12. 1980: January 21. The columns of April 29, 1963; June 19, 1963; and August 8, 1964, consider *Pacem in Terris*.
42. *Y* January 7, 1963.
43. Ibid.
44. Ibid.
45. *Y* April 22, 1963.
46. *Y* February 17, 1964. See also *Y* January 21, 1980, where Higgins—in his comments concerning three booklets written for the National Right to Work Committee (one by a Catholic scholar, one a Protestant scholar, and the other a Jewish scholar)—reaffirmed the moral acceptability of the union shop and revisited the debate of 1963.
47. *Y* February 17, 1964, emphasis is in the original. The quote uses the word *syndicates*, the European word for workers' associations or trade unions.
48. *Y* April 4, 1964. This theme was also considered in *Y* June 10, 1963. Here Higgins addressed the labor–management cooperation that is called for in the first part of *Pacem in Terris*. He related this to the labor–management cooperation and economic planning and development on the local, regional, and international levels.
49. *Y* August 17, 1964.
50. *Y* August 19, 1968. This column drew from a *Concilium* article by the German professor Philipp Herder-Dorneich. For a complete description of this shift, see John Mahoney, *The Making of Moral Theology: A Study of the Roman Catholic Tradition* (Oxford: Clarendon Press, 1987), 302–47.
51. Joseph A. Komonchak, "The Struggles for the Council during the Preparation of Vatican II (1960–1962)," in *History of Vatican II*, vol. 1, *Announcing and Preparing Vatican Council II: Toward a New Era in Catholicism*, ed. Guiseppe Alberigo and Joseph A. Komonchak (Maryknoll, N.Y.: Orbis, 1996), 197. Regarding Higgins' involvement at the Second Vatican Council, see Gerald M. Costello, *Without Fear or Favor: George Higgins on the Record* (Mystic, Conn.: Twenty-third Publications, 1984), 119–41.
52. Komonchak, "The Struggles for the Council," 196.
53. Ibid., 199.
54. Jan Grootaers, "The Drama Continues between the Acts: The 'Second Preparation' and Its Opponents," in *History of Vatican II*, vol. 2, *The Formation of the Council's Identity: First Period and Intercession, October 1962–September 1963*, ed. Giuseppe Alberigo and Joseph A. Komonchak (Maryknoll, N.Y.: Orbis Press, 1997), 436.
55. Evangelista Villanova, "The Intercession (1963–1964)," in *History of Vatican II*, vol. 3, *The Mature Council: Second Period and Intercessions, September 1963–1964*, ed. Guiseppe Alberigo and Joseph A. Komonchak (Maryknoll, N.Y.: Orbis, 2000), 387n123.

56. Ibid., 390.
57. *Y* January 20, 1964.
58. Ibid.
59. Austin P. Flannery, ed., *Documents of Vatican II* (Grand Rapids, Mich.: Eerdmans, 1975), 974.
60. *Y* January 24, 1966.
61. *Y* March 28, 1966.
62. *Y* April 11, 1966.
63. *Y* May 14, 1966.
64. *Y* October 9,1972.
65. *Y* November 22, 1965.
66. *Y* July 19, 1976. Higgins contrasted the mood of the country at the time of its bicentennial in July 19, 1976. He noted the difference of mood at the time of the nation's founding, its centennial, and its bicentennial. The year 1776 was a time when the founders were boldly sure of the success of the nation's experiment with freedom. The year 1876 was a *post-bellum* time when the nation had high optimism and self-confidence. The year 1976 was a time when the nation had lost its idealism, hope, and innocence. The bicentennial was celebrated with the raw remembrance of the war in Vietnam, its failure to eradicate poverty, the continuance of racism, the disgrace of President Nixon, and economic recession.
67. *Y* May 26, 1975. This signaled an end to the old "thesis–hypothesis" position that gave the church preferential treatment.
68. *Y* January 3, 1977.
69. Flannery, *Documents of Vatican II*, 741–42.
70. See *Y* July 21, 1978.
71. Ibid.
72. Ibid.
73. Thirty-six *Y* columns are devoted to Catholic–Jewish relations in the post-conciliar period: January 25, March 15, June 28, July 26, November 1, 1965; March 14 and 21, 1966; March 6 and December 4, 1967; November 4, 1968; February 10, 1969; January 26, 1970; March 1, 1971; February 7, April 3, and December 11, 1972; December 2, 1974; January 13 and 27, February 24, November 3, and December 1, 1975; February 23, March 22 and 29, 1976; May 9 and November 7, 1977; May 1, June 5 and 12, July 24 and 31, September 18, 1978; May 26, June 23, and December 8, 1980. Three *Y* columns consider an incipient anti-Jewish racism on the part of militant black activists and the beginnings of tension in African American–Jewish relations: February 26, August 27, and October 1, 1979. Higgins considered black anti-Semitism just as despicable as white anti-Semitism. He also reminded African Americans that "the Jewish community . . . can legitimately claim to have done at least as much and probably more than any other ethnic or religious group to atone for the past and to advance the cause of equal justice and opportunity for black Americans." *Y* February 10, 1969.
74. *Nostra Aetate* was not a political document. However, the beginning of a new era required delicate political and religious dialogue with Melkite Catholics and other Christian Arabs in the Middle East during the council sessions and, afterward, during the Camp David agreements in 1980. See *Y* January 25, 1965; February 23, March 22 and 29, 1976; May 26 and December 8, 1980. In the United States there was a need for sociological data to determine whether preaching, catechesis, liturgy, and popular religion contributed to anti-Semitism.
75. *Y* November 1, 1965.
76. See *Y* November 1, 1965; January 13 and 27, February 24, 1975.
77. *Y* March 21, 1966; November 4, 1968; and February 7, 1972.

78. Monsignor John M. Oesterreicher, an illustrious pioneer in Catholic–Jewish studies at Seton Hall University in New Jersey, was one of the first Catholics to indicate the religious significance of the land of Israel. See *Y* February 14, 1972. The meaning of the land became a political issue during the six-day Arab–Israeli war in 1967. See *Y* December 4, 1967, and January 26, 1970. It featured prominently at the Catholic–Moslem meeting in Tripoli, Libya (February 1–6, 1974). Two resolutions (out of twenty-eight) that passed at the meeting were hostile to Israel. Jews anguished over the anti-Zionism tonality of the meeting and its two resolutions. The issue came up again when the General Assembly of the United Nations passed a resolution that sided with Palestinian Arabs and equated Zionism with racism. See *Y* March 22, 1976; November 7, 1977; and May 26 and December 8, 1980.

79. *Y* January 19, 1975.

80. The first meeting of the International Catholic Jewish Liaison Committee was held in Paris in 1972. Subsequent meetings were held in Marseilles, France; Antwerp, Belgium; and Rome, Italy. Higgins attended the fifth annual meeting (March 1–3, 1976), at the Martin Buber Center of Hebrew University in Jerusalem; and the sixth annual meeting (March 28–30, 1977), in Venice. See *Y* February 23, March 22 and 29, 1976; and May 9, 1977.

81. *Y* June 5, 1978.

82. *Y* October 18, 1971.

83. *Y* January 17, 1972.

84. Ibid.

85. *Y* November 1, 1971.

86. *Y* October 23, 1971.

87. *Y* November 15, 1971.

88. See *Catholic Social Thought: The Documentary Heritage*, ed. David J. O'Brien and Thomas A. Shannon (Maryknoll, N.Y.: Orbis Books, 1992) 295.

89. *Y* March 18 and June 3, 1963; March 30 and May 11, 1964; January 3 and 24, August 1, 1966; February 20, May 1 and 22, November 27, 1967; January 1 and August 26, 1968; February 24 and June 16, 1969; July 19, 1971; January 17 and 24, July 10, 1972; March 19, 1973; November 11, 1974; June 9, 1975; April 4 and October 3, 1977; March 6 and 13, May 8, 1978; January 2 and 9, 1978; April 23, 1979.

90. The quotation comes from *Tomorrow's Christian*, a book by Ed Marciniak, who is a deeply and effectively involved Catholic social activist in Chicago. Marciniak uses the phrase *secular Christian* to refer to the laity and its role in transforming the everyday world.

91. His use of the phrase does not intend to denigrate the importance of marches and demonstrations on behalf of civil rights and racial justice. Higgins stood shoulder to shoulder in public witness with people of color. He lent his name and moral suasion to causes for racial dignity and social change. Nor does the phrase intend to downplay the importance of the clergy's participation in public protest and interfaith witness. Higgins consistently stood side by side with interfaith and interracial activists.

92. *Y* June 16, 1969.

93. *Y* April 4, 1977. This column was originally an encomium in honor of Bishop James Rausch. Rausch had been the secretary-general at the National Conference of Catholic Bishops–United States Catholic Conference. He was installed as ordinary of the diocese of Phoenix on March 22, 1977. This column was an abbreviated version of remarks Higgins made at a reception in Washington, DC, shortly before Rausch's installation.

94. *Y* March 18, 1963. See also *Y* June 3, 1963, and August 26, 1968.

95. *Y* November 27, 1967.

96. *Y* March 30, 1964, and November 27, 1967.

97. *Y* March 19, 1973.
98. *Y* May 1, 1967.
99. *Y* January 2, 1979.
100. Ibid.
101. *Y* May 25, 1964; August 21, October 2, 1967; June 24, 1968; March 10, 1969; March 2, 1971; October 9, 1972; January 1, March 26, August 13, 1973; September 22, 1975; August 28, 1980. These columns are examples of the ways moral theologians were relating social teaching to its foundation in systematic theology.
102. *Y* August 21, 1967.
103. *Y* March 10, 1969.
104. *Y* June 24, 1968; September 22, 1975; and August 28, 1980.
105. *Y* January 1 and March 26, 1973.
106. *Y* May 25, 1964.
107. *Y* columns regarding racism: February 4 and 25, March 4, April 1, June 17 and 24, August 26, and September 23, 1963; January 24, April 3, and September 4, 1967; November 11, 1968; October 4, 1971; October 7, 1974; June 21 and August 9, 1976; September 9 and 16, 1978; June 25, and October 29, 1979. *Y* columns regarding civil rights: August 5, 1963; April 13, September 14, 1964; April 5, August 9, 1965; July 17, 1967; April 15, July 15, 1968, March 10, 17, 24, April 7, September 8, 1969; March 23, 1970; February 26, August 27, October 1, 1979; and September 22, 1980.
108. Emphasis in the original. Higgins' definition of racism comes from Anthony Downs' *Racism in America and How to Combat It*. This is congruent with recent definitions that understand racism as discrimination, marginalization, and exclusion of others because of the color of their skin. It manifests itself not only in the attitudes and actions of individuals and groups against people of color but also in unjust systems and structures that deliberately function to discriminate, marginalize, and exclude others solely on the basis of skin color. The consequences of racism are manifested in the binaries of superiority/inferiority, entitlement/exclusion, dominance/powerlessness, and privilege/second-class status. Long-standing racism eventually invades the air that a society breathes, incarnates itself in structures of sin, and creates an ethos that is difficult to unmask and dismantle. For a treatment of racism by the Catholic bishops of the United States, see Bryan N. Massingale, "James Cone and Recent Catholic Episcopal Teaching on Racism," *Theological Studies* 61 (2000): 700–730, especially 712–26. See also Mary Elizabeth Hobgood, *Dismantling Privilege: An Ethics of Accountability* (Cleveland, Ohio: Pilgrim, 2000), 63–106 and 138–53; and David R. Roediger, *The Wages of Whiteness: Race and the Making of the American Working Class*, rev. ed. (New York: Verso, 2000).
109. Higgins was deeply influenced by James Baldwin, an African American novelist and essayist. In *The Fire Next Time* Baldwin passionately communicates that the quest for racial equality is an urgent matter.
110. *Y* August 26, 1963. See also Y February 4, 1963. Higgins was not infrequently accused of being prolabor and antimanagement. One critic wrote, "Management . . . may be readily damned by anyone, but no one may criticize any practice of the unions, not even that of denying membership to Negroes, as many of them do." Higgins felt compelled to respond. "This allegation," he wrote, "which, in context, was obviously directed at the author of the *Yardstick*, is so completely contrary to fact and so damaging in its implications that I feel I simply have to challenge it for the sake of the public record. It leaves the impression that this column is unconcerned about the problems of racial discrimination in the labor movement and . . . that the author . . . is doggedly determined to squelch any criticism of unions which are guilty of dis-

criminating against Negro workers. The fact is that the *Yardstick* has already criticized these unions. . . . Moreover, many of the 15 to 20 annual Labor Day sermons which this writer has delivered to predominantly labor audiences and many of the talks which he has delivered at union conventions have likewise called attention to the essential immorality of racial discrimination by unions. Ditto for several of the annual Labor Day Statements of the NCWC Social Action Department with which this writer happens to be associated" (Y June 17, 1963).

111. Higgins admired and praised Bayard Rustin—one of the most articulate African American intellectuals and one of the nation's most influential activists—for his singular commitment to organized labor. Rustin supported organized labor because he recognized its emancipatory power for African Americans in their quest for a better life, for better jobs, and for better economic citizenship. Rustin also opposed black anti-Semitism. See Jervis Anderson, *Bayard Rustin: Troubles I've Seen; A Biography* (Berkeley: University of California Press, 1998), 322–32. Rustin joined A. Philip Randolph, his trusted friend and "the chief," in linking jobs with civil rights. Both played crucial parts in the historic national march on Washington for jobs and freedom on August 28, 1963. Randolph epitomized the goal in the following words: "We are the advance guard of a massive moral revolution for jobs and freedom. . . . We know that real freedom will require many changes in the nation's political and social philosophies and institutions. . . . We must destroy the notion that . . . property rights include the right to humiliate me because of the color of my skin. The sanctity of private property takes second place to the sanctity of the human personality. All who deplore our militancy, who exhort patience in the name of false peace, are in fact supporting segregation and exploitation. They would have social peace at the expense of social and racial justice. They are more concerned with easing racial tensions than enforcing racial democracy" (in *Labor Leaders in America*, ed. Melvyn Dubofsky and Warren Van Tine [Urbana, Ill.: University of Illinois Press, 1987], 276–77). Jervis Anderson considered the ways that Randolph obtained recognition within organized labor for African Americans. See his *A. Philip Randolph: A Biographical Portrait* (Berkeley: University of California Press, 1986), 151–225 and 229–332. For an analysis of the march on Washington movement, the struggle for civil and economic rights, and the development of the Brotherhood of Sleeping Car Porters, see Beth Tompkins Bates, *Pullman Porters and the Rise of Protest Politics in Black America, 1925–1945* (Chapel Hill: University of North Carolina Press, 2001), 148–87. For a treatment of the conflict between Irish immigrants and African American workers in organized labor, see Noel Ignatiev, *How the Irish Became White* (New York: Routledge, 1995), 92–121.

112. Y April 13, 1964. In this column Higgins pointed out that extreme right-wing organizations had remained silent regarding civil rights legislation. Some groups linked their opposition to civil rights with their anticommunism stand. Higgins confronted the newspaper columnist David Lawrence regarding his opinion that religious communities should not support civil rights legislation. Higgins indicated that Lawrence was masking a prejudice against interracial marriages.

113. Y August 5, 1963.

114. Y June 24, 1963.

115. Y April 5, 1965.

116. Y April 15, 1968. Here Higgins quoted from *Toward a Democratic Left: A Radical Program for a New Majority* by Michael Harrington.

117. Costello, *Without Fear or Favor,* 149.

118. John Kenneth Galbraith, *The Affluent Society*, 40th-anniv. ed. (New York: Mariner / Houghton Mifflin, 1998), 242.

119. Irving Howe, in the introduction to Michael Harrington, *The Other America: Poverty in the United States* (New York: Touchstone / Simon and Schuster, 1997), xiv.

120. *Let Us Now Praise Famous Men* was published in the mid-1930s. Agee wanted to do more than just report the desperation of farmers and farming families dwelling on dust-bowl lands during the Depression. He wanted to create a new literary form that would grip his readers. Thus *Let Us Now Praise Famous Men*, deriving from a figurative phrase reminiscent of the biblical book of Sirach and the Letter to the Hebrews, combined reporting with narratives of testimony and the graphic black-and-white photographs of Walker Evans.

121. Maurice Isserman suggests that Harrington may have borrowed the idea of invisibility from Ralph Ellison, the African American novelist. "In choosing to describe the poor as 'invisible,' Michael may have been harkening back, consciously or not, to Ralph Ellison's *Invisible Man*, which he had reviewed for the *Catholic Worker* ten years earlier." See *The Other American: The Life of Michael Harrington* (New York: Public Affairs, 2000), 402n66.

122. "The 'culture of poverty' had been the guiding concept of *Five Families: Mexican Case Studies in the Culture of Poverty*, a then recently published ethnographic study by the radically inclined anthropologist Oscar Lewis. Sociologists had long studied the 'way of life of the poor,' but until Lewis no one had argued that this way of life functioned as a distinct 'subculture.' Lewis contended that being poor was not simply a condition marked by the absence of wealth or material comfort; rather, poverty created 'a subculture of its own,' one that cuts 'across regional, rural-urban, and even national boundaries.' In other words, however different their cultures of origin, poor people in Azteca, Mexico, might have more in common with their counterparts in San Juan—or, for that matter, New York—in terms of family structure, inter-personal relations, time orientation, value systems, and spending patterns than with other, better off people form their own communities. Echoing Lewis, Michael argued in *Commentary* that American poverty constituted 'a separate culture, another nation, with its own way of life.'" See Isserman, *The Other American*, 180. In addition, "the publication of Lewis' widely discussed *Children of Sanchez* in 1961 would further popularize the notion of the 'culture of poverty.'" See ibid., 399n16.

123. Ibid., 198.

124. Harrington, *The Other America*, 159–60.

125. Isserman, *The Other American*, 208–20.

126. In addition to reading *The Other America*, Higgins also read Harrington's *Toward a Democratic Left* (published in 1968; see n. 118) and *Socialism* (published in 1972). Higgins wrote about poverty in Y September 2, 1963; February 3, March 16, August 10 and 17, 1964; February 8, 1965; March 7, 1966; June 24 and July 15, 1968; March 10, 1975; February 6, 1978; September 10 and October 8, 1979; July 14, November 10, and December 1, 1980.

127. Y March 7, 1966.

128. Y March 10, 1975.

129. Y February 8, 1965.

130. Y March 10, 1975.

131. Y March 16, 1864.

132. Y September 10, 1979.

133. Y August 10, 1964.

134. Y November 10, 1980.

135. Ibid. In this column Higgins commemorates the tenth anniversary of the *Campaign for Human Development* (this was renamed the Catholic Campaign for Human Development in 1999; hereafter, CCHD). The bishops had begun the CCHD as a kind of Catholic crusade against poverty in 1970. It also was an educational and action program. Its goal was long-range, effective change. The CCHD had given grants of $80 million to "fund self-help projects controlled by poor people and designed to eliminate the causes of poverty. . . . CCHD is not a

handout, but rather a way out of poverty. Groups of poor and low-income people design their own plans to eliminate the causes of poverty" (*Y* July 14, 1980).

136. *Y* June 24, 1968.

137. Costello, *Without Fear or Favor*, 169.

138. Ibid., 230. The fact that the AFL-CIO endorsed the war and that the war was perceived and promoted as a deterrent to communism may have influenced Higgins. For an historical assessment of the war, see George C. Herring, *America's Longest War: The United States and Vietnam, 1950–1975*, 3rd ed. (New York: McGraw-Hill, 1996); Amanda Porterfield, *The Transformation of American Religion: The Story of a Late Twentieth-Century Awakening* (New York: Oxford University Press, 2001), 88–134; Marilyn B. Young, *The Vietnam Wars, 1945–1990* (New York: Harper Perennial, 1991). In addition, many Americans born after 1973 learned about the war though novels and films.

139. Costello, *Without Fear or Favor*, 238. Here Costello quotes from *Y* October 16, 1972.

140. Some wondered why Higgins did not write more frequently on these important issues. There are two reasons. First, the responsibility for considering these issues in depth lay with other members of SAD or with other departments within the USCC. Second, no one—not even someone with Higgins' erudition, interests, and insight—could have been expected to have had the energy, the passion, and the time to consider every issue. Higgins devoted himself to his principal areas of responsibility and interest—namely, labor–management issues, the renewal of organized labor, and the quest for ecojustice for farm laborers and farmhands.

141. Costello, *Without Fear or Favor*, 181.

142. The church considered the family as the foundational unit in society. It promoted the traditional view that women gave the family its vitality, strength, and stability. Women contributed to the moral and spiritual development of their husbands and children. SAD publications, beginning in the 1930s, presented and promoted the role of women in the home. Linna E. Bresette, in her testimony before Congress, endorsed the role of women as keepers of the hearth. Church departments such as SAD maintained that employers had a responsibility to provide men with a living wage so that their earnings would be sufficient for their families to live in modest comfort. When women entered the workplace during the Second World War, and when economic necessity forced them to work outside the home, SAD and other Catholic agencies continued to promote the ideal.

143. Costello, *Without Fear or Favor*, 184–88.

144. *Y* September 7, 1964.

145. *Y* May 8, 1967.

146. *Y* March 2, 1970.

147. *Y* February 21, 1966.

148. Ibid.

149. *Y* September 11, 1967.

150. March 24, 1973.

151. *Y* May 13 and 27, July 1, August 19, 1963; April 20, 1964; May 24, 1965; October 3, 1966; May 8, December 25, 1967; May 13, June 17, 1968; October 27, 1969; January 19, February 2, March 2, May 4 and 25, November 23 and 30, December 14 and 21, 1970; February 1, August 30, September 13, 1971; August 21 and 28, September 11, November 13, 1972; January 22, June 11 and 18, September 10, 1973; June 3, July 1, 1974; February 10, March 17, October 27, 1975; October 25, 1976; January 24, February 14, May 2 and 23, September 19, 1977; February 5, July 23, 1979; June 16, August 25, 1980.

152. *Y* October 3, 1966.

153. *Y* May 24, 1965.

154. Y May 13, 1963.

155. Y August 25, 1980.

156. Y June 16, 1980.

157. Y August 28, 1972, took issue with revisionist historians who critiqued labor history through a Marxist hermeneutic and who viewed the labor movement from the ideological stance of the socialist International Workers of the World. Higgins had a long memory for history. He often praised the courage and radicalism of Samuel Gompers, John L. Lewis, Phil Murray, Walter Reuther, and George Meany.

158. Y March 2, 1970.

159. Y referred to the civil rights movement as the "negro freedom movement."

160. Higgins became the first Catholic priest to address a UAW convention. Y reported that he preached them a sermon at the 1957 convention. He was also an original member of the PRB. As chair of the PRB he presented a ten-year report on its achievements in 1968. See note 8.

161. Y May 2, 1977. For the history of the UAW–Flint sitdown strike see Sidney Fine, "The General Motors Sit-Down Strike: A Re-examination," *American Historical Review* 70 (1969): 691–712. Higgins esteemed Biemiller as a friend and as a lobbyist who had devoted twenty-five years "to bring about the enactment of progressive legislation in the field of social welfare, labor-management relations and civil rights." See Y February 5, 1979.

162. Ibid.

163. Y June 16, 1980.

164. Y May 20, August 12, 1963; February 8, May 17, 1965; July 18 and 25, October 3, 1966; September 4, 1967; February 12, August 5, September 16, December 2, 1968; January 6, September 15, November 10, 1969; March 16, April 27, May 11, June 8 , August 24, 1970; April 5, June 28, August 9, 1971; April 10, June 12 and 19, July 3, August 7 and 14, September 18, 1972; February 4, 12, 26, March 5, April 23 and 30, May 7, 21, 28, July 2, 9, 16, 30, August 20 and 27, September 3, October 1 and 8, November 26, 1973; January 14, March 11, 18, 25, April 15, 22, 29, May 13 and 27, June 17, July 29, August 12 and 19, September 23, October 14 and 21, December 9 and 23, 1974; January 20, February 17, March 31, April 21 and 28, May 5 and 12, June 2 and 17, July 14 and 28, September 29, 1975; February 16, April 26, August 16, September 13, 1976; January 31, February 7, March 14, July 25, August 1 and 22, 1977; January 16, August 7 and 14, September 11, October 23, 1978; March 5, April 2, May 7 and 21, 1979; February 25, March 25, July 21, September 1, 1980.

165. The word *bracero* refers to the strong arms that guest workers needed to pick the produce of the fields. Farm labor required workers to use a short hoe, *el cortito* (the short one), also known as *el brazo del diablo* (the devil's arm). Only twenty-four inches long, *el cortito* forced the worker to bend and stoop all day. This led to debilitating, lifelong back injuries and chronic pain. Maurice "Mo" Jourdaine and his associates at the California Rural Legal Assistance worked seven years to have the short-handled hoe declared illegal in 1975. Guest workers were also brought into the United States to work on the railroads during the Second World War. The United States and Mexico successfully fulfilled their agreement in this little-known bracero program. See Barbara A. Driscoll, *The Tracks North: The Railroad* Bracero *Program of World War II* (Austin: University of Texas Press, 1999).

166. The United States began importing guest workers in the mid-19th century. A plentiful, cheap manual-labor force was needed when cattle ranches expanded in Texas and New Mexico and when fruit-bearing production increased in California during the 1850–1880 period. The Chinese came first. Over two hundred thousand Chinese workers were contracted for the cultivation of Californian fields, but the racist and the xenophobic attitudes of Anglos influenced

the passage of the Chinese Exclusion Act in 1882. Japanese workers were then imported and replaced by Filipino workers in 1903. With the construction of the railroad between Mexico and the United States between 1880 and 1890, many Mexican workers got jobs as railroad workers. Fifty-five thousand Mexican workers immigrated to Texas, New Mexico, and California between 1850 and 1880. Between 1910 and 1917, fifty-three thousand Mexican workers per year immigrated freely into the United States. They worked in agriculture, industry, and the service areas during the First World War. When the U.S. Border Patrol was founded in 1924, the status of Mexican workers changed. They became illegal aliens. For the earlier history of guest workers, see the "Bracero Project" at www.farmworkers.org. For the history of California farm labor in the era just before the First World War see David Vaught, *Cultivating California: Growers, Specialty Crops, and Labor, 1875–1920* (Baltimore: Johns Hopkins Press, 1999). For the history of the bracero agricultural program, see Otey M. Scruggs, "The Bracero Program under the Farm Security Administration 1942–1943," *Labor History* 3 (1962): 149–68; and Patrick J. Sullivan, *Blue Collar–Roman Collar–White Collar: U.S. Catholic Involvement in Labor Management Controversies, 1960–1980* (Lanham, Md.: University Press of America, 1987), 1–37.

167. Scruggs, "The Bracero Program," 149–51.

168. Secretary of labor James Mitchell appointed Higgins and two others to a committee to study the possibility of reviving the bracero program in 1973. Higgins served as chair. They decided against it because it would have provided a docile, guaranteed workforce; it would have been unfair to U.S. agricultural workers; and it would have delayed a solution to the farmworkers' problems. *Y* July 9, 1973; October 21 and December 9, 1974.

169. *Y* July 9, 1973, and August 1, 1977.

170. *Y* July 9, 1973; October 21 and December 9, 1974; March 31, 1975; August 1, 1977; March 5 and May 7, 1979.

171. *Y* May 17, 1965.

172. "Address by Cesar Chavez, President, United Farm Workers of America, AFL-CIO, the Commonwealth Club of California, November 9, 1983—San Francisco," 2. Available from the Cesar E. Chavez Foundation, www.ufw.org/fast.htm.

173. Ibid., 3.

174. Ibid., 4.

175. Ibid., 7.

176. This quote is from page six of "Address of Cesar Chavez, President, UFW, AFL-CIO, the Commonwealth Club of California, November 9, 1984, San Francisco, CA. Available from www.ufw.org/commonwealth.htm.

177. John C. Hammerback and Richard J. Jensen, *The Rhetorical Career of Cesar Chavez* (College Station: Texas A & M Press, 1998), 14. Juana Chavez used these traditional forms of speech to keep her family together in difficult and painful times. She also used them to teach moral values. Cesar Chavez used these rhetorical devices to teach his audiences about sacrifice, suffering, hard work, courage, Mexican history, and the powerful image of blood; and to solidify his identity with Mexican Americans, in form and in content.

178. Cletus E. Daniel, "Cesar Chavez and the Unionization of California Farm Workers," in Dubofsky and Van Tine, *Labor Leaders in America*, 366.

179. Ibid., 368–69.

180. Chavez undertook three public fasts during his life. The first, mentioned earlier, lasted twenty-five days. The second lasted twenty-four days (May 11–June 4, 1972). Chavez began this fast in Phoenix to protest a recently passed law that took away the farmworkers' right to strike or boycott. The third, his last and longest, took place in Delano, California, when Chavez was sixty-one. This fast lasted thirty-six days (July–August 1988). It enabled Chavez to call attention to the plight of those farmworkers and their families who suffered from illnesses caused by pesticides. He

explained the reason for this fast in an address he presented at Pacific Lutheran University in March 1989: "The fast was first and foremost directed at myself. It was something I felt compelled to do to purify my own body, mind, and soul. The fast was an act of penance for our own members who, out of ignorance or need, cooperate with those who grow and sell food treated with toxics. The fast was also for those who know what is right and just. It pains me that we continue to shop without protest at stores that offer grapes, that we eat in restaurants that display them, that we are too patient and understanding with those who serve them to us. The fast, then, was for those who know that they could or should do more—for those who, by not acting, become bystanders—in the poisoning of our food and the people who produce it. The fast was, finally, a declaration of non-cooperation with supermarkets that promote, sell, and profit from California table grapes. They are as culpable as those who manufacture the poisons and those who use them." See Susan Ferriss and Ricardo Sandoval, *The Fight in the Fields: Cesar Chavez and the Farmworkers Union* (San Diego, Calif.: Hartcourt Brace, 1998), 65–123.

181. Daniel, "Cesar Chavez and the Unionization," 369–70.

182. Yolanda Broyles-Gonzalez, *El Teatro Campesino: Theater in the Chicano Movement* (Austin: University of Texas Press, 1994), 241–42.

183. In 1967 Luis Valdez described the process that ETC used in creating its plays. "'We take a real situation—often something that happens on the picket line—and we improvise around it. When we get an improvisation that we like, we're ready. An *acto* is never written down.' All *Teatro Campesino* performance pieces went through various transformations and discussions before being committed to memory (not to written form). Yet that form was always subject of new improvisation, not least of all during performance. . . . Born of and for the working-class farmworker community, the . . . *actos* directly enacted the physical sociocultural memory of that community's experience. Memory indeed was the prime conduit for all performance work within ETC. And the power and instrumentality of memory, rooted in the community and in the body, made possible the immediacy, authenticity, and vitality characteristic of the ensemble's work." Broyles-Gonzalez, *El Teatro Campesino*, 22–23.

184. Hammerback and Jensen, *The Rhetorical Career of Cesar Chavez*, 30.

185. Sullivan, *Blue Collar–Roman Collar–White Collar*, 37–171.

186. U.S. Bishops, "Statement on Farm Labor," *Catholic Mind* 67 (January 1969): 4.

187. Ibid.

188. Ibid.

189. Ibid.

190. Ibid.

191. Hugh A. Donohoe, "Collective Bargaining for Farm Workers," *Catholic Mind* 68 (January 1970): 24–25.

192. Ibid., 25.

193. Daniel Lyons, "Three Statements on the California Grape Strike," *Catholic Mind* 68 (October 1970): 1–5. Higgins confronted Lyons in Y March 10, 1974. He said that Lyons had written more anti-Chavez and anti-UFW articles and disseminated more misinformation than anyone else in the Fourth Estate. Lyons wrote that the lettuce and grape boycotts were immoral in his article "The Church and the Boycott," which appeared in the *National Catholic Register* on March 10, 1974. The same article also stated that the U.S. bishops were against the boycotts and the UFW. Higgins set the record straight. The bishops had endorsed the boycott at their November 1973 meeting. They also endorsed legislation at their 1974 meeting that would give farmworkers the same rights that the National Labor Relations Act guaranteed for workers in the other industries. See Y June 16 and July 14, 1975.

194. Lyons, "Three Statements on the California Grape Strike," 1.

195. Ibid., 5.

196. Ibid.

197. Ibid., 6.

198. Higgins and Joseph F. Donnelly, an auxiliary bishop of the Hartford Archdiocese, were lifelong friends and esteemed colleagues in the social apostolate. Higgins esteemed Donnelly's work in social action–labor education in New Haven, Connecticut, and his work in labor–management relations. Donnelly's episcopal motto was "Peace, the Work of Justice." Donnelly died on June 30, 1977. Cesar Chavez read one of the Scripture readings at his funeral on July 6, 1977. See Y July 25, 1977, in appendix G, document 5 (p. 238). Donnelly served with four other bishops on the committee: Archbishop Timothy Manning of Los Angeles; Bishop Hugh A. Donohoe of Fresno, California; Bishop Walter W. Curtis of Bridgeport, Connecticut; and Bishop Humberto S. Medeiros of Brownsville, Texas. Higgins and Mahony represented the bishops' committee at an historic meeting on August 11, 1970, between the United Farm Workers Organizing Committee and the Western Conference of Teamsters. Higgins and Mahony brought both sides together for an all-night meeting that resulted in a contract on the morning of August 12. See Y August 24, 1970, in appendix G, document 1 (p. 230).

199. Y May 27, 1974, and April 21, 1975. Higgins made it clear that he went to California not to beat the drum for Cesar Chavez nor to oppose the growers. He went to offer official assistance. He did not go as a neutral bystander. Y August 7, 1972, indicated that he stood for the workers' right to organize and bargain collectively. "No one speaking from the social tradition of the church could be neutral." The same *Yardstick* column put the current struggle into the context of the larger labor movement. He stated that the struggle to organize was thirty-five to forty years late. "Labor's right to organize and bargain collectively in those (auto and steel) and other major industries is finished business. The problem now is how to make collective bargaining work more effectively." The tragedy, as he saw it, was that the farm labor crisis was back where the other industries had been two or three generations ago. The small growers were in trouble. He recommended that all parties take the first step—that is, sit down and do collective bargaining. Then they could proceed to the next step, to jointly address the problems of the industry. He maintained that cooperation would be possible only if there were a strong union and a strong growers' association.

200. Higgins wrote, as early as 1966, about Chavez as "a man of extraordinary genius and unsurpassable integrity" (Y July 18, 1966). Higgins and Bishop Donnelly succeeded in getting Cesar and Helen Chavez a private audience with Pope Paul VI in 1974. Higgins stated that "Chavez stands on the side of the angels and is not a dangerous revolutionary" (Y December 23, 1974). Reactionaries such as Father Dan Lyons, S.J., and Father Cletus Healy, S.J., as well publications such as *The Wanderer, National Catholic Register,* and *Twin Circle,* continued to attack Chavez. They held that the UFW was a menace to the nation. E. Norris Hall, the leader of the Grange in New Hampshire, warned people to "beware of Cesar Chavez and the black eagle program, . . . a one man Communist move to control the food supplies of America" (Y December 23, 1974).

201. Higgins had been participating in liturgies for farmworker justice for years. Y July 18, 1966, reported that Higgins joined Bishop Humberto Medeiros at a rally and liturgy in San Juan, Texas. Higgins said, "I felt, for once, that the Church could still claim to be the Church of the poor." The same *Yardstick* column reported that Higgins thought Mexican American farmworkers were on the verge of an historic breakthrough and that the Delano *huelga* was the beginning of a social movement (*la causa*). He concluded, "Organized cooperation (between growers and workers) is their only hope." Y August 20, 1973, reported that he celebrated the liturgy for over forty priests, religious, and rank-and-file farmworkers who had been jailed for eleven days.

202. Y March 16, 1970.

203. Y May 11, 1970.
204. Y June 8, 1970.
205. Y February 5, 1973.
206. Quoted in Y March 11, 1970.
207. Ibid.
208. Y September 3, 1973.
209. Y March 5, 1973.
210. Y April 23, 1973.
211. Ibid.
212. Y May 21, 1973.
213. Y May 5, 1975.
214. Y February 16, 1976.
215. Y September 23, 1974.
216. Y July 21, 1980. Higgins is here referring to a congressional commission studying U.S. immigration policies. See also Y February 7, March 14, August 4, 1977; January 16 and August 14, 1979; February 25, May 24, September 1, 1980.
217. Y January 31, 1977. See appendix G, document 3 (p. 235).
218. Y December 24, 1973; February 4, March 4, April 8, September 16, 1974; October 19, 1977. See also Sullivan, *Blue Collar–Roman Collar–White Collar*, 200–214.
219. Y April 8, 1974.
220. Sullivan, *Blue Collar–Roman Collar–White Collar*, 213.
221. Y October 10, 1977.
222. Y November 10, 1975; August 15, 1977; January 1, March 12, May 21, 1979; April 28, November 3, 1980. See also Sullivan, *Blue Collar–Roman Collar–White Collar*, 215–52.
223. Y November 10, 1975.
224. Y January 1, 1975.
225. Y May 21, 1979.
226. Y November 19, 1979.
227. Y May 19, 1980.
228. Y columns regarding hospital workers: July 6, 1964; March 25, 1958; May 10, 1976; July 2, 1979; September 29, 1980. Y columns regarding janitors: August 5, 1975. Y columns regarding public employees: March 4, 1968; March 3, August 18, 1969; September 15, 1975. Y columns regarding teachers: October 9, 1967; May 27, 1968; March 3, 1969; August 11, 1975; October 18, November 1, 1976; August 29, 1977; April 9, 1979.
229. Y July 6, 1964.
230. Y September 29, 1980.
231. Y March 25, 1968.
232. Y October 18, 1976; August 29, 1977; April 9, 1979.
233. Y February 11, 1963; October 21, 1968.
234. Y June 1, 1964; January 18, June 14, 1965; February 23, 1970.
235. Y January 23, March 20, April 24, June 26, July 10, 1978.
236. Y January 23, 1978.
237. Y March 20, 1978.
238. Ibid.
239. Y May 23, June 13, 1966; July 12, 1971; May 24, 1976; June 20, July 4, 11, 18, September 1977; February 27, 1978; March 3, 1980.
240. Y September 8, 1980.

241. Y December 25, 1972; June 14, 1971; October 3, 1977; November 13, 1978. The June 14, 1971, column placed Pope Paul VI "on the side of the angels."

242. Y June 19, 1978.

243. Y August 21, 1978.

244. Y September 9, 1974.

245. Y March 25, 1963.

246. Y April 18, 1966.

247. Y May 19, 1969. He repeated this column in memoriam on June 4, 1979. Randolph died at age ninety on May 16, 1979.

248. Y December 25, 1972. See also Gary Gerstle, *American Crucible: Race and Nation in the Twentieth Century*, (Princeton, N.J.: Princeton University Press, 2001), 268–310, especially 278–79.

249. Y May 18, 1970.

250. Ibid.

251. Ibid.

252. Y December 3, 1979.

253. Ibid.

254. Ibid.

255. See appendix G, document 7 (p. 241).

256. Y September 3, 1979.

257. Y November 25, 1975. See appendix G, document 2 (p. 233).

258. Clancy: Y June 21, 1971. Connolly: Y April 30, 1979. Smith: Y January 15, 1968. Donnelly: Y July 25, 1977; see appendix G, document 5 (p. 238). Lucey: Y June 20, 1974.

259. Y May 31, 1976.

260. Ibid.

261. Ibid.

262. Y December 15, 1980.

263. Y January 30, 1978.

264. Y February 11, 1980. For a contextual, albeit brief, treatment of the role that Blanshard and the Protestant organization played in the anti-Catholicism of the late 1940s and following, see Leo P. Ribuffo, "Religious Prejudice and Nativism," in *Encyclopedia of the American Religious Experience: Studies of Traditions and Movements*, ed. Charles H. Lippy and Peter W. Williams (New York: Charles Scribner's Sons, 1988), 3:1525–1546, especially 1552b–1554a. Ironically Blanshard died in a Catholic hospital.

265. Ibid.

266. Y January 6, 1969. The quotation is taken from an article on labor unions that Ryan published in volume 8 of the 1910 edition of the *Catholic Encyclopedia*.

267. Ibid. See also April 12, 1972; March 25, 1974; and July 14, 1975.

268. Y March 10, 1974. Higgins had earlier confronted Healy in November 10, 17, and 24, 1969. Healy's booklet, *Battle for the Vineyards*, promoted the position that the church only tolerated the "secular" kind of unionism that Higgins championed for United States. Higgins read him chapter and verse *Quadragesimo Anno*, a commentary on *Quadragesimo Anno* by Father Oswald von Nell Breuning, *Mater et Magistra*, and a commentary on *Mater et Magistra* by Monsignor Pietro Pavan. He told Healy that the issue had been settled when Cardinal Gibbons went to Rome to defend the right of U.S. Catholics to join the Knights of Labor. The church in the United States had approved of "secular" unions. In fact, it prefered them to the so-called confessional or Christian unions. "Father Healy is beating a dead horse in tying to revive this ancient controversy" (Y November 17, 1969). See Y December 23, 1974.

269. Y December 28, 1970.
270. Y April 12, 1971.
271. Ibid.
272. Y April 19, 1971.

Chapter 5

1. 1993 *LDS*, 1. For the 1993 *LDS*, Ricard assembled a series of quotes from George G. Higgins, *Organized Labor and the Church: Reflections of a "Labor Priest,"* with William Bole (New York: Paulist, 1993).
2. Ibid., 3. See also *LDS* 1998 and Higgins, *Organized Labor and the Church*, 181.
3. For a listing of the *LDSs* (1981–2001) issued by the Department of Social Action and World Development, United States Catholic Conference, see the bibliography, section D under Primary Sources (p. 352).
4. 1987 *LDS*, 1; and 1995 *LDS*, 2.
5. 1996 *LDS*, 2; and 2000 *LDS*, 2.
6. 1997 *LDS*, 1–2.
7. 1994 *LDS*, 3.
8. *LDSs* 1994, 1985, 1996, 1997, 1998, 2001.
9. 1997 *LDS*, 2.
10. 1998 *LDS*, 2.
11. 1999 *LDS*, 2.
12. 1994 *LDS*, 3.
13. 1997 *LDS*, 3. The U.S. bishops issued a statement giving ten ethical principles to guide Catholics in reflecting, judging, and acting in the economic life of the nation. The full text is found in appendix H.
14. 2001 *LDS*, 3.
15. Ibid., 2.
16. 1999 *LDS*, 2.
17. 1994 *LDS*, 3.
18. 1999 *LDS*, 1.
19. Ibid.
20. 1996 *LDS*, 2.
21. 1994 *LDS*, 1.
22. 1998 *LDS*, 2.
23. Henry A. Giroux, *Public Spaces, Private Lives: Beyond the Culture of Cynicism* (New York: Rowman and Littlefield, 2001), 2.
24. Y 1981: February 2 and 9; March 2, 16, and 30; June 8; and August 17, 24, and 31. 1982: October 18, 1982. 1983: May 23.
25. Y February 2, 1981.
26. Ibid.
27. Y March 2, 1981.
28. Ibid.
29. Y March 16, 1981.
30. Y March 30, 1981.
31. Y August 24, 1981.

32. Ibid.

33. Nine *Y* columns consider particular unions. UAW: February 23, 1981, and July 17, 1989. PATCO: August 24, 1981; October 18, 1982; April 23, 1990; and April 1, 1991. GM: August 31, 1981; May 24, 1982. Janitors for Justice: January 4, 1988. Five *Y* columns look back on union history: November 30, 1981 (the one-hundredth anniversary of the AFL-CIO), February 16 and December 14, 1987, and January 28 and February 4, 1991 (the one-hundredth anniversary of *Rerum Novarum*). Two Y columns—February 1, 1982, and April 1, 1991—treat union leadership. Four Y columns—September 7, 1981; August 27, 1984; September 5, 1988; and August 20, 1990—investigate the meaning of Labor Day. The role of working women is considered in *Y* November 23, 1981; August 2, 1982; December 26, 1983; and October 29, 1984. Other specific and more universal issues are discussed in *Y* January 19 and October 12, 1981; March 1 and 15, April 19, July 12, October 4, and November 8, 1982; August 22, October 10, November 13 and 28, and December 5, 1983; April 2 and 30, September 10 and 17, and November 12, 1984; January 28, February 4, March 18, April 22 and 29, August 12 and 19, September 5, and October 7, 1985; February 24, September 1 and 15, and October 13, 1986; March 30, May 25, June 29, September 14, November 9 and 16, 1987; January 11 and 18, March 7 and 21, May 9 and 30, and November 7, 1988; May 8 and 22, July 31, August 14, and October 23, 1989; January 8 and 15, March 5, April 9 and 30, June 18, October 29, December 3 and 31, 1990; July 15, 1991; June 1, October 5 and 19, and November 16, 1992; March 22, April 5 and 22, and June 28, 1993; January 24, February 21, April 4 and 18, and July 25, 1994.

34. *Y* September 7, 1981. See also *Y* January 15, 1990.

35. *Y* February 23, 1987.

36. *Y* June 22, 1987.

37. Ibid.

38. Ibid.

39. *Y* September 18, 1988.

40. Ibid.

41. Ibid.

42. *Y* March 7, 1994.

43. Ibid.

44. *Y* January 4, 1988. See also Jane Williams, "Restructuring Labor's Identity: The Justice for Janitors Campaign in Washington, DC," in *The Transformation of U.S. Unions: Voices, Visions, and Strategies from the Grassroots*, ed. Roy M. Tillman and Michael S. Cummings (Boulder: Rienner, 1999) 203–17.

45. *Y* January 4, 1988.

46. Ibid.

47. Higgins' most representative column on gender bias was that of April 5, 1993. He considered the role of working women in the columns of November 23, 1981; August 2, 1982; December 26, 1983; and October 29, 1984.

48. *Y* November 23, 1981.

49. Ibid.

50. *Y* March 1, 1982.

51. *Y* March 15, 1982.

52. *Y* October 10, 1983. See also *Y* November 2, 1992.

53. *Y* July 12, 1982.

54. *Y* December 5, 1983. See also *Y* November 12, 1984.

55. *Y* July 12, 1982. See also *Y* April 9, 1990.

56. Y October 4, 1982.
57. Y February 24, 1986.
58. Y October 16, 1989.
59. Higgins devoted twenty-one Y columns to the Solidarity labor movement: October 19 and November 16, 1981; February 15, March 8, May 3, and December 20, 1982; May 9, 1983; May 7, 1984; May 23, 1988; May 15, September 18, October 30, November 13 and 20, 1989; May 7, October 1, and December 10, 1990; June 10, 1991; July 9 and November 15, 1993; and January 10, 1994.
60. Y May 23, 1988.
61. Ibid.
62. Ibid.
63. Y February 15, 1982.
64. Y December 20, 1982.
65. Y May 15, 1989.
66. Y October 1, 1990.
67. Y July 1, 1991.
68. *Laborens Exercens* became a *locus theologicus* for the *LDS*s of the 1980s and 1990s (see the first section of this chapter); affected the pastoral letters, the bishops in Canada, and the United States issues on the economy; and gave birth to theological reflection on the meaning of work and related topics in the writings of Gregory Baum in Canada and Christine C. Gudorf, Giles Meilander, Edward C. Vacek, and Miroslav Wolf in the United States.
69. Pope John Paul II develops the meaning of solidarity in this encyclical. A case can be made for solidarity as a new cardinal virtue. For a treatment of the theological development of solidarity, see Marie Vianney Bilgrien, *Solidarity: A Principle, an Attitude, a Duty? Or the Virtue for an Interdependent World?* (New York: Peter Lang, 1999).
70. Y May 18, 1991.
71. Y September 28, 1981.
72. Y June 13, 1991.
73. Ibid.
74. Y April 15, 1991.
75. Y May 20, 1991.
76. Y October 3, 1983; March 4, 1985; March 16, 1987; and August 15, 1988.
77. Y October 3, 1983.
78. Ibid.
79. Y March 16, 1987.
80. *Economic Justice for All*, nos. 329–331.
81. Y September 2, 1985. Higgins commended the laity for their initiative in social action. In particular, he praised the work of Paul Weber, a member of the Detroit chapter of the Association of Catholic Trade Unionists in the late 1930s and 1940s, and the work of Ed Marciniak, once the editor of *Work*, the newspaper of the Chicago Catholic Labor Alliance. Higgins hoped that others would follow in their footsteps. "May their tribe increase," wrote Higgins, as he concluded this *Yardstick* with one of his favorite phrases.
82. Ibid.
83. In Y September 13, 1982, Higgins noted the political prophetic role of Pope John Paul II in defending solidarity and the role of the U.S. bishops in addressing abortion, human rights, and nuclear warfare. See also Y March 29, 1982; February 14, 1983; August 13, 1984; February 25, 1985; July 29, 1991.

84. Y November 30, 1987; April 4, 1988; and March 12, 1990.
85. Y September 27, 1982.
86. Y November 5, 1990.
87. Ibid.
88. Y July 30, 1990.
89. Y March 23, 1992.
90. Y October 10, 1988.
91. Higgins devoted seventeen Y columns to Catholic–Jewish relations: April 20, June 15, and November 9, 1981; January 18, 1982; February 21 and 28, 1985; July 21 and 28, August 4, and September 8, 1986; January 26, 1987; April 25, 1988; January 9 and 23, 1989; July 9, 1990; May 31, 1993; and June 24, 1994. He also wrote on the meaning of the Holocaust in four Y columns: May 11, 1981; March 21, 1983; October 26; 1987; and May 3, 1993.
92. Y July 9, 1990.
93. Ibid. See also Y July 28, 1986.
94. Y June 15, 1981.
95. Y August 4, 1986.
96. Y August 23, 1982; April 4 and 11, August 29, and September 19, 1983; January 30, April 16, July 23 and 30, and September 28, 1984; November 4, 11, and 25, 1985; January 20, October 27, 1986; September 21, 1987; June 3, 1988; January 2, February 13, May 29, and June 19, 1989; April 15, May 14, June 11, October 15 and 22, 1990; January 7 and 21, 1991; July 27, 1992; and March 7, 1994.
97. Y July 23, 1984.
98. Ibid.
99. Ibid.
100. Y September 24, 1984.
101. Ibid.
102. Y September 19, 1983.
103. Ibid.
104. Y January 21, 195. See also Y for October 15 and 22, 1990.
105. The most noteworthy Y columns of this period are responses to the religious Right—namely, the following. *The Wanderer*: January 12, 1981, and May 10, 1982. The writings of Michael Novak: July 11, 1983, and December 10, 1984. Articles critical of *Economic Justice for All*: June 7 and July 19, 1982. A column on Neuhaus' "Catholic Moment," November 24, 1986; as well as a response to Neuhaus on *Centissimus Annus*, May 27, 1991. The religious Right: January 2, 1984; June 2, 1986; and July 25, 1988.
106. Y December 10, 1984.

Conclusion

1. Barbara Ehrenreich, *Nickel and Dimed: On (Not) Getting By in America* (New York: Metropolitan Books, 2001), 221.

~

Bibliography

Primary Sources

Archival Sources

Archives of the Archdiocese of Boston

O'Connell, William. "Relations between Employers and the Employed." Advent 1912.

Archives of the Catholic University of America (ACUA), Washington, DC

Bresette, Linna E. "Report and Activities of Linna E. Bresette, Field Secretary, Department of Social Action, National Catholic Welfare Conference." ACUA files of the Social Action Department, box 25, file 1.

Higgins, George G. "The Underconsumption Theology in the Writings of Monsignor John A. Ryan." Unpublished master's diss., Catholic University of America, 1942.

———. "Voluntarism in Organized Labor in the United States, 1930–1940." Unpublished PhD diss., Catholic University of America, 1944.

———. *The Yardstick: Catholic Tests of a Social Order (1945–1994)*. The *Yardstick* columns. ACUA (see appendix I).

A. The Yardstick columns by George G. Higgins (1945–1994)

See appendix I.

B. The Yardstick columns by Guest Columnists (1949–1977)

See appendix I.

C. Other writings by George G. Higgins

1. ACUA 129, box 36: Subject files, hospital union folder

Letter of Charles J. Harrington to Monsignor George Higgins, July 31, 1974.

Letter of Monsignor George G. Higgins to Charles Harrington, August 6, 1974.

McBrien, Richard. "Let's Do Justice in this Workplace." *Catholic Messenger* (Davenport, Iowa). April 22, 1993.

2. *ACUA 129, box 115*

Higgins, George G. "Address at Labor Day Conference, San Francisco, September 5, 1983."

———. "Address at Labor Day Rally, Milwaukee County Labor Council AFL-CIO, September 6, 1993."

———. "Draft: Labor Day Statement, 1983."

———. "Homily at Labor Day Mass, Shrine of the Sacred Heart, Washington, September 7, 1992."

———. "On the Origins of Labor Day, 1986."

3. *Other publications*

Higgins, George G. "American Contributions to the Implementation of the Industry Council Plan." *American Catholic Sociological Review* 13 (1952): 10–24.

———. "Farm Workers: Assuring Basic Necessities for Human Dignity," *Origins* 15, no. 38 (March 6, 1986): 621–22.

———. "Laetare Medal Ceremony." University of Notre Dame, May 20, 2001 (unpublished manuscript).

———. "Organized Labor and Collective Bargaining at the Crossroads." *Blueprint for Social Justice* 51 (April–May 1998): 1–10.

———. "Organized Labor 1964." *Catholic Mind* 62 (November 1964): 47–54.

———. *Organized Labor and the Church: Reflections of a "Labor Priest."* With William Bole. New York: Paulist Press, 1993.

———. "Poverty and the Migrant Worker." *Catholic Mind* 63 (May 1965): 32–40.

———. "Random Observations on My 50 Years as a Priest." *Origins* 20 (June 7, 1990): 62–64.

———. *Subsidiarity in the Catholic Social Tradition: Yesterday, Today, and Tomorrow.* Albert Cardinal Meyer Lecture. Mundelein, Ill.: Mundelein Seminary University of St. Mary of the Lake, 1994.

———. "Toward a New Society." *Catholic Mind* (1956).

———. "Twenty-five Years of *Quadragesimo Anno.*" *America* 95 (1956): 130–33.

D. Bishops' Labor Day Statements, 1946–1999

1. *ACUA 129, boxes 114 and 115*

1946–1967: Social Action Department, National Catholic Welfare Conference

1946	McGowan, Raymond A.	*Labor Day Statement*
1947	McGowan, Raymond A.	*Labor Day Statement*
1948	McGowan, Raymond A.	*Labor Day Statement*
1949	McGowan, Raymond A.	*Labor Day Statement*
1950	McGowan, Raymond A.	*Labor Day Statement*
1951	McGowan, Raymond A.	*Labor Day Statement*
1952	McGowan, Raymond A.	*Labor Day Statement*
1953	McGowan, Raymond A.	*Labor Day Statement*
1954	McGowan, Raymond A.	*Labor Day Statement*
1955	Higgins, George G.	*Labor Day Statement*
1956	Higgins, George G.	*Labor Day Statement*
1957	Higgins, George G.	*Labor Day Statement*

1958	Higgins, George G.	*Labor Day Statement*
1959	Higgins, George G.	*Labor Day Statement*
1960	Higgins, George G.	*Labor Day Statement*
1961	Higgins, George G.	*Labor Day Statement*
1962	Higgins, George G.	*Labor Day Statement*
1963	Higgins, George G.	*Labor Day Statement*
1964	Higgins, George G.	*Labor Day Statement*
1965	Higgins, George G.	*Labor Day Statement*
1966	Higgins, George G.	*Labor Day Statement*
1967	Higgins, George G.	*Labor Day Statement*

1968–1971: Division for Urban Life, Social Development Department, United States Catholic Conference

1968	Higgins, George G.	*Labor Day Statement*
1969	Higgins, George G.	*Labor Day Statement*
1970	Baroni, Geno C., and George G. Higgins	*Labor Day Statement*
1971	Higgins, George G.	*Labor Day Statement*

1972–1978: Secretary for Research, United States Catholic Conference

1972	Higgins, George G.	*Labor Day Statement*
1973	Higgins, George G.	*Labor Day Statement:* The Farm Labor Problem
1974	Higgins, George G.	*Labor Day Statement*
1975	Higgins, George G.	*Labor Day Statement*
1976	Higgins, George G.	*Labor Day Statement:* Liberty and Justice for All, Some Notes on the Bicentennial
1977	Higgins, George G., and John Carr	*Labor Day Statement:* Full Employment
1978	Higgins, George G.	*Labor Day Statement*

1979–1980: Secretary for Special Concerns, United States Catholic Conference

1979	Higgins, George G.	*Labor Day Statement*
1980	Higgins, George G.	*Labor Day Statement*

1981–2000: Department on Social Development and World Peace, United States Catholic Conference

1981	Kreitemeyer, Ronald T.	*Labor Day Statement:* Reflections on the Economic Crisis in Light of the Church's Social Teaching
1982	Kreitemeyer, Ronald T.	*Labor Day Statement:* Reflections on the Papal Encyclical, On Human Work
1983	Hurley, Mark J.	*Labor Day Statement:* Jobs and Justice
1984	O'Connor, John J.	*Labor Day Statement:* Reflections on the Forthcoming Pastoral Letter on Catholic

		Social Teaching and the U.S. Economy
1985	O'Connor, John J.	*Labor Day Statement:* The Right to Health Care
1986	O'Connor, John J.	*Labor Day Statement:* Addressing the Issues of Work and Family
1987	Sullivan, Joseph M.	*Labor Day Statement:* The Need for New and Renewed Partnerships
1988	Sullivan, Joseph M.	*Labor Day Statement:* Solidarity and American Catholics
1989	Sullivan, Joseph M.	*Labor Day Statement:* Freedom, Justice, and the Role of Unions
1990	Higgins, George G.	*Labor Day Statement:* On the Condition of Labor
1991	Malone, James	*Labor Day Statement:* A Time for Action
1992	Malone, James	*Labor Day Statement:* Work and Family: New Challenges
1993	Ricard, John	*Labor Day Statement:* Msgr. George Higgins: A "Labor Priest" Challenges Us
1994	Ricard, John	*Labor Day Statement:* Work: Still the Center of the Social Question
1995	Ricard, John	*Labor Day Statement:* A Shifting, Churning Economy
1996	Skylstad, William S.	*Labor Day Statement:* An Economy of Paradoxes
1997	Skylstad, William S.	*Labor Day Statement:* Economic Progress: Looking Beyond the Numbers
1998	Skylstad, William S.	*Labor Day Statement:* Labor Day: Not a Picnic for Everybody
1999	Mahony, Roger A.	*Labor Day Statement:* Social Security and Solidarity
2000	Mahony, Roger A.	*Labor Day Statement:* A Jubilee for Workers: Challenges and Opportunities for the New Millennium
2001	Mahony, Roger A.	*Labor Day Statement:* The Dignity of Work and Workers: The Message of *Laborem Exercens*
2002	McCarrick, Theodore E.	*Labor Day Statement:* Monsignor George G. Higgins: Faithful Priest and Voice for Workers

2003	McCarrick, Theodore E.	*Labor Day Statement*. Labor Day 2003: Recommitting to Justice for Farm Workers

E. Social Action Department (SAD): National Catholic Welfare Conference (NCWC) / United States Catholic Conference (USCC)

Cuban Catholic Action and the Social Action Department, National Catholic Welfare Conference. *Statement of the Second Inter-American Catholic Seminar on Social Studies*, 23–29. Washington, DC: SAD/NCWC, 1946.

Diocese of Brooklyn, N.Y. "Principles of Social Justice." In *Course of Catechetical Instructions for the Ecclesiastical Year 1937–1938*, part III, 16–35. ACUA, NCWC/USCC, SAD 10, box 67, folder 22.

McGowan, Raymond A., and John A. Ryan. *Organized Social Justice: An Economic Program for the United States Applying Pius XI's Great Encyclical on Social Life. 133 Signers. Notes and a Study Outline*. New York: Paulist Press, 1935; and SAD/NCWC. ACUA, NCWC/USCC, SAD 10, box 68, folder/section 1930–1939.

Ryan, John A. *Roosevelt Safeguards America*. ACUA, NCWC/USCC, SAD 10, 1930–1936, box 67, folder 18, Ryan—Miscellaneous Publications. Washington, DC: Democratic National Committee, October 8, 1936.

———. *The Equal Rights Amendment in Relation to Protective Legislation for Women*. Washington, DC: SAD/NCWC, 1924.

F. Other Primary Documents

Administrative Committee of the National Catholic War Council. "Program of Social Reconstruction." In *Pastoral letters of the United States Catholic Bishops*, vol. 1, *1792–1940*, ed. Hugh J. Nolan, 255–71. Washington, DC: National Council of Catholic Bishops / United States Catholic Conference, 1984.

Bishops' Ad Hoc Committee on the Farm Labor Dispute. "Three Statements on the California Grape Strike." *Catholic Mind* 68 (October 1970): 1–7.

Commission for Catholic–Jewish Relations of the National Conference of Catholic Bishops. "Guidelines for Catholic–Jewish Relations." *Catholic Mind* 65 (June 1967): 62–65.

Department of Social Development of the U.S. Catholic Conference. "USCC Supports Farm Labor Rights." *Catholic Mind* 68 (May 1970): 5–6.

Division for Poverty of the U.S. Catholic Conference. "USCC's Statement on Mexican Workers." *Catholic Mind* 68 (February 1970): 3–5.

Gibbons, Cardinal James. "Defense of the Knights of Labor, February 20, 1887." In *The Encyclopedia of American Catholic History*, ed. Michael Glazier and Thomas J. Shelley, 772–77. Collegeville, Minn.: Liturgical Press, 1997.

Social Action Department of the National Catholic Welfare Conference. "The Problem of Poverty." *Catholic Mind* 62 (May 1964): 54–63.

U.S. Bishops. "Letter to President Wilson on the Establishment of the National Catholic Welfare Council and Pledge of Catholic Loyalty." In *Our Bishops Speak*, ed. Raphael M. Huber, 173–74. Milwaukee, Wisc.: Bruce, 1952.

———. "Statement on Farm Labor." *Catholic Mind* 67 (January 1969): 4–6.

Secondary Sources

Books

Abell, Aaron I. *American Catholicism and Social Action: The Search for Social Justice, 1865–1950*. Garden City, N.Y.: Doubleday, 1960.

Ahlstrom, Sydney E. *A Religious History of the American People*. Garden City, N.Y.: Doubleday, 1975.

Allitt, Patrick. *Catholic Converts: British and American Intellectuals Turn to Rome*. Ithaca, N.Y.: Cornell University Press, 1997.

———. *Catholic Intellectual and Conservative Politics in America, 1950–1985*. Ithaca, N.Y.: Cornell University Press, 1993.

Anderson, Jervis. *A. Philip Randolph: A Biographical Portrait*. Berkeley: University of California, 1986.

———. *Bayard Rustin: Troubles I've Seen; A Biography*. Berkeley: University of California, 1998.

Appleby, R. Scott. *"Church and Age Unite!" The Modernist Impulse in American Catholicism*. Notre Dame, Ind.: University of Notre Dame Press, 1992.

Arnesen, Eric. *Brotherhoods of Color: Black Railroad Workers and the Struggle for Equality*. Cambridge, Mass.: Harvard University Press, 2001.

Aronowitz, Stanley. *From the Ashes of the Old: American Labor and America's Future*. Boston: Houghton Mifflin, 1998.

Avella, Steven M. *This Confident Church: Catholic Leadership and Life in Chicago, 1940–1965*. Notre Dame, Ind.: University of Notre Dame Press, 1992.

Badger, Anthony J. *The New Deal: The Depression Years, 1933–1940*. New York: Hill and Wang, 1989.

Bates, Beth Tompkins. *Pullman Porters and the Rise of Protest Politics in Black America, 1925–1945*. Chapel Hill: University of North Carolina Press, 2001.

Baum, Gregory. *The Priority of Labor: A Commentary on "Laborem Exercens."* New York: Paulist, 1982.

Beckley, Harlan R., ed. *Economic Justice: Selections from "Distributive Justice" and "A Living Wage."* Louisville, Ky.: Westminster John Knox Press, 1996.

Bellah, Robert N. *The Broken Covenant: American Civil Religion in Time of Trial*. New York: Seabury Press, 1975.

Bellah, Robert N., Richard Madsen, William M. Sullivan, Ann Swidler, and Steven M. Tipton. *The Good Society*. New York: Alfred A. Knopf, 1991.

———. *Habits of the Heart: Individualism and Commitment in American Life*. Berkeley: University of California Press, 1985.

Berry, Thomas. *The Great Work: Our Way into the Future*. New York: Bell Tower, 1999.

Betten, Neil. *Catholic Activism and the Industrial Worker*. Gainesville: University Presses of Florida, 1976.

Black, Allida M. *Casting Her Own Shadow: Eleanor Roosevelt and the Shaping of Postwar Liberalism*. New York: Columbia University Press, 1996.

Blantz, Thomas E. *George N. Shuster: On the Side of Truth*. Notre Dame, Ind.: University of Notre Dame Press, 1993.

Blewett, Mary H. *Constant Turmoil: The Politics of Industrial Life in Nineteenth-Century New England*. Amherst: University of Massachusetts Press, 2000.

———. *Men, Women, and Work: Class, Gender, and Protest in the New England Shoe Industry, 1780–1910*. Urbana: University of Illinois Press, 1988.

———. *We Will Rise in Our Might: Workingwomen's Voices from Nineteenth-Century New England*. Ithaca, N.Y.: Cornell University Press, 1991.

Bluestone, Barry, and Irving Bluestone. *Negotiating the Future: A Labor Perspective on American Business*. New York: Basic Books, 1991.

Boyle, Kevin. *The UAW and the Heyday of American Liberalism, 1945–1968*. Ithaca, N.Y.: Cornell University Press, 1995.

Brecher, Jeremy. *Strike!* Rev. and upd. Boston: South End Press, 1997.

Brenda, Saul E. *Social Justice and Church Authority: The Public Life of Archbishop Robert E. Lucy*. Philadelphia: Temple University Press, 1982.

Broderick, Francis L. *Right Reverend New Dealer: John A. Ryan*. New York: Macmillan, 1963.

Brody, David. *In Labor's Cause: Main Themes on the History of the American Worker*. New York: Oxford University Press, 1993.

———. *Workers in Industrial America: Essays on the Twentieth Century Struggle*. New York: Oxford University Press, 1983.

Brown, Dorothy, and Elizabeth McKeown. *The Poor Belong to Us: Catholic Charities and American Welfare*. Cambridge, Mass.: Harvard University Press, 1997.

Browne, Henry J. *The Church and the Knights of Labor*. Washington, DC: Catholic University of America Press, 1949.

Broyles-Gonzalez, Yolanda. *El Teatro Campesino: Theater in the Chicano Movement*. Austin: University of Texas Press, 1994.

Burns, Jeffrey M. *Disturbing the Peace: A History of the Christian Family Movement, 1949–1974*. Notre Dame, Ind.: University of Notre Dame Press, 1999.

Byers, David M., ed. *Justice in the Marketplace: Collected Statements of the Vatican and the United States Catholic Bishops on Economic Policy, 1891–1984*. Washington, DC: United States Catholic Conference, 1985.

Byrnes, Timothy A. *Catholic Bishops in American Politics*. Princeton, N.J.: Princeton University Press, 1991.

Cady, Linell. *Religion, Theology, and American Public Life*. Albany: State University of New York Press, 1993.

Calvez, Jean-Yves. *The Social Thought of John XXIII: "Mater et Magister."* Chicago: Henry Regnery, 1964.

Calvez, Jean-Yves, and Jacques Perrin. *The Church and Social Justice*. London: Burns and Oates, 1961.

Camp, Richard L. *The Papal Ideology of Social Reform*. Leiden, Neth.: E. J. Brill, 1969.

Carnes, Mark C. *Secret Ritual and Manhood in Victorian America*. New Haven, Conn.: Yale University Press, 1989.

Casanova, Jose. *Public Religion in the Modern World*. Chicago: University of Chicago Press, 1994.

Cashman, Sean Dennis. *America in the Age of the Titans: The Progressive Era and World War I*. New York: New York University Press, 1988.

Chadwick, Owen. *The Secularization of the European Mind in the Nineteenth Century*. New York: Cambridge University Press, 1975.

Chinnici, Joseph P. *Living Stones: The History and Structure of Catholic Spiritual Life in the United States*. New York: Macmillan, 1989.

Clements, Kendrick A. *Woodrow Wilson: World Statesman*. Chicago: Ivan R. Dee, 1999.

Coburn, Carol K., and Martha Smith. *Spirited Lives: How Nuns Shaped Catholic Culture and American Life, 1836–1920*. Chapel Hill: University of North Carolina Press, 1999.

Coffey, Joan L. *Leon Harmel: Entrepreneur as Catholic Social Reformer*. Notre Dame, Ind.: University of Notre Dame Press, 2003.

Cohen, Lizabeth. *A Consumers' Republic: The Politics of Mass Consumption in Postwar America*. New York: Alfred A. Knopf, 2003.

Coleman, John A. *An American Strategic Theology*. New York: Paulist, 1991.

Conway, Martin. *Catholic Politics in Europe, 1918–1945*. New York: Routledge, 1997.

Corrin, Jay P. *Catholic Intellectuals and the Challenge of Democracy*. Notre Dame, Ind.: University of Notre Dame Press, 2002.

Costello, Gerald M. *Without Fear or Favor: George Higgins on the Record*. Mystic, Conn.: Twenty-third Publications, 1984.

Craig, Robert H. *Religion and Radical Politics: An Alternative Christian Tradition in the United States*. Philadelphia: Temple University Press, 1992.

Cronin, John F. *Catholic Social Action*. Milwaukee, Wisc.: Bruce, 1948.

———. *Catholic Social Principles: The Social Teaching of the Catholic Church Applied to American Economic Life*. Milwaukee, Wisc.: Bruce, 1950.

Crosby, Donald F. *God, Church, and Flag: Senator Joseph R. McCarthy and the Catholic Church, 1950–1957*. Chapel Hill: University of North Carolina Press, 1978.

Cross, Robert D. *The Emergence of Liberal Catholicism in America*. Cambridge, Mass.: Harvard University Press, 1958.

Curran, Charles E. *American Catholic Social Ethics*. Notre Dame, Ind.: University of Notre Dame Press, 1982.

———. *The Origins of Moral Theology in the United States: Three Different Approaches*. Washington, DC: Georgetown University Press, 1997.

Cushman, Philip. *Constructing the Self, Constructing America: A Cultural History of Psychotherapy*. New York: Addison-Wesley, 1995.

Davis, Cyprian. *The History of Black Catholics in the United States*. New York: Crossroad, 1990.

Dawley, Alan. *Struggles for Justice: Social Responsibility and the Liberal State*. Cambridge, Mass.: Harvard University Press, 1991.

Delbanco, Andrew. *The Real American Dream: A Meditation on Hope*. Cambridge, Mass.: Harvard University Press, 1999.

Dolan, Jay P. *The American Catholic Experience: A History from Colonial Times to the Present*. Garden City, N.Y.: Doubleday, 1985.

———. *Catholic Revivalism: The American Experience, 1830–1900*. Notre Dame, Ind.: University of Notre Dame Press, 1979.

Dorr, Donald. *Option for the Poor: A Hundred Years of Vatican Social Teaching*. Maryknoll, N.Y.: Orbis, 1983.

Dorrien, Gary J. *Reconstructing the Common Good: Theology and the Social Order*. Maryknoll, N.Y.: Orbis, 1990.

———. *Soul in Society: The Making and Renewal of Social Christianity*. Minneapolis, Minn.: Fortress, 1995.

Dries, Angelyn. *The Missionary Movement in American Catholic History*. Maryknoll, N.Y.: Orbis, 1998.

Driscoll, Barbara A. *The Track North: The Railroad Bracero Program of World War II*. Austin: University of Texas Press, 1999.

Dubofsky, Melvyn. *The State and Labor in Modern America*. Chapel Hill: University of North Carolina Press, 1994.

———. *We Shall Be All: A History of the Industrial Workers of the World*. Abr. ed. Edited by Joseph A. McCartin. Urbana: University of Illinois Press, 2000.

Dudziak, Mary L. *Cold War Civil Rights: Race and the Image of American Democracy*. Princeton, N.J.: Princeton University Press, 2000.

Dulles, Foster Rhea, and Melvyn Dubofsky. *Labor in America: A History*. 5th ed. Wheeling, Ill.: Harlan Davidson, 1993.

Ellis, John Tracy. *American Catholicism*. 2nd ed. Chicago: University of Chicago Press, 1969.
———. *The Life of James Cardinal Gibbons, 1834–1921*. 2 vols. Milwaukee, Wisc.: Bruce, 1952.
Ellwood, Robert E. *The Sixties Spiritual Awakening: American Religion Moving from Modern to Postmodern*. New Brunswick, N.J.: Rutgers University Press, 1994.
Engelhardt, Tom. *The End of Victory Culture*. Amherst: University of Massachusetts Press, 1995.
Etzioni, Amitai. *Next: The Road to the Good Society*. New York: Basic Books, 2001.
Fergusson, David. *Community, Liberalism, and Christian Ethics*. New York: Cambridge University Press, 1998.
Ferris, Susan, and Ricardo Sandoval. *The Fight in the Fields: Cesar Chavez and the Farmworkers Movement*. San Diego, Calif.: Hartcourt Brace, 1997.
Fisher, James Terence. *The Catholic Counterculture in America, 1933–1962*. Chapel Hill: University of North Carolina Press.
———. *Dr. America: The Lives of Thomas A. Dooley, 1927–1962*. Amherst: University of Massachusetts Press, 1996.
Flynn, George Q. *American Catholics and the Roosevelt Presidency, 1932–1936*. Lexington: University of Kentucky Press, 1968.
Fogarty, Gerald P. *The Vatican and the American Hierarchy from 1870–1965*. Collegeville, Minn.: Michael Glazier, 1985.
Foner, Philip S. *History of the Labor Movement in the United States*. 10 vols. New York: International Publishers, 1947–1994.
Fones-Wolf, Ken. *Trade Union Gospel: Christianity and Labor in Industrial Philadelphia, 1965–1915*. Philadelphia: Temple University Press.
Fox, Mary Harrita. *Peter E. Dietz: Labor Priest*. Notre Dame, Ind.: University of Notre Dame Press, 1953.
Franklin, R. W., and Robert L. Spaeth. *Virgil Michel: American Catholic*. Collegeville, Minn.: Liturgical Press, 1988.
Fraser, Jill Andresky. *White-Collar Sweatshop: The Deterioration of Work and Its Rewards in Corporate America*. New York: W. W. Norton, 2001.
Freeman, Joshua. *Working Class New York: Life and Labor since World War II*. New York: New Press, 2000.
Freidel, Frank. *Franklin D. Roosevelt: The Apprenticeship*. Boston: Little, Brown, 1952.
Galbraith, John Kenneth. *The Affluent Society*. 40th anniv. ed. New York: Mariner/Houghton Mifflin, 1998.
Gearty, Patrick W. *The Economic Thought of Monsignor John A. Ryan*. Washington, DC: Catholic University of America Press, 1953.
Gerstle, Gary. *American Crucible: Race and Nation in the Twentieth Century*. Princeton, N.J.: Princeton University Press, 2001.
Gilkey, Langdon. *On Niebuhr: A Theological Study*. Chicago: University of Chicago Press, 2001.
Gleason, Philip. *The Conservative Reformers: German-American Catholics and the Social Order*. Notre Dame, Ind.: University of Notre Dame Press, 1968.
———. *Keeping the Faith: American Catholicism Past and Present*. Notre Dame, Ind.: University of Notre Dame Press, 1987.
Glickman, Lawrence B. *A Living Wage: American Workers and the Making of the Consumer Society*. Ithaca, N.Y.: Cornell University Press, 1997.
Goen, C. C. *Broken Churches, Broken Nation: Denominational Schisms and the Coming of the Civil War*. Macon, Ga.: Mercer University Press, 1985.
Gorn, Elliott J. *Mother Jones: The Most Dangerous Woman in America*. New York: Hill and Wang, 2001.

Gribble, Richard. *Catholicism and the San Francisco Labor Movement, 1896–1921*. Lewiston, N.Y.: Edward Mellen Press, 1993.

Grimes, Marcy C. *The Knights in Fiction: Two Labor Novels of the 1880s*. Urbana: University of Illinois Press, 1986.

Griswold Del Castillo, Richard, and Richard A. Garcia. *Cesar Chavez: A Triumph of Spirit*. Norman: University of Oklahoma Press, 1995.

Haas, Francis J. *Man and Society*. 2nd ed. New York: 1952.

Halsey, William M. *The Survival of American Innocence: American Catholicism in an Era of Disillusionment, 1920–1949*. Notre Dame, Ind.: University of Notre Dame Press, 1980.

Hammerback, Jack, and Richard J. Jensen. *The Rhetorical Career of Cesar Chavez*. College Station: Texas A & M Press, 1998.

Hammond, Phillip E. *With Liberty for All: Freedom of Religion in the United States*. Louisville, Ky.: Westminster John Knox Press, 1998.

Harrington, Michael. *The Other America: Poverty in the United States*. New York: Touchstone / Simon and Schuster, 1997.

Heilbroner, Robert L. *The Worldly Philosophers: The Lives, Times, and Ideas of the Great Economic Thinkers*. New York: Simon and Schuster, 1953.

Heineman, Kenneth J. *A Catholic New Deal: Religion and Reform in Depression Pittsburgh*. University Park, Penn.: Pennsylvania State University Press, 1999.

———. *Put Your Bodies upon the Wheels: Student Revolt in the 1960s*. Chicago: Ian R. Dee, 2001.

Hennesey, James. *American Catholics: A History of the Roman Catholic Community in the United States*. New York: Oxford University Press, 1981.

Herberg, Will. *Protestant-Catholic-Jew: An Essay in American Religious Sociology*. Garden City, N.Y.: Doubleday, 1955.

Herman, Arthur. *Joseph McCarthy: Reexamining the Life and Legacy of America's Most Hated Senator*. New York: Free Press, 2000.

Herring, George C. *America's Longest War: The United States and Vietnam, 1950–1975*. 3rd ed. New York: McGraw-Hill, 1996.

Hicks, Douglas A. *Inequality and Christian Ethics*. New York: Cambridge University Press, 2000.

Himes, Michael J., and Kenneth R. Himes. *Fullness of Faith: The Public Significance of Theology*. New York: Paulist, 1993.

Hobgood, Mary Elizabeth. *Dismantling Privilege: An Ethics of Accountability*. Cleveland, Ohio: Pilgrim, 2000.

Hollenbach, David. *Claims in Conflict: Retrieving and Renewing the Catholic Human Rights Tradition*. New York: Paulist, 1979.

———. *The Common Good and Christian Ethics*. New York: Cambridge University Press, 2002.

———. *The Global Face of Public Faith: Politics, Human Rights, and Christian Ethics*. Washington, DC: Georgetown University Press, 2003.

———. *Justice, Peace, and Human Rights: American Catholic Social Ethics in a Pluralistic Context*. New York: Crossroad, 1988.

Huff, Peter A. *Allen Tate and the Catholic Revival: Trace of the Fugitive Gods*. New York: Paulist, 1996.

Hunter, Tera W. *To 'Joy My Freedom: Southern Black Women's Lives and Labors after the Civil War*. Cambridge, Mass.: Harvard University Press, 1997.

Huthmacher, J. Joseph. *Senator Robert F. Wagner and the Rise of Urban Liberalism*. New York: Atheneum, 1968.

Hutsen, James H. *Religion and the Founding of the American Republic*. Washington, DC: Library of Congress, 1998.

Ignatiev, Noel. *How the Irish Became White*. New York: Routledge, 1995.

Isacsson, Alfred. *The Determined Doctor: The Story of Edward McGlynn*. Second Edition. Tarrytown, N.Y.: Vestigium Press, 1998.

———. *Edward McGlynn: Studies Marking the Centenary of His Death*. Tarrytown, N.Y.: Vestigium Press, 1999.

Isserman, Maurice. *The Other American: The Life of Michael Harrington*. New York: Public Affairs, 2000.

Isserman, Maurice, and Michael Kazin. *America Divide: The Civil War of the 1960s*. New York: Oxford University Press, 2000.

Jacoby, Robin Miller. *The British and American Women's Trade Union Leagues, 1890–1925*. Brooklyn, N.Y.: Carlson, 1994.

Jardin, Andre. *Tocqueville: A Biography*. Baltimore: Johns Hopkins Press, 1998.

Kammen, Michael. *Mystic Chords of Memory: The Transformation of Tradition in American Culture*. New York: Vintage, 1993.

Kammer, Fred. *Doing Faithjustice*. New York: Paulist Press, 1991.

———. *Salted with Fire: Spirituality for the Faithjustice Journey*. New York: Paulist Press, 1995.

Kane, Paula M. *Separatism and Subculture: Boston Catholicism, 1900–1920*. Chapel Hill: University of North Carolina Press, 1994.

Kantowicz, Edward R. *Corporation Sole: Cardinal Mundelein and Chicago Catholicism*. Notre Dame, Ind.: University of Notre Dame Press, 1983.

Kauffman, Christopher J. *Ministry and Meaning: A Religious History of Catholic Health Care in the United States*. New York: Crossroad, 1995.

Kochan, Tomas J., Harry C. Katz, and Robert B. McKersie. *The Transformation of American Industrial Relations*. Ithaca, N.Y.: Cornell University Press, 1994.

Laderman, Gary. *The Sacred Remains*. New Haven, Conn.: Yale University Press, 1986.

Laurie, Bruce. *Artisans into Workers: Labor in Nineteenth-Century America*. Urbana: University of Illinois Press, 1997.

Leach, William. *Land of Desire: Merchants, Power and the Rise of a New American Culture*. New York: Vintage, 1993.

Lears, T. Jackson. *No Place of Grace: Antimodernism and the Transformation of American Culture, 1880–1920*. New York: Pantheon Books, 1981.

Leuchtenburg, William E. *The FDR Years: On Roosevelt and His Legacy*. New York: Columbia University Press, 1995.

Licht, Walter. *Industrializing America: The Nineteenth Century*. Baltimore: John Hopkins Press, 1995.

Lictenstein, Nelson. *State of the Union: A Century of American Labor*. Princeton, N.J.: Princeton University Press, 2002.

Lindley, Susan Hill. *"You Have Stept Out of Your Place": A History of Women and Religion in America*. Louisville, Ky.: Westminster John Knox Press, 1996.

Lischer, Richard. *The Preacher King: Martin Luther King Jr. and the Word That Moved America*. New York: Oxford University Press, 1995.

Lovin, Robin W. *Reinhold Niebuhr and Christian Realism*. New York: Cambridge University Press, 1995.

Martin, Christopher R. *Framed! Labor and the Corporate Media*. Ithaca, N.Y.: ILS Press / Cornell University Press, 2004.

Marty, Martin E. *Modern American Religion*. Vol. 1, *The Irony of It All, 1893–1919*. Chicago: University of Chicago Press, 1986.

———. *Modern American Religion*. Vol. 2, *The Noise of Conflict, 1919–1941*. Chicago: University of Chicago Press, 1991.

———. *Modern American Religion*. Vol. 3, *Under God, Indivisible, 1941–1960*. Chicago: University of Chicago Press, 1996.

———. *The One and the Many: America's Struggle for the Common Good*. Cambridge, Mass.: Harvard University Press, 1997.
———. *The Public Church*. New York: Crossroad, 1981.
———. *Religion and Republic: The American Circumstance*. Boston: Beacon, 1987.
Massa, Mark A. *Catholics and American Culture: Fulton Sheen, Dorothy Day, and the Notre Dame Football Team*. New York: Crossroad, 1999.
Massey, Douglas S., and Nancy A. Denton. *American Apartheid: Segregation and the Making of the Underclass*. Cambridge, Mass.: Harvard University Press, 1993.
Matthiesen, Peter. *Sal Si Puedes: Cesar Chavez and the New American Revolution*. Berkeley: University of California, 2000.
May, Henry F. *Protestant Churches and Industrial America*. New York: Harper and Row, 1949.
McAvoy, Thomas T. *The Great Crisis in American Catholic History, 1895–1900*. Chicago: Henry Regnery, 1957.
McCarraher, Eugene. *Christian Critics: Religion and the Impasse in Modern American Social Thought*. Ithaca, N.Y.: Cornell University Press, 2000.
McCartin, Joseph A. *Labor's Great War: The Struggle for Industrial Democracy and the Origins of Modern American Labor Relations, 1912–1921*. Chapel Hill: University of North Carolina Press, 1997.
McCarthy, Timothy G. *The Catholic Tradition: The Church in the Twentieth Century*. Rev. and exp. 2nd ed. Chicago: Loyola Press, 1998.
McCool, Gerald. *From Unity to Pluralism: The Internal Evolution of Thomism*. New York: Fordham University Press, 1989.
———. *The Neo-Thomists*. Milwaukee, Wisc.: Marquette University Press, 1994.
McDermott, Gerald R. *One Holy and Happy Society: The Public Theology of Jonathan Edwards*. University Park, Penn.: Pennsylvania State University Press, 1992.
McElroy, Robert W. *The Search for an American Public Theology: The Contribution of John Courtney Murray*. New York: Paulist Press, 1989.
McGraw, Barbara A. *Rediscovering America's Sacred Ground: Public Religion and Pursuit of the Good in a Pluralistic America*. Albany: State University of New York Press, 2003.
McGreevy, John T. *Parish Boundaries: The Catholic Encounter with Race in the Twentieth-Century Urban North*. Chicago: University of Chicago Press, 1996.
McMath, Robert C., Jr. *American Populism: A Social History, 1877–1898*. New York: Hill and Wang, 1993.
McShane, Joseph M. *"Sufficiently Radical": Catholicism, Progressivism, and the Bishops Program of 1919*. Washington, DC: Catholic University of America Press, 1986.
Merriman, Brigid O'Shea. *Searching for Christ: The Spirituality of Dorothy Day*. Notre Dame, Ind.: University of Notre Dame Press, 1994.
Miller, Vincent J. *Consuming Religion: Christian Faith and Practice in a Consumer Culture*. New York: Continuum, 2004.
Misner, Paul. *Social Catholicism in Europe*. New York: Crossroad Publishing, 1991.
Mitchell, John J. *Critical Voices in American Economic Thought*. New York: Paulist Press, 1991.
Molony, John. *The Worker Question: A New Historical Perspective on "Rerum Novarum."* Dublin: Gill and Macmillan, 1991.
Montgomery, David. *The Fall of the House of Labor: The Workplace, the State, and American Labor Activism, 1865–1925*. New York: Cambridge University Press, 1987.
Mooney, Christopher F. *Public Virtue: Law and the Social Character of Religion*. Notre Dame, Ind.: University of Notre Dame Press, 1986.
Moore, R. Lawrence. *Religious Outsiders and the Making of Americans*. New York: Oxford University Press, 1986.

———. *Selling God: American Religion in the Marketplace of Culture*. New York: Oxford University Press, 1994.

Moorehead, James H. *World without End: Mainstream American Visions of the Last Things, 1880–1925*. Bloomington: Indiana University Press, 1999.

Morris, Charles R. *American Catholic: The Saints and Sinners Who Built America's Most Powerful Church*. New York: Vintage, 1997.

Munier, Joseph David. *Some American Approximations to Pius XI's "Industries and Professions."* Washington, DC: Catholic University of America Press, 1943.

Murray, John Courtney. *We Hold These Truths: Catholic Reflections on the American Proposition*. Kansas City, Mo.: Sheed and Ward, 1988.

Nelson, Bruce. *Divided We Stand: American Workers and the Struggle for Black Equality*. Princeton, N.J.: Princeton University Press, 2001.

Neuhaus, Richard John. *The Naked Public Square: Religion and Democracy in America*. 2nd ed. Grand Rapids, Mich.: Eerdmans, 1995.

———. *Time toward Home: The American Experiment as Revelation*. New York: Seabury Press, 1975.

Niebuhr, H. Richard. *The Responsible Self*. New York: Harper and Row, 1963.

Niebuhr, Reinhold. *The Irony of American History*. New York: Charles Scribner's Sons, 1952.

———. *Moral Man and Immoral Society*. New York: Charles Scribner's Sons, 1960.

Nisbet, Robert A. *The Quest for Community: A Study in the Ethics of Order and Freedom*. San Francisco: Institute for Contemporary Studies Press, 1990.

Nordholt, Jan Willem Schulte. *Woodrow Wilson: A Life for World Peace*. Berkeley: University of California Press, 1991.

Oates, Mary Jo. *The Catholic Philanthropic Tradition in America*. Bloomington: Indiana University Press, 1995.

O'Brien, David J. *American Catholics and Social Reform: The New Deal Years*. New York: Oxford University Press, 1968.

———. *Public Catholicism*. Maryknoll, N.Y.: Orbis, 1996.

———. *The Renewal of American Catholicism*. New York: Doubleday, 1972.

O'Connor, Alice. *Poverty Knowledge: Social Science, Social Policy, and the Poor in Twentieth-Century U.S. History*. Princeton, N.J.: Princeton University Press, 2001.

O'Connor, Brian. *Civil Society: The Underpinnings of American Democracy*. Hanover, N.H.: Tufts University, 1999.

O'Rourke, Lawrence M. *Geno: The Life and Mission of Geno Baroni*. New York: Paulist Press, 1991.

Orren, Karen. *Belated Feudalism: Labor, the Law, and Liberal Development in the United States*. New York: Cambridge University Press, 1991.

O'Toole, James M. *Militant and Triumphant: William Henry O'Connell and the Catholic Church in Boston, 1859–1944*. Notre Dame, Ind.: University of Notre Dame Press, 1992.

Patterson, James T. *America's Struggle against Poverty in the Twentieth Century*. Cambridge, Mass.: Harvard University Press, 2000.

Pecklers, Keith F. *The Unread Vision: The Liturgical Movement in the Unites States of America, 1926–1955*. Collegeville, Minn.: Liturgical Press, 1998.

Phelan, Craig. *Divided Loyalties: The Public and Private Life of Labor Leader John Mitchell*. Albany: State University of New York Press, 1994.

———. *Grand Master Workman: Terence Powderly and the Knights of Labor*. Westport, Conn.: Greenwood Press, 2000.

———. *William Green: Biography of a Labor Leader*. Albany: State University of New York Press, 1989.

Phillips, Paul T. *A Kingdom on Earth: Anglo-American Social Christianity, 1880–1940*. University Park: Pennsylvania State University Press, 1996.

Piehl, Mel. *Breaking Bread: The Catholic Worker and the Origins of American Catholic Social Radicalism*. Philadelphia: New Society Publishers, 1983.

Porter, Jean. *Natural and Divine Law: Reclaiming the Tradition for Christian Ethics*. Grand Rapids, Mich.: Eerdmans, 1999.

Porterfield, Amanda. *The Transformation of American Religion: The Story of a Late Twentieth-Century Awakening*. New York: Oxford University Press, 2001.

Putnam, Robert D. *Bowling Alone: The Collapse and Revival of American Community*. New York: Simon and Schuster, 2000.

Rauschenbusch, Walter. *Christianity and the Social Crisis*. Louisville, Ky.: Westminster John Knox Press, 1991.

———. *A Theology for the Social Gospel*. Nashville, Tenn.: Abingdon Press, 1990.

Richey, Ronald C., and Donald G. Jones, eds. *American Civil Religion*. New York: Harper and Row, 1974.

Rifkin, Jeremy. *The End of Work: The Decline of the Global Labor Force and the Dawn of the Post-market Era*. New York: G. P. Putnam's Sons, 1996.

Roberts, Nancy L. *Dorothy Day and the Catholic Worker*. Albany: State University of New York Press, 1984.

Rodgers, Daniel T. *Atlantic Crossings: Social Politics in a Progressive Age*. Cambridge, Mass.: Harvard University Press, 1998.

Roediger, David R. *The Wages of Whiteness: Race and the Making of the American Working Class*. Rev. ed. New York: Verso, 2000.

Rourke, Thomas R. *A Conscience as Large as the World*. Lanham, Md.: Rowman and Littlefield, 1997.

Ryan, John A. *Capital and Labor*. Huntington, Ind.: Our Sunday Visitor Press, 1920.

———. *Economic Justice: Selections from "Distributive Justice" and "A Living Wage."* Edited by Harlan B. Beckley. Louisville, Ky.: Westminster John Knox Press, 1996.

Schor, Juliet B. *The Overworked American: The Unexpected Decline of Leisure*. New York: Basic Books, 1992.

Schuck, Michael J. *That They Be One: The Social Teaching of the Papal Encyclicals, 1740–1989*. Washington, DC: Georgetown University Press 1991.

Schulman, Bruce J. *The Seventies: The Great Shift in American Culture, Society, and Politics*. New York: Free Press, 2001.

Seaton, Douglas P. *Catholics and Radicals: The Association of Catholic Trade Unionists and the American Labor Movement from Depression to Cold War*. Lewisburg, Penn.: Bucknell University Press, 1981.

Sellers, Charles. *The Market Revolution: Jacksonian America, 1815–1846*. New York: Oxford University Press, 1991.

Shields, John C. *The American Aeneas: Classical Origins of the American Self*. Knoxville: University of Tennessee Press, 2001.

Shklar, Judith N. *American Citizenship: The Quest for Inclusion*. Cambridge, Mass.: Harvard University Press, 1991.

Silk, Mark. *Spiritual Politics: Religion and America since World War II*. New York: Simon and Schuster, 1988.

Slawson, Douglas J. *The Foundations and First Decade of the National Catholic Welfare Council*. Washington, DC: Catholic University of America Press, 1992.

Spalding, Matthew, and Patrick J. Garrity. *A Sacred Union of Citizens: George Washington's Farewell Address and the American Character*. Lanham, Md.: Rowman and Littlefield, 1996.

Sparr, Arnold. *To Promote, Defend, and Redeem: The Catholic Literary Revival and the Cultural Transformation of American Catholicism, 1920–1960*. Westport, Conn.: Greenwood Press, 1990.

Stone, Brad. *Robert Nisbet: Communitarian Traditionalist*. Wilmington, Del.: ISI Books, 2000.

Sullivan, Patrick J. *Blue Collar—Roman Collar—White Collar: U.S. Catholic Involvement in Labor Management Controversies, 1960–1980*. Lanham, Md.: University Press of America, 1987.

Sutton, William R. *Journeymen for Jesus: Evangelical Artisans Confront Capitalism in Jacksonian Baltimore*. University Park: Pennsylvania State University Press, 1998.

Sweeney, John J. *America Needs a Raise: Fighting for Economic Security and Social Justice*. Boston: Houghton Mifflin, 1996.

Thiemann, Ronald E. *Constructing a Public Theology: The Church in a Pluralistic Culture*. Louisville, Ky.: Westminster John Knox Press, 1991.

———. *Religion in Public Life*. Washington, DC: Georgetown University Press, 1996.

Tocqueville, Alexis de. *Democracy in America*. New York: Harper Collins 1988.

Trehey, Harold Francis. *Foundations of a Modern Guild System*. Washington, DC: Catholic University of America Press, 1940.

Vaught, David. *Cultivating California: Growers, Specialty Crops and Labor, 1875–1920*. Baltimore: Johns Hopkins Press, 1999.

Weiler, Paul C. *Governing the Workplace: The Future of Labor and Employment Law*. Cambridge, Mass.: Harvard University Press, 1990.

Weir, Robert E. *Beyond Labor's Veil: The Culture of the Knights of Labor*. University Park: Pennsylvania State University Press, 1996.

Werner, Stephen A. *Prophet of the Christian Social Manifesto: Joseph Husslein, S.J., His Life, Work, and Social Thought*. Milwaukee, Wisc.: Marquette University Press, 2001.

Wilson, John F. *Public Religion in American Culture*. Philadelphia: Temple University Press, 1979.

Wilson, William Julius. *When Work Disappears: The World of the New Urban Poor*. New York: Alfred A. Knopf, 1996.

Wuthnow, Robert. *Christianity and Civil Society: The Contemporary Debate*. Valley Forge, Penn.: Trinity Press International, 1997.

Young, Marilyn. *The Vietnam Wars, 1945–1990*. New York: Harper Perennial, 1991.

Zieger, Robert H. *American Workers, American Unions*. 2nd ed. Baltimore: Johns Hopkins University Press, 1994.

Zoller, Michael. *Washington and Rome: Catholicism in American Culture*. Notre Dame, Ind.: University of Notre Dame Press, 1999.

Zweig, Michael. *The Working Class Majority: America's Best Kept Secret*. Ithaca, N.Y.: Cornell University Press, 2000.

Articles

Abell, Aaron I. "American Catholic Reaction to Industrial Conflict." *Catholic Historical Review* 41 (1955): 385–407.

———. "The Bishop's Program of Social Reconstruction." In *American Catholic Teaching on Social Questions*, edited by Aaron I. Abell. New York: Bobbs-Merrill, 1968.

———. "The Catholic Factor in Urban Welfare: The Early Period, 1850–1880." *Review of Politics* 14 (1952): 289–324.

———. "Monsignor John A. Ryan: An Historical Interpretation." *Catholic Historical Review* 8 (1946): 128–34.

———. "Origins of Catholic Social Reform in the United States: Ideological Aspects." *Review of Politics* 11 (1949): 295–309.

———. "The Reception of Leo XIII's Labor Encyclical in America, 1891–1919." *Review of Politics* 7 (1945): 464–95.

Arnal, Oscar L. "Toward a Lay Apostolate of the Worker: Three Decades of Conflict for the French Jeunesse Ouvriere Chretienne (1927–1956)." *Catholic Historical Review* 73 (1987): 211–27.

Arx, Jeffrey von. "Cardinal Henry Edward Manning." In *Varieties of Ultramontanism*, edited by Jeffrey von Arx, 61–84. Washington, DC: Catholic University of America Press, 1998.

Avella, Steven M. "Reynold Hillenbrand and Chicago Catholicism." *U.S. Catholic Historian* 9 (1990): 335–51.

Barrett, James R. "Militants and Migrants: Immigrant Workers in the United States, 1880–1920." *International Labor and Working-Class History* 37 (1990): 41–51.

Baxter, Michael J. "Following Jesus at the Job Fair." *Logos* 3 (2000): 15–33.

Bellah, Robert N. "Civil Religion in America." *Daedalus* 96 (1967): 1–21.

———. "Is There a Common American Culture? Diversity, Identity, and Morality in American Public Life." In *The Power of Religious Publics: Staking Claims in American Society*, edited by William H. Swatos Jr. and James K. Wellman Jr., 53–67. Westport, Conn.: Praeger, 1999.

———. "The Quest for the Self." *Philosophy and Theology* 2 (1988): 374–86.

———. "Religion and the Legitimation of the American Republic." In *Varieties of Civil Religion*, edited by Robert N. Bellah and Phillip E. Hammond. San Francisco: Harper and Row, 1980.

———. "Religion and the Shape of National Culture." *America* 181 (July 31–August 7, 1999): 9–14.

Beretta, Simona. "Wealth Creation and Distribution in the Global Economy: Human Labor, Development and Subsidiarity." *Communio* 27 (2000): 474–89.

Berman, Hyman. "Labor." In *Dictionary of American History*, rev. ed., edited by Louise Bilebof Ketz, 4:60–78. New York: Charles Scribner's Sons, 1976.

Betten, Neil. "John Ryan and the Social Action Department." *Thought* 46 (1971): 227–46.

———. "Urban Catholicism and Industrial Reform 1937–1940." *Thought* 44 (1969): 434–50.

Billington, Monroe L. "Roosevelt, the New Deal, and the Clergy." *Mid-America* 54 (1972): 20–33.

Billington, Ray Allen. "American Protective Association." In *Dictionary of American History*, rev. ed., edited by Louise Bilebof Ketz, 1:111. New York: Charles Scribner's Sons, 1976.

Blantz, Thomas E. "Francis J. Haas: Priest and Government Servant." *Catholic Historical Review* 59 (1972): 571–92.

———. "Francis Joseph Haas (1889–1953)." In *The Encyclopedia of American Catholic History*, edited by Michael Glazier and Thomas J. Shelley, 609–10. Collegeville, Minn.: Liturgical Press, 1997.

———. "George N. Shuster and American Catholic Intellectual Life." In *Studies in Church History in Honor of John Tracy Ellis*, edited by Nelson H. Minnich, Robert B. Eno, and Robert F. Trisco, 345–65. Wilmington, Del.: Michael Glazier, 1985.

Bole, William. "The Labor Movement and American Catholics." In *The Encyclopedia of American Catholic History*, edited by Michael Glazier and Thomas J. Shelley, 783–87. Collegeville, Minn.: Liturgical Press, 1997.

Bowden, Witt. "William Bauchop Wilson." In *Dictionary of American Biography*, edited by Dumas Malone, 10:348–49. New York: Charles Scribner's Sons, 1936.

Breitenbach, William. "Religious Affections and Religious Affectations: Antinomianism and Hypocrisy in the Writings of Edwards and Franklin." In *Benjamin Franklin, Jonathan Edwards, and the Representation of American Culture*, edited by Barbara B. Berg and Harry S. Stout. New York: Oxford University Press, 1993.

Brinkley, Alan. "The Problem of American Conservatism." *American Historical Review* 99 (1994): 409–29.

Broderick, Francis L. "The Encyclicals and Social Action: Is John A. Ryan Typical?" *Catholic Historical Review* 55 (1969): 1–6.

Brown, Bernard E. "Tocqueville and Publius." In *Reconsidering Tocqueville's Democracy in America*, edited by Abraham S. Eisenstadt. New Brunswick, N.J.: Rutgers University Press, 1988.

Browne, Henry J. "Archbishop Hughes and Western Colonization." *Catholic Historical Review* 36 (1950): 257–83.

———. "Peter E. Dietz, Pioneer Planner of Catholic Social Action." *Catholic Historical Review* 33 (1948): 448–56.

———. "Terence V. Powderly and Church–Labor Difficulties of the Early 1880s." *Catholic Historical Review* 32 (1946): 1–27.

Brusher, Joseph "Peter C. Yorke and the A.P.A. in San Francisco." *Catholic Historical Review* 37 (1951): 129–50.

———. "Rerum Novarum in the San Francisco Strike of 1901." *American Ecclesiastical Review* 141 (1959): 103–16.

Burns, Jeffrey M. "Cesar Chavez (1927–1993)." In *The Encyclopedia of American Catholic History*, edited by Michael Glazier and Thomas J. Shelley, 321–24. Collegeville, Minn.: Liturgical Press, 1997.

———. "John Augustine Ryan." In *The New Dictionary of Catholic Social Thought*, edited by Judith A. Dwyer, 851–56. Collegeville, Minn.: Liturgical Press, 1994.

———. "John Augustine Ryan (1865–1945)." In *The Encyclopedia of American Catholic History*, edited by Michael Glazier and Thomas J. Shelley, 1226–30. Collegeville, Minn.: Liturgical Press, 1997.

———. "Knights of Labor." In *The Encyclopedia of American Catholic History*, edited by Michael Glazier and Thomas J. Shelley, 771–77. Collegeville, Minn.: Liturgical Press, 1997.

———. "Knights of Labor." In *The New Dictionary of Catholic Social Thought*, edited by Judith A. Dwyer, 513–15. Collegeville, Minn.: Liturgical Press, 1994.

———. "Peter Yorke (1864–1925)." In *The Encyclopedia of American Catholic History*, edited by Michael Glazier and Thomas J. Shelley, 1533–34. Collegeville, Minn.: Liturgical Press, 1997.

Butler, Gregory S. "Visions of a Nation Transformed: Modernity and Ideology in Wilson's Political Thought." *Journal of Church and State* 39 (1997).

Byron, William J. "Catholicity and Creativity in the Collective Bargaining Process." In *Issues in the Labor–Management Dialogue: Church Perspectives*, edited by Adam J. Maida, 207–15. St. Louis, Mo.: Catholic Health Association, 1982.

Cady, Linell E. "H. Richard Niebuhr and the Task of a Public Theology." In *The Legacy of H. Richard Niebuhr*, edited by Ronald F. Thiemann, 107–26. Minneapolis: Fortress Press, 1991.

Cahill, Edward. "The Catholic Social Movement: Historical Aspects." In *Readings in Moral Theology No. 5: Official Catholic Social Teaching*, edited by Charles E. Curran and Richard A. McCormick, 3–31. New York: Paulist Press, 1986.

Campbell, Debra. "A Catholic Salvation Army: David Goldstein, Pioneer Lay Evangelist." *Church History* 52 (1983): 322–32.

———. "David Goldstein and the Rise of the Catholic Campaigners for Christ." *Catholic Historical Review* 72 (1986): 33–50.

———. "The Heyday of Catholic Action and the Lay Apostolate, 1919–1959." In *Transforming Parish Ministries: The Changing Roles of Catholic Clergy, Laity, and Women Religious*, edited by Jay Dolan, R. Scott Appleby, Patricia Byrne, and Debra Campbell, 222–52. New York: Crossroad, 1989.

Carey, Patrick W. "American Catholic Romanticism, 1830–1888." *Catholic Historical Review* 74 (1988): 590–606.

———. "Republicanism within American Catholicism, 1785–1860." *Journal of the Early Republic* 3 (1983): 413–37.

Chenu, Marie Dominique. "Catholic Action and the Mystical Body." In *Restoring All Things: A Guide to Catholic Action*, edited by John Fitzsimons and Paul McGuire, 1–15. New York: Sheed and Ward, 1938.

Chinnici, Joseph P. "Virgil Michel and the Tradition of Affective Prayer." *Worship* 62 (1988): 225–36.

Chmielowski, Philip J. "Copartnership." In *The New Dictionary of Catholic Social Thought*, edited by Judith A. Dwyer, 237–41. Collegeville, Minn.: Liturgical Press, 1994.

———. "Oswald von Nell-Breuning." In *The New Dictionary of Catholic Social Thought*, edited by Judith A. Dwyer, 676–78. Collegeville, Minn.: Liturgical Press, 1994.

Cline, Catherine Ann. "Priest in the Coal Fields: The Story of Father Curran." *Records of the American Catholic Historical Society* 68 (1952): 67–84.

Cochran, Clarke E. "Sacrament and Solidarity: Catholic Social Thought and Health Care Policy Reforms." *Journal of Church and State* 4 (1999): 475–98.

Coleman, John A. "Neither Liberal nor Socialist: The Originality of Catholic Social Teaching." In *One Hundred Years of Catholic Social Thought, Celebration, and Challenge*, edited by John A. Coleman, 25–42. Maryknoll, N.Y.: Orbis, 1991.

———. "Vision and Praxis in American Theology: Orestes Brownson, John A. Ryan, and John Courtney Murray." *Theological Studies* 37 (1991): 3–40.

Cort, John C. "Association of Catholic Trade Unionists." In *The Encyclopedia of American Catholic History*, edited by Michael Glazier and Thomas J. Shelley, 300–302. Collegeville, Minn.: Liturgical Press, 1997.

———. "Association of Catholic Trade Unionists." In *The New Dictionary of Catholic Social Thought*, edited by Judith A. Dwyer, 51–54. Collegeville, Minn.: Liturgical Press, 1994.

———. "The Association of Catholic Trade Unionists and the Auto Workers." *U.S. Catholic Historian* 9 (1990): 335–51.

———. "The Labor Movement." *Commonweal* 51 (December 23, 1949): 316–18.

Cronin, John F. "Forty Years Later: Reflections and Reminiscences." In *Readings in Moral Theology No. 5: Official Catholic Social Teaching*, edited by Charles E. Curran and Richard A. McCormick, 69–76. New York: Paulist Press, 1986.

———. "Quadragesimo Anno: An American Symposium." *Social Order* 6 (1956): 2–13.

Craypo, Charles, and Patrick J. Sullivan. "Unions and Catholic Health Care Facilities." In *Issues in the Labor–Management Dialogue: Catholic Perspectives*, edited by Adam J. Maida, 14–46. St. Louis, Mo.: Catholic Health Association, 1982.

Cross, Robert D. "The Changing Image of the City among American Catholics." *Catholic Historical Review* 48 (1962): 33–52.

Curran, Charles E. "Natural Law in Moral Theology." In *Readings in Moral Theology No. 7*, edited by Charles E. Curran and Richard A. McCormick, 247–95. New York: Paulist, 1991.

Curran, Robert Emmett. "Confronting 'The Social Question': American Catholic Thought and the Socio-Economic Thought in the Nineteenth Century." *U.S. Catholic Historian* 5 (1986): 186–94.

———. "'The Finger of God Is Here': The Advent of the Miraculous in the Nineteenth-Century American Catholic Community." *Catholic Historical Review* 71 (1987): 41–61.

———. "The McGlynn Affair and the Shaping of the New Conservatism in American Catholicism, 1886–1894." *Catholic Historical Review* 66 (1980): 184–204.

———. "Prelude to 'Americanism': The New York Academia and Clericalism in the Late Nineteenth Century." *Church History* 47 (1978): 48–65.

Daniel, Cletus E. "Cesar Chavez and the Unionization of California Farm Workers." In *Labor Leaders in America*, edited by Melvyn Dubofsky and Warren Van Tine, 350–82. Urbana: University of Illinois Press, 1987.

Davis, Allen F. "The Women's Trade Union League: Origins and Organization." *Labor History* 5 (1064): 3–17.

Deedy, John G., Jr. "The Catholic Press: The Why and Wherefore." In *The Religious Press in America*, edited by Martin E. Marty, 67–121. New York: Holt, Rinehart, and Winston, 1963.

De Hueck, Catherine. "I Saw Christ Today." *Orate Fratres* 12 (1938): 305–10.

Delio, Ilia. "The First Catholic Social Gospelers: Women Religious in the Nineteenth Century." *U.S. Catholic Historian* 13 (1995): 1–22.

Deslippe, Dennis A. "'A Revolution of Its Own': The Social Doctrine of the Association of Catholic Trade Unionists in Detroit, 1939–1950." *Records of the American Catholic Historical Society* 102 (1991): 19–36.

DeVault, Ileen A. "'Give the Boys a Trade': Gender and Job Choice in the 1890s." In *Work Engendered: Toward a New History of American Labor*, edited by Ava Baron, 191–215. Ithaca, N.Y.: Cornell University Press, 1991.

DiBacco, Thomas V. "National Association of Manufacturers (NAM)." In *Dictionary of American History*, rev. ed., edited by Louise Bilebof Ketz, 4:461. New York: Charles Scribner's Sons, 1976.

Doherty, Robert E. "Thomas J. Hagerty, the Church, and Socialism." *Labor History* 3 (1962): 39–56.

Donahue, James A. "Religious Institutions as Moral Agents: Toward an Ethics of Organizational Character." In *Issues in the Labor–Management Dialogue: Church Perspectives*, edited by Adam J. Maida, 139–59. St. Louis, Mo.: Catholic Health Association, 1982.

Donahue, Thomas R. "From Rerum Novarum to Laborem Exercens: A United States Labor Perspective." In *Readings in Moral Theology No. 5: Official Catholic Social Teaching*, edited by Charles E. Curran and Richard A. McCormick, 384–410. New York: Paulist Press, 1986.

Donohue, Hugh A. "Collective Bargaining for Farm Workers." *Catholic Mind* 68 (January 1970): 24–27.

Dorn, Jacob H. "The Rural Ideal and Agrarian Realities: Arthur E. Holt and the Vision of a Decentralized America in the Interwar Years." *Church History* 52 (1983): 50–65.

Dowling, Austin. "The National Catholic Welfare Conference." *Ecclesiastical Review* 9 (October 1928): 337–54.

Dubofsky, Melvyn. "Organized Labor and the Immigrant in New York City, 1900–1918." *Labor History* 2 (1961): 182–201.

———. "Success and Failure of Socialism in New York City, 1900–1918." *Labor History* 9 (1968): 361–75.

Editorial. "A New Deal for the Negro." *America* 53 (May 11, 1935): 98–99.

———. "The President's Forecast." *America* 53 (May 11, 1935): 97–98.

———. "The President's Plan." *Commonweal* 18 (August 4, 1933): 335–36.

———. "The Wagner Bill." *America* 50 (March 24, 1934): 582.

Egan, John J. "Liturgy and Justice: An Unfinished Agenda." *Origins* 12 (September 22, 1983): 245–53.

Ellis, William E. "Catholicism and the Southern Ethos." *Catholic Historical Review* 69 (1983): 41–50.

Ellwood, Robert S. "Occult Movements in America." In *Encyclopedia of the American Religious Experience, Studies of Traditions and Movements*, edited by Charles H. Lippy and Peter W. Williams, 2:711–22. New York: Charles Scribner's Sons, 1988.

Elsbernd, Mary. "Work and Workers in the Pastoral Letters of the United States Conference of Bishops." *Louvain Studies* 19 (1994): 212–34.

Euart, Sharon. "Ten Years after the Pastoral on the Economy." *Origins* 26 (November 21, 1994).

Faherty, William Barnaby. "The Clergyman and Labor Progress: Cornelius O'Leary and the Knights of Labor." *Labor History* 11 (1970): 175–89.

Faue, Elizabeth. "Paths of Unionization: Community, Bureaucracy, and Gender in the Minneapolis Labor Movement of the 1930s." In *"We Are All Leaders": The Alternative Unionism of the Early 1930s*, edited by Staughton Lynd, 172–98. Urbana: University of Illinois Press, 1996.

Fine, Sidney. "The General Motors Sit-Down Strike: A Re-examination." *American Historical Review* 70 (1965): 691–712.

Finn, Daniel Rush. "Economic Order." In *The New Dictionary of Catholic Social Thought*, edited by Judith A. Dwyer, 310–27. Collegeville, Minn.: Liturgical Press, 1994.

Fiorenza, Francis Schussler. "Social Mission." In *The New Dictionary of Catholic Social Thought*, edited by Judith A. Dwyer, 151–71. Collegeville, Minn.: Liturgical Press, 1994.

Fisher, James T. "John M. Corridan, S.J., and the Battle for the Soul of the Waterfront, 1948–1954." *U.S. Catholic Historian* 16 (1998): 71–87.

Fogarty, Gerald P. "Cardinal Henry Edward Manning." In *Varieties of Ultramontanism*, edited by Jeffrey von Arx, 118–46. Washington, DC: Catholic University of America, 1998.

———. "The Catholic Hierarchy in the United States between the Third Plenary Council and the Condemnation of Americanism." *U.S. Catholic Historian* 11 (1993): 19–35.

Foner, Philip S. "Songs of the Eight Hour Movement." *Labor History* 10 (1972): 571–88.

Fones-Wolf, Elizabeth, and Ken Fones-Wolf. "Lending a Hand to Labor: James Myers and the Federal Council of Churches, 1926–1947." *Church History* 68 (1999): 62–86.

Fraser, Nancy, and Linda Gordon. "A Genealogy of *Dependency*: Tracing a Keyword of the U.S. Welfare State." *Signs* 19 (1994): 309–36.

Gabin, Nancy. "'They Have Placed a Penalty on Womanhood': The Protest Actions of Women Auto Workers in Detroit-Area UAW Locals, 1945–1947." *Feminist Studies* 8 (1982): 373–98.

———. "Time Out of Mind: The UAW's Response to Female Labor Laws and Mandatory Overtime in the 1960s." In *Work Engendered: Toward a New History of American Labor*, edited by Ava Baron, 351–74. Ithaca, N.Y.: Cornell University Press, 1991.

Gall, Gilbert. "Labor Unions." In *Dictionary of American History: Supplement*, edited by Robert H. Ferrill and Joan Hoff, 356–57. New York: Charles Scribner's Sons, 1996.

Gauchat, William. "Helping the Hobo to God." *Orate Fratres* 15 (1941): 385–89.

Gauvreau, Michael. "From Rechristianization to Contestation: Catholic Values and Quebec Society, 1931–1970." *Church History* 69 (2000): 803–33.

Gerstle, Gary. "The Protean Character of American Liberalism." *American Historical Review* 99 (1994): 1043–73.

Giblin, Marie J. "Quadragesimo Anno." In *The New Dictionary of Catholic Social Thought*, edited by Judith A. Dwyer, 802–13. Collegeville, Minn.: Liturgical Press, 1994.

Gini, Al. "Meaningful Work and the Rights of the Worker: A Commentary on *Rerum Novarum* and *Laborem Exercens*." *Thought* 67 (1992): 225–39.

Gleason, Philip. "American Catholics and Liberalism." In *Catholicism and Liberalism, Contributions to American Public Philosophy*, edited by R. Bruce Douglas and David Hollenbach, 45–75. New York: Cambridge University Press, 1994.

———. "The Catholic Church in American Public Life in the Twentieth Century." *Logos* 3 (2000): 85–99.

Gobel, Thomas. "Becoming American: Ethnic Workers and the Rise of the CIO." *Labor History* 29 (1988): 173–98.

Gould, Lewis L. "The Gilded Age." In *The Oxford Companion to U.S. History*, edited by Paul S. Boyer, 308–10. New York: Oxford University Press, 2001.

Gould, Rebecca Kneale. "Getting (Not Too Close) to Nature: Modern Homesteading as Lived Religion in America." In *Lived Religion in America: Toward a History of Practice*, edited by David D. Hall, 217–42. Princeton, N.J.: Princeton University Press, 1997.

Green, Archie. "The Death of Mother Jones." *Labor History* 1 (1960): 68–80.

Green, Thomas R. "The Catholic Conference on Industrial Problems in Normalcy and Depression." *Catholic Historical Review* 77 (1991): 437–69.

Greenbaum, Fred. "The Social Ideas of Samuel Gompers." *Labor History* 7 (1966): 35–61.

Greene, Julie, "Dinner-Pail Politics: Employers, Workers, and Partisan Culture in the Progressive Era." In *Labor Histories: Class, Politics, and the Working-Class Experience*, edited by Eric Arnesen, Julie Greene, and Bruce Laurie, 71–96. Urbana: University of Illinois Press, 1998.

———. "Negotiating the State: Frank Walsh and the Transformation of Labor's Political Culture in Progressive America." In *Organized Labor and American Politics, 1894–1994*, edited by Kevin Boyle, 71–102. Albany: State University of New York Press, 1998.

Greenleaf, William. "Clayton Antitrust Act." In *Dictionary of American History*, rev. ed., edited by Louise Bilebof Ketz, 2:71–72. New York: Charles Scribner's Sons, 1976.

Gribble, Richard. "A Conservative Voice for Black Catholics: The Case of James Martin, Gillis, C.S.P." *Catholic Historical Review* 85 (1999): 420–34.

———. "*Rerum Novarum* and the San Francisco Labor Movement." *U.S. Catholic Historian* 9 (1990): 275–88.

———. "Social Catholicism Engages the American State: The Contribution of Archbishop Edward J. Hanna." *Journal of Church and State* 42 (2000): 737–58.

Griffin, John J. "The Spiritual Foundations of Catholic Action." *Orate Fratres* 9 (1935): 455–64.

Grob, Gerald N. "The Knights of Labor, Politics, and Populism." *Mid-America* 40 (1958): 3–21.

———. "Terence V. Powderly and the Knights of Labor." *Mid-America* 39 (1957): 39–55.

Grootaers, Jan. "The Drama Continues between the Acts: The 'Second Preparation' and Its Opponents." In *History of Vatican II*. Vol. 2, *The Formation of the Council's Identity: First Period and Intercession, October 1962–September 1963*, edited by Giuseppe Alberigo and Joseph A. Komonchak, 359–513. Maryknoll, N.Y.: Orbis, 1997.

Guilday, Peter. "The Catholic Church in the United States: A Sesquicentennial Essay." *Thought* 1 (1926): 3–20.

Gutman, Herbert G. "Protestantism and the Labor Movement: The Christian Spirit of the Gilded Age." *American Historical Review* 62 (1966): 74–101.

Hammond, Phillip E. "Constitutional Faith, Legitimating Myth, Civil Religion." *Law and Social Inquiry* 14 (1989): 377–91.

Handy, Robert T. "The American Religious Depression, 1925–1935." *Church History* 29 (1960): 3–16.

Harlow, Alvin F. "Collective Bargaining." In *Dictionary of American History*, rev. ed., edited by Louise Bilebof Ketz, 2:110–13. New York: Charles Scribner's Sons, 1976.

Harris, Howell John. "Industrial Democracy and Liberal Capitalism, 1890–1925." In *Industrial Democracy in America: The Ambiguous Promise*, edited by Nelson Lichtenstein and Howell John Harris, 43–66. New York: Cambridge University Press, 1996.

Harvey, Thomas J. "The Catholic Health Care Facility: Roots in the Gospel and in the Nation." In *Issues in the Labor–Management Dialogue: Church Perspectives*, edited by Adam J. Maida, 176–88. St. Louis, Mo.: Catholic Health Association, 1982.

Hatch, Nathan O. "The Democratization of Christianity and the Character of American Politics." In *Religion and American Politics from the Colonial Period to the 1980s*, edited by Mark A. Noll. New York: Oxford University Press, 1990.

Hehir, J. Bryan. "Church-State and Church-World: The Ecclesiological Implications." *Catholic Theological Society of America Proceedings* 41 (1986): 54–74.

———. "The Discipline and Dynamic of a Public Church." *Social Thought* 11 (1985): 4–8.

———. "Forum: Public Theology in Contemporary America." *Religion and American Culture* 10 (2000): 20–27.

———. "The Public Church: The Implications of Structural Pluralism." *Origins* 14 (May 31, 1984): 40–43.

Heideain, Eustas O. "Socialization." In *The New Dictionary of Catholic Social Thought*, edited by Judith A. Dwyer, 891–96. Collegeville, Minn.: Liturgical Press, 1994.

Hennesey, James. "Leo XIII's Thomistic Revival: A Political and Philosophical Event." In *Celebrating the Medieval Heritage: A Colloquy on the Thought of Aquinas and Bonaventure*, edited by David Tracy. Chicago: University of Chicago, 1978.

Henry, Patrick. "'And I Don't Care What It Is': The Tradition-History of a Civil Religion Proof-Text." *Journal of the American Academy of Religion* 49 (1981).

Himes, Kenneth R. "Eucharist and Justice: Assessing the Legacy of Virgil Michel." *Worship* 62 (1988): 201–24.

Hite, Jordan. "Members of Religious Comminutes and Unions." In *Issues in the Labor-Management Dialogue: Church Perspectives*, edited by Adam J. Maida, 91–111. St. Louis, Mo.: Catholic Health Association, 1982.

Holland, Joe. "The Call for a Prophetic Catholic Health Care System." In *Issues in the Labor-Management Dialogue: Church Perspectives*, edited by Adam J. Maida, 189–206. St. Louis, Mo.: Catholic Health Association, 1982.

Hollenbach, David. "Afterword: A Community of Freedom." In *Catholicism and Liberalism: Contributions to American Public Philosophy*, edited by R. Bruce Douglas and David Hollenbach, 323–43. New York: Cambridge University Press, 1994.

———. "Catholics as Citizens: Pastoral Challenges and Opportunities." *Logos* 3 (2000): 57–69.

———. "Civil Society: Beyond the Public-Private Dichotomy." *Responsive Community* 5 (1994–1995): 15–23.

———. "The Common Good in the Postmodern Epoch: What Role for Theology?" In *Religion, Ethics, and the Common Good*, edited by James Donohue and M. Theresa Moser, 3–22. Mystic: Twenty-third Publications, 1996.

———. "The Common Good Revisited." *Theological Studies* 50 (1989): 70–94.

———. "A Communitarian Reconstruction of Human Rights." In *Catholicism and Liberalsim: Contributions to American Public Philosophy*, edited by R. Bruce Douglass and David Hollenbach, 127–50. New York: Cambridge University Press, 1994.

———. "Contexts of the Political Role of Religion: Civil Society and Culture." *San Diego Law Review* 30 (1994): 879–901.

———. "Freedom and Truth: Religious Liberty as Immunity and Empowerment." In *John Courtney Murray and the Growth of Tradition*, edited by J. Leon Hooper and Todd David Whitmore, 129–48. Kansas City: Sheed and Ward, 1996.

———. "The Growing End of the Argument." *America* 153 (November 30, 1985): 563–66.

———. "The Market and Catholic Social Teaching." In *Outside the Market No Salvation?* edited by Dietmar Mieth and Marciano Vidal, 67–76. Maryknoll, N.Y.: Orbis, 1997.

———. "Politically Active Churches: Some Empirical Prolegomena to a Normative Approach." In *Religion and Contemporary Liberalism*, edited by Paul J. Weithman, 291–306. Notre Dame, Ind.: University of Notre Dame Press, 1997.

———. "Public Reason/Private Reason? A Response to Paul J. Weithman." *Journal of Religious Ethics* 22 (1994): 39–46.

———. "Public Theology in America: Some Questions for Catholicism after John Courtney Murray." *Theological Studies* 37 (1976): 290–303.

———. "Religion and Public Life." *Theological Studies* 52 (1991): 87–106.

———. "Virtue, the Common Good, and Democracy." In *New Communitarian Thinking: Persons, Virtues, Institutions, and Communities*, edited by Amitai Etzioni, 143–53. Charlottesville: University of Virginia Press, 1994.

Hollenbach, David, Robin Lovin, John A. Coleman, and J. Bryan Hehir, "Theology and Philosophy in Public: A Symposium on John Courtney Murray's Unfinished Agenda." *Theological Studies* 40 (1979): 700–715.

Hopkins, Vincent C. "New Deal." In *Dictionary of American History*, rev. ed., edited by Louise Bilebof Ketz, 5:43–48. New York: Charles Scribner's Sons, 1976.

Hughson, Thomas. "Public Catholicism: An American Prospect." *Theological Studies* 62 (2001): 701–29.

Hunnicutt, Benjamin K. "Monsignor John A. Ryan and the Shorter Hours of Labor: A Forgotten Vision of 'Genuine' Progress." *Catholic Historical Review* 69 (1983): 384–402.

Isacsson, Alfred. "Edward McGlynn (1837–1900)." In *The Encyclopedia of American Catholic History*, edited by Michael Glazier and Thomas J. Shelley, 882–85. Collegeville, Minn.: Liturgical Press, 1997.

Issel, William, and James Collins. "The Catholic Church and Organized Labor in San Francisco, 1932–1958." *Records of the American Catholic Historical Society* 109 (1999): 81–112.

Jacoby, Robin Miller. "The Women's Trade Union League and American Feminism." *Feminist Studies* 3 (1975): 126–40.

Jaeger, Leo. "The Liturgical Movement in Relation to Catholic Action." *Catholic Mind* 33 (1935): 11–18.

Jeffrey, Kirk. "The Family as Utopian Retreat from the City: The Nineteenth-Century Contribution." In *The Family, Communes and Utopian Societies*, edited by Sallie TeSelle, 21–41. New York: Harper and Row, 1972.

Joy, William. "The National Labor Relations Act: Ethical Considerations for Catholic Health Institutions." In *Issues in the Labor–Management Dialogue: Church Perspectives*, edited by Adam J. Maida, 47–61. St. Louis, Mo.: Catholic Health Association, 1982.

Kealy, Robert L., and James A. Serritella. "New Realities in Employment Matters: Counseling Catholic Health Care Institutions." In *Issues in the Labor–Management Dialogue: Church Perspectives*, edited by Adam J. Maida, 62–76. St. Louis, Mo.: Catholic Health Association, 1982.

Kelleher, Margaret M. "Liturgy and Social Transformation: Exploring the Relationship." *U.S. Catholic Historian* 16 (1998): 58–70.

Kelly, John E. "The Influence of Aquinas' Natural Law Theory on the Principle of 'Corporatism' in the Thought of Leo XIII and Pius XI." In *Things Old and New: Catholic Social Teaching Revisited*, edited by Francis P. McHugh and Samuel M. Natale, 104–43. Lanham, Md.: University Press of America, 1993.

Kenny, Kevin. "The Molly Maguires and the Catholic Church." *Labor History* 36 (1995): 345–76.

Kent, Peter C., and John F. Pollard. "A Diplomacy Unlike Any Other: Papal Diplomacy in the Nineteenth and the Twentieth Centuries." In *Papal Diplomacy in the Modern Age*, edited by Peter C. Kent and John F. Pollard, 11–21. Westport, Conn.: Praeger, 1994.

Kimmel, Michael S. "Baseball and the Reconstitution of American Masculinity, 1880–1920." In *Baseball History from Outside the Lines: A Reader*, edited by John E. Dreifort, 47–61. Lincoln: University of Nebraska Press, 2001.

Kleiler, Frank M. "National Labor Relations Act." In *Dictionary of American History*, rev. ed., edited by Louise Bilebof Ketz, 3:466–67. New York: Charles Scribner's Sons, 1976.

Komonchak, Joseph A. "The Significance of Vatican Council II for Ecclesiology." In *The Church as Gift*, edited by Peter Phan, 69–92. Collegeville, Minn.: Liturgical Press, 2000.

———. "Subsidiarity in the Church: The State of the Question." In *The Nature and Future of Episcopal Conferences*, edited by Herve Legrand, Julio Manzanares, and Antonio Garcia y Garcia, 298–349. Washington, DC: Catholic University of America Press, 1988.

———. "The Struggle for the Council during the Preparation for Vatican II." In *History of Vatican II*. Vol. 1, *Announcing and Preparing Vatican Council II: Toward a New Era in Catholicism*, edited by Giuseppe Alberigo and Joseph A. Komonchak, 157–356. Orbis: Maryknoll, 1995.

Kreuter, Joseph. "Catholic Action and the Liturgy." *Orate Fratres* 3 (1929): 165–70.

Laba, Gerald. "Renewing Person and Society: The Lay Retreat Movement as Presented in *The Sign*: 1921–1930." *Passionist*, no. 29 (1955): 21–30.

Labue, Wayne. "Public Theology and the Catholic Worker." *Cross Currents* 26 (1976): 270–85.

Lamb, Matthew. "Solidarity." In *The New Dictionary of Catholic Social Thought*, edited by Judith A. Dwyer, 908–12. Collegeville, Minn.: Liturgical Press, 1994.

Lamoureux, Patricia. "Irish Catholic Women and the Labor Movement." *U.S. Catholic Historian* 16 (1998): 24–44.

Larsen, Charles E. "Westbrook Pegler." In *Dictionary of American Biography, Supplement Eight 1965–1970*, edited by John A. Garraty and Mark C. Carnes, 497–99. New York: Charles Scribner's Sons, 1988.

Laslett, John H. M. "Haymarket, Henry George, and the Labor Upsurge in Britain and America during the Late 1880s." *International Labor and Working-Class History* 29 (1986): 62–82.

———. "Samuel Gompers and the Rise of American Business Unionism." In *Labor Leaders in America*, edited by Melvyn Dubofsky and Warren Van Tine, 62–88. Urbana: University of Illinois Press, 1987.

Lauer, Eugene F. "Service Strikes: The New Moral Dilemma." In *Issues in the Labor-Management Dialogue: Church Perspectives*, edited by Adam J. Maida, 77–90. St Louis: Catholic Health Association, 1982.

Lefebvre, G. "Catholic Action and the Liturgy." In *Restoring All Things: A Guide to Catholic Action*, edited by John Fitzsimons and Paul McGuire, 16–50. New York: Sheed and Ward, 1938.

Leonard, Thomas C. "John Thomas Flynn." In *Dictionary of American Biography: Supplement Seven, 1961–1965*, edited by John A. Garraty, 249–50. New York: Charles Scribner's Sons, 1981.

Lichtenstein, Nelson. "American Trade Unions and the 'Labor Question': Past and Present." In *What's Next for Organized Labor? Report of the Century Fund Task Force on the Future of Unions*, 57–117. New York: Century Foundation Press, 1999.

———. "Epilogue: Toward a New Century." In *Industrial Democracy in America: The Ambiguous Promise*, edited by Nelson Lichtenstein and Howell John Harris, 275–83. New York: Cambridge University Press, 1996.

———. "From Corporatism to Collective Bargaining: Organized Labor and the Eclipse of Social Democracy in the Postwar Era." In *The Rise and Fall of the New Deal Order, 1930–1980*, edited by Steve Fraser and Gary Gerstle, 122–52. Princeton, N.J.: Princeton University Press, 1989.

———. "Great Expectations: The Promise of Industrial Jurisprudence and Its Demise, 1930–1960." In *Industrial Democracy in America: The Ambiguous Promise*, edited by Nelson Lichtenstein and Howell John Harris, 113–41. New York: Cambridge University Press, 1996.

Lichtenstein, Nelson, and Howell John Harris. "Introduction: A Century of Industrial Democracy in America." In *Industrial Democracy in America: The Ambiguous Promise*, edited by Nelson Lichtenstein and Howell John Harris, 1–19. New York: Cambridge University Press, 1996.

Linder, Robert D. "Universal Pastor: President Bill Clinton's Civil Religion." *Journal of Church and State* 38 (1996): 733–49.

Link, Arthur S. "What Happened to the Progressive Movement in the 1920s?" *American Historical Review* 64 (1959): 833–51.

Lucey, Robert. "Apathy: Our Scourge." *Homiletic and Pastoral Review* 36 (1936): 468–77.

———. "Are We Fair to the Church?" *Commonweal* 28 (1938): 490–92, 521–33.

———. "Economic Disorder and Quadragesimo Anno." *Homiletic and Pastoral Review* 35 (1935): 858–64.

———. "Labor in the Recession." *Commonweal* 28 (1938): 47.

McAvoy, Thomas T. "American Catholics and the Second World War." *Review of Politics* 6 (1944): 131–50.

———. "Americanism: Fact and Fiction." *Catholic Historical Review* 31 (1945): 133–53.

———. "Bishop John Lancaster Spalding and the Catholic Minority (1877–1908)." *Review of Politics* 12 (1950): 3–19.

———. "The Catholic Church in the United States between Two Wars." *Review of Politics* 4 (1942): 409–31.

McCarraher, Eugene B. "The Church Irrelevant: Paul Hanly Furfey and the Future of American Catholic Radicalism." *Religion and American Culture* 7 (1997): 163–94.

McCarthy, Donald G. "The Catholic Vision of Work in the World." In *Issues in the Labor–Management Dialogue: Church Perspectives*, edited by Adam J. Maida, 1–13. St. Louis, Mo.: Catholic Health Association, 1982.

McCartin, Joseph A. "'An American Feeling': Workers, Managers, and the Struggle over Industrial Democracy in the World War I Era." In *Industrial Democracy in America, The Ambiguous Promise*, edited by Nelson Lichtenstein and Howell John Harris, 67–86. New York: Cambridge University Press, 1996.

McGowan, Raymond A. "Government and Social Justice." *Catholic Mind* 36 (1938): 222–26.

———. "An Indictment of the Wage System." *Catholic Charities Review* 1 (1917): 75–79.

———. "The National Industrial Recovery Act." *Catholic Action* 15 (July 1933): 12 and 31.

———. "A Plan of Industrial Organization." *Catholic Charities Review* 1 (1917): 139–43.

———. "The Priest and the Industrial Crisis." *The Ecclesiastical Review* 89 (1933): 225–34.

———. "Testing the NRA by Catholic Teaching—I, II, III." *Catholic Action* 15 (October 1933): 23–24 and 31; 15 (October 1933): 28–29; 16 (January 1934): 11–12 and 31.

McKeown, Elizabeth. "Apologia for an American Catholicism: The Petition and Report of the National Catholic Welfare Council to Pius XI, April 25, 1922." *Church History* 43 (1974): 514–28.

———. "Catholic Charities." In *The Encyclopedia of American Catholic History*, edited by Michael Glazier and Thomas J. Shelley, 242–45. Collegeville, Minn.: Liturgical Press, 1997.

———. "The National Bishops Conference: An Analysis of Its Origins." *Catholic Historical Review* 66 (1980): 566–74.

McKeown, Elizabeth, and Dorothy M. Brown. "Saving New York's Children." *U.S. Catholic Historian* 13 (1995): 77–95.

McShane, Joseph M. "Bishops' Program of Social Reconstruction." In *The New Dictionary of Catholic Social Thought*, edited by Judith A. Dwyer, 88–91. Collegeville, Minn.: Liturgical Press, 1994.

———. "'The Church Is Not for the Cells and the Cave': The Working Class Spirituality of the Jesuit Labor Priests." *U.S. Catholic Historian* 9 (1990): 289–304.

———. "'To Form an Elite Body of Laymen . . .': Terence J. Shealy, S.J., and the Laymen's League, 1911–1922." *Catholic Historical Review* 78 (1992): 557–80.

———. "A Survey of the History of the Jesuit Labor Schools in New York: An American Social Gospel in Action." *Records of the American Catholic Historical Society* 102 (1991): 37–64.

Mandel, David, and Alfred J. Petit-Clair Jr. "Taft-Hartley Act." In *Dictionary of American History*, rev. ed., edited by Louise Bilebof Ketz, 6:456–57. New York: Charles Scribner's Sons, 1976.

Marable, Manning. "The Rainbow Coalition: Jesse Jackson and the Politics of Ethnicity." *Cross Currents* 34 (1984): 21–42.

Marburger, Daniel R. "Whatever Happened to the 'Good Old Days'? The Evolution of Baseball's Labor–Management Relations." In *Baseball History from outside the Lines: A Reader*, edited by John E. Dreifort, 246–80. Lincoln: University of Nebraska Press, 2001.

Marini, Stephen A. "Religion, Politics, and Ratification." In *Religion in a Revolutionary Age*, edited by Ronald Hoffman and Peter J. Albert, 184–217. Charlottesville: University Press of Virginia, 1994.

Marlett, Jeffrey. "Harvesting an Overlooked Freedom: The Anti-urban Vision of American Catholic Agrarianism, 1920–1950." *U.S. Catholic Historian* 16 (1998): 88–108.

Marty, Martin E. "Public Religion." In *Encyclopedia of Religion and Society*, edited by William H. Swatos Jr., 393–94. Walnut Creek, Calif.: AltaMira Press, 1998.

Massingale, Bryan N. "James Cone and Recent Catholic Episcopal Teaching on Racism." *Theological Studies* 61 (2000): 700–730.

Mattern, Johannes. "Thoughts on the New Deal." *Catholic Mind* 32 (1934): 369–75.

May, Martha. "The Historical Problem of the Family Wage: The Ford Motor Company and the Five Dollar Day." *Feminist Studies* 8 (1982): 399–424.

May, William F. "The Religious Underpinnings of the Marketplace." *Logos* 3 (2000): 59–79.

Michel, Virgil. "Catholic Workers and Apostles." *Orate Fratres* 13 (1939): 28–30.

———. "City or Farm." *Orate Fratres* 12 (1938): 367–69.

———. "Defining Social Justice." *Commonweal* 23 (February 14, 1936): 425–26.

———. "The Liturgy: The Basis of Social Regeneration." *Orate Fratres* 9 (1935): 536–45.

———. "Our Social Environment." *Orate Fratres* 12 (1938): 318–20.

———. "Social Aspects of the Liturgy." *Catholic Action* 16 (May 1934): 9–11.

———. "Social Justice." *Orate Fratres* 12 (1938): 129–32.

Milkman, Ruth. "Redefining 'Women's Work': The Sexual Division of Labor in the Auto Industry during World War II." *Feminist Studies* 8 (1982): 337–72.

Miscamble, Wilson D. "The Limits of American Catholic Fascism: The Case of John A. Ryan." *Church History* 59 (1990): 523–38.

Misner, Paul. "Wilhelm Emmanuel von Ketteler." In *The New Dictionary of Catholic Social Thought*, edited by Judith A. Dwyer, 503–6. Collegeville, Minn.: Liturgical Press, 1994.

Mize, Sandra A. Yocum. "Peter E. Dietz." In *The New Dictionary of Catholic Social Thought*, edited by Judith A. Dwyer, 283–84. Collegeville, Minn.: Liturgical Press, 1994.

———. "Peter E. Dietz (1878–1947)." In *The Encyclopedia of American Catholic History*, edited by Michael Glazier and Thomas J. Shelley, 434–36. Collegeville, Minn.: Liturgical Press, 1997.

———. "Terence V. Powderly (1849–1924)." In *The Encyclopedia of American Catholic History*, edited by Michael Glazier and Thomas J. Shelley, 1162–64. Collegeville, Minn.: Liturgical Press, 1997.

Moloney, Diedre M. "Combatting 'Whiskey's Work': The Catholic Temperance Movement in Late Nineteenth-Century America." *U.S. Catholic Historian* 16 (1998): 1–23.

Montgomery, David. "Industrial Democracy or Democracy in Industry? The Theory and Practice of the Labor Movement, 1870–1925." In *Industrial Democracy in America: The Ambiguous Promise*, edited by Nelson Lichtenstein and Howell John Harris, 20–42. New York: Cambridge University Press, 1996.

———. "Labor Movement." In *The Encyclopedia of the Irish in America*, edited by Michael Glazier, 525–31. Notre Dame, Ind.: University of Notre Dame Press, 1999.

———. "William H. Sylvis and the Search for Working-Class Citizenship." In *Labor Leaders in America*, edited by Melvyn Dubofsky and Warren Van Tine, 3–29. Urbana: University of Illinois Press, 1987.

———. "The Working Classes of the Pre-industrial American City, 1780–1830." *Labor History* 9 (1968): 3–22.

Montgomery, Royal E. "Norris-La Guardia Anti-injunction Law." In *Dictionary of American History*, rev. ed., edited by Louise Bilebof Ketz, 5:111–12. New York: Charles Scribner's Sons, 1976.

Moody, Joseph N. "Leo XIII and the Social Crisis." In *Leo XIII and the Modern World*, edited by Edward T. Gargan, 65–86. New York: Sheed and Ward, 1961.

Mooney, Edward A. "The Duty of the Catholic Worker to Join Organized Labor." *Catholic Mind* 38 (1939): 569–71.

Mundelein, George Cardinal. "Catholic Action for Social Justice." *Catholic Mind* 36 (February 8, 1939): 47–49.

Murphy, William C. "The New Deal in Action." *Commonweal* 18 (May 5, 1933): 11–13.

Murray, John Courtney. "Leo XIII on Church and State: The General Structure of the Controversy." *Theological Studies* 14 (1953): 1–30.

———. "Leo XIII: Two Concepts of Government." *Theological Studies* 14 (1953): 551–67.

———. "The Return to Tribalism." *Catholic Mind* 60 (1962): 5–12.

———. "Revising the Secularist Drift." *Thought* 24 (1949): 36–46.

National Catholic Alumni Federation. "A Program of Social Justice." *Catholic Mind* 31 (1933): 281–88.

Nell-Breuning, Oswald von. "The Drafting of Quadragesimo Anno." In *Readings in Moral Theology No. 5: Official Catholic Social Teaching*, edited by Charles E. Curran and Richard A. McCormick, 60–68. New York: Paulist Press, 1986.

Nichols, Aidan. "Thomism and the Nouvelle Theologie." *Thomist* 64 (2000): 1–19.

Novak, Michael. "A Letter to Roberto." *Logos* 3 (2000): 70–84.

Novitsky, Anthony. "Peter Maurin's Green Revolution: The Radical Implications of Reactionary Social Catholicism." *Review of Politics* 37 (1975): 83–103.

O'Brien, David J. "American Catholics and Organized Labor in the 1930s." *Catholic Historical Review* 52 (1966): 323–49.

———. "The American Priest in Social Action." In *The Catholic Priest in the United States: Historical Investigations*, edited by John Tracy Ellis. Collegeville, Minn.: Liturgical Press, 1971,

———. "The Historical Context of North American Theology: The U.S. Story." *Catholic Theological Society of America Proceedings* 41 (1986): 1–15.

———. "The New Deal and American Catholics." In *The Encyclopedia of American Catholic History*, edited by Michael Glazier and Thomas J. Shelley, 1031. Collegeville, Minn.: Liturgical Press, 1997.

———. "Social Teaching, Social Action, Social Gospel." *U.S. Catholic Historian* 4 (1986): 195–224.

O'Brien, John J. "George G. Higgins and the Yardstick Columns." *U.S. Catholic Historian* 19 (2001): 87–101.

O'Hara, Edwin V., and Karl J. Alter, "Christian Social Order: Some Basic Principles." *Catholic Mind* 36 (1938): 220–22.

O'Shea, William. "Liturgy in the United States, 1889–1964." *American Ecclesiastical Review* 150 (1964): 176–96.

Ostreicher, Richard. "Terence V. Powderly, the Knights of Labor, and Artisnal Republicanism." In *Labor Leaders in America*, edited by Melvyn Dubofsky and Warren Van Tine, 30–61. Urbana: University of Illinois Press, 1987.

Parsons, Wilfrid. "The Function of Government in Industry." *Catholic Mind* 31 (March 1943): 7–15.

———. "What Are Vocational Groups?" *Thought* 17 (1942): 464–69.

Paulhus, Normand J. "Uses and Misuses of the Term 'Social Justice' in the Roman Catholic Tradition." *Journal of Religious Ethics* 15 (1987): 261–82.

Pawlikowski, John. "The American Catholic Church as a Public Church." *New Theology Review* 1 (1988): 8–29.

Paxon, Frederick Logan. "Robert Marion LaFollette." In *Dictionary of American Biography*, edited by Allen Johnson and Dumas Malone, 5:541–46. New York: Charles Scribner's Sons, 1933.

Pope, Stephen J. "Rerum Novarum." In *The New Dictionary of Catholic Social Thought*, edited by Judith A. Dwyer, 828–44. Collegeville, Minn.: Liturgical Press, 1994.

Purcell, Richard J. "John A. Ryan, Prophet of Social Justice." *Studies* 35 (1946): 153–74.

Putnam, Robert D. "Democracy in America at Century's End." In *Democracy's Victory and Crisis*, edited by Axel Hadenius. New York: Cambridge University Press, 1997.

Quinn, Joseph. "Mary Harris ('Mother') Jones (1830–1930)." In *The Encyclopedia of American Catholic History*, edited by Judith A. Dwyer, 731. Collegeville, Minn.: Liturgical Press, 1997.

Ramirez, Ricardo. "What Cesar Chavez Believed." *Origins* 23 (May 27, 1993): 17–20.

Reinhold, Hans A. "ACTU and Liturgy." *Orate Fratres* 14 (1939): 32–34.

———. "House of God and House of Hospitality." *Orate Fratres* 14 (1939): 77–78.

———. "Liturgy and the 'New Order.'" *Orate Fratres* 15 (1940): 77–79.

———. "A Social Leaven!" *Orate Fratres* 25 (1951): 515–19.

Ribuffo, Lee P. "Religious Prejudice and Nativism." In *Encyclopedia of the American Religious Experience, Studies of Traditions and Movements*, 2:1525–46. New York: Charles Scribner's Sons, 1988.

Rice, Charles Owen. "Confessions of an Anti-Communist." *Labor History* 30 (1989): 449–62.

Rosato, Philip J. "The Transocialization of the Eucharistic Elements: Rereading the Tradition in the Light of a Metaphysics Based on Justice." *Gregorianum* 81 (2000): 493–540.

Rose, Margaret. "'From the Fields to the Picket Lines: Huelga Women and the Boycott, 1965–1975." *Labor History* 31 (1990): 271–93.

Ross, Theodore. "The Personal Synthesis of Liturgy and Justice: Five Portraits." In *Living No Longer for Ourselves: Liturgy and Justice in the Nineties*, edited by Kathleen Hughes and Mark R. Francis, 17–35. Collegeville, Minn.: Liturgical Press, 1991.

Rosswurm, Steve. "The Catholic Church and the Left-Led Unions: Labor Priests, Labor Schools, and the ACTU." In *The CIO's Left-Led Unions*, edited by Steve Rosswurm, 119–37. New Brunswick, N.J.: Rutgers University Press, 1992.

Rouner, Leroy S. "To Be at Home: Civil Religion as Common Bond." In *Civil Religion and Political Theology*, edited by Leroy S. Rouner, 125–37. Notre Dame, Ind.: University of Notre Dame Press, 1986.

Rourke, Thomas R. "Contemporary Globalization: An Ethical and Anthropological Evaluation." *Communio* 27 (2000): 490–510.

Ryan, John A. "Aims of the New Deal Explained." *Catholic Action* 16 (May 1934): 14.

———. "American Catholics and American Socialism, *Ecclesiastical Review* 87 (1932): 584–92.

———. "Cardinal Mermillod and the Union of Fribourg." *America* 45 (1919): 200–201.

———. "The Church and the Workingman." *Catholic World* 89 (1909): 776–82.

———. "Economic Internationalism." *Commonweal* 19 (1935): 657–59.

———. "Economists on the Depression." *Sign* 15 (1936): 335–37.

———. "The Experts Look at Unemployment: I. Higher Wages for the Masses." *Commonweal* 10 (1929): 612–13.

———. "The Experts Look at Unemployment: II. A Shorter Work Period." *Commonweal* 10 (1929): 636–38.

———. "High Wages and Unemployment." *Commonweal* 13 (January 7, 1931): 259–61.

———. "Labor and Labor Legislation." *Catholic Encyclopedia* 8 (1910): 719–24.

———. "Labor's Program of Reconstruction." *America* 20 (1919): 466–68 and 493–95.

———. "Labour Unions." *Catholic Encyclopedia* 8 (1910): 724–28.

———. "Mr. Hoover and the Depression." *Commonweal* 12 (1930): 436–38.

———. "New Deal and Social Justice." *Commonweal* 19 (1934): 657–59.

———. "A New Social Order." *Catholic Action* 14 (October 1932): 15, 18, 31.

———. "The New Things in the Encyclical." *Ecclesiastical Review* 87 (1931): 1–14.

———. "Organized Social Justice." *Commonweal* 23 (1936): 175–76.

———. "The Personnel of the Industrial Relations Commission." *Catholic World* 98 (1913): 221–24.

———. "Pope Pius XI and A New Social Order." *Catholic Action* 16 (June 1934): 14–15, 18.

———. "A Programme of Social Reform by Legislation." *Catholic World* 89 (1909): 433–44 and 608–14.

———. "Roosevelt and Social Justice." *Review of Politics* 7 (1945): 297–305.

———. "The Senate Looks at Unemployment: I. Important Facts Which It Clearly Saw." *Commonweal* 10 (1929): 550–52.

———. "The Senate Looks at Unemployment: II. Important Facts Which It Failed to See." *Commonweal* 10 (1909): 578–80.

———. "The Sit-Down Strike." *Ecclesiastical Review* 96 (1937): 419–21.

———. "Unemployment: Causes and Remedies." *Catholic World* 128 (1929): 535–42.

Salvatore, Nick. "Eugene V. Debs: From Trade Unionist to Socialist." In *Labor Leaders in America*, edited by Melvyn Dubofsky and Warren Van Tine, 89–110. Urbana: University of Illinois Press, 1987.

Sanks, T. Howland. "The Social Mission of the Church: Its Changing Context." *Louvain Studies* 25 (2000): 23–48.

Schatz, Ronald W. "American Labor and the Catholic Church, 1919–1950." *U.S. Catholic Historian* 3 (1983): 178–90.

Schindler, David L. "Homelessness and the Modern Condition: The Family, Evangelization, and the Global Economy." *Logos* 3 (2000): 34–56.

Schleifer, James T. "Tocqueville as Historian: Philosophy and Methodology in the *Democracy*." In *Reconsidering Tocqueville's* Democracy in America, edited by Abraham S. Eisenstadt, 46–67. New Brunswick, N.J.: Rutgers University Press, 1988.

Schmandt, Raymond H. "The Life and Work of Leo XIII." In *Leo XIII and the Modern World*, edited by Edward T. Gargan, 15–48. New York: Sheed and Ward, 1961.

Schofield, Kent. "The Public Image of Herbert Hoover in the 1928 Campaign." *Mid-America* 51 (1969): 278–93.

Schrecker, Ellen W. "McCarthyism and the Labor Movement: The Role of the State." In *The CIO's Left-Led Unions*, edited by Steve Rosswurm, 139–57. New Brunswick, N.J.: Rutgers University Press, 1992.

Schuck, Michael J. "Modern Catholic Social Thought." In *The New Dictionary of Catholic Social Thought*, edited by Judith A. Dwyer, 611–32. Collegeville, Minn.: Liturgical Press, 1994.

Scibilia, Dominic. "The Christological Character of Labor: The Theology of Mary Harris ('Mother') Jones." *U.S. Catholic Historian* 13 (1995): 49–61.

———. "Edward McGlynn, American Social Catholic." *Records of the American Catholic Historical Society of Philadelphia* 101 (1990): 1–16.

———. "Thomas McGrady: American Catholic Millennialist Millennial Social Catholic." *Records of the American Catholic Historical Society of Philadelphia* 195 (1994): 32–46.

Shain, Barry Alan. "Individualism." In *The Encyclopedia of Politics and Religion*, edited by Robert Wuthnow. Washington, DC: Congressional Quarterly, 1998.

Shanaberger, Manuel S. "Edward McGlynn: A Missionary Priest and his Social Gospel." *U.S. Catholic Historian* 13 (1995): 23–47.

Shannon, Thomas A. "Catholic Social Teaching in America." In *The Encyclopedia of American Catholic History*, edited by Michael Glazier and Thomas J. Shelley, 295–98. Collegeville, Minn.: Liturgical Press, 1997.

Shapiro, Edward S. "Catholic Agrarian Thought and the New Deal." *Catholic Historical Review* 65 (1979): 583–99.

Shaw, Stephen J. "The Cities and the Plains: A Home for God's People; A History of the Catholic Parish in the Midwest." In *The American Catholic Parish: A History from 1850 to the Present*, edited by Jay P. Dolan, 2:327–54. New York: Paulist Press, 1987.

Skerrett, Ellen. "The Irish in Chicago: The Catholic Dimension." In *Catholicism: Chicago Style*, edited by Ellen Skerrett, Edward R. Kantowicz, and Steven M. Avella. Chicago: Loyola University Press, 1993.

Slater, Joseph. "Public Workers: Labor and the Boston Police Strike of 1919." *Labor History* 38 (1997): 7–27.

Slawson, Douglas J. "'The Boston Tragedy and Comedy': The Near Repudiation of Cardinal O'Connell." *Catholic Historical Review* 77 (1991): 616–43.

———. "John J. Burke, CSP: The Vision and Character of a Public Churchman." *Journal of Paulist Studies* 4 (1994–1996): 47–93.

———. "National Catholic Welfare Council." In *The Encyclopedia of American Catholic History*, edited by Michael Glazier and Thomas J. Shelley, 1005–7. Collegeville, Minn.: Liturgical Press, 1997.

———. "Thirty Years of Street Preaching: Vincentian Motor Missions, 1934–1965." *Church History* 62 (1993): 60–81.

Smith, John S. "Organized Labor and Government in the Wilson Era; 1913–1921: Some Conclusions." *Labor History* 3 (1962): 265–86.

Solomon, Albert. "Tocqueville's Philosophy of Freedom." *Review of Politics* 1 (1939): 400–431.

Stehlin, Stewart A. "The Emergence of a New Vatican Diplomacy during the Great War and Its Aftermath, 1914–1929." In *Papal Diplomacy in the Modern Age*, edited by Peter C. Kent and John F. Pollard, 75–85. Westport, Conn.: Praeger, 1994.

Steinfels, Peter. "The Failed Encounter: The Catholic Church and Liberalism in the Nineteenth Century." In *Catholicism and Liberalism: Contributions to American Public Philosophy*, edited by R. Bruce Douglas and David Hollenbach, 19–44. New York: Cambridge University Press, 1994.

Strom, Sharon Hartman. "Challenging 'Women's Place': Feminism, the Left, and Industrial Unionism in the 1930s." *Feminist Studies* 9 (1983): 359–86.

Stromquist, Shelton. "Class Wars, Frank Walsh, the Reformers, and the Crisis of Progressivism." In *Labor Histories: Class, Politics, and Working-Class Experience*, edited by Eric Arnesen, Julie Greene, and Bruce Laurie, 97–114. Urbana: University of Illinois Press, 1998.

Sultan, Paul E. "Closed Shop." In *Dictionary of American History*, rev. ed., edited by Louise Bilebof Ketz, 2:80–81. New York: Charles Scribner's Sons, 1976.

Swanson, Merwin. "The 'Country Life Movement' and the American Churches." *Church History* 46 (1977): 358–73.

Syracuse Diocesen Employment Guidelines. "The Church as Employer." *Origins* 13 (September 22, 1983): 253–57.

Terrar, Toby. "Thomas McGrady: American Catholic Socialist." *Ecumenist* 21 (1982): 14–16.

Thiemann, Ronald F. "Public Religion: Bane or Blessing for Democracy?" In *Obligations of Citizenship and Demands of Faith: Religious Accommodation in Pluralist Democracies*, edited by Nancy L. Rosenblum, 73–89. Princeton, N.J.: Princeton University Press, 2000.

Thompson, Heather. "Another War at Home: Reexamining Working Class Politics in the 1960s." *Mid-America* 81 (1999): 297–318.

Thorning, Joseph Francis. "Economic Organization and the Encyclical of Pius XI." *Catholic Mind* 33 (1935): 21–27.

———. "Principles and Practice of NRA." *Catholic Mind* 32 (1934): 361–68.

Tipton, Steven M. "Public Theology." In *The Encyclopedia of Politics and Religion*, edited by Robert Wuthnow, 624–28. Washington, DC: Congressional Quarterly, 1998.

Verter, Bradford. "Nativism." In *The Encyclopedia of Politics and Religion*, edited by Robert Wuthnow, 557–61. Washington, DC: Congressional Quarterly, 1998.

Villanova, Evangelista. "The Intercession (1963–1964)." In *History of Vatican II*. Vol. 3, *The Mature Council: Second Period and Intercession, September 1963–September 1964*, edited by Giuseppe Alberigo and Joseph A. Komonchak, 347–490. Maryknoll, N.Y.: Orbis, 2000.

Vizzard, James L. "The Agricultural Revolution." In *The Church and Social Progress: Background Readings for Pope John's "Mater et Magister,"* edited by Benjamin Masse. Milwaukee, Wisc.: Bruce, 1966.

Wakestein, Allen M. "The National Association of Manufacturers and Labor Relations in the 1920s." *Labor History* 10 (1969): 163–76.

Walker, Samuel. "Terence V. Powderly, the Knights of Labor and the Temperance Issue." *Societas* 5 (1975): 279–93.

Wandersee, Winifred D. "'I'd Rather Pass a Law Than Organize a Union': Frances Perkins and the Reformist Approach to Organized Labor." *Labor History* 34 (1993): 5–32.

Washington, George. "The First Inaugural Speech." In *George Washington: A Collection*, edited by W. B. Allen. Indianapolis, Ind.: Liberty Fund, 1988.

Weakland, Rembert. "The Urban Poor and the Churches." *Origins* 26 (November 14, 1996): 360–36.

Weber, Leonard J. "Labor Unions and Two Concepts of Social Justice." In *Issues in the Labor–Management Dialogue: Church Perspectives*, edited by Adam J. Maida, 160–75. St. Louis, Mo.: Catholic Health Association, 1983.

Weir, Robert. "Powderly and the Home Club: The Knights of Labor Joust among Themselves." *Labor History* 34 (1993): 84–113.

Welch, Richard E., Jr. "Sherman Antitrust Act." In *Dictionary of American History*, rev. ed., edited by Louise Bilebof Ketz, 6:276–77. New York: Charles Scribner's Sons, 1976.

Werpeikowski, William. "Labor and Capital in Catholic Social Thought." In *The New Dictionary of Catholic Social Thought*, edited by Judith A. Dwyer, 516–27. Collegeville, Minn.: Liturgical Press, 1994.

White, Ronald C., Jr. "Lincoln's Sermon on the Mount: The Second Inaugural." In *Religion and the American Civil War,* edited by Randall M. Miller, Harry S. Stout, and Charles Reagan Wilson, 208–25. New York: Oxford University Press, 1998.

Wimberley, Ronald C., and William H. Swatos Jr. "Civil Religion." In *Encyclopedia of Religion and Society,* ed. William H. Swatos Jr., 94–96. Walnut Creek, Calif.: AltaMira Press, 1998.

Windmuller, John P. "International Labor Organization." In *Dictionary of American History,* rev. ed., edited by Louise Bilebof Ketz, 3:454–55. New York: Charles Scribner's Sons, 1976.

Withorn, Ann. "Why My Mother Slapped Me." In *For Crying Out Loud: Women's Poverty in the United States*, edited by Ann Withorn and Diane Dujon. Boston: South End Press, 1996.

Wood, James E., Jr. "Public Religion vis-à-vis the Prophetic Role of Religion." In *The Power of Religious Publics: Staking Claims in American Society,* edited by William H. Swatos Jr. and James K. Wellman Jr., 35–51. Westport, Conn.: Praeger, 1999.

Wuthnow, Robert. "Civil Religion." In *The Encyclopedia of Politics and Religion,* edited by Robert Wuthnow, 153–57. Washington, DC: Congressional Quarterly, 1998.

Yonke, Eric. "Cardinal Johannes von Geissel." In *Varieties of Ultramontanism,* edited by Jeffrey von Arx, 12–38. Washington, DC: Catholic University of America Press, 1998.

Zotti, Mary Irene. "The Young Christian Workers." *U.S. Catholic Historian* 9 (1990): 387–400.

Dissertations

Batdorf, Sylvia M. "The Work of the Social Action Department of the National Catholic Welfare Conference in All Phases of Industrial Relations." Master's diss., Catholic University of America, 1933.

Blantz, Thomas E. "A Priest in Public Service: Francis J. Haas and the New Deal." PhD diss., Columbia University, 1968.

Cerny, Karl H. "Monsignor John A. Ryan and the Social Action Department." PhD diss., Yale University, 1955.

Czuchlewski, Paul Edward. "The Commonweal Catholic: 1924–1960." PhD diss., Yale University, 1972.

Elsbernd, Mary. "Papal Statements on Rights: A Historical Contextual Study of Encyclical Teaching from Pius VI to Pius XI (1791–1939)." PhD diss., Catholic University of Louvain, 1985.

Lee, William James. "The Work on Industrial Relations in the Social Action Department of the National Catholic Welfare Department, 1933–1945." Master's diss., Catholic University of America, 1946.

Lescher, Bruce. "The Spiritual Life and Social Action in American Catholic Spirituality: William J. Kerby and Paul H. Furfey." PhD diss., Graduate Theological Union, 1990.

Miller, Mark A. "The Contribution of the Reverend Raymond A. McGowan to American Catholic Social Thought and Action 1930–1939." Master's diss., Catholic University of America, 1979.

Mize, Sandra Ann Yocum. "The Papacy in Mid-Nineteenth-Century American Catholic Imagination." PhD diss., Marquette University, 1987.

Pastor-Zelaya, Anthony Sean. "The Development of Roman Catholic Social Liberalism in the United States, 1887–1935." PhD diss., University of California, Santa Barbara, 1988.

Paulhus, Normand Joseph. "The Theological and Political Ideals of the Fribourg Union." PhD diss., Boston College, 1983.

Prentiss, Craig Russell. "Taming Leviathan: The American Catholic Church and Economics, 1940–1960." PhD diss., The University of Chicago, 1997.

Scibilia, Dominic P. "Edward McGlynn, Thomas McGrady, and Peter C. Yorke: Prophets of American Social Catholicism." PhD diss., Marquette University, 1990.

Stroh, Paul. "Catholic Clergy and American Labor Disputes, 1900–1937." PhD diss., Catholic University of America, 1939.

Tonn, Mari Boor. "The Rhetorical Personae of Mary Harris 'Mother' Jones: Industrial Labor's Maternal Prophet." PhD diss., University of Kansas, 1987.

Index

~

About the Author

John J. O'Brien is a Passionist priest living at Calvary Retreat Center in Shrewsbury, Massachusetts. A graduate of the doctoral program in historical theology at Weston Jesuit School of Theology in Cambridge,

Massachusetts, he is currently involved in teaching, preaching retreats, research, and writing. He has published in liturgical and historical journals and is doing archival research to connect American Catholic church history with liturgical praxis and the search for worker justice and environmental spirituality.